Pieces of String Too Short to Save

A Memoir About Life, Journalism and Foreign Service

By

Bob Chancellor

Cover Design by Bruce Helm, Helm Graphics

CONTENTS

INTRODUCTION

My maternal grandmother, Mary Louise Nunnelly Tearle, was frugal. She lived alone as a widow for more than 20 years, maintaining an apartment and an independent life style in Kansas City. She did not have a great deal of money. Her husband, Arthur Tearle, had died at the age of 55, and had not had the opportunity to amass much in the way of retirement funds. Grandmother Tearle worked for many years as a clerk in the Emory Bird Thayer Department Store in Kansas City, but retired on little more than social security.

Thus, she saved paper bags, aluminum foil and string. At the time she was moved to a nursing home late in 1965, my Aunt Phoebe was helping to clean out accumulated possessions in grandmother's apartment, which included a large ball of string which had been saved and wound up for many years. And in that same cabinet, Phoebe found a full cardboard box, labeled "pieces of string too short to save."

That is sort of the way with this work – there is not enough here to make a full ball, just a lot of little snippets which don't really wind together. But, I hope, there are at least enough "pieces of string too short to save" to fill a box.

In the past, children learned about their family history by hearing the stories of their elders, or by eaves-dropping on adult conversations. But today, with families scattered across the nation and across the world, when grandparents and great grandparents are not so much in evidence around the home, children often are not aware of the rich history and background of their families.

And usually, children do not really care about that history until it is too late and the people who can relate that are gone. I find that is true in my case. Now that I am the patriarch of my clan, I cannot recall much of the family lore that was passed on to me orally by my parents and grandparents. And I know that my children and grandchildren will ask, "Who were those people?"

I will make an effort here to answer some of those questions. It is not a genealogy, and I make no claim to being a genealogist. For that, you will have to draw on my brother, Sam Chancellor, or on the excellent genealogy completed a few years ago by William Clarke Wroe of Edgewater, Maryland. Cousin Bud Wroe spent years and much energy preparing his genealogy, "*The Wroe and Chancellor Families.*"

The two families, Wroe and Chancellor, have a strong inter-linking. In early Virginia history, the Chancellor family produced four daughters, and each of them married a brother in the Wroe family. That created the link that was fortunate for us, since Bud Wroe had to research the Chancellor family history in order to know the history of the Wroes.

This also will not be a true and exact history because I am not a historian. Thus, I will feel free to pass on stories which may not in fact be true, but which I believe to be true, or at least be true representation of events which were passed on to me. I will attempt to label as speculation those items which are speculation, and as lore those items which are not known positively.

As I move forward into my own life, I will try to recollect events and times. Some of the memories were kindled by a project when I sorted and digitized several thousand photographic slides that had been accumulating for 50 years.

I need to thank my aunt, Phoebe Popham, who for years has told me I should write this book. She was right – and she was the one who discovered the box of string too short to save.

Letters which I wrote to and received from my wife, Linda Hulston Chancellor, make up a large part of this, as well as letters she wrote to our parents. Without her diligence in writing home, this project would not have been feasible. Without her sharing in this life-long adventure, this story would not have happened. She also is my primary editor and advisor; this story is as much hers as mine, and this book is dedicated to her.

INTRODUCTION

We travelled a long way during our 50+ years together, from our beginnings in Missouri, to Asia, the Middle East, Africa and the southwestern United States. One piece of advice to anyone who is about to embark on such an adventure — even if you are just starting life and not sure you will ever have such an adventure—is to keep a diary or journal because it is amazing how many of those experiences, and names and places will escape your memory in the years to come.

Linda and I celebrated our 50th anniversary in 2008. As part of the celebration, we took the whole family on a seven-day Caribbean cruise out of Galveston: our kids, our grandkids, my brothers and some of their kids. There were 19 of us in the party, and on the first day at sea, we all appeared in identical tee shirts designed by grandson Kyle Carter. Emblazoned over the art shown below were the lines "Bob and Linda, 50 year World Tour," and on the back: locations and years where we had lived and worked, like some sort of aging rock band. The symbolism in the design will be discerned as you read this book.

BOB AND LINDA

Springfield, MO 1956-1959
St. Joseph, MO 1960-1962
Springfield, MO 1963
Alexandria, VA 1963-1964
Bowie, MD 1965-1967
Bangkok, Thailand 1967-1969
Tokyo, Japan 1969-1972
Bowie, MD 1972-1975
Nairobi, Kenya 1975-1979
Springfield, MO 1979
Jerusalem, Israel 1980
Johannesburg, South Africa 1981-1984
Austin, TX 1984-1985
Seabrook, TX 1985-1989
Springfield, MO 1990 —

50 year WORLD TOUR

CHAPTER 1 — THE FIRST CHANCELLORS

An early Chancellor family history was prepared in 1895 by Dr. C.F. Chancellor, a physician who served as the U.S. Consul in Havre, France. Some of it, unfortunately, has not been proven out in later years, but it still provides a fascinating insight into our family. He wrote:

The original founder of the Chancellor Family was M. Gaultier, a French law officer of the Crown, who crossed over into England at the time of the Norman Conquest, 1066, with William the Conqueror. At that time he wrote his name "Gaultier, le Chancelier," to indicate his position as Chief law officer of the Crown. Subsequently his descendants dropped the surname of "Gaultier" and assumed successively that of "Le Chancelier," "Le Chancelour," "Chancelor," and finally, after the fourteenth century, the name was written "Chancellor."

Dr. C. F. Chancellor also wrote about the first Chancellors in America. He may have been right or wrong; certainly some of his findings were not supported by Bud Wroe. But Dr. Chancellor provided the following exciting and romantic tale.

The founder of the family in America was Richard Chancellor, who left England in 1682 and settled in Westmoreland County, Virginia. He had been a soldier in the service of Charles II, with the rank of Captain, but being a zealous whig, devoted to the Protestant religion, he joined the party of Monmouth, Essex, Russell and Sidney and others, who were disposed to levy war and raise the nation in arms against the encroachments of the government of Charles II upon the Established Church of England, but the plot being discovered, Captain Chancellor found it necessary to escape by flight the penalty of death or perpetual imprisonment...and accordingly emigrated to America. As related

by Captain Chancellor, in order to escape the fate of his conferes, he "laid conceiled for some days under London bridge and finally through the aid of female adroitness and generosity, was able to board a vessel bound for America."

Was there really a Captain Richard, who made a daring escape to America? According to Bud Wroe's research, it is questionable and unproven, but the time was right. The Chancellors of Shield Hill in Scotland had become an important family, holding land for five centuries and thus it is likely a young man of the family might achieve rank in the King's army. According to Bud Wroe, no evidence has ever been produced of a Richard Chancellor. There is reliable documentation, he says, that <u>two</u> persons by the name of Chancellor arrived in America in the period between 1670 and 1688, probably as early as 1672, and that they were the younger brothers of Robert Chancellor, the laird of Shieldhill, 1642-1661. That time fits with the ascendancy of Charles II to the throne in May 1660, which caused religious turmoil and occasional bloody battles.

Bud Wroe summarizes: *Up to this point, we have the two brothers of Sir Robert Chancellor, who crossed the Atlantic. We believe this occurred a few years after Charles II came to power and we believe that they came to America. We do not know how either of the brothers paid for their transportation or exactly where they first set foot in this country. Beyond that, we have accounts that one of them had been a soldier who fled to this country to escape prosecution for conspiracy and there were certain items which reportedly would document that claim, if only they could be located.*

That evidence, according to the Rev. Melzi Sanford Chancellor, writing in 1886, included a silver

QUE JE SURMONTE

Chancellor

mounted sword and a military tactics book, which were destroyed in a fire which destroyed Rev. Chancellor's house during the Civil War Battle of Chancellorsville in May, 1863. Tradition has it there also was a Bible in which Captain Chancellor wrote that he "laid concealed in London for some time, but finally, through female adroitness and generosity, was enabled to board a vessel bound for America and after landing, remained some years incognito." The Bible has never since been found.

Bud Wroe writes that 1672 is the earliest known documented information on anyone named Chancellor in this country; this in the records of Somerset County, Maryland: John Chansler [sic] and a woman named Abigail Harrington were indentured servants of a Richard Kimball. In March, 1673, they were indicted and tried for the crime of fornication: John was sentenced to "twenty nine lashes well laid on upon his bare back," and Abigail "twenty lashes well laid on upon her bare shoulders."

In 1675, Kimball was in court again to complain that John and Abigail "continued in evil" resulting in the birth of a child, which deprived Kimball of their services. The court ordered John and Abigail to pay Kimball two hundred pounds of tobacco each to satisfy his loss. John received another twenty lashes. In 1676, their indenture to Kimball ended and they were married. (An indentured servitude would have been one way that Captain Chancellor could have managed to finance passage to America. Was Abigail Harrington the adroit and generous female who helped his escape?)

Bud Wroe writes: *A few years after the first record of John Chancellor in Somerset County, Maryland, another Chancellor, by the name of Thomas, appears in Westmoreland County, Virginia. No, this is not the son of John Chancellor, because John's son was born in 1691 and there is proof that this person was in Westmoreland County, Virginia, as early as 1688, by which time he was old enough to sign as a witness to a will. This would seem to indicate that he was of a generation prior to that of Thomas, the son of John of Somerset.*

There are records of Thomas marrying a widow, Katherine Robinson, in 1692. They had a son, also named Thomas, very close in age to Thomas, the son of John of Somerset County. Rev. Melzi Chancellor quoted his grandmother, "they came from England and his name was <u>John</u> and he was a captain in the British army…." From that point forward, Wroe's genealogy relates to Thomas, of the second generation, who probably, but not certainly, was the Thomas who was the son of John of Somerset County.

It is likely that the Thomas of Westmoreland County, Virginia, was John's brother. This all is complicated even more by the fact that John, Abigail, their illegitimate daughter Mary and their son Thomas, also had moved to Westmoreland County, Virginia.

Confused? So is everyone, because apparently there were two Chancellors from England. Perhaps this is enough of the early family history. There are other Chancellors in the United States, including a large clan in Alabama, to whom links have never been established, and some people in Alabama believe their progenitor came from Germany, not England. There is even a town named "Chancellor" south of Dothan and Enterprise in south Alabama.

Shieldhill Castle, one of the oldest in Scotland, originally built in 1199 near Edinburgh. It was the family seat of the Chancellor family over 700 years. While altered by renovation and extensions, there are still many original features. The castle now is privately owned and managed as a hotel, where rooms rent for about $250 per night.

CHAPTER 2 — THE GUY AT FOUR CORNERS

Four Corners is the point where the four states of Colorado, New Mexico, Arizona and Utah, all meet. A monument there shows the state lines. A person can climb on the monument and squat, putting one foot in each of two states and a hand in each of two states and be in all four states at one time.

There are a lot of locations where three states meet but there is no other place in America where you can be in four states at once. There is a tri-state marker south of Joplin, Missouri, where Missouri, Kansas and Oklahoma all meet. When I was a youngster, we went there on a Sunday drive, but it was just marked by a small concrete pylon and was very unimpressive.

Four Corners had always intrigued me. Geography had always intrigued me. I love looking at maps. That probably resulted from a board game we had as children, called "Topography." It was a map of the United States, with many, many cities marked by small holes. To play, we would spin a dial to get a letter, such as "W" and then we would have two minutes (as determined by an egg timer) to place markers in as many cities as we could that began with that letter, such as "Washington" and "Walla Walla." I became pretty good at that game, and knew the location of most of the cities and all of the states (many of which I have visited over the years).

But most intriguing was the Four Corners. There was no hole there for a peg, but the concept that one could stand there and be in four states at once captured my imagination. It only took me 57 years to get to Four Corners, a destination reached after travels to the Far East, Africa, the Middle East, and much of the United States. Linda (my wife, friend and traveling companion) took a picture of me there, and then we visited the Indian souvenir shops that surround the monument.

My interest in geography was furthered by two books by Richard Halliburton at the Webb City Public Library, *The Occident* and *The Orient*. These were travel books written for young people in 1937 and 1938. Packed with black and white photographs, and texts of history and description, he took his young readers from the Golden Gate Bridge to Niagara Falls to the Panama Canal and Gibraltar to Pompeii. *The Orient* moved on to the Pyramids, the Dead Sea, Victoria Falls, Angkor Wat and the Great Wall of China, and many other marvels in between. I read both books, cover to cover, several times.

Let me introduce the seeker of the Four Corners. I am Robert Tearle Chancellor, always known as Bob, born in Boonville, Missouri, January 18, 1936. My father was Bonham Monroe Chancellor. He was from New Franklin, Missouri, just across the river from Boonville, and was the third generation of Chancellors to be born and live in Howard County. He was in Boonville because he was a school teacher there, and because he had married Frances Marie Tearle of Boonville, one of the prettiest girls in town.

Soon after my birth, the family moved to Shelbina, Missouri, a small town in the northeast part of the state. Although I went to first grade in Shelbina, I have almost no memories of the town. We do have pictures that my mother and father took of me in those wonderful days when I was the first, and only, child. In them, I seemed to have a costume for every occasion – a cowboy suit, an Indian suit – a tricycle, lots of toys and a Spitz dog named Patty, which I remember as being very ill tempered.

My reign as "only child" ended in Shelbina, October 3, 1940, with the birth of a little brother, Sam Bonham Chancellor. There was no hospital in Shelbina, and Sam was born at home.

Bob, Bonham and Sam, biking in Shelbina in the summer of 1942

The family moved in the summer of 1943. World War II was underway. In Shelbina, the war had gone almost un-noticed by a six year old kid. Dad was not eligible for the draft, and his effort to join the Navy failed because of a mis-shapen tailbone. My father, Bonham Chancellor, had taken a job as Principal of Webb City High School.

Nearby Joplin had an airport, and Navy training planes from Chanute, Kansas, would fly over Webb City each night on training missions. It took several days to convince me that we were not under attack. We lived for a year in a house near the high school at 815 West Second Street, while I attended second grade at Eugene Field School. My teacher was Miss Reed. For the next year, we moved to another rental house, on Liberty Street, (in the lesser north part of town) in the Webster School district, where I attended 3rd through 6th grade. (The house on Liberty no longer exists. It was torn down, I was told, when the black next-door neighbor wanted to buy it).

SCHOOLDAYS 1945

315 N Roane

After one year, we moved to another house, at 315 North Roane, still in the Webster School district –

that is the place I consider my boyhood home. I still drive by the one-story, two-bedroom house whenever I visit Webb City – it is virtually unchanged. It had a huge side yard, big enough for football and baseball games, plus a garden. It was a six block walk to Webster School and four blocks to the high school.

I got my first job when I was in the fifth grade: delivering a weekly, free newspaper, *The Graphic Review*, to about 200 houses. I would pick up the papers on Thursday night, fold them, and deliver them by bicycle early Friday morning. Sometimes my mother would help with the folding, and she or Dad would drive me on the paper route on snowy days. I earned 75 cents for each delivery. A couple of years later, I got a job delivering a daily newspaper, the Joplin News Herald, where I made $5 per week.

Early proceeds from the jobs went to purchase a Philco portable radio. It had a battery about the size of a brick, weighed a good five pounds, and I would carry it around on my shoulder, like young men would do years later with their ghetto blasters. But the long term goal of working was to save to buy a motor bike, which never happened.

By the time I was in the ninth grade, I got a really glamorous job as an usher in the Civic movie theater. That paid $2 per day, six or seven days a week. Some nights I would work from 5:30 P.M. until 9:30 P.M., but on alternate days I had to stay and close up, about midnight. Often, the manager and his wife, Howard and Dixie Larsen, would take me out for coffee or a hamburger after closing, and I wouldn't get home until nearly 1 A.M. Those hours caused some consternation at home (in fact, I am surprised the folks let me do it) but it was a great job. I got to see all the movies, free, and got paid for it. And being an usher was a great opportunity to flirt with girls.

Once, when I was an usher, the theater hosted a live show by a travelling magician. Before the show, he arranged for me to come up on stage during the performance and help him as he put his lady assistant into a trance and made her float freely in the air. He said he was using me because I "could keep my mouth shut" about what I might see. I did it and didn't see anything that I could tell. I know she was not in a trance, because she

whispered to him, "careful." She levitated, and he passed a ring all around her body to show there were no wires. Later, I was asked many times how he did it, and I had to admit I didn't know.

After I left show business, I washed dishes and cleaned a café. I got a job sacking groceries for 75 cents an hour. I worked in three different supermarkets during my final years in high school and got as much as $1.25 an hour at Safeway, as well as a union membership, stocking shelves and preparing produce.

Bonham had a theory that a person should have more than one profession to fall back on in hard times. Although I had no idea what I wanted to do with my life, he suggested that I learn a trade, that of being a motion picture projectionist. We found a Webb City man who had a couple of small, non-union, theaters in the neighboring towns of Carl Junction, Missouri, and McCune, Kansas. Every Wednesday and Saturday, I would ride with Charlie (last name forgotten) to his theater in McCune, where he would sell tickets and I would run the films. I got no pay, just training, a hamburger at the end of each trip, and all the popcorn I could eat.

(For those who have grown up in the digital age, or in modern cinemas, here is an explanation of what a projectionist did. A feature film would fill four to six large reels. Reel one would be placed on projector one, the carbon arc lamp lit, and the film started. Nearing the end of reel one, the projectionist would light up the lamp in projector two; and watch the screen for a cue mark – a white dot that would flash in the upper right corner of the screen. On the first cue mark, the projectionist starts the motor of projector two; upon a second cue mark, he switches either manually or electronically, to projector two, turning off the first machine, which then was loaded with reel three. If done correctly, this "changeover" as it was called, was undetectable to the audience. If the cue was missed, allowing the film to run out and the bright, white light to fill the screen, the audience felt free to boo while the projectionist scurried to make a correction).

Webb City was a great town to grow up in, small enough to be safe and for everyone to know who you were and keep you out of trouble. It had been the center of a big lead and zinc mining area many years before, and the outskirts of town had huge piles of gravel, or chat, called tailing piles, remaining from the mines. There were also remaining open mine shafts and the foundations and relics of mills. The children of Webb City were all warned not to play on the chat piles, but those mounds of loose gravel, looking like the sand dunes of the desert, were too tempting and were visited often.

We could ride bicycles almost anywhere, including two miles north of town to Center Creek, where we would skinny dip, hiding under the bridge when a car came by. When I got older, the corner drug store downtown was a favorite hangout, as was the (forbidden) pool hall across the street.

One favorite summer time pursuit was the Hatten Park Swimming Pool, a large pool built in what was once the basement of a college building.

Bob (L) clowning at the pool with Jan Jester and Howard Phillips (R). 1954

Draining the pool required a certain degree of courage, or recklessness. It involved climbing down a rickety wooden ladder into a manhole, then opening the 12 inch pipe, which would allow the pool water to begin gushing into the manhole and out to a ditch. When I started helping there — no pay but free swimming — a board was pried between the metal plate capping the pipe and the wall. Eight nuts and bolts were removed, then you climbed out and yanked on a rope from the top to remove the board and allow the water to flow. Later, they installed a large valve, which was even worse, because you had to stand in the bottom of the manhole cranking open the valve while the water began rushing in around your legs and trunk If you were too slow opening the valve, the water would be to chin level before the task was finished.

Another summertime task was to help set up for Friday night band concerts in the park. Two or three kids would meet at the high school band room, load 50 folding chairs, plus sousaphones, drums and music stands into a truck, then ride to the memorial park to set up the bandstand. After the concert, it all had to be returned to the school. No pay, but we received free passes for miniature golf for our labors.

For 25 cents, we could get on a bus and ride to Joplin, and play basketball at the YMCA. If we spent the bus fare on some treat, we could hitchhike back home. In summer, we would camp out in the back yard, in tents, often for several consecutive nights. And for a week each summer, we would go to a real camp – Boy Scout, or YMCA or church camp.

In junior and senior high school, we had free dances almost every week after football or basketball games, or on special occasions. During my junior year, an itinerant evangelist, Braxton Sawyer, held a week-long revival and preached about sin and corruption at the high school. That sin was dancing, and he convinced about half the kids in my class. Several were saved, the prom was threatened and the debate raged on through that spring, but it seemed to be forgotten by the next school year.

We had only one school bus, and it brought in kids from outlying towns. Everybody else walked, or those lucky enough to have cars, drove. There was no cafeteria – you either walked home and back for lunch or carried your lunch in a brown bag. There was a store across from the high school, Couraw's, where you could get a coke, and a hot dog for ten cents. The ten-cent hot dog was split lengthwise into quarters, one sliver of meat was slipped into a bun, along with a smear of greasy chili.

My youngest brother, Stephen Monroe Chancellor, was born August 21, 1947. Being the oldest, at twelve, I was often drafted into duty as a baby sitter. I even learned how to change dirty diapers and sterilize milk bottles for the baby – skills that would come in handy in future years.

I had two real close friends through my grade school and high school years. One was Montford "Monte" Handley, the other, John Charles Wallace, both of whom lived about a block from our house.

John was an only child who had all the toys known to man. His mother was a piano teacher, and he usually could not have company at his house during lesson times, so John spent many, many hours at 315 N. Roane. Although he had chemistry sets and bicycles and stuff, his big interest always was photography. From an early age he declared that he intended to join the Navy and become a photographer. And he did – he realized his life's dream at the age of 20 and even advanced to being an official White House photographer, but unfortunately died of a heart attack before he reached the age of 33.

Monte lasted longer. He died at the age of 64, but he had been ill for many years. He was a big kid, tall and husky, but very gentle and not at all athletic. He had grown up in a house full of older sisters, and in fact, was a bit of a sissy. But he was a great dancer – in demand by all the girls because most of the rest of us could not, would not, did not venture onto the dance floor very often. Monte went to California to become a movie star, had one bit part in a TV show, became an airline ticket agent and eventually returned to Webb City to work as a hairdresser. He and I spent many spare hours at his house, smoking, drinking coffee and gossiping with his mother.

David Larsen, whose family owned the Civic Theater, was another friend, as was Jan Jester.

The James kids, all grown up at a 2006 reunion. (L-R) Walt, Janet, Terry (now deceased), Mary Curtis and Bobby.

And then there were the Jameses: mother Madge James, kids Janet, Terry, Jim, Mary Curtis and Bob. Madge was the secretary to the school superintendent, and a rarity in those times, a single mother. There was a father, who was around only on the rarest of occasions – Madge raised her large family on her salary and they all turned out to be great people. Janet, Terry and Jim were all older than me, Mary Curt just a bit younger, and Bobby was the age of my brother Sam. They lived just a block from us and we were often at one another's house.

I had to start wearing glasses during my sophomore year of high school. It was traumatic – I hated them. Dad had befriended a new optician who had moved to Webb City, and was encouraged to bring his kids in for an examination. I failed. So did Sam. The doctor put me in a pair of bi-focals (although I learned much later in life that I could have gotten by with just lenses for distant vision) and told me to wear them all the time. Well, they spent half the time in their case in my pocket, except when Dad was around and insisting I put them on. I refused to wear them on dates, even though I could even admit to myself that I couldn't really see enough to be driving at night. I never really became accustomed to the glasses until I was in college and got a pair of horn rims, which were more stylish. A friend had advised me to wear horn rims, so people would know I had on glasses, instead of the narrow steel rims which blended in and became part of my persona.

We have to speak of smoking. I started sneaking around puffing on cigarettes in the 7th grade. By the time I was sixteen, I announced at home that I smoked, and was told in no uncertain terms by my father, "No, you don't." He would not permit it (even though he had smoked in prior years). "I tried it, and didn't like it," he reasoned, "so there is no reason for you to do it." Of course, that did not dissuade me.

At the age of 16, the most important thing in a kid's life is the right to drive the family car. After several discussions about smoking, the mandate was handed down: "If you want to smoke, then you can't drive my car." That was a heavy penalty, so I professed to give up the evil habit, although I didn't; I just didn't smoke openly. During my senior year of high school, I got caught – and I was banned from using the car. That was a prohibition which lasted the rest of the school year; if I had a date requiring wheels, or needed to go somewhere, I had to bum a ride with a friend. That was a genuine hardship on a high schooler.

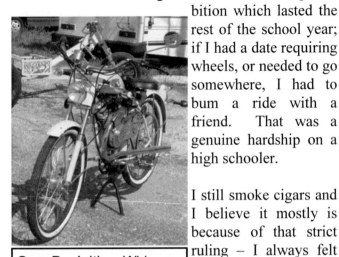

Gee, Pop! It's a Whizzer. Spotted recently along old Highway 66 between Springfield and Webb City.

I still smoke cigars and I believe it mostly is because of that strict ruling – I always felt that I had earned the privilege. If my father had taken a more understanding tack, I might not have been so insistent.

And then there were motorbikes. Many kids in town had Whizzer motorized bikes, or Cushman motor scooters, a few even had small motorcycles. My father would not allow me to have one. I had my own money to buy it, and I had a need for one with the paper route which stretched out over several miles. That continued even after I turned 16 and wanted to buy a car. No way. In fact, several years later, when I was in college and living at home, he still would not permit me to buy a car until I was 21. You can be sure that the day I turned 21, I went out and bought my first car, a 1954 maroon Ford convertible.

He got easier to deal with in later years. Sam was allowed to buy a car before he turned 21, and later, he even bought a motor scooter for Steve when he was 14 or so. There is a certain burden to being the oldest. My father and I really did not get along. He was stubborn and so was (am) I. We did not have a strong, warm father-son relationship; he rarely praised me for any accomplishment.

I have never understood why we had that relationship. Perhaps if I had been a star athlete I might have received praise, but I was lousy at athletics. I went out for football a couple of years, played a

little junior high basketball. He was not an athlete either. I was smart and a pretty good student, but I was always told I could do better if I would apply myself. I acted in the senior class play, and was selected for the National Honor Society. Even working a lot and earning my own money never gained praise. I think he was driven by the tension of being the school principal and responsible for 500 kids, because he mellowed in later years when he went back to classroom teaching.

I thought I did all the right things, but often they were not right. In the 6th grade, it was suggested I might like to take band. "Great," I said, "I want to play drums." "Nope," Bonham said, "You can't serenade a girl with drums; here's a trumpet." Well, that lasted just a couple of years.

I think that tension showed in another way, too. He was a public figure in a small town. When I was about 12, he overheard me and some other kids talking about drinking and acting like we were drunk. He took me to the basement and revealed a big secret – never to be discussed. He had a locked cabinet, and in it he had…beer. He would drive to the far side of Joplin to buy it. He and his friends would drink beer at home, after closing the blinds so snoopy neighbors couldn't see.

The Webb City junior and senior high schools were combined into one building – thus I spent six years in the school where my father was the principal. That was a burden for me because I was expected to behave and not cause trouble. But I was no angel – when I was a junior he caught me smarting off to a new, young teacher, and took me to his office and paddled me. And he left the office door open so everyone on the second floor could hear. The study hall teacher across the hall announced: "That's Bob Chancellor in there getting it."

Obviously, he was a stern disciplinarian. Many of the kids called him "the warden" because he had once taught in Boonville, which happened to be the location of the State Reform School for Boys. It was a nickname which he disliked intensely – but he was strict enough that it really fit.

Example: one year, the junior class decided it would have a "skip day" in the spring. "No," said the warden. "There is no provision in the school calendar for a skip day and it will not be permitted." The entire junior class (about 80 students) ignored that prohibition, and took their "skip day" anyway. His response was to suspend each and every one of the absent students – their parents had to bring each one back to school to get them reinstated as students. It was not a popular move – our home phone nearly rang off the wall that night – but he insisted that he, and not the students, was in charge of the school. These days, when I see the attitude and lack of discipline shown by many youngsters, I become convinced the warden probably was right.

He also was a stickler for good sportsmanship and would not tolerate booing or jeering at Webb City High School basketball games, where he ran the scoreboard and public address system. He posted signs all around the gym: "Be a good sport," and "Webb City doesn't boo." I remember one game the fans were upset by a referee's call and began booing. He stopped the clock, rang the buzzer and announced that the game would not continue until the crowd shut up. They then began booing him, but he just sat there with his arms crossed until the gym got quiet, and then he resumed the game.

During my junior year, the Korean War was underway, and many young men were being drafted into the army right after high school. One way to avoid being drafted was to be a member of the National Guard, so as a junior, at the minimum age of 17, I joined Company B, 135th Tank Battalion, 35th Division – the Missouri National Guard. I had no interest in driving tanks (though it did look like fun) so I was assigned as a radio mechanic, knowing nothing about that either.

The highlight of the National Guard was summer camp. For two weeks, all us guardsmen would go off to a military camp and play soldier. My first year, we went by truck convoy to Fort Knox, Kentucky, where I learned some basics about radio operation. (I also learned how to pee off the back of a moving truck during that two-day-plus truck ride to camp). The second year, we traveled by train to Camp McCoy, Wisconsin.

There was another fringe benefit of being in the Guard – they had several jeeps that needed driving regularly. The sergeant in charge of the armory

Bob and Sam on the steps at 315 North Roane. The cat's name was Scalawag, and he lived to be 19 years old.

would let David Larsen (a fellow guardsman) and me each check out a jeep many afternoons after school, and we would zip around town, playing tag over the two-way radios the vehicles carried.

Many of my fellow guardsmen were also high school students, or young men who had just recently finished high school. One of them was Dewey Joe Phillips. He was three or four years older than me – by then he was attending Joplin Junior College. We were not at that time good friends – more like acquaintances – although everybody in Webb City pretty well knew everybody else. But remember the name – Dewey Joe Phillips – because our acquaintanceship would later have a very important influence on my life and my career.

I graduated from Webb City High School in May, 1954. The summer after high school graduation, I worked for the State Highway Department in Joplin – I became a sign painter and road sign installer. I really had no idea what I wanted to do. College was a foregone conclusion. The default plan: I would attend Joplin Junior College for two years, and then go on to the Rolla School of Mines for a degree in electrical engineering. Later in this tale, you will learn how that plan changed, radically.

Webb City High School Class of 1954
(Right) 40th Year Reunion
(Below) 45th Year Reunion
(Bottom) 50th Year Reunion

CHAPTER 3 — THE FLYING PROFESSOR

Late in the war, my father became intrigued with flying and obtained a private pilot's license. It was an expensive hobby, but he worked summers at the airport, cleaning and caring for planes, and took his pay in flying hours. The following is excerpted from an article I wrote, which was published in the Webb City Sentinel, in January 2011, based on his flying log books.

Bonham Chancellor moved his family to Webb City in the summer of 1943, to take up the position as principal of the junior-senior high school. We moved from Shelbina, MO., where there was no airport; and he had grown up around Boonville, MO., where there was no airport, so the move to Webb City was certainly his first exposure to airports and flying. But his interest and enthusiasm for flying took effect quickly and strongly.

His first flight, a 30-minute demonstration, was logged October 9, 1943 with pilot/instructor Tim Merritt. He next flew in February of 1944, and had been in the air 21 times by the end of June. These were all dual hours, with instructor N.A. (Gus) Skoglund, a former Navy pilot. Simultaneously with flying, he was taking the required ground training courses, and in May, 1944, he applied for a student pilot license.

At least 60 hours of flying time, both dual accompanied by an instructor, and solo, were required before the student pilot could attain a private flying license. The instructed hours included lots of take-offs and landings: circle the field, land and take-off again; emergency landing, plot and follow a course to Pittsburg, KS, or Neosho.

With 10 hours 40 minutes under his belt, Bonham Chancellor made his first solo flight June 23, 1944. That was followed by a few more instructed hours and lots of solo time, reaching for the goal of 60: take-off, turns, stalls, landing, and "playing around."

Flying activity in those days was centered at a large hangar, right by the highway between Webb City and Joplin. There were two or three trailers that functioned as offices for the various flying services -- there was no Joplin air terminal or commercial air service at that time. The airplanes were single-engine, high-wing aircraft: Cessna 120's or 140's, Luscombes or Aeronicas.

Bonham Chancellor's big day came more than a year after his first solo flight. With 63 hours of solo time and 85 hours total air time, he was tested and awarded his Private Pilot's License, October 14, 1945. Now, he could take up passengers. That was a beginning of a chapter in which many people in Webb City, young and old, would take their first airplane ride.

His first passenger was my younger brother, Sam, who was five years old. The next ride was mine; I was nine. And then my mother. It appears that he hoped Mother would get the flying bug, and perhaps take instruction for her own license – during the first year she was his most frequent passenger and he even purchased her own log book.

There was a notation in his log book that his license had cost $571: $184 for instructed time and $387 for solo time plane rental. That sounds incredibly cheap for these times, when earning a private license can cost 8 to 10 thousand dollars. But those were the days of 20 cent gasoline, and as principal of the high school, he earned $6000 per year, so learning to fly was a substantial investment.

But the flying professor found a way to finance his expensive hobby. During the summer vacation periods, he worked for the flying service, maintaining and cleaning planes, pumping gas and pushing aircraft into and out of the hangar. He also worked on the apron, spinning and starting propellers in those days when small planes did not have electric starters. For pay, he took one hour of flying time for each hour of ground work. He did this for several summers and amassed a large balance of free flying time.

He loved to fly. I think it was because of the precision and preparation it took. And he loved to share his enthusiasm of flying. He always was looking for someone to fly with him. After receiving his license, he made 513 flights; 390 of those times he took a passenger. In fact, the first 63 flights after he was licensed, he had a passenger with him.

I flew with him 32 times, amassing 18 plus hours in the air – pretty heady stuff for a pre-teen. My mother surpassed me, with 19 hours in 26 flights and even younger brother Sam, barely able to see over the dashboard, made 20 flights and logged nearly 11 hours.

Sometimes it is difficult to determine the names or partial names, or initials entered into his flight log books, but over the four year period, he took more than 205 people aloft, many for their first flight ever. His passengers included high school students, friends, fellow teachers, Lions Club members, or if you were just hanging around the airport when it was time to go flying, you were invited. Over the years, I have been told by many people that they had flown with my father. Some are not even listed in the log books; often he would take up a passenger, make a 15 minute circle over the Webb City vicinity, then land, taxi to the hangar, and exchange passengers.

In mid-1946, he had passed the examination for his Commercial Pilots license, which meant he could be paid for flying, and many of the logged flights appear to be familiarization flights for prospective students. He was not licensed as an instructor, however. And many flights were not paid flights – he took people aloft for the sheer joy of flying.

By 1949, the pace and the enthusiasm had slowed down, in part because he had used up most of the accumulated flying hours from his summers of work, and the costs of a family of three boys forced him to seek remunerative summer employment elsewhere.

He had attained a Ground Instructors license, and taught aeronautics for the Civil Air Patrol, in which he was an officer, and for Finley's Flying Service. He also taught aeronautics in 1948 at Webb City High School; one of the few public high schools in the country to offer such a course. And of course, he and his class painted the famous navigation aid sign on the high school roof, which showed the latitude and longitude of Webb City and pointed to both the north and the nearest airport at Joplin.

Bonham Chancellor's last logged flight was a 35 minute jaunt on March 28, 1953, at which point he had logged 355 hours flying time. Ironically, he was never again in an airplane until 1972 when he boarded an airliner from St. Louis to Washington, D.C. for the wedding of his first passenger, Sam Chancellor.

CHAPTER 4 — THE GOAT

This is a story from my youth, which I wrote as a short article, but then never had published. It is true. It was prompted one day, about 1992, when I read an ad in the Springfield newspaper that reminded me of this youthful adventure.

The antique dealer's ad in the newspaper brought it all back.

"FOR SALE. A SADDLE MOUNTED ON A METAL SPRING, ON WHEELS, WITH GOAT HORNS ATTACHED. FROM SOUTHWEST MISSOURI. WE BELIEVE THIS WAS USED IN SOME SORT OF LODGE OR CLUB RITUAL BUT KNOW NOTHING MORE ABOUT IT. $250."

Indeed. It was known as "the goat," and I met it on a spring evening during my senior year in high school

The word had been going around school for a couple of weeks about this great new club, or lodge, several of the guys had joined.

Members of the football team had been the first to join the club known as ATA. They always set the style. When I expressed an interest, my level-headed and practical father discouraged it. "There is nothing to it, it is only an excuse for an initiation, and it is a bunch of older men. It's not for kids."

He did not need to say more. The next Thursday evenings, while I was hanging out at the drug store, the recruiters for ATA came by and soon two friends and I were on our way toward the inner circle.

The ATA Lodge Hall was about five miles out of town, an old white-frame building at a country crossroads. It looked as if it had been there a long time. So did some of the members.

ATA stood for "Anti-Theft Association." It was explained to us prospective new members that

once it had been the "Anti Horse-Theft Association," but it had recognized modern times. We were assured that for our $3 annual dues, we would be joining a group of community minded leaders dedicated to the prevention of theft and other crime.

In addition to a membership card, each new member would receive an "ATA window decal," the mere presence of which was enough to deter any car thief.

"Your fellow members will go to any length to apprehend the thief who dares to take your car," we were told.

"The initiation was a mere formality," they said. We attended a ten-minute lecture on the philosophy of ATA and the prevention of crime.

That was a piece of cake for a fairly good student who paid attention. Time for a quiz on what we had learned. One by one, we faced this last hurdle prior to full membership. "Did you bring any valuables with you?" our instructor asked. "No."

"Are you sure?" The active members looked on attentively. "No, nothing but this Timex wrist watch"

"But what about these family jewels?" the interrogator asked, popping his hand into my crotch.

"He lied. He lied. Unacceptable," the membership cried in unison. Someone suggested, "Make him ride the goat. The goat. The goat."

At this point, a contraption was rolled into the room. It was a saddle mounted on a metal spring, with goat horns attached. My punishment for lying, it was explained, was to ride on the metal goat while it was being bounced by my mentors. No one mentioned the blindfold until I confidently climbed aboard.

Even blindfolded, it was not a difficult ordeal. The bouncing was rough, but not severe. Until someone turned on the transformer from a Model

`A Ford, which was attached to a battery, which was wired to metal studs in the saddle, and in the hand grips alongside the goat's head. Then, the punishment for my "lie" began to feel severe, even shocking.

The ride on the goat lasted only a few minutes, and once it stopped, I was welcomed into the fold of the ATA. I even benefited from being the first, since I got to watch my fellow initiates fail the test and ride the goat. All in good fun and fellowship.

The initiation was followed by a formal business meeting. We were all sitting in chairs arranged around the periphery of the room. It looked like it had once been a Masonic meeting hall. We were steeped in fellowship and enjoying our first really adult club meeting when the discussion took on a serious tone.

The new treasurer reported to the membership that the books he had inherited from Edgar Nealy were not in balance. In fact, there was a shortage of several thousand dollars.

Now, I knew Edgar Nealy. He was one of the few adults in the room that I did know. I played baseball with his son, Eddie, who was an earlier member of ATA. Edgar was a strange, quiet man, heavy-set, 6'4 or so, a farmer who lived in town and made his meager living running a herd of cows on the outskirts. Strange, distant, a loner, but not a thief. He was even a neighbor and a member of our church.

Not Edgar, not a thief. There were others among the gathering who agreed. The discussion became heated. Did Edgar purloin several thousand dollars from the Anti Theft Association, or did he not?

Eventually Edgar got up and stormed out of the hall. "No one calls me a thief," he shouted on his way to the door. Several of his supporters stormed out in support of him, including Eddie.

I was appalled. Here I had gone through the rigors of an initiation, and had been admitted to the inner council of an adult, responsible and respected organization, only to have it begin to crumble on my first night. "Do my loyalties to the Nealy family, to Eddie, require me to leave also or should I stay with my new lodge brothers?" I stayed.

The business discussion moved on, to what I don't remember. But the buzz continued in the room about Edgar. It had only been continuing for a few minutes when the doors burst open, and Edgar came running back into the lodge hall, shouting and cursing, "You bastards, you should not accuse me of being a thief. I won't take that."

His angry outburst was accompanied by the biggest handgun I had ever seen, a long barrel .38, which Edgar waved around the room, pointing at various people, but mostly at the innocent newcomers among us, instead of his accusers.

"You sons-of-bitches," he yelled, as he began pulling the trigger. Bang! Bang! Bang! Half a dozen shots rang out in the stunned hall. We new members were directly in the line of fire. Was I to die merely for attending a club that my father considered a bunch of foolishness?

Only then did the assemblage begin to laugh. The shots, of course, were blanks. Old weird Edgar had been shooting up ATA Lodge initiations for years. The second, and final, phase of the initiation was ended. The meeting ended.

I never went back to an ATA meeting. I wasn't really interested in crime prevention. Besides, I didn't even have a car to safeguard from theft. And graduation was looming. Also, there were no more guys in my class to initiate.

But I remember the goat. And I wonder if the antique dealer ever found out what ritual it was used for.

CHAPTER 5 — EARLY CHANCELLORS AND BONHAMS

It is time to introduce my family more fully. My great-grandfather was Brown Monroe Chancellor, born on Christmas Eve, 1832, in Faquier County, Virginia. He was in the sixth generation of Chancellors in America. He was the fifth of six children born to John Hore Chancellor and Elizabeth Rogers. The family at some time moved to Kentucky, and then on to the Missouri River bottoms at Franklin, Missouri. I know very little about them other than that they were farmers attracted to what was very rich farm land along the river.

Brown Monroe was 34 years old when he married Hannah Gearhart of Howard County, Missouri.

Father Isaac Gearhart apparently had been a very successful farmer, amassing a large acreage of farm land which he divided among his six children. Brown farmed Hannah's share.

Brown and Hannah had five children, the youngest of whom was my grandfather, Ernest Monroe Chancellor, born March 17, 1879. His sister, Sarah, who I knew as "Aunt Sally" was born in 1871. Brown's farm was divided among Ernest, Sarah, and perhaps others. The other children were Ella, Horace and John G., known as "Hardy."

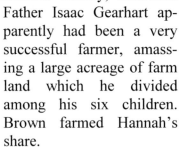

Brown Monroe Chancellor
& Hannah Gearhart Chancellor

Ella married Virgil Blankenbaker, a cousin, from another prominent Howard County family, and they headed out to Montana, where they established a sheep ranch and many businesses along the Missouri River about 75 miles northwest of Great Falls. He amassed a huge tract of land, stretching fifteen miles along the river. They also founded a town there, naming it Virgelle (for Virgil and Ella). They established a Mercantile Store and Bank (the buildings now house a bed and breakfast) and Virgil was elected to the state legislature.

Ella's brother, John. G., or Hardy, and his wife Pauline, known as Jessie, also went to Virgelle, where Hardy had a ranch and ran the store. They had one child, Irene. Our family took a summer vacation trip to Montana when I was a teenager. Irene, who was sort of a homely tom-boy, married a Czechoslovakian immigrant ranch hand, Jim Cervany and they ran the ranch after her parents' death. They raised registered breeding-stock cattle, only about 200 of them, and Jim knew each one by name and pedigree.

I remember one day that summer, when Jim and I were riding around the ranch in a pickup, he spotted a wild goose in the field, and proclaimed "a goose dinner would be good." He jumped out of the truck, chased and caught the goose, wrung its neck and threw it in the back. It was good. They never had children, and died leaving a half million dollar estate to various charities of Montana.

My grandfather, Ernest Chancellor, with his first grandson (me). Below, my grandmother, Margaret Lavinia Bonham Chancellor.

Brown Monroe Chancellor, my great-grandfather, also went to Montana in 1910 after the death of Hannah. He died five years later and his body was returned for burial at Clark's Chapel in Howard County. Hardy lived until 1947. I don't remember Hardy, but I do

remember Sarah, "Aunt Sally" who married Luther Lee and lived in the farm adjacent to my grandparents.

My grandfather, Ernest, was given half of the Brown and Hannah Chancellor land, a farm of 120 acres. He received a high school education at the Military Academy at Mexico, Missouri, before going into farming. I remember visiting their farm, just north of the river from Boonville, until I was a teen-ager. By then, he was in his 60's and 70's and didn't actively farm – he rented his land out to sharecroppers, milked a cow or two, and kept chickens and pigs. He also dabbled in botany, and grew and helped develop small seedless watermelons, about the size of a bowling ball.

I remember that they did not have electric power service until well after the war, even though they were only two miles from Boonville. No electricity meant no running water or indoor toilets. They did have electric lights, provided by a gasoline powered Delco power plant in the basement, but that didn't provide enough power to operate water pumps, and the Delco was only operated at night.

Ernest married a "city" girl, Margaret Lavinia Bonham of Fayette, the elder of two daughters of Dr. Vaughn Quain Bonham, a respected physician who himself was the descendent of a well-known family whose history stretched back to the Mayflower.

V.Q. Bonham's father, Nehmiah McDaniel Bonham, also had been a doctor in Howard County. (Of particular interest to the Texans in my family, Nehmiah Bonham was a great uncle of James Butler Bonham, the hero of the Alamo).

Margaret was born in July of 1881. For two years, she attended Hardin College and Conservatory of Music in Mexico, Missouri. At the age of 23 she moved from the more sophisticated life of the

city of Fayette, to the farm at New Franklin. They built a modest two-story house, surrounded by huge maple trees, and named it Maple Manor. That house stood until the big Missouri River floods of 1994 – nearly 90 years. In all that time, the house had never flooded although floods were frequent in the river bottom land. After the big flood, the land and home site were purchased by the government.

My father, Bonham Monroe Chancellor, was born in that house June 27, 1908, as was his sister, Louise Bonham Chancellor, in 1905. (you can see the reverence for the prestige of Doctor Bonham, in that his name was given to both his grandchildren).

Dr. V.Q. Bonham and Nanny Boggs Bonham. Photos are dated 1880.

Ernest and Margaret Chancellor built this house in the Missouri River bottom in 1904, near New Franklin and across the river from Boonville. They named it Maple Manor. Both my father, Bonham Chancellor, and his sister, Louise Bonham Johns, were born here. The house was on high enough ground that it never flooded during frequent high water periods, until 1994 when it got up to two feet deep inside. After that, the property was purchased by the government and razed.

The "Monroe" in his name harkens back several generations in the Chancellor family to Jane Monroe, an aunt of the fifth President of the United States, James Monroe. She was John Hore Chancellor's grandmother. And of course, both Ernest and his father, Brown, also carried the tradition of a middle name honoring the link to the president. (That tradition was continued into the next generation as well: my brother Sam carries the middle name "Bonham" and youngest brother Steve is "Stephen Monroe").

Poor Bonham Monroe Chancellor was saddled with carrying both family names, and always resented that he had to carry that baggage. According to my mother, he wished he had a simple name, but he never made an effort to change it, or even to go by a nickname, such as "Bud" which was suggested by mother. He just carried on as Bonham, or sometimes his initials, "B.M." which also has some negative connotations.

Young B.M. attended elementary school at Clark's Chapel, a country school and church about two miles from Maple Manor. Did he walk, or ride a horse? I don't know, but once when he said he often walked to school in the snow, an older relative remarked: "Why, Bonham, you did not, when it snowed, your mother got out the car and drove you to school."

The Clark's Chapel school is closed now, but the

Church is still in operation, and several generations of Chancellors are buried in its cemetery, on the crest of a hill overlooking the lush river valley below. When Bonham died in Boonville in 1980, we held his funeral service in Clark's Chapel, although he was buried back across the river in Boonville.

He graduated from high school in Boonville in 1925, then enrolled at Central College in Fayette, taking classes up to 1928 and in the summer of 1929. He then did three years of "high school work" (this would be the modern day equivalent of student teaching) at New Franklin High School. During the summers of 1930 and 1931, he attended Missouri State Teachers College at Warrensburg and also took University of Missouri Extension classes in

Bonham's freshman year photo, 1926. The notation reads: "Chancellor is the name of a good cigar and a good man."

1930. He then returned to Central College in 1932 to finish his degree. At some point after, perhaps the following year, he taught and coached basketball for one year in the tiny town of Bertrand, in extreme southeast Missouri, then returned to Boonville to teach, where he also met my mother. In 1938, he received a Master of Arts degree from the University of Missouri.

His sister, Louise, three years older, attended New Franklin High School, and then attended Howard Payne Junior College in Fayette as a high school student, from 1919 to 1923. She took piano lessons and piano related classes and did graduate from Howard Payne in Piano at the high school level. She attended Central College in Fayette from 1923 thru 1925, but she did not receive a degree from Central College. She taught music for a time in Memphis, Tennessee.

Louise Bonham Chancellor Johns, and her husband, Fleming Marshall Johns. He was from Boonville, hated his given name and always was known as "Skipper." He was a foreman for the state highway department, stationed in Jefferson City and then Fredericktown, MO. Skipper was swashbuckling to me as a kid because he drove a state pick-up truck.

At left is Aunt Lily, younger sister of my grandmother Margaret. She was married, but widowed the entire time I knew her. She was kowtowed to by my father and Aunt Louise because of the belief she had gotten more than her share of the estate when Dr. Bonham and his wife Nanny died, and the only way to get the money and a large farm back was to treat her with great deference. It didn't work — upon her death many years later, she left some money to survivors, but the farm went to someone else.

Bob (L) at Clark's Chapel and our kids (above) there. The adjoining cemetery has more than 20 Chancellor family graves, although Ernest and Margaret Chancellor as well as Bonham and Frances Chancellor, are buried across the river in Boonville. Bob, Sam and Stephen jointly own a burial plot at Clark's Chapel, and probably will make use of it among the family ghosts.

Bob at Maple Manor, after the flood and after the house was condemned. It was razed soon after this picture was taken. During this visit, we dug up a wild shoot from the maple trees that once lined the front of the home, and re-planted the sapling at our home at 2152 E. Berkeley in Springfield, where it has grown into a substantial, 30-foot tree. Unfortunately, we had to move away from that house and leave the tree behind.

CHAPTER 6 — THE TEARLES

Frances Marie Tearle was born October 20, 1913, in Carthage, Missouri, but her family moved to Chicago when she was a baby. Thirty years later, she would return to the vicinity of Carthage for the first time when our family moved to Webb City, just ten miles away. Frances always talked fondly of her early childhood in Chicago – particularly the beaches along Lake Michigan. Her father was head of the copy-writing department for the *Dry Goods Economist*. The family then moved to Sedalia and to Boonville which she really considered her home town.

Mother went through elementary and high school in Boonville, and for two years, attended Christian College, an all girls junior college, in Columbia. I know that at Christian, she was interested in modern dance, because one time *Life Magazine* did a photo feature about those dancers and she was among them. After college, for a time, she worked at the *Boonville Daily News* as a secretary and typist. She told me one of her main jobs was to take dictation daily from the Associated Press, which would call with a summary of the state and national news. Apparently the *Daily News* did not have a teletype machine. She was a pretty girl and a pretty woman. Everyone who knew Frances was struck by how sweet and gentle she was.

Her father was Arthur Tearle, a dry goods merchant, born in Stanbridge, Bedforshire, England in October, 1881. He immigrated to the United States at the age of 22, arriving at Ellis Island aboard the ship Carpathia, on June 10, 1904. (The steamship Carpathia would later gain fame when it rescued 705 survivors of the Titanic in April, 1912, and later again when it was torpedoed and sunk by a German submarine in 1918.)

He listed his occupation as a draper. I remember my mother saying that for a time he worked at a hospital, where he saw and cared for drunks, reinforcing his aversion to alcohol. Phoebe, her younger sister, is not aware of this story. Anyway, so far as is known, he never drank liquor and both he and his wife were strongly opposed to it. He listed his destination as Kansas.

After finishing public schools, he had become an apprentice in the dry good business in England, holding posts in London, Northampton and Reading. He decided to come to the U.S. while doing social settlement work in Northampton, when he became enthused about the U.S. by a couple whose wife had lived here. Arthur worked at a dry goods store in Fairfield, Iowa, and then attended Koster Window Trimming and Advertising School in Chicago.

He became window trimmer and publicity man for the Rush Store in Cherryvale, Kansas, where he met Mary Louise Nunnelly.
A Cherryvale newspaper article in 1910 states: *Arthur Tearle made a little trip to Independence (Kansas) this morning, returning with two*

LIST OR MANIFEST OF ALIEN PASSENGERS FOR THE U. S. IMMIGRATION OFFICER AT PORT OF ARRIVAL.

very important documents. One was his marriage license and the other was the proof that he is now a full fledged citizen of the United States. Mr. Tearle came to the United States six years ago. This morning he foreswore allegiance to the new King George by taking out naturalization papers. (Not quite true that he became "a full-fledged citizen," this was his original naturalization application, and precedes his Certificate of Naturalization by the required five years.)

They were married May 18, 1910. Another article in the *Cherryvale Daily Journal*, notes Miss Nunnelly had had a short residence in Cherryvale, coming after the Christmas holidays as a special supervisor of music in the public schools.

"Mr. Tearle," the newspaper said, *"is also an important factor in musical circles, possessing a cultivated tenor voice. He has made himself very popular in Cherryvale as well as proved himself a successful young business man."*

He became a naturalized American citizen on June 14, 1915. The naturalization certificate by the U.S. District Court at Joplin, Jasper County, Missouri, shows he was married at the time to Mary Louise Tearle, whose address was 1136 Maple Street, Carthage, Missouri; and had a minor child, Frances Marie Tearle, of the home. Judging from this time table, he was still a British citizen at the time of my mother's birth.

From Chicago, the family had moved to Missouri, where he was in charge of advertising for the Chasnoff stores of Sedalia, Warrensburg and Boonville. In 1922, he became manager of

Arthur Tearle and baby Frances in Carthage.

Chasnoff's Boonville store and became its owner in 1927, doing business as the Tearle Dry Goods Store on Main Street.

From the *History of Cooper County*, by E.J. Melton, 1937: *"From early boyhood he sang in choirs, first of the State church in England, and*

then in his adopted country. He was director of the Presbyterian choir in Boonville, a deacon in the church and active in the Knights of Pythias lodge. (According to Phoebe, her mother also was a member of the choir and they often sang duets. He also had been the choir director of the Broadway Presbyterian Church in Sedalia.)

At the time of his death (of a heart attack, at age 55) in January, 1936, he was a member of the Boonville Chamber of Commerce and was honored by a resolution of that organization. He died fourteen days before my birth – that fact led to my fascination in researching his history. And you will notice, I am his only descendent in this country to carry his surname as my middle name.

"Tearle" is a very unusual name both in this country and in England, although there is a society of Tearles in the U.K. His obituary said he was survived by four sisters in England and was the youngest of a large family. The sisters were twins Kate and Eliza born in 1873 and died in 1954; Sabina, 1875-1915 and Phoebe 1877-1953. He was pre-deceased by sister Annie, and brothers Frederick and Thomas. His father, John Tearle, was born in 1840 and was the Stanbridge Church sexton.

In an article in the History of Cooper County, written some time after his death, Arthur Tearle was described as quiet and self-effacing, "but his idealism, steadfast character and thorough capacities put him in a position of leadership."

In an interview with the writer of the Cooper County History article, in December, 1934, Arthur Tearle reminisced about Christmas in England and said he would enjoy a visit. *"However, I know I would find things different over there. Time and change bring disillusionment when one returns to old haunts. A short stay, I am sure, would forever cure recurring homesickness for scenes of my boyhood. There is greater opportunity here than in England and I love the country of my adoption."* He never returned to England.

I knew my maternal grandmother, Mary Louise Nunnelly Tearle better than any of my other grandparents. In fact, I lived with her for part of a year in 1955. Her full name was Mary Louise, but she apparently always just went by Louise. She was born September 27, 1883 at Danville, in Montgomery County, Missouri. Her parents were John Theophilus Nunnelly, born in 1837, and Mary Frances Bush, born in 1842. Louise was the youngest of seven children, and I remember her talking about her sisters, Eva, Ora and Gertrude, and brother, Guy. There was another brother, Luther, and a sister, Birdella, who died at the age of three.

John and Mary Nunnelly

Mr. Nunnelly was a mill operator and implement dealer in Montgomery City, where Grandmother Tearle went to school, but she never talked about her life as a girl. She next appears in my records in Cherryvale, Kansas, as a music teacher and fiancée of Arthur Tearle. She moved with her husband to Carthage, Chicago, Sedalia and to Boonville, where she raised her family. The Tearles lived in a two-story brick house high atop a hill at the south end of Main Street. The house is still there – my mother told of the car running out of gas and being able to coast all the way down the Main Street hill to a service station to refill the tank.

My aunt Phoebe was born October 15, 1920 in Sedalia and was in high school in Boonville when her father died. Louise had worked in the store alongside her husband on occasion, but neither Frances nor Phoebe ever worked there. Upon Arthur Tearle's death, Mr. Malone, a rival merchant who apparently had some investment in the Tearle store, took over the store and closed it. Phoebe remembers "it was not a pleasant situation and it upset mother greatly." Another competitor, Mr. Koppel, was described by Phoebe as being a lot of help after Arthur died, and offered Louise the job of running his store, the Sunny Day, a dress shop. Being the widow of a successful Boonville merchant apparently had not left Louise and Phoebe too well off.

About four years later, in 1940, Louise and Phoebe moved to Kansas City where grandmother went to work at Emory Bird Thayer, in the linen department, and Phoebe says she enjoyed that job very much. She worked there nearly 20 years. Phoebe recalls they moved to Kansas City because Phoebe wanted to attend the Edna Marie Dunn School of Fashion Illustration and Design. "Mother didn't want me to go to K.C. by myself and she had no reason to stay in Boonville, so we moved. I've always felt bad about that because she had such nice friends in Boonville. I think her life would have been much more pleasant there than in Kansas City."

The Tearle family visits Frances at Christian College, Columbia

In Kansas City, Grandmother Tearle can best be described as "indomitable and energetic." She was short, buxom and had white hair, which had turned at an early age. She never had a car, but walked long distances – often the 30 or so blocks to work – and rode public transit to work and to shop, always wearing a hat and little red gloves. She always lived in apartments, first near the Country Club Plaza and later on Armour Blvd. To my knowledge, she never had a boyfriend, nor any interest in re-marriage although she did tell me she had had opportunities. When she retired from the store, she stayed on in her apartment until dementia forced Mother and Phoebe to place her in a nursing home. She died in July, 1968, at the age of 85. At the time we were living in Thailand and unable to attend her funeral.

Phoebe and me (Bob). While in high school, she used me at a home economics project,

Marsh Kennedy, preparing to attack the snow in Buffalo, NY

Phoebe, who was an accomplished artist, also worked at Emory Bird Thayer in the advertising department after finishing the Dunn school. Then she got a job at Trans World Airlines in the advertising department but was put in the reservations department "to get a feel for the airline." She liked that so much that she just stayed in reservations from 1943 to 1946. While working there, she met Marshal S. Kennedy, a college roommate of her boss. They were married in September, 1946, in Buffalo, New York, and lived two years in Youngstown, New York, on the banks of the Niagara River where it flows into Lake Ontario. There they spent a lot of time sailing on his parent's 28 foot boat.

Marsh Kennedy worked for a time with TWA, and then with Bell Aircraft Company. I remember when I first met him, he gave me some Bell Co. pictures of the XS-1 experimental rocket-powered airplane, which was a Bell project. To me, he was an exciting creature, who drove an MG sports car. Their first daughter, Laura, was born in Youngstown, May 3, 1948. Then they moved back to Kansas City where Marsh worked for the Bendix Aviation Corporation. The company was a prime contractor to the Atomic Energy Commission, and while Marsh could not talk much about his job, he did travel frequently to New Mexico to observe nuclear bomb tests.

They lived at Lake Quivira, west of Kansas City, from 1951 to 1965, and their second daughter, Kristin, was born August 23, 1951. In 1965, the family moved to Jacksonville, Florida, where Marsh worked for Mason, Hanger, Silas, Mason engineering company until his death July 11, 1967. Phoebe and the girls moved back to Kansas

City in 1968, and not too long afterward, Phoebe married Arthur C. Popham, a successful lawyer and member of a prestigious Kansas City family.

Art, like Marsh, was a flamboyant character – he had done a lot of big game hunting and had a house full of African trophies, as well as several dioramas of his animals at the Kansas City Museum. He, too, was a car aficionado, having been the owner of a Cord in his younger days. He died September 23, 2009 at the age of 94.

Phoebe's eldest daughter, Laura, married and since divorced a journalist, Richard Olive, in 1977, and they had one son, Andrew Kennedy Olive, born November 17, 1980. Laura died in San Francisco on September 16, 2002.

Kristin married Larry Bowen in Houston on June 30, 1984, and they had two children, Marshall Thibideaux Bowen, born September 28; 1985 in Kansas City, and Marguerite (Maggie) Louise Bowen, born October 11, 1988. She was named after Louise Tearle. Larry, a master professional chef, died June 24, 2009.

Boonville was revisited in 1990 by my aunt Phoebe, (second from left) when she took my brother Steve, his wife Kay (at left) and her daughters Kristin (in front) and Laura (at right) on a tour of her old home town.

CHAPTER 7 — PIZZA AND POLIO IN KANSAS CITY

Some time back — before I digressed into the goat and flying and other stuff — I mentioned that my somewhat vague plans about what would follow high school were changed. In September, 1954, I had what can only be described as a life-altering experience. It was called polio.

Fresh out of high school, I had spent the summer working two jobs, for the highway department, and evenings and weekends clerking at the Safeway Supermarket in Webb City. College was to start in September, so I decided I needed a brief vacation. I went to Kansas City by bus to stay with my grandmother, and to visit a long-time friend who lived in Kansas City.

Richard Ballard was my age, the son of friends of my parents — his father was a teacher and his mother was related to someone my family knew (perhaps even a distant cousin) in Howard County. Richard and I had been summer playmates at the farm, where his aunt and uncle had a neighboring farm, and I had visited him before in Kansas City. I had always enjoyed the city, and was looking forward to a good time. We went to a couple of parties with his classmates at Southwest High School, and I even tasted pizza for the first time at Jimmy and Mary's Steakhouse.

But then I began feeling sick, and it wasn't the pizza. It felt like the flu. I was headachy, my back was sore and I was lethargic. I took to bed and stayed there for two days. (At Grandmother Tearle's apartment, there was only one bed, a pull-down Murphy bed, and I had been sleeping on the sofa, but I was feeling so bad that she gave me the bed and used the sofa herself.)

After two days of this, she became concerned and called my mother, who suggested she contact Dr. Needles, (really his name) then in Kansas City, but who had once been our family doctor in Webb City. Dr. Needles came to her apartment and immediately diagnosed my illness as polio. He called an ambulance and I was quickly transferred to the isolation ward at St. Mary's Hospital. That was my first, and so far, only ambulance ride.

In those days, polio was the scourge of summer for young people – thousands of kids would catch it each year and many remained crippled for life. I was a little old at 18 to be catching it; it usually seemed to hit younger children. There was not yet a polio vaccine – in fact, ironically, I was still in isolation about three weeks later when I heard a news announcement about the discovery of the Salk vaccine. That was just a little too late for my case.

I was a really sick puppy. At one point early on, I may have been near death. My breathing was affected and for a few days I was put in an iron lung – a really frightening, claustrophobic experience. Mother came up from Webb City and stayed with me. Dad came up on weekends, but had to go back for the start of the school year.

Short of the Salk vaccine, which was not yet available, the only known preventative for people who had been exposed to polio was a gamma globulin injection. GG was a blood extract, and its injection caused a large, painful lump in the hip of everyone who received it. As a preventative, many of my friends, including Richard and his school mates in Kansas City, and my girlfriend and friends in Webb City, were advised to see their doctor and get a sore souvenir of my illness.

After three weeks or so, I was no longer contagious, and was removed from isolation. Then began the rehabilitation process – a long, painful experience. At that point, I had no use of either leg, very little use of my right arm, and no strength in my back or abdomen.

The first element of treatment was what were called Sister Kinney hot packs. Twice a day, the patient (me) would be wrapped in steaming-hot wet wool blankets, and then a plastic sheet. The heat was supposed to relax constricted muscles, but what it created mostly was discomfort — first with the intense heat and then itching when the wet wool began to cool against my skin.

That's when I met Sister Mary Bede – who was to be my torturer, helper and friend for the better part of the ensuing year. A tall, lanky nun, probably not more than six years older than me, she was the physical therapist at St. Mary's.

Her family name was Boland and she was from Washington, MO. She left the order of the Sisters of St. Mary some time after my hospital time. My efforts to contact her since have been unsuccessful — I would like to have thanked her for being an important part of my life.

Rehabilitation consisted of twice daily immersions into a whirlpool tank of hot water, followed by her stretching and exercising my limbs and back. The stretching pain was severe. It was several weeks before she could move my legs through their full range of motion. I regained strength in my left leg and arms, but never regained anything in my right leg. It was shot.

The next phase was learning to walk with crutches and a brace on the right leg, then learning to get up and down stairs with them. The secret of recovery was exercise, exercise, exercise. I came to hate it. My father hung a sign on my bed: "If you want to walk, exercise." And at that time, my smoking habit came to be tolerated; not accepted, but tolerated. I suppose there were just much more important things in life than that.

Some of my fellow physical therapy sufferers. The small guy is Gary Spinks, about 5. To my left is Connie, about 16, who was a terrible, complaining polio patient. To her left is a girl whose name I don't recall — she did not have polio, but had a leg amputated because of diabetes and was learning to use an artificial leg — she was a real trooper.

A lot of the time, when not in therapy, I was in a wheel chair, and wheeled myself all over the hospital. Even before the wheel chair, I could lay on a gurney with big wheels at one end, and wheel myself up and down the hallway of Three North. I got to know a lot of people, both staff and patients. I was sort of a pet. I even went to a dance at the nursing school with a student nurse date.

I was an in-patient at St. Mary's for three months, and then released as an outpatient, still required to spend most of every day there in physical therapy. For a while, I lived with my grandmother, but I became too much for her to handle (an episode where I stayed out all night with friends put an end to that arrangement). So I moved into a rooming house next to the hospital, where several members of the staff lived.

Sister Mary Bede was a great therapist, but a lousy administrator. She liked me and hired me as a part time assistant to try to get her records and books up to date, and to provide me with some spending money. I was a real hospital bum – I spent my days either in treatment or at work; I spent my evenings with hospital staff people, and enjoying the night life of Kansas City. I ate most of my meals in the hospital cafeteria.

Sister Mary Bede encouraged me to get out and to get around. On one occasion, she prevailed on another patient to take me to Webb City for a quick visit home. He had had surgery on his arm and could not use his right arm or hand, but he could still drive home for a visit. Never mind that his home was in Pittsburg, Kansas, some 50 miles from Webb City and out of his way. I was still on crutches and a brace and had difficulty walking. We stopped for dinner enroute, and he had to help me get into the restaurant, and I had to cut his food for him. We made a great pair. But he delivered me to my front porch in Webb City for an unannounced surprise weekend visit. Then he made the trip out of his way again to take me back to Kansas City on Monday. Did I mention that Sister Mary Bede was persuasive?

I did improve. I got off the crutches, and walked with a cane. I had two surgeries, one to stabilize my right ankle, the other transplanting a tendon in my right foot. Eventually, I gained enough control of my right leg that I got out of the brace and walked by locking my right knee back. I was nearing the end of my career as a hospital bum, and in August, 1955, I was released and ready to resume my college career. Of course, being in this environment, and so intensely involved in it, I made a change in career plans. Once I get out of this, I decided, I will become a doctor.

CHAPTER 8 — LINDA AND JOURNALISM 101

Remember the old joke: "My parents moved and did not leave a forwarding address." Well, it almost was like that. During the year I spent in the hospital, my folks moved from Webb City to Springfield, where my father had gotten a teaching job. He was fed up with being an administrator and wanted to get back into the classroom. And Springfield had a good, well-paying school system, and a state college, Southwest Missouri State Teachers College, as it was known then.

They bought a house just three blocks from the campus, at 916 South Fremont. I never saw the house until I settled in there; in fact, I had only been in Springfield one time on a school excursion.

Tuition at SMS was only $26.50 per quarter, and I could walk to school and live at home. That was not really what I wanted to do – hey, I had lived pretty much on my own for the better part of a year – but there did not seem to be much other choice. Plus, for the first time in my life, I had a bedroom of my own.

In the few days before the start of the fall term, my mother and I were shopping downtown for school clothes. In the National Shirt Shop, just off the square in Springfield, I ran into a clerk, Dewey Joe Phillips (you remember him from my stint in the National Guard). He learned that I was planning to attend SMS, where he was a senior, and suggested I might consider his fraternity, Tau Kappa Epsilon. To that point, I had never thought about a fraternity – and my father was dead set against it because it would cost too much and would interfere with my studies. As it turned out, he was certainly right about the second part.

I had enough of my own money remaining from Kansas City (and even from the previous summer at the highway department) that I could afford it. So I signed up for rush, and became a member of TKE. It was without doubt the strongest, most prestigious fraternity on the campus at that time; I was one of 35 new members.

The Tekes did not want me because of my sterling personality – in fact, my personality had become a bit withdrawn and shy from being (I thought) the only kid on the campus who walked with a serious limp. And I certainly had nothing to offer in terms of intramural sports. No, Dewey Joe remembered that I was a pretty smart kid back in Webb City, and the fraternity needed a few scholars to help balance their overall grade point average.

I was still a pledge (probationer) in TKE when one of our members, Don Burns, was named editor of *The Southwest Standard*, the college newspaper. Don was a navy veteran (a drummer in the Navy Band in Washington) and a former editor of the newspaper before going into the service. He came to a fraternity meeting, seeking staff for the paper. I was picked (actually assigned) to become the Sports Editor. My fellow pledge and good friend, John Harlin, would be features editor. I have since decided it was because we were among the few pledges who could spell – I certainly did not have any interest, training or background in journalism and not a whole lot of interest in sports.

Burns said he would teach me, and he did. He became my mentor, and a good friend. Don had contracted myasthenia gravis while in the navy – a disorder which caused him frequently to lose control of his facial muscles and lose his ability for talk for a short period of time. I think we became friends because we both were self-conscious about our disabilities. He not only taught me the basics of journalism, he edited papers which I prepared for English classes, always pointing out ways to get a better, more dramatic lead and fuller content. He was a good editor and a good teacher.

My grades in English classes thrived because of his help. At the same time, my grades in chemistry and mathematics (prerequisites for pre-med) suffered because of the amount of time I was spending with fraternity functions and the newspaper staff. The newspaper was fun – staff members with an hour off would hang around the small office, talking or playing cards – a lot more fun than toiling in the chemistry lab. By the end of my freshman year, it was pretty obvious that I was not enough of a dedicated scholar to become a doctor.

At that point I was not yet considering journalism as a career – it was just something to do. But the classes I enjoyed most were those that would aid a future journalist: political science, history, sociology, economics, and English composition. By the start of my sophomore year, I had wangled one of the two paying jobs at the Standard, that of Business Manager. I sold and laid out advertising and ran the newspaper's budget, while still continuing to write. I was out of sports by then, doing general assignment stories, a weekly column, and was the defacto assistant editor.

At right, Don Burns and Bob discuss the layout with printers

Southwest Standard staff gather around a table as famous for games of Hearts and Spades as journalism. John Harlin, Bill Kelsay, Harmon Chapman, Claire Chalmers, Jo Ann Harris, Everett Underwood, Wayne Holsinger, Betsy Dimond, Bill Parrish, me and Linda Hulston.

It's a cliché often used in magazines and TV talk shows: "My wife (husband) is my best friend." But it can be true. One of the newspaper staff members that first year was Linda Hulston. She had a lot more experience in journalism than I did: she had worked on the Central High School newspaper in Springfield and had worked one summer

for the real newspaper, the *Springfield News Leader*. In addition to her contribution to the *Standard*, she also wrote a twice weekly column for the *News Leader* about news from SMS (as she had done from Central High School).

Linda and I didn't date – in fact she was going steady with one of my fraternity brothers. We were often on double dates, and at the same parties, and she was the best friend and sorority sister of a girl that I had a serious crush on. Besides that, I enjoyed her company. We were friends.

We even got in trouble together – on a double date at a college hangout called "Doc's 21 Club," which was raided by police. Unfortunately, I was not 21 and I had a beer. Pictures of the raid, and of Linda and me and others with black bands hiding our eyes, appeared on the front page of the Sunday newspaper. Linda's parents were pretty understanding about it since she wasn't drinking. I was in trouble at home, and got a real chewing out.

Linda dropped out of college midway in her sophomore year to go to work at KTTS radio as a copy writer and music librarian. She recommended me as her successor to write the twice weekly SMS column for the *News Leader*. I had become a published and paid journalist. Later that year, I got an even better job as a journalist, working four hours per evening for the *Daily News*, the sister paper of the *News Leader*. There I was thrown into writing obituaries, re-writing stories from the afternoon paper, and occasionally assigned a real news story to do. I was still doing the SMS column, and I continued as *Standard*

Linda with my first car, a 1954 maroon Ford convertible. Obviously from her dress, this was taken after we married and were expecting a passenger. Linda did help me pay off the car.

business manager, until I lost Don Burns' favor (over a girl) and I was replaced.

By then, I was launched into a career, not really of my making, but one I enjoyed and apparently had some talent for. I became an English major. (That was a no brainer, when I had one of the best writers on campus looking over one shoulder, and a very talented girl friend over the other.)

Before long, in the revolving door of Springfield media, I was hired as the afternoon and evening newswriter for KYTV – one of two television stations in town. The pay was better than the newspaper – in fact, I made enough money so that the day I turned 21, I was able to go out and buy my first car.

At KYTV, I was not on the air, I just wrote the 10 P.M. newscast and handed the script over to an announcer. I also clipped pictures from the UPI photo machine, and mounted them for showing on the air. It was a two member news department, headed by Sol Mosher, who left to become a Washington press aide to Congressman Durward Hall.

I was still in college at the time, and active in fraternity affairs, serving as secretary and historian of the chapter. During this time, I started dropping by KTTS, where my friend Linda worked. It also had a TV station and its policy was that the news-

writers also were news broadcasters. When an opportunity arose, I switched stations and became a newsman (writer, reporter and broadcaster) for KTTS radio and television. The newsroom there was in the basement, the radio and TV studios on the second floor, of an old converted mansion in downtown Springfield.

Linda and I became interested in being more than just best friends. We began dating, fell in love, she wore my fraternity pin, and we even occasionally discussed marriage in the future. She says she trapped me by coming to visit when I was in the hospital for another tendon transplant. Her aunt Betty, who was a hospital volunteer, claimed she saw me first and picked me out for Linda. The night I got out of the hospital, we went on a double date with a good friend, Bob Sims and his girl, and Linda and I decided we were pretty interested in each other. I had dated a lot in college, but Linda was really my first serious girl friend. Then disaster loomed. Linda's stepfather, Fred Hunt, was about to take a new job, that would cause him to move to Wichita, Kansas, taking along his wife, Georgia, and Linda. This caused a lot of worry for both of us – how would we stay together. My mother and father resolved that dilemma one eve-

1331 S Pennsylvania

ning: "If you like the girl that much, why don't you just marry her?" They owned a small rental house at 1331 Pennsylvania Avenue, near the campus, which they offered us for a minimal rent of $25 per month. The proviso: I had to finish college.

Delighted with that outcome, Linda and I became officially engaged at Christmas time, 1957, and started planning to get married March 7, 1958. As it turned out, we did not have to be in such a hurry – Fred changed his plans and they did not move to Wichita. Ever. (In later years, I would joke with Fred that the whole thing had been a con job to capture Linda a husband.)

KTTS radio and TV were housed in this old mansion in downtown Springfield. Note the antenna on the roof.

Bob and Linda were married March 7, 1958, at First and Calvary Presbyterian Church in Springfield. At left, Bonham and Frances Chancellor, at right Georgia and Fred Hunt. Completely by chance, the wedding date was the same as Bonham and Frances' wedding date in 1935.

Bob's moment of fame, or shame, was not welcomed when it appeared in the Sunday newspaper

The first interviewed by Howard was a youth of 20.

The boy immediately opened the conversation with, "Will there be any publicity about this? I don't want my dad to hear about it, if I can help it."

* * *

Howard told the boy that he couldn't answer that—that it would be up to other officials.

Howard then asked the boy for his draft registration card, and copied his name, address and age. He then obtained the names of the youth's father and mother (her maiden name), explaining that he wanted this information only to get a birth certificate on the boy.

Howard had a bottle of beer from which the boy had been drinking. He asked the boy if he had bought the beer, and, on receiving an affirmative reply, asked how much he paid for it.

"Too damn much—30 cents," said the boy. "And 25 cents for a coke (the price at the Stein Club) is even worse."

The boy then asked Howard, "Why'd you pick on me, out of all these kids?"

Howard answered, "We didn't pick on just you, son; there are a lot of kids who are going to be questioned tonight."

Howard then asked him, "Why did you start giving me a hard time (when Howard had first questioned the boy, he had admitted he wasn't 21, but denied drinking any beer, although Howard had seen him drinking it); why didn't you tell me the truth at first?"

Youth—"I just didn't want any trouble."

* * *

Howard—"Not telling me the truth could have meant a lot more trouble for you—we'd have had to pull you in for questioning."

After having the boy initial the bottle of beer, Howard permitted him to leave.

DISHONEST JOURNALISM LESSON: THE PERSON TAKING NOTES ON THIS INTERVIEW NEVER IDENTIFIED HIMSELF AS A REPORTER.

CHAPTER 9 — LINDA'S CLAN

Linda Lea Hulston was born in Springfield, October 4, 1937. Her mother was Georgia Helen Mace, born August 23, 1915, in Iberia, Missouri, but she and her sister Eileen (Betty) and brothers Maurice and James Robert, all grew up in Springfield.

Betty Mace with baby Georgia

Linda's father was Frederick Cecil Hulston, a Springfieldian born June 15, 1914. Georgia and Fred married the summer she finished high school and kept it secret for a year. Georgia and Fred lived with his parents on North Douglas street when Linda was born, and then they all moved to 1643 E. Belmont. Early proof of baby Linda's existence still is at that location – when

Fred Hulston and Linda

she was a toddler, a new concrete driveway was poured and her footprint was put in the wet cement. It is still there.

Georgia and Fred had a rocky marriage and Linda felt the consequences. Her parents divorced in the early 1940's and Linda and her mother lived with a family named Golden on east Locust street. Then Georgia and Fred remarried and moved to a home at

Fred and Georgia. Boats were one point of contention between the two; Fred loved boats, Georgia hated them.

800 North Jefferson. Linda attended the second, third and fourth grades at Bailey School. They divorced again and Georgia and Linda moved into the Camp Manor Apartments at 423 East Elm, in 1947.

Georgia had to work to keep the family together, and Linda spent many hours with a succession of sitters, or with her grandmother and grandfather, Leroy Christopher Hulston and Mabel Hill Hulston. Georgia worked as a bookkeeper at the Carr Shade Factory from 1939 until 1952. Then she went to work for Laura Traylor at the welfare office for six months, until Mrs. Traylor's husband hired Georgia away to work at his Ozark Typewriter Company. Georgia worked for Ozark Typewriter until her retirement many years later.

Linda and Grandmother Mabel Hulston

Mary and Clyde Bilyeau

Summers, Linda would be shipped to Iberia to stay with her other grandmother, Mary, (Georgia's mother) and step grandfather, Clyde Bilyeu. Fred Hulston took a second wife, Bonnie Pitts DeGraffenreid; and Georgia took a second husband, Fred Stewart Hunt, born January 29, 1919 in Garrison, Missouri.

Fred Hunt had moved to Springfield after his service in World War Two, and had become a sales-

Fred Hunt

man, eventually opening his own Farmers Insurance Agency. He was proud of his military service as a truck driver – "the best damned driver in the outfit" – with the third Armored Division, which landed at Omaha Beach on "D-Day plus 8." He was a local golfer of some note, with two lifetime holes in one and was active in veterans' organizations. He pretty much became Linda's de-facto father. Fred and Georgia celebrated their 50th wedding anniversary in January, 2000, just a few months before his death September 14 of that year.

Linda's father, Fred Hulston, also served in the war, but because of a medical problem – flat feet – he was allowed to choose his posting and he chose O'Reilly General Military Hospital in Springfield. For many years, he was a salesman for Oregon Saw Chain Company until he and Bonnie moved to Hickory County and began development of real estate and the Holiday Marina at Pomme de Terre Lake. He died in May, 1975.

Linda and her grandfather Leroy Hulston

Linda's grandfather, Leroy Hulston, was born in 1885 near Greenfield, Missouri, where his family operated Hulston Mill. He died in 1970. Linda's grandmother Hulston was a stern woman of German stock, whose fam-

Biggie & Grandpa Cuckoo

ily came to Missouri from Peoria, Illinois. She died when Linda was young, in 1945. Her grandfather re-married Frances Eaves, a widow from Memphis, Tennessee, who was known to her grandchildren, to Linda and eventually to our children, as "Biggie."

The name "Hulston" carries a lot of weight in Springfield — but not because of anything Linda's

direct family had done. Leroy's brother, also a Fred, was a businessman and banker at Ash Grove, and his son, John K. Hulston was a well known lawyer, historian, author and philanthropist who funded the Hulston Cancer Center at Cox Hospital.

Linda and her mother stayed close, sharing hardships and poverty together, until, as they say, "we married Fred (Hunt)." We always teased Georgia that she had chosen her second husband with special care – she didn't even have to change her monograms.

Another great influence in Linda's life was her Aunt Betty, Hazel Eileen Mace, born July 25, 1913. Betty, as she was always known, had been married and divorced from Leonard Pierce, and had re-married Granville Pearson Ward.

G.P., or G. Pearson, or just Pearson, was a broadcasting pioneer in Springfield. He had started the city's first radio station in 1922 in the Heer's Department Store, as a vehicle to popularize and sell radios. In 1942, he and several local businessmen started a commercial radio station, KTTS, and even later, in 1953, the city's first television station, KTTS-TV. He was its vice president and general manager, and thus, my boss when I went

Aunt Betty Ward and (below) Pearson

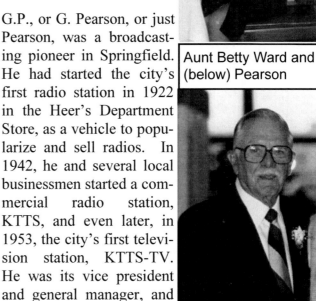

to work there from KYTV. Pearson also was very active in the Springfield Chamber of Commerce and was chosen as "Springfieldian of the Year;" and with the YMCA, where daily he played volley ball. He died October 18, 1987, several years after retiring. After his death, the Y was named for him.

Betty and Pearson were a glamorous couple by Springfield standards. Because of his affiliation with a CBS television station, they made frequent trips to New York or Los Angeles, where they would meet and be photographed with a parade of celebrities. They were better off than the rest of the family and belonged to Hickory Hills Country Club, but they were generous in sharing their good fortune. Betty was noted especially for her lavish gifts at Christmas and birthdays.

In 1972, Betty decided she wanted to go into business, so she and Pearson bought (ironically) the Carr Shade Factory, in partnership with Johnny Fittro, a long time employee. Betty worked at the plant as a bookkeeper and manager for 27 years, until her death December 22, 1999. In the latter years, the factory did not do a lot of business, but she kept it afloat, mostly because it gave her something to do. In the meantime, the television station had been sold, leaving her a wealthy woman (much later to the benefit of our family).

Zsa-Zsa and Ferd

When Linda and I were married, and later when Kimberly Ann Chancellor was born, November 3, 1958, we were surrounded by family. There was the notable scene, while Linda was still in the hospital, of her mother and stepmother coming into the room arm in arm to congratulate her and see the baby.

There was a lot of traffic to our house because of Kim — Georgia and Fred, Fred and Bonnie, my mother and father and brothers Sam and Steve, Betty and Pearson, Grandfather Hulston and Biggie. It's a wonder the poor child ever got any sleep. But we had lots of free baby-sitting, and when we were short on money, which was frequently, we could always find a place to be invited to dinner. Being surrounded by family like this made it difficult to leave when the time came to leave Springfield and set out on a career in broadcasting.

A few months after Kim's birth, my folks announced they were moving to St. Louis, but brother Sam would stay behind in Springfield to finish college. They owned another rental house, larger than our bungalow on Pennsylvania, and we moved to 1221 W. University Street, with Sam living in an apartment in the basement. Within a

few months we would move away ourselves, leaving Sam behind – not the last time we would abandon him.

A quick word about nicknames imposed on all these fine folks by our children. Georgia became "Zsa-Zsa" because Kim could not pronounce Georgia, and Georgia was not at all interested in being known as grandmother. The older of us did, and still do, call her "George." Fred Hunt became "Grand Ferd," because "Ferd" is what Linda's best friend, Martha, always called him. Grandfather Hulston became "Grandpa Cuckoo" because of the clock he had on his wall. Biggie was always Biggie. Fred Hulston would come to be known as "Grandpa Truck" because he had a Jeep pickup. Betty and Pearson were always Betty and Pearson. My folks were known as "Nana" and "Grand daddy."

While on the subject of nicknames: my mother was known to high school and college friends as "Titter," which was Aunt Phoebe's baby pronunciation of "sister."

426 E. Bennett. The home of Fred S. and Georgia Hunt, and the house where Linda grew up. For many years, this also served as our official address when we were overseas.

The Mace kids of Iberia and Springfield. L-R: Maurice, Eileen (Betty), Georgia, James Robert.

Fred Hulston, Linda and Linda's stepmother, Bonnie.

This is Fred Hulston where he would most want to be — fishing on Pomme de Terre Lake.

At left, Leroy Christopher Hulston visits the Hulston Mill, on the Sac River, in Dade County near Greenfield. Roy grew up at the family owned mill and for a time operated it.

The Hulston family took over and modernized the mill in 1892 and operated it until 1897, then leased it out until 1906.

The mill was established in 1840 at the confluence of the Sac River and Turnback Creek. The mill played a role in the Civil War, furnishing food supplies for the Union troops in Springfield, before and after the Battle of Wilson's Creek, the first Civil War battle west of the Mississippi.

When the Stockton Dam was built in 1967, the Hulston Mill site was to be flooded, so the mill building was moved to dry ground about a mile away and preserved as a historic site.

Lower left, Linda visits the Hulston Mill in its new location.

CHAPTER 10 — ST. JOE, FRANK, AND THE KISSIN' KUSN

My strongest recollection of Frank Smith is at a lumber yard fire shortly after I began working as a newsman at KFEQ Radio and Television in St. Joseph, Missouri. Frank was standing in the middle of a street intersection, in water nearly up to his knees, with fire hoses snaking all around and firefighters bustling to and fro. He was trying to photograph the blazing structure only a few feet away.

That should not be an exceptional picture of a small town TV News Director – except that Frank had had a severe case of polio a few years earlier, and was required to use crutches and wear braces on both his legs, up to his waist. His disability never stopped him from covering the news. He traveled all over St. Joseph in his car, with hand controls, jumping out to take pictures, lumbering into the court house, city hall or the police station, to check with news sources.

The television studio at KFEQ was on a lower level of the building from the offices and newsroom, and for every TV newscast, at least twice a day, Frank would make the arduous climb down a long flight of stairs to the studio, carrying scripts and pictures, and after the program, climb back up to the newsroom. He never complained about it.

I met Frank late in 1959, a few weeks after I had finished college at Southwest Missouri State. I had gone out searching for a job away from Springfield, where the broadcasting industry paid notoriously low wages. I really wanted to work in radio and TV in Kansas City, but being fresh out of college, I knew I needed some grounding elsewhere first.

I had made a lot of contacts with news directors around the state by mail and phone, and had even gone to Moberly and Hannibal in Northeast Missouri, and to Sioux City, Iowa, to apply for jobs. Going home to Springfield from this job search, I passed through St. Joseph, but for some reason did not stop there, having not made any contact there. I had not been home more than a couple of days when Frank Smith called me, saying he had heard

I was looking and that he needed a newsman. I quickly drove back to St. Joseph for an interview, and was offered a job. And it was for more money. In Springfield, I was earning $75 per week; KFEQ was willing to pay $100 per week, plus a $5 car allowance.

KFEQ, then, was a fairly big-time radio station, one of the original high-powered radios in the Midwest with a signal that could be heard over several states. They were big on local news and farm programming, and played middle-of-the-road and some popular music. KFEQ television was a CBS affiliate, but faced the competition of bigger, richer TV stations in Kansas City. Its biggest asset was that it was a home town station and the only television station in town. (Everyone in St. Joseph also watched the three network stations in Kansas City.)

The news department consisted of Frank and me. We shared work space with a two-man farm department and with two staff announcers who handled sports and weather. We did not shoot film, and video was way off in the future, but we all carried Polaroid Instamatic cameras with us at all times, and used those still pictures, as well as wire photos from AP, to make up TV newscasts. Breaking news for radio was covered by calling in from the scene of a story by telephone (usually by borrowing some neighbor's telephone) and ad-libbing the story to tape, which was then carried to the studio and put on the air (or included in a newscast if it was not of bulletin importance).

I worked the early morning shift for radio newscasts, then went out to check on the police station and city hall before returning to the station to do noontime newscasts on radio and television. Each newscast was 15 minutes. In the afternoon, I would cover the court house, or other events, bringing material back for the evening. Frank began work at mid-day and did the 6 P.M. and 10 P.M. television news. But we both were on call – if there was breaking news in the morning, I would call Frank at home and send him out, and after 6 P.M., when I was off, he would call me out to cover accidents and events around town.

Frank and I became close friends as well as working colleagues. When I first took the job in St. Joseph, I rented a spare room in his house until I could find a place to live, and bring Linda and Kim to join me. Frank and his wife, Betty, often would take rides around town in the evening – it was his way of keeping track of what was going on in his town. And as the new kid, I often rode with them, learning the lore of St. Joseph.

In 1960, St. Joseph was the third largest city in Missouri, a few thousand larger than Springfield. But even then, it was obvious that it was not as progressive a city as Springfield, which soon would surpass it in size and importance. It was an old Missouri River city, with lots of ancient buildings and some pretty grimy industrial areas. (Although everybody in Missouri referred to the city as "St. Joe," tradition was that no one liked that shortcut, and on the air we were prohibited from using that name.)

Two years passed, and I took the opportunity to

Above: First house in St. Joseph at 2725 Oakland
Below: Second house, 3126 Miller Avenue.

keep up contact with TV stations in Kansas City, still with the hope of working there some day. That looked like big time, with ten to fifteen member news staffs, cameramen who shot film for news, remote units and two way radios in station owned news vehicles.

We moved to St. Joe in the fall of 1959, and David Alan Chancellor was born January 7, 1960, at Missouri Methodist Hospital. Craig Robert Chancellor followed a year later, on June 12, 1961. We lived at first in a small two bedroom house at 2725 Oakland, but our growing family prompted a move to a larger house at 3126 Miller Avenue.

The times in St. Joseph were good; we had a lot of friends among the station staff and some neighbors. And we were known in the community – it was a good example of being a big duck in a small pond, everybody in town seemed to know the number two newscaster at the only TV station in town.

One venture involved wheel chair basketball. Frank Smith was the instigator of that; he rounded up eight guys with disabilities who could qualify

Wheelchair basketball. That's Frank Smith nearest to the camera.

for wheel-chair competition, and found a sponsor who donated five special sports chairs to the team. Most of the players were ambulatory; I was the most ambulatory of the group and I was not a very effective athlete sitting down. But I was important to the team because I could be sent running off on errands, and help the others in transporting the chairs. We even played once out of town. A local manufacturer, the Anchor Serum Company, allowed us to fly to Indianapolis, Indiana in their company plane for a game.

I even did some acting with the St. Joseph Little Theater group. I still remember the opening lines from my first play, *Detective Story:* "My name is Sims. Endicott Sims. I'm an attorney." In makeup for that role, the hair at my temples was brushed white. Linda liked the look; little knowing that soon enough that graying would come naturally.

Since high school, I had been a jazz fan, particularly a fan of the Stan Kenton band. I heard them play once at Drury College during my freshman year at SMS. St. Joseph had a big dance hall, the Frog Hop Ballroom, and one night, the Kenton band was playing the Frog Hop. Linda and I bought tickets which we couldn't afford and went. Stan Kenton had been a Teke, and while we were standing just in front of the stage, I mentioned to him that I, too, was a Teke. "Where are you sitting?" he asked. I pointed out our table, and he said, "I'll talk to you at intermission." And at intermission, he came directly to our table, sat down and we proceeded to chat throughout the break. We talked about college and children and music, just long-time buddies, until the band starting playing the theme song, *Artistry in Rhythm*, and he headed back to his piano. It was a wonderful experience.

I met Richard and Pat Nixon in St. Joe. They were campaigning there for President against John Kennedy in 1960. I took a Polaroid picture of each, and asked them to autograph it. Nixon seemed amazed at the technology of instant photography.

After John Kennedy defeated Nixon, he appointed Newton Minow to be the head of the Federal Communications Commission. And Minow made a speech describing television as "a vast wasteland." The management of KFEQ was quite distressed that I used that story in a newscast. I didn't even use the full quote from his speech to the National Association of Broadcasters:

When television is good, nothing — not the theater, not the magazines or newspapers — nothing is better. But when television is bad, nothing is worse. I invite each of you to sit down in front of your television set when your station goes on the air and stay there for a day without a book, without a magazine, without a newspaper, without a profit and loss sheet or a rating book to distract you. Keep your eyes glued to that set until the station signs off. I can assure you that what you will observe is a vast wasteland.

But I thought then — and still do — that Minow was right. And television now is worse.

I also had the interesting experience of interviewing Oral Roberts when he brought his revival to St. Joseph. I think he recognized my skepticism as he described his ability to bring God's healing down to individuals in his audience, but he retained a calm, placid demeanor. I went away with this conclusion: I don't believe he can heal, but I believe he believes he can.

Being in St. Joe with the only grandchildren in the family meant we had a steady stream of visitors – Georgia and Fred from Springfield, Mother and Dad and Stephen from St. Louis. And we were able to get away to Springfield or St. Louis and even to the Lake of the Ozarks occasionally.

We would go to Kansas City frequently to visit with Phoebe, Marsh and the girls. We appreciated the chance to play in Lake Quivira and we enjoyed their company a lot. They had been awfully good to me when I was recuperating from polio, having me and occasionally a date, out to their house for the day. When I was looking for a job, as you will soon learn, Marsh introduced me to his bosses at Bendix – they had no need for a journalist, but thought I might be useful in a management team for my skill in writing and collating reports. No job was ever offered.

However, during this time (unbeknownst to me) the KFEQ management decided they did not like my style or presentation of news on TV. To my surprise one day, I was introduced to Jon Poston, who had been hired, I thought, as the third member of our news team, only to learn that he had been hired to replace me. Frank was not happy about this but had no power to stop it. I was instructed to take Jon Poston around and introduce him to my news sources as my replacement, which I reluctantly and begrudgingly did.

One of the people to whom I introduced him was Magistrate Judge Margaret Young. She, too, was unhappy about the way I was being treated and she did something about it. She contacted a good friend who was the Coca Cola distributor in St. Joseph, and he, in turn, contacted KFEQ with the message that if I was let go, he would withdraw his advertising from the station. With that threat, I was retained at KFEQ and we had a three-man news staff, although I was now relegated to radio news only.

During this unsettled period, I was contacted by Ward Wright, manager of KUSN radio in St. Joseph, who said he wanted to create a local news presence on his station. It was a highly-rated rock-and-roll broadcaster, which carried no news except what could be ripped and read from the UPI wire. He offered me $110 per week, which was what I was making at KFEQ by then. This being before the intervention of Coca Cola, I accepted, but then after Coca Cola, I called him back and declined the job, telling him I was staying at KFEQ.

"But I thought you were out of a job," he said. "I was," I replied, "but I am not now." At that point, he offered me $125 per week, which there was little chance of making at KFEQ. In fact, that was a salary equal to Frank's, and I would have the title of News Director. I was still reluctant, because I believed news coverage was serious business and I was not sure this rock-and-roll pop-music teakettle was as serious about it as I was. Wright assured me that he was serious about news, and that my hiring was not a ploy to in-

crease rating, but a long term commitment to the community, so I accepted.

At KUSN –"Your Kissin' Cousin" as they said on the air – I stayed with the concept of news being a serious business and not a part of the rock-and-roll scene. We did build up some audience for news, and had some successes. Our newscasts had a brighter sound than those at KFEQ, and we did on-air editorials which were a first for St. Joseph broadcasting. Wright and I had some disagreements about how bright and flashy the newscast should be, but I usually managed to keep them in a style that I felt was acceptable and responsible. Frank Smith and I remained good friends and in contact with one another even as competitors, to the point of protecting one another when major stories occurred.

In many ways, KUSN was very much like the television program *WKRP In Cincinnati*. Ward Wright was the chief salesman as well as manager and part owner. The secretary/receptionist was a pretty woman, though no Loni Anderson, who had more common sense than anyone else on the staff. We had a chief engineer with whom I shared an office, but I never felt obliged to put yellow tape on the floor to delineate the newsroom.

There were never more than two or three announcers on staff. KUSN was a daylight only operation, and usually had one DJ from opening to noon, and another from noon to closing, plus one who mostly did promotions and commercials. One consistent problem was that our early morning DJ, who was supposed to open up at 5:30 or 6 A.M., often overslept, and did not have a phone. So I would come in to work for the morning news, and put on an LP record (which did not fit our rock and roll format) and leave the building to go wake him up.

During the year, the management also installed an FM transmitter, the first in St. Joseph, and for a few nights (until an automated system was installed) I got to play late night disk jockey with jazz. I was the first voice on the air for KUSN-FM for its world premier.

Unfortunately, Ward Wright's commitment to community affairs was not as strong as his commitment to the ratings, and KUSN was unable to dislodge KFEQ radio from its top rating in the key 7 A.M. newscast. (That was, after all, the same 7 A.M. newscast that I had done on KFEQ for two years.) Almost exactly one year after he hired me, Wright said he was letting me go because we had not beaten out KFEQ. This chilling announcement came at the time of Thanksgiving, 1962, and he gave me until Christmas to find another job.

It was a devastating time and a bleak Christmas. I did not immediately find another job although I had been actively keeping my resume out in front of all sorts of news directors around the Midwest, and also had letters out seeking a job in public relations. That was the way broadcasting worked in those days (and still does today). To advance, you had to move on to another, hopefully bigger, job in a bigger market.

One of the contacts I had made had been with Voice of America. I had seen an item in the good old *Southwest Standard* from SMS that VOA was looking for announcers and news-writers to work in Washington, D.C. I sent off an application, and wrote a sample newscast for them from a *New York Times* newspaper as requested. They seemed interested, but said it would be a matter of several months before anything could be done about hiring me. And in the present circumstances, we did not have several months: I needed a job immediately.

St. Joseph really didn't leave me with any good memories and no desire to go back. Linda and I did make a quick trip there from Kansas City one time, but we no more than hit the city limits when it began to snow, and we got the hell out of town.

But forty-one years after leaving with my tail between my legs, in April 2004, I did return to St. Joseph for a Sertoma Club regional convention. And I decided that I would try to find (or find out about) Frank Smith. I knew from some source or another that Frank had quit KFEQ, and had gotten a job doing public relations for the college in St. Joseph. There had always been a Junior College, but there had been a long term campaign to make it a four-year school, an effort led in large part by attorney John Downs, who had been a good friend of mine and Frank's. And not long after I left

town, the effort had succeeded. Frank's assignment there probably had a great deal to do with John Downs' influence.

In my search for Frank Smith, I contacted Richard Dahms, another attorney and a teammate from our wheel-chair basketball days. Dahms told me Frank and his wife, Betty, had divorced, and that Frank had died in 1980. He did remember that Betty had worked for some office in town, so I called there. Eventually, someone remembered that Betty, too, had died. They had a daughter, Marci, who had married, but no one remembered her name. The News Express newspaper was no help – they had no information in their morgue. Neither did the public library. No help at the university.

I went out to KFEQ television, still in the same location, except the muddy road up the hill had been paved. Same dumpy brick building, nestled under the TV tower; same long steep flight of steps to the studio. No one remembered Frank Smith – one staff member told me "Five years here makes you an old-timer."

The city of St. Joseph looked more depressed than ever. Downtown was dotted with vacant lots – it looked like it had been bombed. There are still some pretty residential areas, but it is no place I would want to live, or even re-visit.

The whole episode of trying to find Frank reminded of a tribute to journalists written by Stanley Walker for the New York Herald Tribune in 1934:

"What makes a good newspaperman? The answer is easy. He knows everything. He is aware not only of what goes on in the world today, but his brain is a repository of the accumulated wisdom of the ages.

He is not only handsome, but has the physical strength which enables him to perform great feats of energy. He can go for nights on end without sleep. He dresses well and talks with charm. Men admire him; women adore him; tycoons and statesmen are willing to share their secrets with him...he hates lies and meanness and sham, but keeps his temper.

He is loyal to his paper and to what he looks upon as his profession; whether it is a profession, or merely a craft, he resents attempts to debase it. When he dies, a lot of people are sorry, and some of them remember him for several days."

We moved to St. Joseph with one little girl — when we left there were three snowbirds. And in St. Joe, we did see snow — lots of it We added Steven Mark to the family just 14 months later, on Groundhog Day, 1964. Because of some dithering on the part of his parents, he came very close to being born on the Memorial Bridge instead of in the D.C. hospital.

This is way out of sequence, but grandmother insists the grandkids' picture has to be in here somewhere. L-R: Shannon Carter, Justin Chancellor, Jenny Chancellor, Kyle Carter. And in the fall of 2010, we added a fifth grandchild when son Craig and Donna adopted two year old Mason Cole Chancellor.

CHAPTER 11 — BACK TO THE OZARKS, BRIEFLY

The idea of working for the Voice of America was intriguing but did not seem to be a reasonable avenue for an unemployed St. Joseph newsman with three children to feed. I started knocking on the doors of the Kansas City media again, and even did interviews in St. Louis. I also investigated the possibility of finding a job in public relations (several of my former Springfield news colleagues had landed such employment with various public service and non profit organizations).

Meanwhile, back in Springfield, KTTS News Director Bill Bowers unfortunately had contracted lung cancer and had undergone surgery. The station needed someone to fill in for him, but Pearson Ward was reluctant to replace him while Bill was still alive and ailing. Father-in-law Fred Hunt to the rescue. He was aware of our situation in St. Joseph and suggested to Pearson that I could come back to KTTS temporarily. So early in 1963, dejected and frustrated, we packed all our belongings in a trailer and began the trek back home.

Things had changed at KTTS during my absence. For one, the pay was much better. The staff had been unionized by the International Brotherhood of Electrical Workers, and newsmen were paid the grand sum of $137.50 per week – a big jump from KUSN. There were four people in the news department, plus a photographer. We were in a new modern building on the edge of town – long gone was the downtown mansion studios (although radio still operated there — we did radio newscasts by remote control from the TV station).

Since we expected we would be in town only temporarily, we found a three bedroom duplex on North Kansas Avenue. We had lots of old friends from past times, and Georgia and Fred, and Betty and Pearson, and Linda's grandparents were in town. Linda's father and stepmother had located in Hickory County, about 50 miles north of Springfield, and were involved in developing real estate and a resort on the newly formed Pomme de Terre Lake, and we made frequent trips there to swim. I was working an early morning shift, doing radio and TV news, and the Noon news, and usually was done by mid afternoon. I even mastered the art of doing live weather forecasts.

Bill Bowers' job remained open and no one was news director. Two of us on the staff were competing to be his eventual replacement; Ron Arnold and me, and I don't know to this day how that competition would have worked out. But during that spring, VOA finally came through.

I had been working hard getting an appointment to VOA, which was an element of the U.S. Information Agency. I contacted my old KYTV boss, Sol Mosher, who was working for Congressman Hall, and Sol promised to shake some doors for me. Pearson wrote to Congressman Hall and to USIA Director Edward R. Murrow on my behalf. A state senator and good friend in St. Joe, John Downs, wrote to U.S. Senator Edward V. Long. But the first I knew that something was about to happen was when I got a warning call from a friend that an FBI agent had been around, asking questions about me. To work even as a lowly newswriter at VOA required what was called a "full field clearance," a security check that would allow me access to top secret information.

One evening I received a call from a gentleman who identified himself as an FBI agent, who said he was working on my clearance. But there was a problem. He had been to SMS to obtain a copy of my college transcript, and they would not give it to him because of "an unpaid debt to the college." That, he said, would be enough to prevent me from receiving the full field clearance and the VOA job. But he gave me a break: if I would go to the college first thing the next morning, and settle the account, he would return to the college in the afternoon, request and obtain my transcript as if nothing had ever happened. I did so the next morning and learned that the outstanding debt was for 75 cents for a transcript I had ordered after graduation. I paid immediately. The matter was settled, but I will always be amazed that my college was prepared to jeopardize a graduate's career over a mere 75 cents.

Fred Hulston and Holiday Marina at Lake Pomme de Terre

Early in May, 1963, I received a call from Washington: VOA was prepared to offer me a job, as a GS-9 newswriter, for $6675 per year, which was $500 less than I was earning at KTTS. After all these months, they wanted to know if I could report for work the following week. I accepted the offer, but said I could not be in Washington until the first of July, because of my current commitments to KTTS and family.

I had some hesitation about accepting at all, because of the lower pay; because we were really enjoying life back in Springfield after the recent trauma in St. Joseph; and because I still had hopes of being named as Bill Bower's successor. I also had a real hot prospect for a public relations job in St. Louis.

We were enjoying the spring and early summer in the Ozarks, especially with the Lake Pomme de Terre so close by. I even wondered if there would be a chance to stay in my home territory and perhaps work at the marina that Fred and Bonnie Hulston were developing.

My father, too, was hesitant, because of the pay. "Civil servants don't make much money," he advised, and especially because of the higher living expenses in far away Washington. The two of us met with a friend of his, a long time federal civil servant, who advised that it was, indeed, a good deal. The rank of GS-9 might be the highest a person could aspire to in the Midwest, he said, but in Washington, the "head shed" as he described it, GS-9 was just a starting point, with great opportunities for advancement. That convinced me, and Dad. The friend was right, within 3 years my salary was over $12,000, surpassing what my father earned.

I did learn later that I accepted appointment too cheap. That same summer, VOA hired a couple of other writers who had less broadcasting experience that I did, at a higher rate of pay. But their rationale was that they were hiring an unknown commodity from a small town in fly-over country.

The *New York Times* once ran a series of advertising for their want ads in which people proclaimed: "I got my job through the *New York Times*." I borrowed from that, and told folks who asked: "I got my job through *The Southwest Standard*." Or to paraphrase an old joke: Q: "How did you get to VOA?" A: "On the Pennsylvania Turnpike."

The last weekend of June, 1963 found me packing our car, a bright red Rambler station wagon. It was loaded to the roof and onto the roof-top rack, with clothes and goods, including two snow tires in mid-summer. I was moving as much stuff as I could while traveling alone – Linda and the kids remained behind in Springfield while I would begin work and find a place to live. It would be a month and a half before they would join me.

CHAPTER 12 — VOA: THIS IS THE BIG TIME?

With a mixture of excitement and trepidation, I headed east into areas unknown. Overnighted with the folks in St. Louis, then onto Highway 66 to the outskirts of Chicago, onto the Indiana and Ohio turnpikes and the fabled Pennsylvania turnpike which I had heard about for years, but of course, had never seen. (We are not in Kansas anymore, Toto.)

It was a two day journey and I pulled into Washington on a sunny Sunday morning, cruising down Connecticut Avenue and mastering a couple of D.C.'s infamous traffic circles.

I found the downtown YMCA, where I had a room reservation, because it was near the U.S. Information Agency headquarters at 1776 Pennsylvania Avenue, just down the street from the White House at 1600 Pennsylvania Avenue. I did a little bit of quick sight-seeing of the Washington Monument and other areas. And I quickly learned about the costs of a major city in the east because it cost me $5 in advance to park the Rambler overnight in a nearby parking lot.

> Letter to Linda, July 1: *The city was a beautiful place as I entered it, coming in on Connecticut Avenue, through the Chevy Chase area. I drove around for a while, driving by Lincoln Memorial, the Washington Monument and the White House. Then I came to the YMCA and checked in. After that, I went back to Washington Monument for the trip to the top, drove along the Potomac, down by fisherman's wharf, looking at cruisers and yachts, and drove around town until I got lost.*

I went to sleep that first night, with a view of the lighted Washington monument out my window.

Early the next morning, I went to the USIA headquarters, only to be met by total puzzlement. VOA, it turns out, was not in that building and they did not know anything about a Robert Chancellor reporting for duty from Missouri. And they weren't particularly helpful. Finally, someone took pity on me and directed me to VOA, in the HEW (Health, Education & Welfare Department) Building at the other end of the mall, nearly 20 blocks away. "There is no place to park down there," they said, suggesting I take a bus. But no one seemed to know what bus would get me there. So leaving my car behind for another $5 per day parking bill, I walked to 3rd and Independence, S.W. I did get to see a better part of the famed Washington mall during that trek and I was amazed by the size and magnificence of the government buildings, the Capital, and the expanse of greenery in the midst of a large city.

Eventually, I checked in at the VOA Personnel Office, was given a quick briefing and was taken to the newsroom on the second floor of the HEW Building. Typically, no one in Personnel was very helpful when I asked about where I might find a place to live, either temporary or permanent – the general response was that whatever I found would be expensive.

The newsroom was massive, with 40 desks in it, and someone at nearly every desk. An ante-room contained 30 or 40 teletype machines clattering away, spewing out yards and yards of paper. Another ante-room had half a dozen people typing away at telex machines. Phones rang constantly, and shouting across the room seemed to be the standard method of communication. After explaining that VOA was taking a big chance on me, because they had never hired anyone off the federal employment register without personal interviews, the News Chief quickly showed me around the room, introduced me to a couple of editors, pointed me toward a desk and left.

It was bewildering at best. There were no radio studios in sight. The writers did their work by re-writing from wire service reports, their desks littered with papers as they parsed through several versions of events from various news agencies, distilling them into one brief story. The central editor's desk – where most of the shouting originated – then compiled these stories into news casts, which went into the nearby telex room for transmission throughout the building. Basically it was a wire service operation, not a radio station. Most of the staff were wire service or newspaper veterans, not broadcasters. Some, it turned out, were diplomats on temporary assignment (more on that later).

I went to lunch with a couple of colleagues from the editors desk, and finally, got some advice on places to live, how to get around D.C. (by bus, they said, and told me the bus route back to the YMCA and my impounded car). In the course of that afternoon, I wrote one news story, about six lines concerning an earthquake in Skopje, Yugoslavia.

Back at the Y that evening, I was not a happy person. I didn't really like Washington – too busy, too big, too unfriendly, too expensive. I seriously considered bailing out my car and heading back to Missouri and the comforts of Springfield, my family and good old KTTS. Besides that, my feet hurt from all the walking. Eventually, we lived a total of seven years in the Washington, D.C., area and despite having friends, sufficient money, good times and interesting work, I never got over those first impressions – I never really liked the place.

Letter to Linda, July 14. *In contrast to the first day or two in the newsroom, when everything was so confusing, I now have come to the conclusion that this job really is rather dull. If I stay here, I hope I can get promoted out of here. The prospect of staying in this room and re-writing wire stories for the next 30 years is not very encouraging. And I have found out one other thing which I was not told as I got interested in this job. Civil service people are not eligible*

for, and do not get, overseas assignments. For that type work, you have to transfer to the Foreign Service, after passing a test and being accepted. It all goes back to the same old thing I debated with myself about before coming. I liked what I was doing, I just didn't see any bright future in it. Now, I don't particularly like what I am doing, and I don't know what the future is. I feel like storming into Ed Murrow's office and asking "just what the hell are my chances around this place.?

Which I guess I could have done, if I knew Ed Murrow and could find his office, which obviously was not in the HEW Building.

Within the first week, I found a temporary apartment to live in at McLean Gardens on Wisconsin Avenue. There I could park my still-loaded car for no charge. I learned the bus routes, met some young newcomers as bewildered as I was, was impressed by the Fourth of July fireworks on the Mall, and started house hunting.

Rental rates were outrageous. But by the first of August, I signed a year's lease for a two bedroom duplex just south of Alexandria, Virginia, and moved out of my McLean Gardens apartment to the house at 1522 Arlington Terrace. No palace, but it had a basement playroom and a fenced yard for the kids for a mere $115 per month, plus utilities.

I began to learn how the Voice worked. I found the studios, where announcers, not newswriters, read the news. And language offices, where translators converted the output of the newsroom into 30 languages, from Russian, Chinese, Spanish and Arabic to Pashto, Lao and Greek. I also learned that VOA newsroom operated 7 days a week, 24 hours a day. I learned this at the end of the first week, when the news chief told me that everyone had to take a turn at working the overnight shift, from 11 P.M. to 7 A.M., and that, as a new guy, that was where I was to go next week. And, yeah, new guys don't get weekends off, their weekends come mid-week.

In fact, this turned out to be beneficial. It gave me weekdays to house hunt, and time to explore the Washington area. And by working nights, I received a 10 percent pay bonus, which was really welcome. Other advantages of working overnight: I didn't have to wear a coat and tie, parking was free, cafeterias were closed so we brown-bagged, there were greater opportunities to do more meaningful work, and there were not a lot of high brass looking over my shoulder.

I also began to learn how VOA and USIA worked together, and against each other. Later, VOA would be described as "at the crossroads of journalism and diplomacy." True, we were a government-owned radio station, but true, also, we were journalists and felt the calling to disseminate news fairly and objectively. It was a struggle that never

A QUICK PRIMER ON HOW IT ALL WORKS

Early in July, I went back across town for a two day orientation on USIA, as it was known in Washington, the United States Information Agency. Overseas, the same organization was known as the U. S. Information Service. Why? I never knew.

VOA was an element of USIA — its radio service (and the largest single element by far.) The agency also had a film division, a press division, it published magazines, and a tiny TV division.

Most of the supervisory jobs were held by Foreign Service Officers on domestic assignment, waiting for their next chance to go overseas. Work and supervision was divided up by regions: Far East, Latin America, Europe, Africa, Middle East. VOA was also divided by those same regions, even in the newsroom where we had separate desks and writers for each region.

Overseas, USIS functions were overseen by the Public Affairs Officer, or PAO, who was a part of the Ambassador's "country team" and the Ambassador's advisor on public affairs. Under the PAO would be a Deputy PAO, an Information Officer or Press officer, a Radio Officer, an Administrative Officer, the director of the USIS Library, and a Cultural Affairs Officer (CAO) who was responsible for sending folks to the United States for study and visits and arranging for visiting Americans to tell the local population about the United States. Along with locally hired assistants and American officers as deputies, a USIS post could range from six to twenty people, and many more in big embassies.

Then there were "the regionals." These were specialists who worked not for an individual USIS post, but for all the USIS posts in the area. There were regional librarians, for example, and in some cases, a regional advisor on film-making or magazine publication.

VOA Correspondents fell somewhere among "the regionals." While assigned to a specific embassy for administrative support, they were not a part of the Ambassador's country team, but were supposed to be controlled by and respond to VOA (the International Broadcasting Service) in Washington.

Sometimes that independence worked; sometimes it was a struggle to keep a PAO, or his minions, from thinking: since you are housed in our USIS post and under the wing of our Embassy, you should answer to our demands and concerns. It was, at best, a system designed for conflict, as you will learn.

ended throughout the 26 years of my career. In the newsroom, we had policy officers whose job it was to represent, and sometimes, impose the view of the bureaucrats, the White House and the State Department. They had access to classified cables from embassies overseas – the reason for my full-field clearance. We had access to every wire service in the world and a good idea of what was really happening. The conflict was built into the system.

The overnight shift was our salvation financially, and a big boost to me professionally. There were fewer than a dozen of us working overnight. The big story at the time was Vietnam, and the overnight shift largely wrote news going back to Asia, in English and translated by Vietnamese, Thai, Lao, Cambodian, Chinese and Korean services. I got to know many of the translators well, and learned from them about their countries. The overnight news chief, Dan Bell, apparently recognized that I had some talents as a newswriter and increasingly gave me responsibility for writing the lead story: The Vietnam War. At night, we did not have to deal with those policy officers – they all worked the day shift.

By mid-August, I was ready for my family. My brother Sam and a friend, Dutch, rented and loaded two trailers with our furniture. I put together two back-to-back mid-week weekends and headed to Missouri. I skidded into Springfield, hitched up one trailer, loaded Linda and the kids, and back east we headed to our new life in Washington. Sam and Dutch hauled the second trailer – giving them a chance to visit Washington as well.

I stayed on the overnight shift two years and learned a great deal about Asia. I also learned to go home to sleep at 8 A.M. until about 4 P.M., then have free time until 11 P.M. Our house full of three young kids – soon to be four when Steven Mark Chancellor was born February 2, 1964 – learned to be quiet all day long while Daddy slept upstairs. The weekends were worst, because then for two days I would try to stay awake during the day and sleep normal hours at night. Without much money to spare, we did all the free tourist things the area had to offer: the monuments, the Capitol building, and the beaches.

We all saw President Kennedy once – he was in a parade on Pennsylvania Avenue riding with Ethiopian Emperor Haile Selassie, just a few weeks before the President was assassinated. The evening of November 22, 1963, I joined the crowd outside the White House, awaiting the return of his body from Dallas, until it was time to go to work.

We spent a lot of time house hunting because we knew we needed more room than the two bedrooms on Arlington Terrace. And it was not the greatest neighborhood. In fact, the kids took to calling it "Ugly-zandria" instead of Alexandria. Dad's friend in St. Louis was right. I got a promotion to GS-11 after one year, and to GS-12 after another. We probably had enough money to afford to buy a house, but we didn't have the cash for a down payment.

At this point, another hero enters our life. Walt McClughan was a veteran news editor at VOA. He often advised me to "buy a house, rent is just money down the drain." When I responded that I didn't have the down payment (and mortgage companies would not permit borrowing of a down payment), Walt

said: "Find a house and then come see me. I will take care of it." We did find a house – or at least a lot – in a new subdivision near Bowie, Maryland, a huge growing development by the Levitt Corporation.

New houses there could be purchased for $16-18,000, for five percent down. We found a model we liked and could afford, on a great lot with woods and a school behind it, for $17,200. I went back to Walt and told him I needed $800 for a down payment. It happened to be payday, and Walt simply took his paycheck, for about $800, from his pocket and endorsed it over to me. "Pay me back when you can," he said, "and when you have the opportunity, you do a favor for someone else."

We made the down payment, and spent three months watching the house being built. I paid Walt back within a few weeks, and he and his wife were our first guests after we moved into 12312 Melody Turn at Christmas, 1965. (A few years later, I was able to pass on the favor, loaning funds to another VOA colleague who was short of cash for a down payment. And we were the first guests at their new house. We had another opportunity to pass on the favor in South Africa – but more about that later.)

Bowie turned out to be a special place. It was the fastest-growing town in America, with 500 new residents each month. The houses were mass produced, almost an assembly line, and everyone on our street had a closing, and moved into their new home on the same day. Most of us worked for the government, made about the same salary, and all had houses full of kids. Dan and Marianne Flavin

next door had two, Bernie and Joan Schuler across the street had four, and we all were in our first homes. We all learned quickly how to care for newly seeded lawns, and the cheapest places to buy curtains. We all socialized together and became close friends. Kim started the first grade at Meadowbrook School, right behind our house. As new suburbanites, we got our first dog, a boxer, Penny, and a new, larger Chevrolet Chevelle station wagon.

Back on the job, Walt McClughan was chief of the evening shift, and after two years of overnight work, I transferred to the evening shift, from 3 P.M. to 11 P.M. Then I carried the rank of editor instead of news writer, and Walt asked for me. I still got most of the bonus pay and continued to work many weekends. I had earned a reputation as a person who knew about broadcasting, and most of my colleagues didn't. We even began to slip sound bites into some of the newscasts I prepared. I received a commendation once because a major story was breaking just as the announcer was headed for the studio and I told him I would hand deliver the copy to him while he was on the air. Apparently no one in the newsroom had ever done that before.

VOA had just a handful of correspondents at this time: one at the White House, one at the State Department, one at the Capital, and some overseas in Munich, Bangkok, New Delhi, Nairobi and in South America. They did not work for the news department, but for an office called "Special Events." The special events staff also had some local staff people, or special events officers, who went out to do taped interviews on occasions. Special Events was the path to being a correspondent, and that's what I wanted. During this time, I was offered a special events job, but I earned the enmity of the division's chief by turning it down because it was day shift work, and I needed the evening shift differential to pay for our new house.

The Voice of America had a new director. John Chancellor, the NBC newsman, had been appointed by President Johnson to head the organization, and he brought from commercial broadcasting some new ideas how VOA should operate and sound. I only met him once, when he toured the newsroom, introducing himself to various writers. "Hi, I'm John Chancellor." "It's nice to meet you, I'm Bob Chancellor." "Well, I'll be damned, we'll have to get together and compare genealogies some time." But we never did and I never learned how, or if, we were related. We did cause some confusion, though – I occasionally got mailed invitations addressed to him and once he received a personal phone call from a doctor intended for me.

We had been back to Missouri during vacations in the summers, and we had a lot of visitors from Missouri: my parents, Linda's parents, Betty and Pearson, and we gave them all the grand tour of the sights of the nation's capital. We knew all the sites from our years of escaping dreary Uglyzandria to the tourist attractions such as the Washington Monument, Lincoln and Jefferson memorials, Arlington cemetery, Dulles Airport, Annapolis and Baltimore in Maryland and Mount Vernon. During this time, my brother Sam moved to the area and began teaching in Maryland, so we had family nearby too.

On my first day back to work on the evening shift, after a summer trip to Missouri in 1966, I received startling news from Vaughn Smartt, then the shift chief. Puffing his ever-present pipe, Vaughn said, "I don't know if I am supposed to tell you this, or not, but you should know. They are talking about sending you to Vietnam." I came to work early the next day to find out what he was talking about.

My old overnight boss, Dan Bell, had been sent out as a correspondent to our bureau in Bangkok, and spent a lot of his time covering Vietnam. Even though the war had not yet become large, the bureau had been expanded to three correspondents with Dan's arrival. Unfortunately, earlier that year, Dan had suffered a heart attack, and while laid up with that, Ed Conley had been sent out from Special Events to fill in for him for three months, to be relieved by Ed Hickey, who also had been out for three months. It was time for Ed Hickey to come home, and I, unknowingly, had been selected to fill in for him for two to three months. I was about to become a correspondent without serving in Special Events.

The VOA headquarters building is at 4th and Independence, SW, Washington, D.C., just a couple of blocks from the Capitol Building. When I first went there, it was known as the HEW Building, and served as the headquarters for the Department of Health, Education and Welfare. VOA had use only of the second floor. Since, VOA has filled the entire building. But it is named the "Cohen Building" after a former Secretary of HEW. In my day, there were no satellite dishes on the roof.

CHAPTER 13 — CHANCELLOR ARRIVES IN SAIGON

Tan Son Nhut airport in Saigon was an overwhelming place for a fledgling foreign correspondent on his first assignment. It was a mix of commercial jetliners from around the world, swarming crowds of passengers and hucksters, unbelievable inefficiency in baggage handling, customs and immigration controls, military helicopters putt-putting overhead, jet fighters screaming in and out, lots of armed guards from U.S. military and Vietnamese police, plus some personal trepidation. What had I gotten myself into?

And there I was – alone. Ed Hickey, who I was in Saigon to relieve, had not gotten the word that I was arriving on this Sunday afternoon, August 21, 1966. I had no idea where I was supposed to go, or what I was supposed to do. So I found a telephone and called JUSPAO – the Joint U.S. Public Affairs Office – and told the duty officer who answered: "This is Bob (I may have mumbled that part) **Chancellor from VOA in Washington**, and I am at the airport and I don't have a way into town."

"I'm sorry, Mr. Chancellor. I don't think we knew you were coming. I will send someone out to get you." Obviously that set the phones ringing around the city on that sleepy Sunday. The director of JUSPAO, Barry Zorthian, the top U.S. public relations guy in Vietnam, was called and responded: "Bring him to my house, he can stay here." A car was to be sent when a foreign service officer jumped in and said he would retrieve the distinguished visitor. Half an hour later, I saw him striding into the Tan Son Nhut terminal and could tell by his demeanor he felt important and was looking for a VIP. "Are you looking for Chancellor?" I asked. "Yes," he said. "I'm him," I responded. He deflated like a damaged balloon, but eventually agreed to take me into town anyway, and dropped me off at the JUSPAO building. Hickey wasn't there either, but I did find the VOA office and dragged my suitcases inside. Did I cause all that confusion intentionally? – well, maybe a little bit. But I did say "Bob," not "John."

From the day of Vaughn Smartt's unofficial warning to me, to this arrival in Saigon, had been a flurry of activity and preparation. It was confirmed to me, the next day at VOA, that I was being sent out for a TDY (temporary duty assignment) of 60, 75, or a maximum of 90 days. I was immediately removed from the evening shift so I could start training about being a correspondent – to learn the format and content of material VOA used. Correspondents were asked to write, voice and transmit CR's (correspondent's reports) of about two and one half minutes, plus shorter news inserts of 45 seconds which would be included within a newscast. Occasionally we would be asked to write a news analysis or commentary, called a grid-iron, with the caveat that those items must be approved by senior officials of JUSPAO before transmission.

Saigon had a regular feed, or transmission, time of 7:15 P.M. (which was 5:15 A.M. in Washington)

The Rex Hotel in Saigon. The bottom three floors housed JUSPAO, the Joint United States Public Affairs Office, which included military and civilian spokesmen, and was the scene of the Five O'clock Follies, as the daily briefing was known. The open floor at the top was a terrace housing an officers club, which was available to journalists and American civilians, as well as JUSPAO staffers. Usually, the elevator didn't work, and it was a five story climb to sustenance. It was the home of five cent slot machines, ten cent gin and tonics and $1 broil-it-yourself steaks. There were movies or entertainment nightly. It was a little piece of America. The middle floors were a bachelor officer quarters for the U.S. military.

at which contact would be made with a studio in Washington. Using a military provided telephone line, all material for the day would be transmitted from Saigon and recorded. Part of my learning process was to come into the office before 5 A.M.- to handle the Washington end of the feed.

Then there were travel arrangements to be made, shots (lots of shots) for smallpox, typhoid fever, the plague, yellow fever, cholera, tetanus, and a bottle of huge orange pills, to be started immediately to guard against malaria. And I had to obtain a passport, and visas for Vietnam, Thailand, Japan, Laos, and other destinations that I might be sent to during my tour.

And there were personal arrangements to be made too. I had been working part-time, two or three days a week, as a speech and newsletter writer for the Transport Workers Union in Washington, to earn some extra income. The chief lobbyist for TWU, Frank O'Connell, was enthusiastic about my opportunity and promised my part-time job back when I returned. But I had to help him recruit a replacement during my absence, and fellow VOA writer Ron Pemstein jumped at that opportunity.

At home, I had always kept the checkbook in balance and paid the bills, so I had to brief Linda on that aspect of domestic life, while assuring her that I would be safe, that this was a great opportunity for me to get out of the newsroom and see some of the world. And this assignment was to have some financial impact – I would be losing the night and weekend bonus pay as well as the extra income from TWU. I was given an $800 travel advance for my per diem, and vowed to live on that, while my regular paychecks would be deposited in Maryland for Linda and the kids to use. But we were aware that the budget would be tight.

I had never traveled abroad before, except for an overnight trip to Windsor, Ontario and Niagara Falls on our just concluded summer vacation. And I had only been on an airliner one time, when Linda and I were taken to a TWU national convention in New York earlier that year.

The long-range plan (my long-range plan, that is) was that I would do my temporary assignment, return to Washington to work in the correspondent's branch, then perhaps receive a permanent assignment, to New Delhi or Athens.

I wrote my folks: *"Linda, at first, was not overly enthusiastic about the assignment because it means a separation for two to three months. But she didn't raise Hell, is resigned to it, and as time passes, I believe is becoming more interested and excited. It will offer a good tryout for correspondents' work and a good chance to prove myself."*

Sunday, August 14th, 7 P.M., I was off. To complicate things, there had been a nationwide airline strike, and reservations were hard to get.

Monday, August 15th. Letter to Linda from Los Angeles: *Obviously I did not get on the Pan Am night flight to Hawaii. I will leave here at 1 P.M. today. Linda, now I know what you meant, it does seem unbelievable that I'm taking off on such a journey. I don't regret it, yet, but it is a little frightening and awing....There is nothing as beautiful as a city at night from the air. The outskirts of LA – while we were still high – looked like something that had been put there just to entertain passengers. Neon lights are vivid and bright...and swimming pools with underwater lights...shine like jewels.*

During my unanticipated overnight stay in Los Angeles, I had a chance to connect with my high school friend, Montford (now Monte) Handley and he drove me to the airport for my next flight to Tokyo via Hawaii. Twelve hours later, I arrived in Tokyo and was met at the airport by Shiro Uyeno of U.S. Information Service, who took me to the Okura Hotel and then out to eat. Another lesson: How to eat with chopsticks (it took me an hour and a half to finish) and about Kobe beef, from cattle raised in the dark, never allowed to exercise and fattened on beer so they don't grow any hard muscle, just flesh.

I spent Wednesday meeting with officials of USIS, and getting in some sight-seeing. I was not overwhelmed by the beauty of Tokyo, just a big, busy, impersonal city. Shiro said I would have to get out into the countryside to see the real Japan (sometime – it will happen).

Letter to Linda: Wednesday night: *Shiro took me night clubbing, an expensive pastime in Tokyo. You have to see the bar girls in action to believe it. Three or four will descend on your table, glasses are brought and they share your beer, all without invitation. In fact, if you don't want B-girls around, you don't go into B's. They are harmless, sort of a modern day version of the traditional geisha. They drink your beer, chatter and giggle, light your cigarettes and try to get you to dance. But when the bars close at 11 P.M., they go home. The girls get a percentage from the house. Some, Shiro says, make more per year than he does.*

The next day, August 18, onward to Bangkok, where I was met at the airport by Dan Bell and a former newsroom colleague, Lee Scanlon. Dan looked good despite the heart attack and said he had never been in better health. He was eager to do something, but had just received orders from Washington not to leave Bangkok. They had anticipated (correctly) that he planned to go to Saigon with me.

I went to the office with Dan on Friday at 10:45 A.M. By noon, we were across the street (Patpong Road) having a beer. And after a great lunch of barbecued shrimp and a little more work at the office, dinner with Dan and his wife, Sue. I could get to like this life.

Letter to Linda: *When Dan took me back to the hotel, I took a walk around a block or two, got propositioned by one streetwalker and one pair of taxi girls. I also had offers from taxi drivers, who offered me "Numbah one girl," blue movies, etc. The next night, I again was asked, "Hey, Joe, you want see blue movies?" My response: "Hell, no, I don't want to see blue movies, I make blue movies. I'm a movie star." Being a typical good natured Thai, he laughed and left me alone.*

Saturday morning, I toured Bangkok's floating market, where merchants in rowboats sell everything from meat and vegetables to radios on the klongs, or canals, that make Bangkok "The Venice of the East." That night, I went night clubbing with Dan and Sue, and Edie Donohue, wife of the Bangkok bureau chief. Her husband, Jerry, was off on a long trip to Malaysia and Indonesia.

Letter to Linda: *We ate at a Chinese restaurant – Peking duck – not bad. I'm getting better with chopsticks. And we went to a dark, loud, dingy Bangkok bar that is typical of the Far East, they said. Bangkok is a great city. I liked it. It is somewhat dirty, crowded, busy and interesting. Tomorrow, I fly into the mouth of the Dragon – Saigon.*

Ed Hickey and I finally connected on that frustrating Sunday afternoon, and he began showing me the ropes around Saigon, introducing me to people who would be helpful, and who would be news sources. But it was a quick indoctrination – he was scheduled to leave for home on Wednesday, and I would be on my own.

Ed and I had dinner one night with Wayne Hyde, a former VOA special events broadcaster, who was in Saigon, working for a CIA sponsored Vietnamese radio station, the Voice of Freedom. Over the ensuing years, Wayne would become one of my best friends and colleagues, and somewhat of a hero to my family. But as Wayne remembered it, our relationship had a rocky beginning. Soon after Ed boarded the "freedom bird back to the world" – the flight home – I had some sort of assignment to fulfill and I didn't have the first idea who to contact or anything else about it. I ran into Wayne in the hall of JUSPAO and asked his advice. He remembered that he just sort of blew me off – "call so and so" – and went on his way. Years later, he apologized profusely for that behavior.

Two locations were central to a VOA correspondent's existence: The Rex Hotel and the Saigon Palace at number 8, Tu Do Street. The VOA office was in the JUSPAO building, which occupied three corner floors of the Rex Hotel and Cinema building. It was on one of the main traffic circles in downtown Saigon.

If the Rex Hotel was a piece of America, the Saigon Palace, about four blocks away, on infamous Tu Do Street, was a piece of colonial Vietnam. That is where VOA maintained an apartment for its correspondents.

Letter to Linda, August 24: *This apartment is really something straight out of the old colonial days – like in the movies. I wouldn't be at all surprised to see Sidney Greenstreet puffing down the hall. You enter the building through the COYA Tailor Shop on the corner, go up a curving staircase, or take the lift, which is a cage, running up and down on two rails, all open. The building is honey-combed with air shafts, where the Vietnamese hang their laundry and which they use as yards. The halls are narrow and often are outside, running along the edge of the airshafts.*

Our apartment is very large – big living-dining room, smaller kitchen. Both bed-

rooms have individual baths. The ceilings are very high, the doors also are tall, with shutters in them. The floors all tile. You should see the bathrooms. They are huge, one is bigger than our dining room (in Bowie). The john is up on a platform, or stoop, so that when you are performing, you feel as if you are on stage. The shower is a large open area, surrounded by a small curb, no stall or curtain.

What I failed to mention to Linda was that the hallways were also filled with rats, so at night when you came home, you shuffled your feet and made a lot of noise to scare them away so you wouldn't step on them. We had a maid (called "Ma Ma" like almost every other maid in Saigon) who came in every day to fix breakfast, clean up the place and do laundry.

Tu Do (Freedom) Street was the sin strip of Saigon, lined with bars and bar girls, panhandlers, pimps, souvenir shops, money changers and Indian merchants. Most of the buildings had apartment complexes over them, like the Saigon Palace. On my corner, the Coya Tailor Shop occupied what had originally been the lobby of the Palace. The tailor's family lived, worked, ate and slept in the shop.

Letter to parents, September 4: *The French, bless their hearts, never did master indoor plumbing or traffic control. There must be 3 million motor bikes and bicycles here – there are only two million people. But the bikes and taxies and jeeps and army trucks all cram onto the streets at once. There is no such thing as staying in lanes, you drive where there's room. The main avenues are wide but the Saigon drivers go up them five and six abreast, plunge into a traffic circle without looking, blow their horn and go. Pedestrians plunge in too – it's the only way to get across, walk out in front of them. Amazingly, few are ever hit. It's evident from what remains that at one time Saigon must have been a beautiful city. Its boulevards are tree lined but it now is run down — the place is filthy and at night rats scurry everywhere.*

The week I arrived, an 11 P.M. curfew was slapped on all Americans in Saigon.

Letter to Linda, August 26: *They said it was because of increased terrorism, but one honcho told me – off the record – the real reason is that Henry Cabot Lodge (the U.S. Ambassador) drove down Tu Do the other night and was appalled by the drunks, whores, etc, being a staid Bostonian. It seems a little unfair to the GI's – they've been out in the heat, the jungle, the war and should be allowed as much chance as possible to get a girl, and a dose. Actually, I am told it is the American construction workers that do the real hell raising.*

Perhaps I was naïve, or stupid, but I was never really concerned about security, or terrorism. I was always alert to what was going on around me and I avoided going into dark alleys alone, but I was that way, even more so, in Washington, D.C. The American and Vietnamese facilities, such as the Rex, were well guarded and sand-bagged. I always felt one America civilian on the street was not worth the price of a grenade to a terrorist – their interest was in hurting or killing a lot of people and sending a message. I pretty much carried that attitude throughout my career – getting hit in a terrorist incident was about the same as being in a train wreck or a tornado – there was not much that could be done to avoid it without cowering in a corner somewhere.

I never had a shot fired at me in anger, and in fact the biggest danger of being shot came from over-zealous rifle-toting allies, be they Vietnamese, Israeli or African nationalists. I never felt any threat from American troops in Vietnam, although I do remember that first day at Tan Son Nhut, when a young GI, perhaps 18, walked by carrying his M-16 on patrol. "He isn't old enough to be carrying a gun," I thought.

Dan Bell kept pressuring Washington to let him join me in Saigon. We intercepted one cable to him from Washington, saying, "Chancellor is young, energetic and capable of handling Saigon on his own." Dan did eventually come to Saigon to relieve me on September 14th. The bureau

chief, Jerry Donohue, was supposed to come to Saigon to help with coverage of an upcoming election and then relieve me, but he never got there.

While there are great advantages to being off working totally on your own, with your bosses ten thousand miles away, there are disadvantages, too. It was hard to get any feedback.

Letter to Linda, August 30: *I don't really know how I'm doing. I feel like I'm doing a good job and producing plenty, but you never know how much they want. And isolated out here, you really don't have any indication whether they like the stuff you send back…I have heard some of my stories played back (to the area) but not all of them by any means.*

Washington had said they did not want much in the way of war coverage, their interest was in political and development issues. And by being required to man the daily 7:15 P.M. feed to Washington, there was not much time for battlefield coverage anyway. As a routine, I would do two or three 45 second news inserts on military news from the daily briefing, and one or two longer correspondent's reports on other subjects.

The correspondent was responsible for handling the feed sent back to some poor soul in Washington who had taken over my job of being in the office at 5 A.M. to receive it

We had a Chinese studio engineer named Chan who was a technical marvel. I remember one day when he was feeding a complicated story with several taped actualities in it: He had one hand on the volume control, his other hand on the start button for a second tape machine, when he needed to shut off a nearby switch. Simple: he slipped out of his flip-flop sandal and reached out with his leg, grabbed the switch with his big toe and made the necessary correction.

The big political story during my first month in Saigon was the forthcoming election of a constituent assembly, or congress, which the Viet Cong had vowed to disrupt.

Letter to Linda, Sunday, September 11: *This is election day in Vietnam, and boy, is this town jittery. If it looked like an armed camp before, it looks like a war operation now. So far, the VC threats to blow the hell out of everything haven't panned out. There have been some bombings, but not really as much as expected.*

Letter to Linda, September 13: *The election was an interesting experience (although a tiring one since I had to cover it alone). It was sort of inspiring to see a voter turnout of eighty percent in a nation that has never really known a democratic form of government, and that has been at war for more than 20 years. Eighty percent is higher than the voter turnout in U.S. elections. The high turnout was partly due to some over-zealous province leaders in the country side, who took to heart the government's pleas for lots of voters. Whole villages were rounded up and marched to the polling places by troops provided for their protection.*

During the period before the election, all U.S. military personnel in Saigon were to be off the streets between 2 P.M. and 4 A.M., to avoid the appearance of intimidation or interference in the election process. It did not apply to civilians. The biggest impact was on Tu Do street where all the bars shut down for lack of business. So much for all the hell raising being done by construction workers.

I spent many evenings just sitting on the front step of Coya Tailors watching the passing scene. And I made some friends there.

Letter to Linda, September 8: *I have another friend on the Saigon Palace corner. His name is Menn, a boy of about ten. Menn is a street urchin, one of thousands that roam the streets, shining shoes, selling candy and picking pockets. Menn one night asked me for a cigarette. I refused, telling him "You Babysan." Ever since, he has liked and respected me. I see him almost every night. He doesn't speak more than a dozen words of English, but we get along. Favorite games; tossing coins at a crack in the sidewalk, or guessing in which hand a coin is held. Every once in a*

while, I slip him a few piastres. Binh (another corner friend) says Menn is one of eight children, no father. I hate to see those kids on the street more than anything else.

Letter to Linda, September 11: *The other night, from the Rex roof, we watched a battle about two miles south of the city. It started with the drop of flares, which light up the countryside like daylight. Flare drops are not unusual, you can see them almost every night around Saigon, since several VC units are in the nearby countryside. But Friday night, the flare drop revealed a gathering of VC ...two armed helicopters were called in and for about an hour we watched machine gun fire pour into the area...It's weird to stand on a hotel roof with a drink in your hand, watching a war. Of course, you can hear heavy artillery firing all night. It's not loud, but just a steady, "whump, whump." After a while, you get so you don't even notice that.*

This is USIS feature writer Joe Dees, with whom I traveled often. He is standing outside a bunker at the Philippine troop base in Tay Ninh Province. Over the years, I would frequently visit the Filipinos, who were great hosts for visiting VIPs. Invariably, after a pleasant evening dinner in the mess hall with all the senior officers, and entertainment by the regimental band, their compound would come under mortar attack. The guests would all be rushed to a bunker to wait out the fusillade, then the "all clear" would come and everyone would go back to their barracks and go to bed. After surviving several "attacks" there, I learned that the incoming mortars were being fired by the Filipinos, for the entertainment of their guests and as a way of putting an exciting climax to the evening's visit. Their commander was Fidel Ramos, who later would become President of the Philippines.

CHAPTER 14 — BANGKOK, LAOS AND PATTAYA

My short-lived escape from Saigon came on Sunday, September 19, when I flew back to Bangkok after four busy and eventful weeks.

I wrote to my parents: *"This is a great city, it is not at all the backwater you might expect from reading. I have never read an article that really reflects the vitality and spirit of Bangkok. There are thousands of shops, all of which are full of merchandise, much of it western. There are more cars than you've ever seen before. The houses are nice...some of the stores are huge department stores, the hotels generally are first class, the people are wonderful (though they, like the Vietnamese, are afflicted with the outstretched palm)."*

The stated standard for VOA correspondents was no more than three weeks in Vietnam at a stretch. The other standing policy was a few days of rest and relaxation after a Saigon tour, so I immediately made plans to go to Pattaya Beach, on the Gulf of Siam, southeast of Bangkok.

Letter to Linda, September 19, from civilization (Bangkok): *I continue to get good comments about my work. Jerry Donohue says I have gotten more reports on the air than any correspondent in the agency. So did Nick Lassiter, whose job is to monitor all VOA programs. Last night, I was telling Lee Scanlon that I plan to make a strong pitch for a permanent correspondent's job, saying that I had been unsure before, but now I feel that my work has been on a par with the other correspondents. "On the contrary," Lee said, "I think your work has been far better than the other correspondents."*

If the lifestyle and city of Bangkok made me want to stay in the area, Pattaya Beach cinched it. I stayed in a beach-front cottage at the U.S. military compound, ate shrimp and seafood at the luxurious Nipa Lodge Hotel and chartered a boat to an off shore island beach.

Letter to Linda, Wednesday, September 21: *I think I am missing you more than I ever have. Maybe it's being here in a place I know you would love and where we could have so much fun. (On the island) there was the most fantastic beach I have ever seen, and no jellyfish. The water here is perfectly clear, and on the island, the sand was gleaming white, almost like sugar. You could see every detail at six feet deep. The beach is narrow, about 30 feet from trees to the waters edge and about a mile long. And it slopes out indefinitely – I was out 100 yards and still chest deep. It was really delightful. I spent about two hours there, most of it wishing you and the kids had been along. If we ever come to Thailand, this beach is one of the first places to be visited.*

There is an expression in the Thai language, "Mai Pen Rai." Literally, it means "never mind," but it is more than that. It is a philosophy that means "don't worry about a thing." Sort of "manana" run rampant. On the bus trip from Bangkok to Pattaya, we passed through a village in a mountainous area, where there obviously had been heavy rains higher up, because there was a small flood in the town; Water was cascading down the valleys, across the highway, into homes. The villagers did not greet this with concern, however, but with delight. Everybody in town was out wading in knee deep water. "So what if the water is in our house and our fields are three feet under. Mai Pen Rai – let's fish while the water's here."

Letter to Linda: *(Foreign life is) not all a bed of roses. Dan Bell said we should be aware there are frustrations -- Mai Pen Rai being one of them. That, plus distance from home, not being able to drink water from the faucet, not being able to get things you want, are some of them. I guess the best way to get along is adopt Mai Pen Rai ourselves.*

I ended my beach sojourn on Thursday, rode back to Bangkok, and boarded a train for points north: Udorn and Nong Khai in Thailand and Vientianne, Laos. The Northeast Express train from Bangkok

was a mix of the Orient Express and the Toonerville Trolley. Old and decrepit, but a romantic adventure in a sort of lurching, rattling way. I had a sleeper, but of course headed off to the dining/bar car where I gained an instant friend –a Thai naval officer who insisted on buying the Singha Beer and toasted everlasting Thai-American friendship. When finally my stomach rebelled and said "food," he ordered Thai fried rice with a fried egg on top, lots of "nam pla prik," or spicy fermented fish sauce. (It sounded awful then, and went down that way – now I love it.) Weaving my way back to my sleeper berth, the train lurched left, I lurched right, reached out for support, grabbed a curtain, pulled the curtain from its support, and awakened and exposed a sleeping Thai gentleman in his BVD's. "Mai Pen Rai," I said, apologetically, and staggered on to my berth.

Daybreak. The morning in Udorn (Udon Thani on the map) was frustrating. I got off the train, hired a pedicab, and made my way to the local USIS office, where I had an appointment with the district's top American official. "Not here, he's in Bangkok." I was directed to the American Library and U.S. Information Officer John Stuckey. "Not here, he's in Bangkok."

I was directed to John Stuckey's home, a wooden house on stilts, like all the other houses. And met John's wife, Marsha, one of the most delightful American girls I have ever run into. And she was so far up in the boondocks that she was excited to see and greet this hung-over stranger from the outer world. I was not in northern Thailand on a whim – there was a major flood on the nearby Mekong River and rumors of an imminent coup in Laos. Marsha, a native of Colby, Kansas, gave me

a better briefing on area affairs than I ever received from officials. Her husband, John, who I met a couple of days later, is from (ta-da!) Webb City, Missouri.

Marsha took me to the Udorn Air Force Base (which officially didn't exist in the never-never land of the early Vietnam war) where I saw hundreds of F-105 American fighter jets (which were not in the country) taking off for missions over North Vietnam (piloted by Americans who also were not in the country). I saw stuff there that no reporter had ever seen (but many had suspected) that I could not do a story on. (You know the old saying, "I could tell you, but then I would have to kill you.)

Transportation in the third world. The Nong Khai landing on the Mekong River, boarding a ferry boat across to Vientiane, Laos.

She took me on to Nong Khai, on the river, where I interviewed the Provincial Governor about the flood, and flood relief. And on to the Mekong River landing where I boarded a ferry (?) across to Laos. The ferry was a flat-bottomed boat, about 10 feet long, with an outboard motor and 50 passengers, who boarded by clambering and sliding down a mud embankment to the water's edge. The Mekong River is as big as the Mississippi, and the ten minute crossing was uneventful, except for white knuckles. Another pedicab took me into Vientiane, the capital city of the Kingdom of Laos. I felt like I had reached the end of the earth.

It is quiet and tranquil at the end of the earth. Very few cars. The pedicabs maneuver for space on the dirt road into town, their bells tinkling for attention and the right-of-way. I remember still the smell of burning sandalwood, a perfumy odor that in America we pay a fortune to match in high priced colognes.

With a couple of interviews, I had pinned down the flood story and sent off a long cable report (no chance of a telephoned voiced report from Vientiane.) The imminent coup? There was nothing to it – apparently there were rumors of an imminent coup monthly in Vientianne. I stayed at the Lane Xang hotel, by far the best in town, where the bar was a hotbed of intrigue and intriguing type people.

Letter to parents: *Vientiane is the absolute end of the civilized world – there are collected all the hangers-on, the connivers, the racketeers, the flotsam of the East. I became acquainted with the Reuters correspondent, a Limey by the name of Tammy Arbuckle. We were sitting in the bar of the Lane Xang Hotel and he started pointing out the people. "He's the city's drunken chief of police, he's a gold dealer, he's an opium smuggler, he's a CIA agent, he's a Chinese agent, he's rich but nobody knows how. There were Frenchmen, Indians (Sikhs with beards and turbans,) Swiss expatriates. I felt like the only normal person in the room. I guess, though I am not quite normal or I wouldn't have been in Vientiane's Lane Xang Hotel either. The town itself is not much to look at – there are many old French buildings from the Colonial period, but generally it has a run down appearance. Many streets are not paved.*

Letter to Linda, September 28: *I ate lunch both days at the American Community Association club house in Vientiane. It's a nice place, with a bar, pool, movies, and the nastiest, most smart alec American kids I have ever seen. If we ever get into the foreign service, I will blister my kids before I have them grow up like the bunch of punks I saw in Vientianne.*

I returned to Udorn on the CIA's Air America flight, which meant I was in Thailand illegally for a couple of days until I could get to Bangkok and straighten it out. Mai Pen Rai. John Stuckey sug-

gested I head south to the town of Khon Kaen, about halfway to Bangkok, where the government was building a new regional university, and where the Americans had built another phantom airfield. A taxi ride to Khon Kaen was arranged – I became the fifth of five passengers in a little bitty Japanese Datsun, and as the last to get aboard, although I was by far the tallest, I got the middle of the back seat over the drive shaft.

I thought I had never been so uncomfortable for a two hour ride in all my life. I thought so until later that night when I returned to Bangkok on the overnight train, sitting up all night in a chair car with seats far too short for a six-footer because my contact in Khon Kaen thought he could save the U.S. government some money by arranging a less than first class ticket.

I toured Khon Kaen for a day, on the back of the contact's motor scooter – the university under construction, the TV station, and the airfield which had a 10,000 foot concrete runway cleared out of the jungle, but nothing else. No airplanes, no

Khon Kaen University Buildings. "Vive Le Roi" was a greeting for the King of Thailand, who was scheduled to visit.

buildings, no personnel. It had been built as a contingency for the war, and never used. To my knowledge, it was never used throughout the whole Vietnam war. But it was a great place to ride a motor scooter.

Letter to parents: *The university only opened in June. It is on a 2000 acre tract on the edge of Khon Kaen, on a beautiful wooded hillside, with a nice view and wonderful breeze. The architecture is straight out of the Frank Lloyd Wright handbook. I visited the TV station – boy, did they have the facilities – two large production studios, one small studio for newscasts and interviews, videotape equipment, four cameras. They do a lot of live entertainment programs and were building sets for some drama when I was there. TV is a big thing in Thailand and even the smallest, most obscure houses, have a television set.*

I had been scheduled to return to Saigon in a couple of days, on October 3.

Letter to Linda, October 4: *Happy Birthday. Your present is on the way. Obviously I am still in Bangkok, though I should have been in Saigon yesterday at noon. I got to the airport to find the flight had been cancelled. Thai International had changed its schedule on the first of October and had not gotten permission from South Vietnam to land. For retribution, Thailand made Air Vietnam cancel its flight for today. There are two flights tomorrow and I am on standby for both of them. Mai Pen Rai.*

(I had really bought in to that philosophy!) I told our parents in a letter:

"In southeast Asia, if something doesn't go wrong, there's something wrong with that. It is just not a place where everything works smoothly. In a way, that makes it interesting, but it also is frustrating."

These are the sort of scenes in Bangkok that so intrigued me and made me want to come back. At right, the Temple of the Emerald Buddha. Below, Chulalongkorn University alongside the Chao Phraya River. Below left, the island beach off Pattaya;, right, Bangkok's, the floating market.

CHAPTER 15 — BACK INTO THE MOUTH OF THE DRAGON

Returning to Saigon was not nearly as daunting as the title of this chapter would suggest. No worries, no concerns. It almost felt like home when I got back. During my two week absence, I had never slept in the same bed more than two nights straight, having crashed at a succession of friend's homes, hotels and beach bungalows. I was scheduled to leave Vietnam for home (the US home) October 24, which was a slight extension of the original 60 day TDY. It was to be quite a bit longer than that.

Letter to Linda: *I do enjoy this work, and the travel and even the uncertainties and frustrations, but it would be much easier if I had a wife and kids to go to at the end of each trip. I am making a pitch for a full assignment here. [name deleted] from the newsroom is supposed to replace Dan Bell in January, but no one here (including the top man at USIS) wants him. And neither does Bill Minehart, the correspondents' chief in Washington. I hope they drop him and need someone to fill his place – I happen to know a good correspondent who knows the area and would be glad to go.*

I was back in Saigon October 5, having caught a military airlift flight so I could relieve Dan and he could return home. He had worked harder during my absence than he should have, given his medical condition. And I think he was glad to go home. The plans for my return to Bowie were indeterminate–as it turned out, it would be another five weeks in Saigon, alone, before I got away, because Defense Secretary McNamara and President Lyndon Johnson intervened.

Letter to Linda, October 9. *LBJ is fouling me up some by his trip to Asia. Washington informed me this week my tour is extended to November 12. I keep shooting for Kim's birthday [November 3] but that may not happen. Washington the other night offered to pay two days per diem if I want to go home by way of Munich. But I think more and more that I will come home the most* direct *route, not even stopping to loll on Waikiki.*

The visit by Defense Secretary Robert McNamara got me out of Saigon and into the Vietnam countryside, at least.

Letter to Linda, October 14*: I'm frustrated from chasing McNamara all over the place. Monday he arrived, I covered that and he promised a news conference before leaving. Tuesday, I covered him when he went to see (Prime Minister Nguyen Cao) Ky. After that meeting—no comment. Wednesday, I followed him to Phu Cat, to watch him walk from a tent to his helicopter—no comment. Thursday, I did not follow him to Cam Ranh Bay, figuring it wasn't worth it. It wasn't. But it wasn't worthwhile to stay in Saigon either–before leaving he made a three minute statement and cancelled the news conference. Thursday night, I got (Chief of Correspondents) Bill Minehart on the feed and he informed me VOA wasn't really very interested in McNamara coverage. Why in the hell didn't they tell me before I chased the man all over South Vietnam?*

Bureau Chief Donohue had not been in Saigon since April, and since he was being relieved in January, he obviously had no intention of coming back. I was really angry that of my 12 weeks in Asia, ten would be spent in Vietnam, alone, filing daily reports while Donohue got to travel around to the more glamorous parts of the region. (Is this time for another "Mai Pen Rai?)

Linda and I kept the post office pretty busy with our exchange of letters. I tried to keep her up to date on my work and my impressions of the area. In the meantime, she was trying to juggle everything at home, including Brownies and PTA, getting three kids back to school in September (Craig bussing to kindergarten, while David and Kim walked through the woods to Meadowbrook School,) working on several remodeling projects, dieting and fending off solicitous neighbors concerned that she would get lonely. She also was working on an SMS alumni reunion to take place in Washington November 12, and she really wanted me home in time for that.

The worst times, for both of us, came on weekends, when the work load was diminished and loneliness (and homesickness on my side) would set in. Oddly enough, the emotion, or the vibes, were running both ways.

> Letter to Linda, October 22: *I sure as hell miss you and wish I was home right now. Nothing outstanding has happened to bring on this feeling, I just am getting tired of being alone. I want my Momma. I had a dream last night about a slim, trim Linda and I chased her all over the house, but never could get to her. Now, by God, I want to get home to prove that ain't so. This is going to be a bad weekend, I can tell now. But at least, there are only two, maybe three, weekends left before I'm home. I think this trip has been important for one reason; I have discovered how much I need you and depend on you. You don't know how much I miss being able to talk to you, to tell you of the day's events, to ask you what I should do about one thing or another, or even to argue with you. I really am convinced that I am only part of a person without you.*

> Letter to Bob, the same weekend: *I'll tell you for sure, you aren't going to go on any more of these things without the whole family, are you? Don't mean to sound shrewish, but I think you feel exactly the same way about it. I just didn't realize how much we shared our feelings – our excitements, disappointments, pats on the back for a job well done – all those thousand things that we go through together in a period of time. It kills me to have done so many things around here that you haven't seen and to have things happen to the kids and you can't possibly know about and to know you are doing so many fascinating things I can't be a part of.*

I did find some pleasant and totally innocent female companionship during this time. A writer from the Vietnamese Division at VOA was sent out to do some special feature stories for them.

Her name was Kayleen Honneck – an Iowa farm girl – and we became good friends. In addition to doing her job for a month or so, she wanted to be close to Lou Polichetti, a former VOA staffer who was serving USIS in the Mekong Delta. Eventually they married – and we will meet them again a couple of times in our life.

President Johnson had scheduled a visit to Manila and Bangkok, and speculation was rife that he would come to Vietnam. My mother wrote, "Wouldn't it be ironic if you saw the President in Saigon, when you have never seen him in Washington?" In the pidgin English language of Tu Do street: "Never happen."

One story, which made the rounds in Saigon, was that the White House advance team in Manila asked for ten air-conditioned busses for the White House press corps accompanying President Johnson. When told there were no air conditioned busses available in the Philippines, the White House said, "Get them." USIS had to order, and air ship in, ten big bus air conditioners. The Hilton Hotel in Manila was asked to build a large, oversized bathtub for the President, and a USIS friend of mine in Manila was ordered to lend his own king-sized bed for the presidential party.

The President flew from Manila to the American built seaport at Cam Ranh Bay one day late in October, and returned the same day to Manila, but the Saigon press corps wasn't there, just the traveling White House press. We were given the runaround all day – "we'll let you know as soon as we know and we'll try to get you there." They never did and I suspect they never intended to, because they wanted to protect coverage for the air conditioned White House press corps. When Prime Minister Ky and President Nguyen Van Thieu got back to Saigon about 7 P.M., they announced Johnson had been at Cam Ranh. When the local wire service offices tried to file it (they still had a beat because the White House crew couldn't get their stories out until they got back to Manila,) the Vietnamese, at the urging of the White House, pulled the plug on all the teletype circuits, stopping the wire services. I was one of the few that did get the story out because I used military telephone lines which were not blocked.

The history books are full of stories about LBJ's visit to Cam Ranh Bay, and his call to nail the Viet Cong's hide to the barn wall. My favorite: LBJ was headed toward a helicopter after a quick stop somewhere, and a Marine stopped him from going to the wrong airship. "That's your helicopter over there, Mr. President." LBJ responded: "They are all my helicopters, son."

Letter to Linda, November 1: *This is a very important day…I got to turn my wall calendar to November and have circled the 10th, and can sit right here and see how close it is, and it makes everything much better. Washington has approved my departure on the 10th and has notified Bangkok to have a replacement here before then.*

Linda had borrowed a short wave radio from a neighbor and had mastered the art of listening through the static and fading, to hear me from Vietnam. Even the kids caught on to listening to shortwave. I think that helped them; I know it helped me knowing that they knew I still existed. My mother in St. Louis also developed the short wave habit, and later told of leaning out her office window, radio in hand, twisting it to obtain the best possible reception.

Letter to Linda, November 1: *This is National Day in Vietnam, celebrating the overthrow of Diem. They had a hell of a big parade today, there must have been ten thousand marchers, and two or three hundred trucks and tanks. Of course, the VC made their contribution – about twenty mortar shells were fired toward the main reviewing stand just before parade time. All fell short, hitting instead a cathedral, a hospital, a school and a seminary. Nice people, those.*

My departure date of November 10th stood. I loaded onto that beautiful Pan Am 707 Clipper at good old Tan Son Nhut, and took off for Hong Kong, Tokyo and the polar route to San Francisco – twelve straight hours of flying – with an immediate connection on United Airlines to Baltimore, arriving at 7 A.M. on the 11th. I would make it to the SMS reunion, among other things.

My last letters home focused more and more on projects I wanted to do when I got there. But there was a prophetic statement in one of them:

As anxious as I am to get home, I kind of hate to see my travels end. I just hope I get another chance to see the world, with you along. I keep hoping we can work something out and maybe get the permanent assignment out here, to Bangkok.

This page and next: Saigon street scenes, including the National Cathedral, traffic and interesting looking people

CHAPTER 16 — A NEW AMBITION

It was even fun to walk into the VOA newsroom when I returned to work. I was sort of a conquering hero – other than Dan Bell, the first person to be taken from the newsroom instead of special events, to be a correspondent. And I hadn't goofed up. Barry Zorthian in Saigon sent a note to John Chancellor "to let you know we think your namesake, Bob Chancellor, did a first-rate job while he was assigned here as a VOA correspondent. I think he is to be commended for his performance, particularly in view of the fact that he was thrown in here cold during some very important events." Chancellor passed the Zorthian comments on to me, with an added note: "I want to add my congratulations on a job well done. Also it is nice to have you back." So far as I know, John never learned of that little event at Tan Son Nhut.

I almost shouted as I came through the door, "I want to go back!" Some major changes had been made during my absence. The coordinator of correspondents had been moved out of Special Events to a desk in the newsroom. Correspondents were now a part of the news operation. The new coordinator was Charles Eberhardt – he was in the pipeline to go to Bangkok as bureau chief at the start of the new year and he promised to do everything he could to make sure I got an assignment to join him.

Charlie was very tall and straight, a former Marine officer and Foreign Service officer in pre-war Vietnam, patrician in manner as he felt befitted his position as a Harvard graduate. But I learned that beneath that stiff exterior, he was a Kansas City boy – a fellow mid-westerner in this den of Yankees. His father had been a Kansas City builder, and in fact, had built a structure I knew well, the Brownhardt Apartments, about a block from my grandmother's apartment on Armour.

With my future apparently sealed, I was kept on the day shift, working as an at-large correspondent, and manning that early morning feed from Saigon. By then, I certainly had more sympathy for the poor correspondent on the other end, struggling with all sorts of difficulties going beyond getting a bad phone line out.

I wrote to my parents: *Linda is happy about the idea. She felt a little left out when I went traveling on my own last time. And the kids are real excited about the prospect. They got the travel bug while I was gone, and by following my adventures on the map and by slides. It's funny to hear the little ones talking knowledgeably about Thailand, Laos and planning stop-overs in Hawaii, California and Hong Kong.*

A promotion was in line first – I was up to $12,873 per year. And I had to transfer officially to the Foreign Service, which meant I had to ap-

Appointed for foreign service

Robert Chancellor was recently appointed by President Johnson and sworn in as a member of the U.S. Information Agency's foreign service. He is the son of Mr. and Mrs. B.M. Chancellor, formerly of Webb City, now living at 2950 No. Waterford dr., Florissant. Chancellor will serve temporary duty in Bangkok. Formerly with the Voice of America, USIA's radio arm, he has been a radio news man in Springfield and St. Joseph, and was on the staff of the Springfield Leader-Press.

Notice Lyndon Johnson in the background? He wasn't really there.

pear before a screening panel. After asking all sorts of innocuous questions about my ambitions, one of the three panelists asked the one that was on all their minds: "You have been with VOA only three years, and you have gotten three promotions. How do you explain that?" The only answer that came to mind quickly was, "I guess I am pretty good at my job." I was approved, and after the interrogation, one of them asked the real question, informally and off-handedly, "What relationship are you to John Chancellor?" I took great delight in answering, "None. I have only met the man once."

There was no hesitation on Linda's part either. She was ready to go for an adventure. We went about amassing information about schools in Bangkok, living conditions, allowances, required clothing and housewares. Linda attended a two-week course at the Foreign Service Institute, designed to train the wives of foreign service officers in the intricacies of serving tea, wearing gloves on formal occasions and carrying engraved calling cards for the required call on the Ambassador's wife. (You were to turn down the corner of the card if the wife did not personally receive you, to indicate that you personally had dropped it by.)

Of course no one in Bangkok wore formal gloves in the 90 degree heat and humidity, and she used a grand total of two formal calling cards in the course of our entire career. But the FSI training was really helpful in practical matters: how to get microbes out of lettuce (soak it in Clorox) and how to deal with the good and the bad of life abroad.

It was decided we would not go out until after the end of the school year. There was a house in Bowie to be rented. Marianne Flavin next door agreed to be our rental agent, and we found renters who took better care of the place than we would have. To prepare for the long absence – we knew it would be at least three years before we could even come home on leave – my parents, and Linda's parents made visits to see us and the kids. There was furniture to be stored – we were allowed only a limited shipment of personal effects, the intent being that we would rent a furnished house in Bangkok. Linda and each kid had to get passports, visas, and all those shots.

Those months went by in a blur of preparation. I did some work for Frank at TWU, writing speeches and newsletters, but eventually yielded that. I did a lot of CR's and features – nothing real notable, but I remember a couple. One week, both Time and Newsweek had the same cover picture, and I researched it by talking to folks in New York and did a report on how rare that occurrence was. (It sort of followed the lines of a research paper I had done in college on the same subject.) And I wrote a feature about a nationwide contest to design the best paper airplane. I learned how to edit audio tape, got some voice coaching, and spent time with producers in the studio to learn how they worked and how I could help from abroad.

There also was a bitter-sweet interlude in July when I flew to Florida to be with Phoebe, Laura and Kristin after Marsh suddenly died. Despite the occasion, we had a nice visit, and I felt I owed them the effort since Phoebe and Marsh had been so good to us over the years.

In July, we put all four kids on a flight to St. Louis, so they could spend some time with their grandparents and other relatives in Missouri and to keep them out from under foot while we sorted and packed. And then with a round of farewells and best wishes, we were ready to head to Springfield and St. Louis, to see the relatives, pick up the kids and head out into the almost unknown.

With our 15 suitcases and trunks, we flew through Los Angeles, but didn't stop (except long enough for Steven to throw up all over the Pan Am terminal) and on to Honolulu, where we had scheduled a three day layover. (Kim threw up at the Honolulu airport.)

The American Bar Association was holding its annual convention in Honolulu, and the only hotel available was the Kahala Hilton – its $100 rooms were way beyond our budget and allowance, but we took it. We couldn't even afford to eat breakfast there – but we had a rental car, and spent most of our days driving around the island, sampling beaches and eating out at family priced restaurants. It was a wonderful interlude.

We flew to Tokyo, where we were met at the airport and visited with correspondent Ray Kabaker and his wife, Diane, and then straight through Hong Kong to Bangkok. Somewhere along the way, one of the kids asked, "Where's Penny?" and we had four tearful children for a while when we explained we had had to leave her behind in Bowie. The kids and I slept from Tokyo to Bangkok, but Linda got off the plane in Hong Kong, where, she said, all she did was sit and yawn in the transit lounge.

We were pretty tired and ragged when we arrived in Bangkok at 11 P.M. on Friday, August 4th, slightly less than one year from the date of my first arrival. Correspondent Roy Heinecke (who I had never met before) was at the airport and took us to the Amarin Hotel. Roy and his wife, Connie, were long-time Far East hands and Roy suggested that Linda call Connie in the morning and begin to plan our settling in.

Roy Heinecke

Linda called Connie the next morning, and as she was introducing herself on the phone, Connie said, "Hold on a minute. There's a cobra on the floor under my dining table." That was probably Linda's "what have I gotten myself into" moment. Later, Connie called back, said that things like that happen (Mai Pen Rai) and they arranged to get together to look at houses and talk about life.

Letter from Linda, August 5: *I can't believe it, but we're here. Bangkok is a lovely city filled with lovely, friendly people and I'm sure we'll love living here even more than we anticipated. Things have gone so smoothly so far, I'm almost afraid we're in the wrong place! Saturday morning, we took a long walk around our immediate area. I can't begin to tell you the fascinating sights, sounds, smells, etc, that we ran into. Evidently, there is no such thing as an ugly Thai. They are either beautiful (male and female) people or they are interesting-looking. Some of the old peddlers with the poles across their shoulders carrying perhaps 50 pounds in each basket, look a thousand years old. All the faces are happy and practically every one of them will greet the children and smile, if not actually stop and touch them. The children love them too.*

Roy Heinecke had spent most of his career in the Marine Corps, much of it as a combat correspondent in Korea. While he was there, Connie got tired of being back in California with her two young boys, so she booked a ship to Japan and lived there so she could be close to Roy. Since the war, they had spent their lives in Asia, mostly in Bangkok, while Roy worked for VOA and other news organizations. Connie had a good eye for fashion, and had been instrumental in starting one of Bangkok's well-known Thai silk factories and stores. Their youngest son, Billy, while still in high school in Bangkok, had started buying and re-selling local radio broadcast time, got into advertising, then hotel development, and was well on his way to being a millionaire by the age of 21. Older son Chip worked in marketing for a Hollywood studio. Needless to say, Connie knew her way around Bangkok and knew everybody in the city worth knowing.

While most of the Americans living in Bangkok had homes east of town, in the Bangkapi neighborhood, the Heineckes live north, off Paholyothin Road, the main avenue to the airport. They spotted a large two-story house on their street, Soi Sri-Fah (Street 15) that they thought would be perfect for the Chancellor family. Linda and I looked at it, and they were right.

Linda described it in a letter: *"The grounds are very large with a circular drive, lots of gorgeous shrubs and trees. We have coconut palms, banana trees, ferns, poinsettias, elephant ears, a lotus garden and dozens of things I can't name yet."*

It was in a walled compound, with a large yard, a klong (pond) off to one side by a beautiful patio. It had three bedrooms and a bath upstairs, a living room, den and dining room down. It was an older

Mrs. Chiem. Her toddler-grandson lived with her, as did a son-in-law and a sister. We also inherited Laddie, a ki-moy (burglar) dog, or watch dog, who came with the house.

We stayed in the Amarin Hotel for a couple of weeks, waiting for our goods to arrive and waiting for the kitchen to be built. The hotel had a pool and the kids got pretty comfortable with it. The pool had underwater windows into the bar, and we could have cocktails while watching the kids swim.

Most Americans lived in the Bangkapi neighborhood because that was the location of the International School of Bangkok, grades 1 through 12. But the summer of our arrival, the school had created a second, satellite campus, grades 1 to 6, which was on our side of town. And the kids enrolled there: Kim in 3rd grade, David 2nd and Craig 1st. There was even a school bus that came to Soi Sri Fah. Two blocks north on Paholyothin Avenue, was the Capitol Hotel, a billet for traveling American servicemen, which had a nice pool, a little PX and a snack bar. We were welcome to use it, and did.

house, with shutters in place of windows and lots of locally made bamboo and teak furniture.

It had two drawbacks: no air conditioning, and a terrible kitchen tucked off to one side of the dining room. That was no problem for Connie – she looked at a large pantry nearby and estimated it could be converted to a modern kitchen fairly cheaply. As poor as we were at the time, it looked to me to be an expensive project, but she was right – local labor and materials were so low cost that even the Chancellors could afford to build a new kitchen.

The air conditioning was a bit more of a problem. The house included one air conditioner, in our bedroom and big ceiling fans in the other bedrooms. Through some quirk of government regulations, people of my rank were not furnished with air conditioners – and they were expensive to buy. People spent most of their time outside, and all our shuttered windows did allow for pretty good breezes, but in nearly constant 90 degree weather, you had to have some respite. Bureau Chief Charles Eberhardt ordered a new AC unit installed in his fully-furnished, fully-air-cooled, government-provided-and-furnished home, and gave us the unit he took out. We installed it in the downstairs den, and that become our hideway from the heat. The kids played there in the hottest of times; Linda and I watched TV there.

Next door in the walled compound lived the owner, an educated English-speaking lady named

Meanwhile, the VOA office was in its same old location, on Patpong Road, on the second floor over the American Library. Patpong Road was sort of Bangkok's Tu Do Street, lined with bars and restaurants. Several other news organizations had offices nearby, and we all tended to use the Patpong Café across the street as a place for a beer, and Mizu's Restaurant, down the block, for lunch. Mizu's – run by a Japanese ex-patriot – had great food, steaks, seafood, and fresh oysters flown in daily.

The office had a car and driver, Su Thep, assigned to it, and every morning, Su Thep would pick up Roy and me and Charles (or whichever of us were in town at the moment) at home and take us to the office. In the evening, he would reverse the trip. Our personal car – the Chevelle station wagon – was shipped to Thailand and was usually available for Linda and her errands.

Letter from Linda October 11: *I will drive here only if the weather is super gorgeous, I am in the highest of spirits, it is not rush hour and I am flat broke and can't afford the price of a taxi. You wouldn't believe the way they drive in this crazy place. The formula seems to be to hang one arm out the window and point at whichever lane you intend to take and keep the other arm glued to the horn. I don't know what they steer with."*

The work routine was pretty relaxed. To the office about 9... across to Patpong Café for a beer at 10:30... back to the office until noon and Mizu's... back to the office to write some stories…a feed to Washington about 5 P.M….and home. Usually there were only one or two of us in town following this routine with another one or two out traveling the area or in Vietnam.

Linda, meanwhile, was learning to cope with servants. Everyone in the U.S. (then and now) will say enviously, "You have servants, isn't that wonderful?" It was, but it also was a chore to get them and keep them and supervise them. However, it was essential given the heat and humidity of Bangkok. First hired was Djan, who washed and ironed, cleaned the upstairs, and mopped every floor in the house every day. Then we hired Lin, who had worked for the Scanlons, and she became cook, server and cleaned the downstairs. And we had a full-time gardener, Boon Rawd, who could make anything grow, who kept the grounds park-like and did those chores an absent Daddy might otherwise take care of.

Over the years this cast of characters would change – at the end of our tour, they were Ratree, Payoon and Gawn, but we never had fewer than three. Linda noted in a letter that with the heat and humidity, every small task would wear her out, *"Not that I'm griping, my tasks are very few with my little group."* And total salaries for the three were less

than $100 per month. The servants lived in rooms behind the main house, and almost became members of the family

Letter from Linda November 28: *The girls were a riot when the shipping arrived and the unpacking began. They squealed and howled over each item, then sat themselves down with all the photo albums and proceeded to ooh and aah over each picture. We didn't get one thing done in that two hours, but when they were finished, the fur really flew. We worked til 11 that first night and I just dropped into bed and thought they did the same. About five minutes later, I heard all this giggling outside and they were merrily riding up and down the driveway on the bicycles. They can be hilarious, touching, stubborn, kind, obtuse, understanding, happy, sad and terribly exasperating all in the space of an hour.*

I anticipated being sent back to Saigon almost immediately, and I was. There had been some substantial changes that made life and work there much better. VOA had moved to a new apartment, on the third floor of the Eden Building, a full square block complex of shops, a cinema, restaurants, offices and apartments. We were on the corner, with a view out at the National Assembly building, Tu Do Street and the Caravelle Hotel, where the TV network people lived and worked.

The Associated Press office was two floors away in the Eden; JUSPAO just a block down the street. Heinecke somehow had finagled to get a military

In the VOA Saigon office.

phone line installed in the apartment, and we made an office of that corner room. There was a nicely furnished living room and a separate bedroom for whatever correspondent was in residence. There also was a spare bed in a corner of the huge 20 by 40 office. We did all our work, including the feeds, from the Eden Building office.

A Vietnamese man who was on the VOA Washington staff, Mr. Thong, was in Saigon at this time, doing some special reportage. But his primary goal of the trip was to find himself a bride, which he did. He and his bride then visited us in Bangkok enroute back to the United States.

Linda wrote: *"She was one of the most beautiful women I've ever seen. She wore the traditional Ao Dai in a flower blue silk, and had that lustrous thick black hair that reached past her waist. Our children were just google-eyed and she in turn loved them. I don't know when I've met a more charming couple."*

When I returned from that first Saigon tour, Charles Eberhardt suggested I go to Singapore and Indonesia. He said to spend two or three weeks just learning your away around, get to know those places. So, while Linda was getting settled in the house and the kids in school, I headed out.

I loved Singapore – it was much cleaner and more modern than Bangkok. I spent two or three days there, then went on to Jakarta, the capital of Indonesia. Charles, and VOA, thought that Indonesia had been vastly under-covered in years past – it was, after all, the fifth most populous country in the world, and had important oil resources. It had recently gone through a very unstable period with the overthrow of President Sukarno and resulting anti-Chinese riots which had led to several thousand deaths at the hands of enraged mobs of Muslim

Indonesians. Jakarta looked like a major city which had been started but never finished. Several sky scrapers, 20 to 40 floors, had been started by Sukarno, but then work had stopped and their rusting skeletons were the predominant landmark on the horizon.

I spent those days in a variety of briefings and familiarization, and it was suggested that I head east by train to Jogjakarta and on to the fabled island of Bali. In Jogja, I was adopted by a group of four college-age Indonesians who wanted to practice speaking English and were more than willing to accompany me as I toured the ruins of the ancient Indonesian capital, and the temples of Borobadur.

Yes, there I was, riding another Asian train. I had an upper berth and was sleeping peacefully at daybreak when I was reminded that I was in a Muslim country. The public address system throughout the train clicked on and a *muezzin* started singing the call to worship. My compartment companion rolled out of his bunk, hit the floor and began praying. (Mecca was toward the rear of the train.) I had to peal myself off the ceiling from being so startled by the loud sound system.

I took another train on to Bali, or at least to the port where I boarded a ferry to the island. I have never been anyplace as pretty, nor as mystical as Bali. Deep green mountains come down to the shore, where there are miles and miles of secluded white sand beaches. I toured in the mountains, visiting craft shops, viewing bright green terraced rice fields, and enjoying Balinese temple dances. I also spent some time on the beach.

When it became time to return home to Bangkok, I had a suitcase full of souvenirs, hundreds of pictures and lots of great memories. It turned out I would be back to Bali two more times. I had done almost no stories, but I felt familiarized and unlike my TDY, here I was going home to my wife and family after three weeks. I thought: "This is going to be a great job," and it was. I no more got back to Bangkok than I was returned to Malaysia, Indonesia, and Bali to cover a visit by Vice President Humphrey.

CHAPTER 17 — WAYNE'S STORY

After my return to Asia, there was more new to working in Saigon than the fancy new office/apartment in the Eden Building. VOA had a new resident correspondent in addition to we souls who commuted from Bangkok.

Wayne Hyde had transferred from his job at Voice of Freedom to work full time for VOA. He had his own apartment across town which he liked, so he stayed there, but worked out of the Eden building. Wayne even had a private car, which was rare for an American in Saigon.

With two of us working there, it made it a lot more practical for one correspondent to get out and around the country, while the other stayed in town, attended the briefings and manned the nightly feed. I was able to get to Danang, Hue, the Mekong Delta, the highlands and even to visit the aforementioned Filipinos in Tay Ninh. Many of these trips I made with Joe Dees, who was a feature writer for USIS. Joe spoke French and loved to eat out, so the three of us spent many evenings together. Joe made one trip to Bangkok, and wanted to meet the children. He had a marvelous way with kids and they were pop-eyed with his stories and antics.

I don't have the benefit of letters home to Linda to remind me of the stories or events of these Saigon sojourns, but we covered a lot of news and features. Bangkok correspondents were sent to Saigon for three week hitches and then were out. Wayne stayed there most of the time, but every couple of months, he would leave the country in the care of us outsiders. The arrangement worked well, and none of us felt overburdened by the need to cover Vietnam, even though it was often a tense and busy job.

Wayne had good reason to stay in Saigon. He had fallen in love with a French lady, Terry Mercier, a diplomat with the French mission. They met when Wayne took French lessons at the Alliance Francais (the French version of USIS). She was of Vietnamese extraction, but a French citizen, pretty, petite and sweet. I often told Wayne that theirs was the most star-crossed love story I had ever heard. Because of her French government connections and her job, they were unable to get together very often despite being in the same city.

Also, she was Catholic and separated from her French planter husband and had family, including older children, who did not approve of her relationship with a Yank. Years later, she was assigned to the French mission in Washington, and Wayne went back to Washington. They even lived together for a time there, but never married. She moved back to Paris and Wayne moved there too. Their story ended tragically when Terry contracted cancer and died in France.

Wayne and I became close friends, worked together, ate many meals together, had many drinks together, and talked a lot. There was a lot more to his story than just Terry. He was small and wiry, and walked with a stiff leg because of injuries suffered as a paratrooper over Europe in World War Two.  He had been a broadcaster in Ohio, and began working for Armed Forces Radio in Europe after the war, until he joined VOA. As a young man, he had been a bantam-weight boxer, had fought professionally, but quit after an opponent died in the ring – that was a story he couldn't tell without tearing up, even after so many years had passed.

Wayne also was a musician, the "boy singer" in one of the dance orchestras that toured the Middle West in the pre-war days. When the leader of the orchestra was drafted early in World War Two, Wayne bought him out and took over the band: bus, 18 musicians, sheet music and all, and continued to tour until he, too, was drafted.

Wayne also was a good and prolific writer. He was the author of several children's books (our kids had the entire series) and wrote short stories, and free lance magazine articles. He was espe-

Wayne Hyde at work in the VOA office in the Eden Building in Saigon.

cially interested in the cowboys of the old west. Often, when he would get away from Saigon for a while, he would go to Bangkok and work – he became a great friend of Linda's, a frequent dinner guest and the kids loved him. Wayne had been married and divorced and had a couple of grown children, but he didn't talk about them much, and I never met them.

As the years passed by, Wayne was back in Washington writing features and special programs. We would get together every time I had occasion to be in Washington, and he flew to Austin, Texas, when our daughter Kim got married in 1984.

We corresponded by mail once or twice a year and had occasional telephone conversations even after he retired and moved to Frederick, Maryland. He continued to write articles, but he would never write the one thing that I constantly nagged him to do — a book about the dance band days and the wild, crazy musicians on his bus.

Some time around 2003, I realized that Wayne and I were no longer communicating. I had retired and was living in Missouri; we even discussed in letters his visiting us in the Ozarks. But he stopped responding to letters and Christmas cards, and there was no answer at his phone.

I was concerned, but felt helpless to do anything until I contacted Pepe Del Rio. Pepe was a Span-

ish broadcaster for VOA, who had spent several stints in Vietnam, and he, Wayne and I had spent a lot of time together.

The three of us had even spent one night in the late 90's reminiscing (and drinking) at Pepe's cabin in the Maryland mountains. I finally managed to contact Pepe, and he, too, was concerned. He had not heard from Wayne in a long time. Pepe began investigating among contacts in the Washington

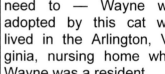

I was sent this picture by Wayne's son. It's entitled "Pals." So far as I knew, Wayne never had any affinity for pets, but he didn't need to — Wayne was adopted by this cat who lived in the Arlington, Virginia, nursing home when Wayne was a resident.

area and reached Wayne's son, only to learn that Wayne had Alzheimer's disease, and was in a nursing home in the Virginia suburbs.

In September, 2004, I went to Washington for a VOA reunion, but primarily for the opportunity to go see Wayne. It was sad. He was living comfortably in a very nice group home in the suburbs, but it was only Wayne's shell that I visited.

I don't believe he knew who I was, but he recognized that I was someone he had known. I tried to steer the conversation to Vietnam, but his only response was "I was in Vietnam once." His memories ran more to his time in World War Two but talking about the band drew a blank.

I got word from Pepe that Wayne died March 25, 2005. In a way I was glad that I had gone to see him a few months earlier, but also sad that I had done so — I would much more like to remember him as I knew him.

And not too many months ago, I got word that Pepe Del Rio also had died.

CHAPTER 18 — LIFE GOES ON IN PARADISE

Perhaps one of the biggest shocks to people who have grown up in the Middle West is to spend Christmas in the tropics. It really convinces them they are in a different world.

Linda described our first Christmas in Bangkok in a letter home: *Another Christmas come and gone – the only thing is, this year I just never did get the spirit. It really was a grand day and we all had a ball, but it never did feel like Christmas. We all wore shorts. Bob did outdoor chores, and for the crowning blow, we had shrimp and rice for dinner. Even so, the children felt it was one of the best Christmases they could remember. One more thing on Christmas – you know we've*

Note the scrawny tree.

been so worried about having a tree ever since we got here – well darned if we don't have two. We bought a potted Thai pine at the Sunday market for an exorbitant price and will put it on the patio during the year and bring it in again next Christmas. It's a wild looking little thing. On the Saturday before Christmas, TWA presented us with a Japanese pine (cut) and we put it in the upstairs hall for the children to decorate themselves.

The children began to learn to speak Thai and were doing well in school. Linda told her mother: *"Their adjustment to foreign living is very reassuring to us since we had no idea how they would*

take it." Linda became proficient in Thai, too. Once she was attending a Foreign Correspondent's Club dinner, seated next to the Tass correspondent. He admitted that he did not speak Thai and was shocked that an American, let alone an American wife, would go to that trouble. "If I never speak another word of the Thai language," Linda said, "it was worth all the lessons I've had just to be able to converse with the waiter in his own language and have to translate for the Russian gentleman."

In the "small world department," Linda was invited to Connie's house for a dinner, at which the President of Haegar Pottery, a Mr. Estes, was the guest of honor. In the course of the conversation, she learned that he had been born in Springfield, Missouri, and was a nephew of a Springfield grocer who she knew well. We also had a visit from Don Sheets, a classmate of mine at Webb City High School, and a friend in Springfield. Don had gone to work for a travel agency and was on a familiarization trip to Thailand.

The Tet Offensive in Vietnam, in February, 1968, surprised everyone. I had been in Saigon for a three-week stint, and had just returned to Bangkok. No news was anticipated during the Tet, the lunar New Year holiday. Vietnam government forces and their American allies seemed to be on top of the situation when, during the holiday, Viet Cong and North Vietnamese forces invaded Saigon, Hue, Danang and other major cities, and overran military outposts all over the country. Historians will long argue whether that surprise attack was a victory for the enemy, or whether it was an act of desperation on the part of the communists and was in fact a victory for our forces as the U.S. military command insisted. History will also show that, in the end, we and the South Vietnamese lost the war and were driven out.

But that argument was on down the road. The present issue was to get back to Saigon, which suddenly had become the most important story in the world. There were no flights and all air traffic had been shut down. It was easy to bravely insist on getting back to the war as long as no planes were available. I made six trips to the airport over three days to try to get a flight, until seats opened up on a U.S. military transport and several journalists, including yours truly, climbed aboard.

> Linda wrote my parents: *I must say I was very glad that Bob had so much trouble getting out early in the crisis – I felt things were much safer when he finally did go than that they would have been on Friday last. He, of course, was fit to be tied after all the futile trips to the airport with suitcases in hand, then having to come back home again – but I was quite thankful every time he came back home.*

Tan Son Nhut was a different place – no Vietnamese customs or immigration officers — everything was under the control of American MPs. No passport check, just a quick security briefing and an ironic, unheeded warning that civilians were not allowed to bring personal weapons into the country or to carry them. We all were carrying and none of us gave up anything.

The city was under strict control. Tu Do street and everything else was closed. There was a 24-hour curfew, we could only be on the streets for official business and then only when accompanied by American military guards. For several days, we made the one block trip from JUSPAO to the Eden Building in an armed jeep. There was still street-to-street fighting in Cholon, the city's Chinese quarter. The siege of Saigon ended within the first week and things began to return to normal.

My only close call came when I was walking past the Saigon USO and a motorcycle carrying two Vietnamese pulled up beside me. The South Vietnamese soldier guarding the USO saw the motorcycle, raised his rifle, took aim and threw a shell into the chamber. Fortunately, he didn't fire, because the bullet would have gone in one of my ears and out the other.

John Charles Daly, another famous broadcaster, had replaced John Chancellor as head of VOA, and once the smoke cleared in Vietnam, he wrote me a nice letter:

> *"Your professional performance in the face of hazard, strain and confusion was an essential element in keeping VOA's coverage timely and accurate and particularly in keeping us clear of many serious pitfalls. Your reporting on the Vietnameese recovery effort and relief work covered an aspect of the story we badly needed and was not available elsewhere in the depth we needed."*

Back in Bangkok, there always was a swirl of parties and receptions, and school events and cub scouts. Life was good, and luxurious.

We had the opportunity to take one long family vacation to Singapore and Malaysia. Our tickets to Bangkok had included an onward flight to Singapore for no additional charge if used within a year and we didn't want to miss that opportunity. I had liked Singapore and was sure Linda and the kids would too. And someone had told me of a thirty-five-foot sail boat off the Malaysian coast which could be rented at a reasonable price, with a two member crew included.

We went at the end of July to make the one-year deadline. Singapore was almost as good a place for shopping as Hong Kong, and we had a list of items we could not get in Bangkok. The kids spent hours exploring the Tiger Balm Gardens with its grotesque statues and jungle walks. We visited the Chinese Museum, we ate on a floating restaurant operated by some journalist friends. We also went to the movies to see "The King And I," a film that was banned in Bangkok. I rented a car in Singapore and arranged to drop it off in Penang, Malaysia, ten days later.

We drove across the causeway into Malaysia and headed for the coastal village of Mersing where our sailboat awaited. We set about the task of buying groceries and provisions for the six of us and two crewmen for four day cruise. No canned soft drinks were available, so we loaded case after case of bottled pop onto the boat, as well as beer and rice and anything else we could find in the Chinese grocery that might keep us from starvation. We set sail into the Gulf of Siam, our destination an island twenty miles offshore. We spent three nights aboard the ketch, anchored at three different islands. The days were spent ashore, lolling on the beach and exploring the nearby woods. None of the islands were inhabited – we did not see another boat or any other people during the entire trip.

From Mersing, we traveled to the Malaysian town of Malacca for a one-night stay. Then we headed for the capital, Kuala Lumpur. I had for several days promised the kids a special treat in K.L., but would not say what it was until we got there. Kuala Lumpur had an A&W root beer store – now there's an American treat you won't find in Thailand – with hotdogs and curly-Q French fries. They though it was great and we ate there a couple of times.

We stayed in a Chinese family hotel, big, barren and noisy – so noisy from the nightclub on the ground floor and the antics in the hallways and neighboring rooms that for once we did not have to shush the kids.

From Kuala Lumpur to the traditional old British resort in the Cameron Highlands, where we walked in the forest and were served afternoon tea on the terrace. The Cameron Highlands are 5500 feet high, and the area is refreshingly cool, but the 38-mile trip up the mountains on a terrible, twisting road took 2 ½ hours.

From the Highlands, we drove to the coastal city of Penang and some more beaches for a day. By then we were so tired we couldn't do much but grumble about the lousy hotel. We did persuade Linda to ride a tram up to the top of a nearby mountain to view the scenery, but she absolutely drew the line and refused to visit the snake temple. We were in Penang to catch a train north to Bangkok – a 26-hour ride in compartments on a train

far more modern than those to which I had become accustomed.

We had taken the family to Pattaya several times after arriving in Thailand. Usually we stayed at a military R and R resort and once Linda and I managed to slip away to the beach for three days without the kids, and luxuriated in a wonderful hotel. A great break came our way when Howard Biggerstaff, who was ending his assignment at USIS, asked us if we would like to take over their one-fourth share of a cottage at Pattaya Beach. We jumped at it — the deal even included ownership of a little Sunfish sailboat. Three other families shared in the cottage, and four other American families shared a neighboring cottage. Every fourth week it was ours, and our partners were very cooperative in trading beach weeks to coincide with my travel schedule.

The cottage was right on the beach, 40 feet from the gentle surf, with two bedrooms, a kitchen and

The Pattaya Beach House

a screened porch overlooking the water. The beach was gentle and shallow, and stretched on for miles. And there were always the fishing boats which would come to the beach and take us out to that marvelous island I had vowed to return to.

We managed to spend at least part of every fourth week at Pattaya for the better part of two years. Usually we would take one or more of the servants along with us, giving us a lot more time for enjoyment. And they enjoyed the experience too. With some help from a GI at the nearby military compound, I learned to sail the Sunfish, and David and Craig became owners of a hand made canoe which

Linda and Ling

they paddled in the surf.

Kayleen Honeck, my friend from Saigon, had married Lou Polichetti and they had moved to Bangkok, where we became close friends. They had a share of the second Pattaya Beach cottage and we spent many trips beachcombing the island with them.

We had acquired a new member of our family – a loveable gibbon named Ling (Thai for monkey) who lived on our back terrace, loved to be held and steal sips from a gin and tonic, and was a great companion and playmate for Steven.

Linda thrived in Bangkok. She worked as the womens' editor of the *Bangkok World* for six weeks during the regular editor's vacation and continued to write features for them. She landed an assignment as a freelance writer for a USIS magazine, *Free World/Horizons*, which was published in Manila and distributed all over Asia. She had no fear of driving in Thailand, telling my folks in one letter: *"As long as I remember that these people are split personalities – in person, gentle and smiling, behind the wheel, absolutely homicidal – I get along."*

After a year on Soi Sri Fah, we moved to another house, a little farther out toward the airport, on Street 32 (Soi Aladin.) It was much more modern, better furniture, bigger, and all three bedrooms and an upstairs den were <u>air-conditioned</u>. It was a good neighborhood. We had doctors on each side of us: one way was a military physician, Col. Beck; the other way, Gordon Perkin, a Canadian expert in family planning, who became a member of Bill Gates' multi-billion dollar charitable foundation for the health of the world's children. General Creighton Abrams, the commander of U.S. forces in Vietnam, had a house just down the street.

Beyond frequent Saigon duties, I had some great assignments out of Bangkok. I was sent (willingly) for six weeks in New Zealand and Australia, to cover a couple of U.N. economic conferences. In arranging the New Zealand trip, I wrote to Fred Foster, who had been a Marine guard and good friend in Saigon. He wrote back that he was getting married to a New Zealand girl and asked if I would serve as his best man. That gave me a chance to meet her family at a farm somewhere north of Wellington. I remember at the wedding reception, I asked one of the ladies for some coffee. "Wait," she said. So I waited, and when she wasn't busy, asked again for some coffee. "Wait," she said again. "But I've been waiting!" She replied: "I asked you how you wanted it. Do you want it wait (white – with cream?) And here I thought I was in an English speaking country.

I visited Wairaki, in the Maori area along the east coast of New Zealand to do a story on the geothermal electric project where they use underground steam from a volcanic field to generate power. And I marveled in Wellington that you could get apples and drink water from the faucet. I also marveled about the beer service — in those days, bars in New Zealand could serve beer only from 5 to 7 P.M., and they had developed an inventive system to keep the glasses filled in that short period of time. The bartender filled glasses from a hose, fed by a pump from an underground beer vat. The vat was filled each day by a tanker truck, via a valve set in the sidewalk.

The Sydney Opera House under construction. Its design was so complicated that many pieces had to be hand crafted in place. And many in Australia wondered whether it would ever be finished.

In Sydney, Australia, I wrote about the controversial Opera House which was just under construction, and the Easter Show, sort of a nation-wide county fair. I was in Canberra for another U.N. economic conference, and made a trip to the Snowy Mountains for a feature on a hydroelectric project.

While I was on this trip – which was supposed to be uneventful and even relaxing – Dr. Martin Luther King was assassinated, and President Johnson announced he would not seek another term in office, so that put a lot of pressure on me to gather comment and reaction from delegates at both international conferences.

The VOA Director, John Charles Daly, was in Sydney at the same time, and we had a chance to spend some time together. I flew to Perth for a visit, and spent a couple of days helping Randall Jesse move into his new house. He had been news director of WDAF in Kansas City – the place I most wanted to work – before he was appointed to the Foreign Service by the Democratic administration at the behest of former President Harry Truman.

I was back in Bangkok from Australia less than two weeks when I was sent back to Sydney in July, 1969, told only to check in with Ed Mason, from NASA. If you ever watch the movie, "The Dish," you will know why. Due to a whole series of circumstances, an Australian government-owned deep-space tracking dish way out away

from everything ("beyond the black stump," in Aussie slang) had been pressed into service to receive the first television signals from the first landing of man on the moon. Somehow the role of Australia and the Parkes Observatory did not capture the attention of the American media – a writer from Readers Digest and I were the only out-of-town reporters in Australia for this event. We were taken to the observatory, walked around on top of the huge dish – and when Neil Armstrong stepped onto the lunar surface, we in Australia saw it first; milli-seconds before anyone else in the world. And we saw it in color, which no one else did because the out-bound satellite relay was in black and white only.

With servants to run the house, and good friends to check up on things, Linda and I were able to travel together some and to go out a lot, to restaurants or to parties.

Letter from Linda May 29, 1968: *I tell you Bob has changed over here so much, it's hard to recognize him. He almost appeared to be stingy sometimes at home, but I think it was just a matter of the fact that we really didn't have the money to buy or do anything and I didn't realize it. Here, he's just delighted to go out anytime, buy anything we can possibly afford and all the time seeing to it that some money is saved. I am finally beginning to realize that he actually didn't care much for the Washington sit-down job – he was never too happy until after the TDY over here and then changing over to correspondent in Washington.*

Linda and I took the train (Yes, the Toonerville Trolley) to Laos, and even got out into the countryside to visit the site of a planned dam on the Mekong River.

Linda, who was usually very circumspect in her letters home, described the situation to her mother: *It was a stupid trip for us to make, since the Pathet Lao (communist guerrillas) work that area very often. We got as far as scampering up a jungle trail and Bob very calmly announced that he and his wife would return to the car, and damn the dam. I was scared spitless, but thought I was just being female, but Bob said I was intelligent to be frightened and he should have been much sooner. Bob said he got his first warning when we ran into a bunch of drying punji stakes farther back.* (Punji stakes were sharpened sticks used to by the communists to make booby traps.)

We had a lot of visitors in Bangkok. The official visitors were primarily the duty of Charles Eberhardt -- we just went to the cocktail receptions for them. Linda's mother and Aunt Betty flew out and spent two weeks with us in October, 1968. For them it was the last stop of a month long tour that included Japan and Hong Kong arranged by Pearson Ward. Luckily, I was home from Saigon during this period, and able to accompany them on many tours around Bangkok. But I drew the line at shopping trips.

For Christmas this year, we had three trees – our potted pine, and gift trees from TWA and from Thai International Airways. I always felt bad that one of them never even got decorated, it spent the holiday hiding in the shower. Just after Christmas, I was able to take Linda to Saigon with me for a few days (it had been forbidden before) and had the opportunity to show her the things I had been talking about for so long. We even had a big party at the VOA office/apartment so I was able to pay back three years worth of accumulated social obligations. She wrote to Georgia that it was one of the best times she had ever had in her life.

Letter, January 6: *Saigon was probably the prettiest city in Southeast Asia five years ago. There are numerous parks in the center of the city, lovely tree-shaded streets, clean, modern shops, and undoubtedly the best restaurants in this part of the world. Now, of course, there are too many guarded buildings, too much barbed wire, too much dire poverty and too many armed soldiers to be a vacation spot, but I never felt one time that I might be in danger.*

I took her to all the briefings and news conferences, and she said she felt much more intelligent and in the know for having spent a week there. In exchange Linda wrangled some money from the government to clean up the VOA office/apartment, re

cover chairs, make drapes and make the place more like a home.

Child rearing sometimes was difficult, partly due to my frequent absences.

In a letter to my mother, Linda said: *"I really think ours are much worse than a year ago. With Bob's occasional weeks here at home, I don't really think it will make much difference. I know he isn't going to start yelling the minute he gets in the door, much less punishing – and by the time they start getting on his nerves enough to really do something about it, he's gone again.*

Letter from Linda February 24, 1969: *As great as it all sounds with servants, etc, you really have to watch children closely to see that they don't decide that this is the normal way to live. I'll never forget the morning that Bob came downstairs unexpectedly when they were getting ready for school and Djan was on her hands and knees under the table, tying David's shoes. Bob nearly had a seizure over that one. Needless to say, David now ties his own shoes.*

Charles Eberhardt was a great boss and a good mentor. He could be critical of your work or some oversight, but God help someone else who dared criticize his colleagues. He was dogged in his determination to prevent the bureaucrats of USIA and the diplomats from the State Department from interfering in VOA news coverage. Unfortunately, for us, he was transferred back to Washington to become Chief

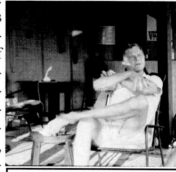

Charles Eberhardt

of the VOA newsroom. Roy Heinecke should have gotten the job as bureau chief, but Charlie was replaced by Roger Cowell, another senior editor in the newsroom. While I knew and liked Roger, I never developed the rapport with him that I had with Charlie – plus, when he got on the scene with a new wife, he almost refused to travel, increasing the burden on Roy and me.

CHAPTER 19 — JAPAN

It should come as no surprise that this idyllic life we were leading in Thailand would have to end. In September, 1969, Washington said I was to be transferred to Tokyo, to be the single correspondent and bureau chief there. We really were not ready to go, to give up our house, our friends, Ling, the kids' school which had just started a new year, and our beach cottage. There were many parts of Thailand we had yet to see, but prepare to go we did.

Linda was more enthusiastic about the transfer than I was. I had been to Tokyo and knew some of its shortcomings. She hadn't, and had always wanted to see Japan. We suspected Charles Eberhardt had arranged the transfer because I was such a junior partner in Bangkok. So, yes, I was being promoted and recognized, but I was not real happy about it.

Linda wrote her mother, September 5: *We are thrilled at the prospect, not only of living there, but of Bob's running his own shop – he will be completely by himself. Naturally, I have mixed feelings about leaving Bangkok, but we've been here over two years now and have loved almost every minute of it. Since change does not bother us nor the children, I think we will adjust easily to Japan.*

Letter from Linda, September 23: *To tell you the truth, I'm a little bit tired of the life of leisure here and am dead to do my own work for a while. I love my servants here but I am definitely in the way in any room in the house. I love to cook – that is out of the question. My adventuresome spirit is still working and I'm still excited about the move, but I must say Bob is getting grouchier about it by the day. There is one huge saving grace for him, however – in 20 years he would never be able to enjoy working for Roger Cowell. If Bob needs the office car for work, it's at the PX with Roger and his wife – lunch is a several hour affair – and perhaps two days out of five, Roger just doesn't come in at all.*

We packed up and loaded out, all in five weeks. Professionally, it was like starting anew. Ray Kabaker and his family had moved away from Tokyo a year and a half earlier, and VOA had had no presence there. I made a quick trip to Tokyo to reconnoiter housing, schools, working conditions, and enroute stopped in Hong Kong to consult with the Kabakers. It would be up to me to re-open the bureau, hire an assistant, and re-establish contacts.

The family stopped over in Hong Kong for several days. There was serious shopping to be done – we had been living in the tropics for two years, and we were going to a climate much more like that at home — cold winters and even snow. There were coats and sweaters and boots to buy. We also stopped for a couple of days in Taiwan just to vacation, but there was urgency to get moved and get the kids back in school.

I managed to get Kim, David and Craig enrolled in Nishimachi International School because of the recommendation of a Bangkok friend who was also the friend of the school's head. They were accepted because we had three boys – the school was heavy with girls. I rented a temporary apartment and insisted to VOA that they would have to rent a 4-bedroom house which could cost as much as $1000 per month.

There was an American school at the U.S. airbase near Tokyo, but attendance there would require a long bus ride. The Kabakers and other friends had talked glowingly about Nishimachi, a small private institution in the center of the city. Nishimachi was founded on the premise that some Japanese children (those of diplomats and businessmen, for example) would benefit from a western, English-language education and that the best way to achieve that would be through a mix of Japanese and western children.

The nationality mix was about 50-50 in grades one through nine. Our kids missed only one week of school in the transition. Steven was too young, and Nishimachi did not have room in kindergarten, so we found kindergarten for him at a nearby Catholic girls school and within a week, he was saying,

"Yes, ma'am." He would move on to Nishimachi for the first grade.

The Polichettis had thrown a wonderful going away party for us in Bangkok. Linda said in a letter *"We will miss lots of good friends but the thing about foreign service is that everybody moves all the time and you will more than likely meet old friends in another post."* That would prove itself true time and time again

We arrived in Tokyo on a Sunday night, and the next morning, the older kids were in school. Linda wrote her mother, *"Kim, David and Craig absolutely love Nishimachi. We were astounded at their enthusiasm for the very first day."*

We took temporary quarters in a two bedroom apartment in the Sendagaya neighborhood while Linda began the arduous task of finding a house. The Kabakers before us had lived in Grew House, a large apartment complex owned by the American Embassy, housing nearly all the American diplomats in Tokyo. But the Embassy, and notably the Public Affairs Officer, Ned Roberts, decided the new VOA correspondent should not be quartered there. That turned out to be a blessing.

Letter from Linda November 9, 1969: *Tokyo is most certainly the biggest city on earth. That, of course, is not just my own observation, but the truth. To me, it means all the scurry and bustle of any big city – its problems and its advantages. The problems are headed by expense – everything costs a lot, and it's dirty. On the other hand, Tokyo has any and everything you could possible want. All six of us are freezing to death. I know by anybody else's standards, it is only late fall and not really cold, but after two years plus in Bangkok, we are suffering with the cold. There is no fear of burglary, walking on the streets after dark or any of the other facts of life becoming so prevalent in Bangkok the past year. The Japanese people are very kind to wandering foreigners and will bend over backwards to help you locate your destination. Frankly, I believe I am culminating a great love affair with Japan that has been going on since my teens. Expense, dirt, what-have-you – with me the advantages of the people and their wonderful customs out weigh all other considerations.*

We quickly learned that we would not be without visitors in Tokyo. The Director of VOA, Kenneth Giddens, his wife and 22 year old daughter, visited during our first month. They would come again early the following year, and we developed what was more a family relationship than a boss/worker relationship.

The Apollo 11 astronauts also came to Tokyo during our first month there as part of a round-the-world tour, and my old friend Ed Hickey was traveling with them for VOA. They did not do autographs on their world tour, but Ed managed to obtain an autographed picture with the inscription: "To the Chancellor children; Kim, David, Craig and Steven – with warmest regards from the Apollo 11 crew," and all three signed it.

By December, we were settled in a house. Linda found a two-story western-style house in the Rappongi neighborhood about two miles from the office, and within walking distance of Nishimachi. It had four bedrooms and a bath upstairs, a living

room, dining room and kitchen down. Right in the middle of Tokyo, we even had a carport for the old green Chevelle station wagon, and a tiny front garden ten feet square. All this for a mere $1000 per month, which was an outrageously high rent for VOA to pay, but I had warned them.

We hadn't been in the home more than a day or two when a Japanese policeman knocked on the door. He just wanted to know who was living in his neighborhood. Between that sort of attention – plus Japan's overall safety and love for children –

we had no concerns about the kids' well-being. They were free to walk and explore the neighborhood and could even ride the subways several miles across the city to visit the zoo. Rappongi even then was known as an area for restaurants and night clubs. Recent visitors report that it is even more so now and probably is not a neighborhood in which to raise children. The site of our house is now a large Mercedes dealership.

At one end of our street was the Japan Defense Ministry; at the other, Hardy Barracks, which was the office and printing plant for the U.S. military newspaper, *Stars and Stripes*, that was distributed all over Asia. Hardy Barracks had a small PX, which we could use and which the kids frequented for candy and treats. For major shopping trips, we would drive or take the train to the big Navy Exchange at Yokohama, an hour away.

Being barred from the Grew House apartments also meant we had to obtain furniture for the VOA house (remember, we had taken only a limited shipment to Bangkok). Linda and I went on a binge of furniture buying at Yokohama – all at VOA expense – and furnished the entire house on one whirlwind shopping trip. The only hitch was in obtaining a washer and dryer, because some USIA regulations said I was not of sufficient rank to rate a washer and dryer (shades of Bangkok air conditioning). I had to contact Washington, and Washington had to send a telegram to USIS before the finance office there would allow the purchase.

PAO Ned Roberts seemed to have antipathy toward VOA, (in later years, his son Doug would be a VOA correspondent and colleague in Africa). He also had a tendency to want to interfere with what I was doing. There was not an office for the VOA correspondent – I was tucked into a temporary space in a corner of the USIS radio section. Fortunately, eight months later, Roberts was replaced by Alan Carter, who liked VOA and never interfered. He even found space for a proper office and separate broadcast studio for VOA. Alan became a good friend, and when we left Japan, he wrote a glowing letter of recommendation to VOA.

As the new year 1970 dawned, I was boarding a plane for Taiwan, Bangkok, Kaula Lumpur, Singapore, Djakarta, Bali, Auckland, Sydney and Hong Kong to cover a tour by Vice President Spiro Agnew. I was eager to go – I had been home for almost three months, except for one quick trip to Korea and another to Osaka. The Agnew trip was a great one to cover – he never said or did much, except arrive and depart and occasionally make a short statement after meeting a host dignitary. No news, but a lot of fun.

Linda was finding the downside of running and cleaning a house with four children, and no help. *"Some days, I'm all but picking up the telephone to call the employment agency for a maid, then other times I'm glad I don't have anyone underfoot. I think what I really want is a built-in baby sitter so I can have the freedom to come and go like I did in Bangkok."* Two or three hours of her day were spent in Japanese classes.

One big story looming on Tokyo's horizon was Expo '70, the world's fair planned for Osaka, Japan, to open in the spring of 1970. The fair site was already under construction, and I went there not long after arrival in the country, to make arrangements for future coverage. I was able to lease an apartment for VOA adjacent to Expo, which would be used in the months to come for whatever VOA staffers came to town. Expo promised to provide a wealth of feature material for VOA, since more than 50 countries would have a presence, many of them countries where we had big audiences. And events such as that attract many high profile visitors and special events.

Over the course of the next nine months, I spent a lot of time at Expo, and story-wise, it was worth every minute. Overall, that assignment was one of the best, the most fun, I ever had, with no political pressures, just the sheer enjoyment of visiting pavilions and preparing features, which were well received at VOA.

Linda and the kids were able to come to Osaka and share the apartment after school ended. They all enjoyed Expo '70, seeing the colorful exhibits and sampling all sorts of exotic food. We did have one frightening adventure while there – the boys were sleeping in an apartment directly across the hall from the VOA place, and somehow, David's pillow slipped off the bed and fell near an electric heater. The pillow caught fire, Steven awoke and smelled the smoke and came for us. By the time we intervened, two mattresses were afire and we dragged them outside to a balcony. We were shocked to find that this eight-story high-rise, one of 60 built near the Expo site, had no fire extinguishers. David and Craig were deferential to Steven the rest of the visit, convinced he had saved their lives.

Tokyo, and Expo also, attracted many more visitors than Bangkok had – and now we were the VOA presence required to take care of them. We went one month with only five days of no company in town. Linda observed: *With Bob running his own office and me running my own house (no servants) entertaining becomes more of a chore and less of a luxury than it was in Bangkok.* She finally did hire a girl to help with cleaning and ironing two days a week.

The Tokyo correspondent was primarily responsible for covering Japan, Korea, Taiwan and Okinawa, with some hitches to Saigon, or Pnom Penh, Cambodia, thrown in. Those trips were fine with me. I got to keep up with events in southeast Asia, and get in some major shopping while passing through Hong Kong enroute.

Late in April, I was off to Vietnam again for a month. But early in May, Steven had a serious accident: He was riding as a passenger on a motorcycle at Hardy Barracks when it went out of control, throwing him headfirst into a solid steel gate. He was taken to an emergency hospital just across the street from our house and received 40 stitches across his forehead and scalp. The *Stars and Stripes* organization felt responsible, since the bike driver was one of their employees, and informed me in Saigon. They arranged a quick military flight back to Tokyo. We took Steven to a U.S. military hospital near Tokyo for further examination. The doctors there could find nothing more wrong with him and praised the needle work of the Japanese doctor. After this encouraging news, I flew back to Saigon to complete my assignment.

Perhaps the most important thing I did in re-establishing the Tokyo bureau was to hire Masaji Ichikawa as an assistant. I started the process of seeking and interviewing candidates for the job

With all the moving (new country, new house) Christmas almost slipped by us. Linda said she just could not get organized, and our Christmas cards didn't go out until December 31st with the following poem enclosed:

Christmas came and Christmas went, and here we sit with our cards unsent!

St. Nick arrived for a visit and left, now all our friends are feeling bereft,

Because from the Chancellors they heard not a line; no greetings from Tokyo at holiday time.

It's obvious we must come up with a reason for fooling around and missing the season.

We've thought of excuses that boggle the mind, but only this one tells why we're behind:

We were moving as October stretched into November, Then 'fore we could gasp, 'twas that day in December.

Our transfer from Bangkok came as one big surprise, from the heat of the tropics to the snow in the skies.

We found a nice house in the heart of the town, where the latch string is out when our friends come around.

The address is the same, just the APO's moved, San Francisco's Postmaster said 96503 is our groove.

We ask our friends please excuse our remissness and pray through the year we do better next Christmas.

Our intentions are great; our bonhomie's intact; it's only the organization we lack.

In closing, let six contrite Chancellors say, Happy New Year to all and Happy Valentine's Day.

soon after arrival in Tokyo, but I was not finding anyone that quite suited me until he came in. Ichikawa-san spoke good English, and was a journalist, who had worked for a couple of Japanese newspapers. But he had an unusual outlook on the work – whereas most Japanese men wanted, and found, employment at one company and stayed there throughout their careers – he was sort of a free spirit. He wanted to experience several different kinds of employment and had jumped from job to job during his career.

Ichikawa-san and I got along great from the beginning. He learned quickly what was expected of him: reporter, translator of newspapers and translator of Japanese customs and culture. He traveled with me most of the time around Japan, and covered the office, filing advisories to the newsroom in those periods when I was out of the country. He was a frequent visitor at our house, and although he had a wife and two children, we never met them until the day of our final departure from Japan. I gave him a nickname which really fit: "Ichi-ban," which means "number one." Ichi-kawa-san means Mr. Ichi-kawa.

Ichi-ban, 1972

He was a valuable and loyal asset to VOA. After I was gone, I remember he filed a news item one day and just happened to mention that his father had died that morning, but he felt he had to perform his duty to VOA first. We had the pleasure, once we were back in the United States, of bringing him back to Washington for a training course, and he stayed in our home with us. For many years, I had lost track of Ichi-ban, but recently we re-established contact and I learned he had worked for the U.S. Cultural Center at Sapporo, for NEC Electronics, at the U.N. headquarters information office in New York and three years as a visiting scholar at the Brookings Institute.

To my mind, the worst part of the Tokyo job was covering South Korea. The American Embassy and USIS just did not like VOA, and they particularly did not like me. It was a prime example of the problems mentioned earlier — VOA being at the crossroads of journalism and diplomacy. I got in more trouble covering Korea stories than at any other time to date. It started in 1969 when I was in Seoul for some international conference. An apartment building collapsed, leaving a good number of people dead. I did just a short news story on it, in which I said faulty, weak cement was the cause of the collapse. (I knew that was

the case, because I went to the scene and picked up pieces of concrete rubble, which crumbled to sand in my hand.) USIS didn't want me to do the story, but I did anyway, saying I did not need their approval for news. (although at that time, I did need their approval for political reports).

The protest cables flew back and forth. VOA supported my position, but warned me to be more circumspect in the future. The Director of VOA, Ken Giddens, was livid that a USIS post had tried to interfere with one of his people. (During home leave in 1970, Giddens took the Seoul PAO and me to lunch, and royally chewed out the PAO in my presence, so they didn't much like me in Seoul afterwards.)

In the revolving door of personnel that was so typical of the USIA/VOA structure, the chief Information Officer in Seoul was Clyde Hess, who took his share of the chewing out and hot cables. Two years later, Clyde Hess was assigned as the Chief of News and Current Affairs at VOA – he became my boss.

I had been to Korea four times prior to this; and On every occasion except one, the post said they did not want me in the country. I went back to Korea a time or two after 1970, including for the 1971 Presidential elections, but I never enjoyed it. The flap did result in some clarification of the rules under which VOA correspondents were to work, as outlined by Ken Giddens in an official letter to USIS in Seoul.

We are aware that conditions vary from area to area and from country to country. We know that in some countries, coverage by VOA correspondents is a regular, routine activity, and that in several other countries the political situation is quite sensitive. We have instructed our correspondents to meet all feed deadlines in the coverage of stories to which they are assigned. If after digging out the facts, checking and consulting with USIS and/or the Embassy, there is substantial disagreement, the correspondents have been told to send their stories...the post may then enter its objections. Our correspondents are thus authorized and indeed required to make the first judgment on the spot.

We began attending an Episcopalian Church in Tokyo because we felt the kids needed that exposure, and because we really liked the pastor, Chris Webber, and his wife, Peg. They, too, had kids in Nishimachi, so we were thrown together often. This was a "high church" Episcopalian congregation, with all the kneeling, standing, sitting, communion every Sunday – what I termed "back door Catholics." Linda and the kids went almost every Sunday, I went when I was forced to, when I was in town, so that I did not have to make up some lame excuse to my friend Chris.

Linda started taking a class in Ikebana (Japanese flower arranging) and another in Chinese cooking. I had to go back to Osaka to close out the Expo '70 set up, and while I was gone, Linda was invited to a U.S. Embassy reception to meet General and Mrs. William Westmoreland. She was impressed.

There were a lot of new people in Tokyo and Linda and I began planning a party for some of them and for some of our long-time friends. The long time friends included Hart and Della Sprager (he was the regional film officer at USIS and they were great partiers who came to Tokyo by way of Rio) and Sandy and Nancy Rosenblum. We picked a disco theme, decorated the house with flashing lights and psychedelic posters, cranked up the stereo and had a great time with 48 people attending. The décor was so authentic that a couple of sailors on leave in Tokyo knocked at the door, thinking it was a club they had missed.

In October I was sent out for what became an eight week trip – the longest time away from home since my 1966 TDY to Saigon. This trip, too, included three weeks in Saigon, and then three more in Pnom Penh, Cambodia, as well as stops in Hong Kong and Bangkok. Meanwhile, Roger Cowell was sitting in Bangkok, not traveling. His attitude forced Roy Heinecke to quit VOA and take a job in Hong Kong.

Cambodia was a new addition to our itinerary. During my time in Bangkok, we could not go there. One of my first hassles in Thailand came when I followed Washington instructions to respond to an open invitation for the press to visit Phnom Penh. The Embassy in Bangkok blocked the trip after several exchanges of cables back and forth.

Now, two years later, VOA had a rented apartment there and was keeping it staffed full time with correspondents from Bangkok, Hong Kong and Tokyo. Duty there was more pleasant than in Saigon, but also more dangerous. More American correspondents were killed in Cambodia in two years time than during the whole of the war in Vietnam.

Phnom Penh was a much nicer place than Saigon. It still had the colonial charm that Saigon had lost in several years of war. The streets were quiet, and we often traveled around town in pedi-cabs. We did have a good setup there, with an all day driver and an assistant/translator, who was necessary because I had no French and Phnom Penh was a French speaking city.

I received national publicity during the first Phnom Penh trip. I had become friends with Jim Foster of Scripps Howard and his wife, Joanne. After a quiet dinner one evening, we happened upon a movie theater just moments after a terrorist bombing. He wrote a dramatic, but true story, about the incident and our efforts to drag the wounded out of the structure before police and other help arrived. Two grenades had been thrown into the movie house (later a third, unexploded grenade was discovered) killing 17 people and wounding about 50. It was Phnom Penh's first real taste of terrorism. I sent a letter to Linda about the incident, but Jim's story ran in the Washington Daily News and several other newspapers, and she received clippings of it before she received my letter.

During my long absence, my cousins Laura and Kristin Kennedy visited the family in Tokyo. They were on the last leg of a round the world trip, courtesy of Phoebe's job with TWA, and by the time they reached Tokyo, were tired and broke. They stayed with Linda and the kids several days, and all had a great time seeing the sights of Japan.

Linda had begun purchasing Japanese and other Oriental antiques and other collectibles. This was at the urging of Connie Heinecke, who told her she could take such items back to the United States and sell them for a fortune. I just laughed; I knew Linda would not part with any of her treasures for any price, and I was right. Here, 39 years later, we still have them.

PIECES OF STRING TOO SHORT TO SAVE

I was sent back to Saigon January 5, 1971. The pressures of travel caused by the non-travelling Bangkok bureau chief were getting to all of us – Kabaker in Hong Kong was going home, Roy Heinecke had already resigned.

> Linda wrote her mother the day I departed: *Tokyo is getting to me. It is just too crowded, the people are too pushy and rude, the traffic is ridiculous, and above all, the air is enough to give anybody anything. (*She had just been diagnosed as having what was termed Tokyo-Yokohama asthma, due to the heavily polluted air there.) *I don't really like the city and Bob just hates it. I think I hate this place simply because Bob is never here anymore. Unfortunately, I just magnify problems all out of proportion when Bob isn't here. Suddenly the traffic is too much, the people are rude and I'm just not fit to live with."*

My travel schedule was heavy: back from Saigon at the end of January, five days at home, then to Sapporo for a Winter Olympics Preview, home for two weeks, then off for another three week stint in Cambodia.

Back in Tokyo after Cambodia, there was good news. The Phnom Penh office had been closed because of the intensifying danger there, and the deaths of several reporters while they were driving roads into the countryside. A good friend of mine from Saigon, Kate Webb of UPI, was believed to be among the casualties, but a couple of months later she was released after being held as a captive. Because of this, I would not have to go back to Southeast Asia until August.

Linda and I had a chance to visit around Japan. I went to Nagoya for the opening of an international table tennis tournament, and I was able to take her along with me. I worked some and we toured some in the castles and gardens of Nagoya and Kyoto and to the Mikimoto pearl island.

The table tennis tournament was notable. An American table tennis team came to Japan to compete and played against the Chinese team, making its first international appearance in five years. Unexpectedly, the Chinese invited the American team to return to China with them for a visit and exhibition matches although at the time China was closed to almost all American visitors. Naturally, their trip was dubbed "Ping Pong Diplomacy" and it helped open the way for President Nixon's historic trip to Peking early in 1972.

Two weeks later the kids were on Spring break, so we took them to Mount Fuji and stayed in a very old, pleasant hotel. The weather was beautiful and Mount Fuji was there. Often Fuji would disappear in the smog that laid over Japan.

We also obtained a beach house, after learning that we would not be leaving Japan this year. It wasn't Pattaya Beach by a long shot. It was crowded on weekends, and the beach was dirty, but it was away from Tokyo. It was about two hours out of the city, and there was train service, so Linda and the kids could drive there during the week and I could join them for weekends. The Rosenblums had their own cabin about a mile away.

> Letter from Linda May 21, 1971: *We finally found our summer place, after several enjoyable trips looking for it. Then out of curiosity, we looked up a for-rent cottage* (from a newspaper ad) *on the bay and were so enchanted with it, we took it for the entire year, until June, 1972. It has two bedrooms and a bath on the first floor and upstairs is the living room, dining room and kitchen, with windows all across the front looking straight out onto the bay. It has a fireplace for the winter months, plus heating. It is fully furnished down to pots and pans and is only a year old. We are taking our first weekend trip next weekend, and as soon as the children are out of school, we will go down for long periods of time.*

Linda and the kids spent most of June and July at the beach. I spent as much time there as I could, between two quick trips to Korea and to Okinawa. The cottage even had a telephone, so I could keep in touch with Ichikawa and determine if there was any news I needed to pursue. We weren't able to use the cabin in August, because I had made a deal with the Deputy PAO of USIS, Dave Hitchcock, to share the place and its expenses. The Hitchcocks also had kids in Nishimachi, about the same ages as ours.

It is just as well we were home in August, Sean Kelly and his family came through Tokyo, enroute to an assignment as VOA correspondent in Bangkok. Roger had been replaced, or had retired.

The Japan beach house was not as private, nor as placid, as the beach house in Thailand.

Ichikawa and I headed up to Mount Fuji, where the international Boy Scout Jamboree was being held, but a typhoon swept across the island and nearly washed them away. We saw a lot of wet, muddy and miserable scouts that day.

Jim Foster, my colleague from the Phnom Penh bombing, came through Tokyo, as did former boss Bill Haratunian and the new bureau chief from Hong Kong, Bill Read.

My time away from southeast Asia stretched from August until November, but finally another Saigon assignment showed up, three weeks, ending Christmas Eve. The schedule held, and I was home in time for Christmas. I missed several anniversaries, a lot of birthdays, and a Thanksgiving or two, but throughout my career, I never missed a Christmas at home.

I went to Taiwan to their big "double ten." October 10 was the anniversary date of the founding of the Republic of China government when Chiang Kai Shek fled the mainland, so double-ten (the tenth day of the tenth month) was celebrated annually. President Nixon's personal representative to the event was a former movie star, the Governor of California Ronald Reagan. (We will hear about him again.)

I sent this News Analysis about the situation, which even was picked up and printed in Japan's Mainichi Daily News, and which gained me a hero-gram from Charles Eberhardt as "one of the best news analyses I have read in a long time."

In the 22 years since the Nationalist Chinese retreated to Taiwan in the face of the advancing Chinese Communists, the Republic of China has experienced growing stability and now it faces with surprising calm the threat of change swirling all around the republic. The republic's closest ally, the United States, is opening communications with Taipei's arch enemy in Peking. The United Nations is considering expelling Taiwan in favor of the Peking regime. Thus, one would have expected a mood of panic and paranoia to prevail in Taipei, but the mood instead is calm. The nationalists obviously do not like the way things are going but seem prepared to cope with the reality. To be sure, President Chiang Kai-Shek in his National Day address made the traditional call for the return to the mainland but that once primary goal of the government seems to have faded.

After the success of Expo '70, there was another big event in Japan in 1972. The Winter Olympics were held at Sapporo, on the northern island of Hokkaido. As at Expo '70, I was responsible for setting up facilities and arrangements for VOA coverage. I was assigned an apartment in the press village, and had phone lines and a telex installed. I hired a driver and car. We covered the winter games with a crew of four: Bill Read, the VOA correspondent in Hong Kong, and Vlad Fleischer from the radio section of JUSPAO in Saigon, were assigned to help Ichikawa and me cover the events.

Bill was there basically to cover the news. Vlad, a Czechoslovakian emigre, came because he was a ice hockey fan and somewhat of an expert in the sport. I had known Vlad for several years in Saigon, and Linda and I had the great pleasure to take him to a Czechoslovakian restaurant in Tokyo, which he loved. He had left his homeland at the time of the communist takeover.

The Olympics were not nearly as much fun as Expo 70 because (1) I hate cold weather and snow and there was a lot of it, and (2) because NBC had the contract to broadcast the Olympics for American television and its contract with the Olympic Committee severely limited the amount of live coverage VOA was allowed. We did live broadcasts of the opening and closing ceremonies, but otherwise our coverage was confined to news reports on winners and events and interviews with participants. What we didn't have, and needed, was a Russian language reporter at an event where the Russians swept up many gold medals. Despite the difficulties, I was commended for my work in organizing the coverage.

Linda had begun working again. She got a job writing articles and doing interviews for a magazine published by the Okura Hotel. The fact that she had a job, and we were fairly happy with life was a precursor to the likelihood that we would be leaving soon.

A series of Viet Cong offensives in April, 1972 drew me back for several weeks. We had three or four correspondents working all over the country. That certainly was a far cry from my ten weeks alone in Saigon during the TDY tour. In many ways, I was sorry to have to leave the area before reaching the end of the story.

April 1st, I covered my first and last prize fight. Mohammed Ali came to Japan for a bout against Mac Foster. It was fitting that it was on April Fools Day, because Ali was in control the whole time. Ali had lost his crown as Heavyweight Champion of the World when he announced he had become a black Muslin and would not serve in Vietnam. The Foster bout was one of several he had against no-name boxers to regain his status and eventually, his championship. I didn't care about prize fighting but as a member of the press, I had a chance at a ringside seat and took advantage of it.

Early in 1972, I was approaching the end of my tour, and had begun communicating with Washington about my next assignment.

> Letter from Linda, January 21, 1972: *As much as I bellyache about Japan, I will certainly miss some of the things that are available only here. Of course, there are some whopping items I won't miss, like smog, rude people, unbelievable crowds everywhere, complete lack of communication and just plain noise. At any rate, Bob Chancellor is leaving Japan after this school year at any cost. He really hates this place, and although I'm not as violent in my opinions of the place, I'll be just as happy to leave.*

Most of our friends were leaving Japan also, and many of them were returning to Washington. Charles Eberhardt wanted me to come back to Washington and be promoted as his deputy in the newsroom – but the bureaucrats nixed that, saying I did not have enough administrative experience. Then Clyde Hess (remember Korea?) asked where I would like to go, and I responded Rome, Athens, London or Munich, in that order. Instead, Hess replied, the intention was to assign me as the deputy bureau chief in New York City. I flatly refused that – we were not the least bit interested in living in New York, or trying to raise four children there as they approached their teen years. Besides, I argued, having lived two years in the world's largest city (Tokyo) I didn't want to go the world's second largest – I'd rather go back to Bowie, Maryland, and the VOA newsroom. (Strategically, it may have been a bad decision – the guy who took that job, Alan Heil, was within two years my boss and eventually the acting Director of VOA.) And that's where it ended. We left Japan on June 17, 1972. Little did I know at the time, but that was an important date – it was the date of the Watergate break-in, an event that would have a great deal of importance for me over the next three years.

Above right: Linda with Nit Noi — That's the Thai word for "little bit — a poodle we (foolishly) bought when we were in Missouri on home leave. In the next chapter you will learn what a hassle it turned out to be bringing him to Japan from the United States. Nit Noi was not a very well behaved dog, in fact, he may not have been very smart. But Sachco-san, a woman who did occasional cleaning for us, loved Nit Noi, and when we were preparing to leave Japan, we gave him to Sachco and her family. They treated the dog like a king and expressed eternal gratitude to us for such a wonderful gift.

One point of contention between the U.S. Government and Japan was the island of Okinawa. The Japanese did not want the U.S. military presence on Okinawa, and they wanted it declared a prefecture of Japan. With the Vietnam war underway, the U.S. was reluctant to relinquish such a strategic place. The Japanese also were not too happy that VOA had a big transmitter facility on Okinawa. I visited there during one trip, and found the facility well away from the general population of the island — and it had an added attraction; it had its own private beach.

CHAPTER 20 — VISITS TO AMERICA

During the summer of 1970, we became eligible for our first home leave, so I abandoned the final days of Expo '70 to Ray Kabaker, and we returned to the United States for the first time in nearly three years. We scheduled it to begin as soon as the school year ended in mid-June.

It would be the family's first trip back to American soil, but the previous September, I had flown back to Anchorage, Alaska to cover the visit of Emperor Hirohito. The Japanese Emperor was stopping over on a trip from Japan to Europe. President Nixon flew to Anchorage to greet him. It was just a one-day event, but I used the opportunity to tour parts of Alaska. I had a great time shopping for items unavailable in Japan, such as certain records, and had time to drive south to look at the glaciers. I had never been to or near Alaska before, but just a few months later, the whole family would visit Alaska for a time on our way back to a stateside assignment.

As home leave neared, Linda had received word that her grandfather, Roy Hulston (Grandpa Cuckoo) was seriously ill, so she and Steven took off early on their own, with me to follow, accompanying Kim, David and Craig, a couple of weeks later. Linda's great misadventure on that trip came in Seattle, where Steven broke out in chicken pox just as they were passing through immigration. But they let the diseased kid into the country anyway – after he had exposed everybody on the Northwest Airlines 707 and most of Seattle's airport. Before the summer was over, the older three also broke out.

The older kids and I rejoined Linda and Steven in Springfield. Her grandfather died during that summer. We spent six-weeks leave in Missouri; with my folks at Lake of the Ozarks where they had bought a cabin, and in Springfield. We spent some days on a houseboat at Lake Pomme de Terre, where Linda's father and stepmother were now running a successful marina. And in a weak moment, we bought a dog – a miniature poodle puppy named Nit Noi.

Our planned return to Japan was elaborate. Government regulations said that on official travel to or from an overseas post, you were entitled to go one way by sea instead of air. But being able to arrange that was rare; the bureaucrats usually found some way or another to block sea passage, because it was so much more expensive. Somehow, we had been approved to return by sea, and booked the American President line's President Wilson for passage from Honolulu to Tokyo. We intended to fly to Los Angeles and visit Disneyland, and fly on to the big island of Hawaii for a few days and then join the ship. The puppy complicated those plans a bit – Hawaii had very strict quarantine rules so that any animal brought onto the island had to be held for six weeks.

This problem took some maneuvering. Eventually, August 10, as we were beginning our journey back, we flew with Nit Noi to Los Angeles where the President Wilson was preparing to depart. We took the puppy aboard ship and put him in the ship's kennel. A crew member promised to watch over and feed him. The dog even had his own ticket for the voyage from Los Angeles to Honolulu. Meanwhile, we headed for two days at Disneyland and Universal Studios, and then on to United Airlines for Hilo.

I learned a trick that day at the Los Angeles airport. We checked in behind a huge tour group, and at the ticket counter we were assigned six center seats scattered throughout the airplane. All the aisle and window seats had been assigned to the tourists. I protested that we were a family flying together and needed to stay together. The ticket agent refused, so I told him "I have four children here, and I intend to show each one of them where the stewardess call button is, and I intend that each one will use it many times since they will not have siblings or parents nearby to restrain them." We were quickly upgraded to first class and had a great flight.

After touring the big island (we put 650 miles on a rented car in four days and even witnessed a volcanic eruption) we rejoined the President Wilson (and Nit Noi) at Honolulu and had a wonderful eight days at sea before arriving back in Yokohama. We made friends on that trip with several American business families returning to Japan, and they joined our social circle.

During home leave in the summer of 1970, my father warned me that he had been having some heart problems, adding that should he die while we were gone, he did not want me to spend a bunch of money trying to get home for a funeral. Just four months later, right before Christmas, on a relaxed Sunday morning, I received the shocking phone call from Washington: my father had not died of a heart attack, my mother had. She was 57, and had had a massive coronary while driving, pulled to the curb and died instantly. It was hard to comprehend because she had never been sick and certainly had never shown any signs of a heart problem. But, her father, Arthur Tearle, had died of a coronary at the early age of 55.

My dad was not aware, and neither was I until then, that the government had a program under which they would pay for me to fly home for compassionate leave. I left that day for St. Louis and she was buried in Boonville three days later. I was much closer to her than to my father and was devastated by this turn of events. (Even today, I will occasionally think of something that I wish I could tell her.)

Linda could not go back for the funeral, but it was a shock to her, too, to lose a mother-in-law she was close to, so soon after losing her grandfather. She had even gotten a long friendly letter from Mother, written three days before her death, and a box of Christmas presents had arrived.

After the funeral at Boonville, Dad, Sam, Steve and I went back to St. Louis, where we put up and decorated a Christmas tree, then I headed back to Tokyo. It was a bleak holiday for Linda and me – the children handled it pretty well.

We received a letter from my father March 7th that really stunned and upset us. He said he was planning to get married June 6, to an old friend in Boonville, Martha Williams, described as a widow with three grown children and a 14-year-old daughter at home. Mother had been dead less than three months. I know he was lonely and upset by Mother's death, but remarriage so soon afterward was unseemly, and I wrote him to tell him so. Everybody in the family was upset about it – my Aunt Louise, his sister, did not approve, and my Great-Aunt Lily was livid.

Linda and I were both angry about his letter. In addition to his glad tidings, asked Linda to send back a piece of Mother's jewelry, a pin, that he had sent home with me after the funeral. He wanted to put a new diamond in it and give it to his bride-to-be. We also learned from Sam that he had changed his will, putting everything in joint custody. It was not that there was much to inherit, but I was concerned about eventually losing the cabin at the lake, since it had been purchased largely with Mother's earnings as a school secretary.

Bonham and Martha

CHAPTER 21 — WASHINGTON REVISITED

The family had had a great trip coming home to the U.S. in 1972. We visited Alaska for several days, touring glaciers and the beautiful countryside near Anchorage and Juneau. We arrived in Anchorage about midnight, and the sun was shining brightly. Between jet lag and the daylight, we had a hard time sleeping, but the midnight sun is a great boon to sightseeing; we could just go forever.

We spent several more days in San Francisco and several weeks visiting relatives in Missouri. We were really reveling in being home – even highly sophisticated Tokyo did not compare with being in the United States.

We had some new family to meet. It was our first time to meet and know my new step-mother Martha. They had been married a year when we arrived; my father had retired from teaching and moved to Boonville. I even had new step-siblings: Melanie, a teen-age daughter who lived with Dad and Martha, and three older, married children.

Martha was a lifelong resident of Boonville and had been divorced (not a widow as previously described) for nearly a dozen years when Dad came along. He sold the house in St. Louis and moved into Martha's large antique-filled home, but they spent as many days as they possibly could in his cabin at Lake of the Ozarks

When Dad had written me in Tokyo that he was planning to re-marry and take on a teen-age daughter, I, as an expert (I already had one) responded that he was about to enter a different phase of life. He did, but not too successfully because he and Melanie never did get along well. She was a little spoiled, and he was still the stubborn warden.

We were prepared not to like Martha, but she was warm and friendly and won us over. Martha was good for Dad. She was jolly, laid back, and could tease him out of a foul mood. And since he no longer had the responsibility for a classroom full of kids that he felt did not want to be there, he became much more relaxed in his attitude. However, visiting them with our brood of four was nerve-wracking to us – in the Boonville house we had to worry that they might damage some of Martha's antiques. At the lake, in that tiny cabin, they seemed to get on everybody's nerves. And he was nervous about them in the water or on the dock – he couldn't swim and just didn't understand that my beachcomber kids were part fish.

The new red convertible I had ordered from the Navy Exchange in Yokohama was ready, and I arranged to pick it up at the Chevrolet factory in Flint, Michigan. I hitched a ride there with my brother Steve and proudly drove it back to Missouri. The old green station wagon also was on its way back to the U.S. from Japan – we had become a two-car family.

We all rode in top-down splendor back to Washington, and moved in on Sam at his apartment in Gaithersburg, Maryland, for a week while we waited for our goods to arrive, and for the renters to vacate the house in Bowie.

My first day back to work at VOA started in a most inauspicious manner. I was tooling down Interstate 70 from Gaithersburg in my brand new convertible, top down, heading for the office, when I ran out of gas. I had to call Sam to bring me more gas, and of course, I was late.

This 1972 Chevelle Malibu is red. And it is my second red convertible. There will be four more red convertibles to come.

89

Once we finally got settled back in our home, in mid-August, we began to realize that life in Bowie just was not the same as it had been before. We all had changed a lot, in attitude, in sophistication and in knowledge from our five years abroad, while our old neighbors had not changed at all. Our best friends tended to be other foreign service or media people who lived in the district or nearby Montgomery County, Maryland, while we were in less prestigious Prince Georges County.

We spent a lot of time socializing with the Rosenblums, who lived in the district and with Bob and Beth Acuff. Bob had gone to school in Springfield with Linda, Beth had been a sorority sister at SMS, and I had dated her. They had lived for a time near Alexandria when we were in that neighborhood, but then had moved on to New York City, and were now back in the Washington area. Wayne Hyde was back in Washington, too, along with Terry.

When the kids resumed school, they, too, were viewed as "different." I remember Craig being upset because his classmates called him "China Boy." Kim and David entered the Bowie Junior High School while Steven and Craig went through the woods and up the hill to Meadowbrook. Prince Georges County was going through the throes of school desegregation and bussing, and some pretty tough black kids were brought daily to our previously all-white neighborhood elementary school

We would liked to have moved, but the old bugaboo, money, intervened – we just could not afford to change houses. We had lived a comfortable, seemingly rich life in Thailand and Japan, but back in Washington we were just another set of poor bureaucrats scraping by. And being an editor for VOA just did not carry the prestige of being a VOA foreign correspondent in a foreign port. We were now little ducks in a big pond.

We didn't have a beach house either. We did manage to take several trips to the beach at Ocean City, Maryland, to Chincoteague Island, and camping on one of the wonderful beaches at Cape Hatteras. Most of our summer vacations we spent in Missouri.

Charles Eberhardt was still chief of the newsroom, and although he could not get me the job he wanted for me, as his deputy, he found a job in which he thought I could do well – that as chief of the assignments desk, which assigned, edited and oversaw the work of all VOA correspondents at home and abroad.

As chief of the assignments desk on the day shift, I was over two other editors (who no doubt resented my being brought in over them) plus assignment editors on the evening and overnight shifts. It was an interesting job, and one for which I felt well-suited, because my experience as a correspondent provided me with an understanding of their problems and difficulties which domestically-based editors might not have. It wasn't reporting, which is what I liked doing best, but it was gaining the sort of "administrative experience" which I apparently lacked and which kept me from the deputy chief's job.

There had been some substantial changes in the VOA news operation. For one thing, the newsroom had been moved to larger, but drabber, dark, airless quarters in the basement of the HEW building. The feature writers and staff of the old special events department had been integrated with the newsroom into a division known as News and Current Affairs. We no longer had to go to a studio to take in audio feeds from Saigon or from other correspondents – that material came directly to an operations studio just off the newsroom, allowing much faster processing of that material and much closer supervision of correspondent's work.

Senator George McGovern was the democratic presidential nominee during the 1972 election campaign, and he tried to bring to the attention of the electorate the transgressions of the Nixon administration in Watergate, but without much success. He had started his quest for the presidency by opposing the Nixon administration policy in Vietnam. In fact, he had visited Southeast Asia and Japan while I was still working in Tokyo, and held a news conference with American journalists in Tokyo to talk about his intention to seek the presidency. I thought at the time that he didn't stand a chance of even getting the nomination, thus I was surprised during that summer of 1972 when he was nominated.

VOA had assigned a correspondent to cover the McGovern campaign throughout the summer and fall. (Our White House correspondent covered the President's campaign.) But late in October, that correspondent fell ill (and I think tired of the relentless work) so I was assigned to cover the final ten days of the McGovern campaign. It was a lot of work, but it was probably as much fun as I have ever had while working really hard.

There were two chartered 727 United Airlines jets in the campaign entourage – the main plane which carried McGovern, his staff and advisers, a few high-powered supporters, and a select group of reporters. VOA had an assigned seat on that plane, and thus I had a chance to get to know McGovern, because he frequently came to the rear cabin to chat with reporters.

The second plane carried other reporters, some secondary staff people, and a huge number of television people – reporters, cameramen, sound recordists and producers. The second plane was called "the zoo" and life aboard it was more relaxed and free-wheeling than that aboard the candidate's aircraft. I know because I flew the zoo on a couple of occasions.

In the final weeks of the campaign, McGovern was making five or six stops each day, widely spread across the country. The routine was that the candidate's plane would always take off first (so TV could get pictures of his departure) but the zoo plane would pass it in the air and land first (so TV could get pictures of his arrival). The media members paid their own way for the trip on the charter, the cost was first class fare plus 50 percent, billed to the news organizations at the end of the campaign. We were responsible for our own hotel and meal charges on the ground, although the campaign staff took care of all the bookings, and even delivered our luggage to our rooms at each stop.

At first class and a half, we could have about anything we wanted in the air. United had assigned particularly attractive and personable flight attendants to the charters, and they went out of their way to make sure we had all the food and drink we desired whenever we wanted it. As we would board the plane through the tail door after a cam-

paign stop, they would be standing at the top of the steps, handing out drinks, or cold beer, or wine, and taking orders for lunch or dinner.

Another aspect of charter flying, we were not required to be seated and belted for take-offs and landings. We would stand around in the aisles chatting. On the zoo plane, cameramen had a game of sitting at the front of the cabin and rolling scrap tail ends of 16 millimeter film down the aisle as the nose arose steeply. At the next stop, crew members would pull these long strips of film out the door and into the trash. It sort of looked like they were disemboweling an animal and I am sure that members of the public who saw the process wondered what was going on. Another fringe benefit was that the cockpit door was always open, and passengers could wander forward to talk with the pilot and co-pilot, and even sit in the jump seat to watch take-offs and landings.

The days went by so fast that I can't begin to remember all the stops or itineraries. My first day out, a Sunday, we flew from Washington to Hartford, Connecticut, where McGovern was scheduled to do a television interview program. I remember that we were several hours late in departing because the candidate wanted to watch the conclusion of a Redskins football game before commencing travel.

In the hectic days that followed, we flew to New York, Philadelphia, Corpus Christi and Waco, Texas; Moline, Illinois; St. Louis; Hibbing, Minnesota; Cincinnatti, Ohio; Grand Rapids and Jackson, Michigan; Gary, Indiana; Pittsburgh; Trenton, New Jersey; Syracuse, New York; and Little Rock, Arkansas. We spent three different nights in New York City, two in Chicago, plus St. Louis, Pittsburgh, and other stops. By this time, the campaign was in a pretty desperate mode – campaign advisers were pretty sure that McGovern was going to be soundly defeated by President Nixon and they were frantically traveling all over to try to shore up support.

There was a memorable stir, I think in Hibbing, when McGovern was being heckled as he walked along a rope-line shaking hands. The heckler said something like, "I like Nixon better than you." McGovern leaned over to the man and whispered:

"Kiss my ass." Unfortunately, members of the press heard it, and reported the candidate's use of a profanity. Several years later, I had another opportunity to travel with McGovern and got to know him pretty well. When I reminded him about his "profanity," he laughed and said, "You guys only caught me that one time. I did it twice."

The final day of the campaign was a real marathon. We started early in the morning with the candidate making a stroll down Fifth Avenue in New York; flew to a rally in Philadelphia; then with a stop in Wichita, Kansas, westward to Long Beach, California for a late night airport rally, where former *Gunsmoke* actor Dennis Weaver was the master of ceremonies. There a beautiful young actress, Candace Bergen, came into the press tent to cuss out "you sons of bitches," blaming the press for McGovern's poor standing with the voters. (Years later, she would have a successful TV program, playing the role of network news correspondent Murphy Brown.) Having flown all the way across the country that day, we then left immediately for McGovern's home state of South Dakota, arriving in Sioux Falls about 2 A.M. on election morning for the final appearance of the campaign.

Election day, November 7, 1972, we all were taken by bus to Mitchell, South Dakota, McGovern's home town, to watch him vote and then return to Sioux Falls to await the inevitable. I missed the bus going back to town but bummed a ride in a limousine carrying a group of McGovern supporters. I sat on Shirley McLaine's lap on the trip back to town.

McGovern's defeat was the worst in American electoral history; he carried only Massachusetts and the District of Columbia. He was philosophical about it on the trip back to Washington and I was sorry to see him lose, because he was such a pleasant man. But at that point, Vietnam was no longer a burning issue, because Nixon and Henry Kissinger said they were on the verge of peace, and Watergate just had not caught on with the voters as an issue that would later lead to Nixon's resignation from office.

As much fun as that campaign trip was, I was ex-hausted and glad to get back home. It had come up so suddenly – and we worked so non-stop during those days, without any return trips to Washington, that I never had a chance to vote. That was the only election I ever missed.

I landed two more out-of-town assignments in the month after the election. Former President Harry Truman was critically ill in Kansas City, and our Chicago correspondent, Bob Lodge, had been there several weeks on a death watch at Research Hospital. Lodge needed a break to go home, so I flew out to Kansas City to fill in for him for a few days. I had met Truman once, in St. Joseph, and had always admired him.

Lodge came back to Kansas City mid-December and I returned home to Washington. By Christmas Eve, Truman was at death's door, but the reporters on the scene were told he was recovering, and they could go home for the holiday. The day after Christmas it was announced that the former President had died. I always suspected that he actually had died before Christmas, but his death was kept secret rather than spoil the holiday for all those journalists and others.

Regardless, I returned to Kansas City, or to be more exact, to Independence, Missouri, where Lodge and I anchored a four-hour live broadcast of the Truman funeral and burial at the Truman Library. Even in those sad circumstances, I remember one funny occurrence: I was on a press platform in front of the library awaiting the motorcade to return the casket from a church service, when a sudden gust of wind blew away all my prepared notes just as the cortège arrived. I had to ad lib for about ten minutes (it seemed like hours) while the casket was carried up a long flight of steps to the library. All I remember saying, in my desperation, was that the casket was being borne up the stairs, slowly, very slowly, step by step by step. It was not a riveting commentary.

The break between the Truman hospital watch, and the funeral, allowed me to be back home for December 22, 1972, when brother Sam married Linda Lear in Silver Springs, Maryland, and I served as his best man. (Fair exchange, he had been my best man many years earlier in Springfield.) We had a great family reunion – Dad flew out for the wedding, his first and only airline flight, and Steve and his girlfriend, Kay Treadway, came because Kay had won money to buy airline tickets in an office baseball pool.

At home we continued to be broke, and Linda volunteered (agreed) to go to work. She had one great opportunity to be the secretary and assistant to an executive at WTOP Television in Washington, and certainly had the credentials for it with all her free-lance journalism work overseas. But we turned it down because of a long commute from Prince George's County to Northwest Washington, and because of our concern that we would never see each other, given our work schedules. The kids were getting old enough that we did not have to be with them all day, but it appeared that we would have too many absences for proper child-rearing.

Linda did take a job as a clerk in a Woodward and Lothrop Department Store at a Prince Georges County mall. She worked in the housewares department, and became a very effective salesclerk, while the job offered flexibility in hours allowing us time together and with the kids. On those evenings when she worked, Kim and I were responsible for preparing dinner, David and Craig were responsible for cleanup.

Aware that we did not want to make the financial sacrifice required to move to a better neighborhood and bigger house in Montgomery County, we had a large addition built on to 12312 Melody Turn. Prior to that, Kim had one upstairs bedroom, the three boys shared another. With the addition of a 16 by 24-foot family room at the back, were able to convert the downstairs dining room into a bedroom for Kim, move David to the small bedroom upstairs, and put up a bookcase partition to separate Craig and Steven. We also installed a swimming pool in the backyard, and our house and pool became the center of a great deal of teenage social life in our community.

Kim turned 16 while we lived in Bowie and began to drive. David had started playing the guitar in Japan, and became a member of a Bowie group called "Majestic" which played a couple of paid concerts and dances, and was pretty good. He was the most musical of the family, but all the kids took piano lessons at one time or another.

During the year 1973, I was assigned as the chief editor of the 3 to 11 P.M. evening shift in the VOA newsroom. During that time we were having trouble getting people to work the off-shifts, so we hired several temporary, or contract, writers. With them, I had a chance to mold a team of great writers and reporters, many of whom would go on to become permanent VOA staff members. John Guerrinni became a VOA foreign correspondent and we worked together years later when he accompanied the Pope to San Antonio, Texas. Margaret Kennedy and Margaret Binda went on to run the African division of the Voice, Al Ortiz became the chief producer of Dan Rather's CBS evening news, Jeff Sandmann, the foreign editor of National Public Radio. I was proud of our little evening group of ten or twelve writers – we produced some of the best written newscasts ever at VOA.

"And now for something completely different," as they used to say on the Monty Python show. Everyone was in agreement that something needed to be done to improve the newsroom quarters in the basement of the HEW Building. The room was dark, crowded, airless and depressing, and the arrangement of the facilities was very inefficient, requiring long walks from the chief editor's desk to the operations studio, so that writers or editors could not easily consult with correspondents as they called in their reports. Noisy teletype machines were scattered throughout the room. As I had observed on my first day at VOA, the main method of communication between desks was to shout across the room. There was a constant din.

Miraculously, someone found money in the VOA budget to improve and modernize the newsroom. Alan Heil, who by then was Chief of News and Current Affairs, and Bernie Kamenske, who was chief of the newsroom, chose me to organize and supervise that effort. I was given the temporary (and unofficial) title of special projects officer and an office adjacent to Heil's.

A small architectural firm had been contracted to design the new facility, and I was to be their liaison to make sure the changes were functional as well as cosmetic. Our first decision was to carpet the newsroom – a heresy because smokers there (me included) had the habit of mashing out burning butts on the floor. OK, we'll get them ashtrays. The benefit of the carpet was to cut down on the noise levels and echoes.

I shopped for and purchased Extel machines – silent teletype machines using what then was new technology, since adopted by all sorts of computer printers – to get rid of the clattering teletypes. New furniture was purchased and arranged together in functional groups. There was a good deal of derision about the lime green trim that the architects applied to mail boxes and room dividers. The editors were moved adjacent to the operations studio and the newswire machines.

New air conditioning ducts were installed to improve air quality – also painted that lime green. We ordered all new telephone and monitoring equipment – it took a special dispensation to install touch tone phones which were then not part of the standard government fare. (We may have been second after the White House to get them.)

A storage area at the back of the room was expanded to create a reference library and break room. A new entry was carved out at the front of the newsroom so visitors did not have to traverse a narrow, dark hallway to get to there.

THE VOA CHARTER

The long-range interests of the United States are served by communicating directly with the peoples of the world by radio. To be effective, the Voice of America must win the attention and respect of listeners. These principles will therefore govern Voice of America (VOA) broadcasts.

1. VOA will serve as a consistently reliable and authoritative source of news. VOA news will be accurate, objective, and comprehensive.

2. VOA will represent America, not any single segment of American society, and will therefore present a balanced and comprehensive projection of significant American thought and institutions.

3. VOA will present the policies of the United States clearly and effectively, and will also present responsible discussions and opinion on these policies.

On the wall at the entrance, we installed a large supergraphic of the VOA Charter. It had been drafted in 1960 and later was signed into law in 1976 by President Ford. It was the guideline we were supposed to follow and that we so often had to fight for.

I saw and purchased my first computer when we ordered the New York Times on-line reference service for our reference library to replace a long rank of metal file cabinets.

It was an enjoyable, but challenging, project, which took up the better part of six months. There were frequent struggles with folks who argued that we always had done it the old way, but I made efforts to solicit opinions from everyone on the staff, and to keep all informed of the plans and benefits. I was even able to recruit several newsroom staffers as volunteers for a Saturday morning, when we stripped all the old furniture out of the newsroom, installed the carpeting and installed new desks. In the course of an eight-hour day, the transformation was done, and not a single newscast was interrupted in the process.

I received a lot of kudos for the project – even among the top brass who just a few months earlier were clamoring for my head. My efficiency report for that year stated that "working with a veteran staff on the reconstruction of the News Division is perhaps the greatest test of anyone's abilities in human relations."

During the remodeling project, I also kept my hand in as a correspondent. My old Hong Kong colleague, Ray Kabaker, was back in Washington as the deputy chief of the features section of VOA and he asked me to travel to the mid-west to prepare some "Postcards from America." They were particularly interested in a story about Hannibal, Missouri, the home of Mark Twain. I added a visit to Eureka Springs, Arkansas, and did an item about visiting the Ozarks. I also spent some time in Kansas City to make preparations for the Democrat Party's planned mid-term convention to be held in 1974, and did a postcard on Kansas City as a travel destination. Of course, the trip also gave me a chance to visit with all the relatives in Missouri.

CHAPTER 22 — WATERGATE

The Watergate Affair began the day we left Japan for the United States — most likely Nixon's henchmen were breaking into the Democratic National Committee headquarters in Washington's Watergate Building at about the same hour as our flight was landing in Anchorage. But the issue would have a big bearing on me in the ensuing three years, for good and bad.

In those early days back at work, Watergate was not a really big story, except in the pages of the *Washington Post;* and the politically attuned VOA policy officers and diplomats wanted to keep it that way. VOA news coverage of Watergate was thin and spotty – we had a rule that a story had to have two sources, and often the Post's Woodward and Bernstein items were the only source. Only when Congress stepped into the picture by forming a Senate special investigating committee did Watergate become a story VOA could really cover.

The newsroom had constant battles with the policy officers, the State Department and particularly the White House over this coverage. A former VOA division chief—a very conservative east European —had been appointed to the National Security Council and considered himself the protector of the Nixon White House's reputation from that bunch of liberals in the news division. I got in the middle of some of those tussles when I assigned correspondents to cover various events, such as Judge John Sirica's hearings for the Watergate burglars at which the defendants first hinted there had been a cover-up of the Watergate burglary.

But when the Senate opened its Watergate hearings in April, 1973, there was little they could do to stop coverage of what was becoming a national event. The policy folks continued to argue that Watergate was a domestic issue which was not important to our foreign audience, but it was news. I assigned myself to cover the opening days of the hearings, partly because I was involved in the decision-making process that put us there, but mostly because I thought it would be a fascinating story to cover. We had an assigned desk in the very crowded Senate caucus room, and a broadcast position in the corridor outside.

After the first couple of weeks I went back to my duties on the assignment desk, leaving the chore in the hands of other correspondents. But I remained active in protecting the coverage, such as the day that John Dean testified that the President "probably lied" about his involvement in the Watergate cover-up. Even as a direct quote, we had to fight for its inclusion in our news reports.

I could have stayed with the hearings, but an opportunity for a foreign trip came my way and I jumped at it. Secretary of State William Rogers was planning to visit Tehran, Iran, for a meeting of the Southeast Asia Treaty Organization, and then on to Copenhagen, Denmark, for a meeting of NATO, the North Atlantic Treaty Organization.

Copenhagen's Little Mermaid, and changing of the guard at the Royal Palace. We feasted on caviar in Tehran and smoked salmon in Denmark

It was good to get out of town for a change, and I enjoyed the trip, traveling aboard one of the special White House 707's. There were no more than half a dozen journalists along for the trip and we enjoyed luxurious treatment. Secretary Rogers was a fine and friendly gentleman (who eventually left the administration in part because of his disgust over the Watergate affair). He even joined some State Department staff people and me in a poker game during the long flight home. (I lost.)

Watergate would just not go away as a bothersome and dangerous issue for VOA. I believed then, and still do, that Nixon's activities in this period provided the greatest danger to the American government in its history. He and his administration were prepared to do anything, legal or illegal, to protect themselves and to continue the cover-up of the Watergate break-in.

I had been assigned to take over as chief editor of the overnight shift, but agreed to come in to work as an editor during the day shift July 4th, 1973. We were short handed because of vacations, and it also was a chance to pick up a 25 percent holiday pay differential. I got in trouble for our coverage that day, and came as close to getting fired as I ever did in my career. Again, it was over Watergate.

One thing that I remember well from that trip to Iran was the reaction of local journalists to VOA's Watergate coverage. The story did not at that time get a lot of major attention in foreign media, but it seemed that everybody in foreign media was listening to our broadcast reports on the subject. They were both amazed that a government owned and operated radio could and would broadcast such news about its national leader, and very congratulatory that we were indeed doing so. That reaction, to me, reinforced the importance of what VOA was doing with this very troublesome "domestic" issue.

VOA had a new Program Director by the name of Nat Kingsley, a loyal Republican who came to us from Radio Free Europe. That July Fourth had been a particularly slow news day so I wrote a couple of news summaries (short 3 minute newscasts) to which he took great exception. Of course, as on previous occasions, the furor started when I was out of town – we had gone back to Missouri for vacation just after the Fourth, and to attend the St. Louis wedding of my youngest brother, Steve, and Kay. Only when I returned to work later that month did I learn I was in trouble.

For this short newscast, I had summarized the

holiday activities this way:

Many other events have marked this fourth of July as Americans around the world celebrated their nation's one hundred ninety seventh birthday.

The July Fourth holiday was marked by an exchange of Chinese-American toasts at the U.S. liaison mission in Peking – the first such celebration in twenty-four years. And in Helsinki, Secretary of State Rogers reportedly discussed the question of future U.S.–East German relations with Foreign Minister Winzer.

The Fourth of July brought announcement that the Chase Manhattan Bank of New York will be the U.S. correspondent bank for the Bank of Peking. And in Europe, the dollar hit new lows on money markets and brought statements of concern.

President Nixon – at his California home—called on Americans to honor the ideals of human equality and dignity set forth in the Declaration of Independence. In Washington, near the White House, young radicals openly smoked marijuana and conducted what they called an "impeach Nixon rally."

Most Americans celebrated the day with picnics, family gatherings, excursions to the beach and fireworks displays. In the state of Alabama, it's an old fashioned Fourth of July political rally, with Senator Edward Kennedy on hand to honor an arch-rival, Governor George Wallace. That event has raised the eyebrows of many political analysts.

Kingsley hit the roof. He honed in on the placement of Nixon toward the end of the story instead of at the top. He took issue with the reference to open dope-smoking on the mall. I knew that was true because I had sent out a reporter to check on it But what he and the other brass found most objectionable were the magic words "impeach Nixon." Never to that point had that phrase had been uttered on VOA, although it was the subject of open discussion elsewhere in the media.

Kingsley called it "bad judgment and poor performance" on the part of the writer (me) and editor (Ed Conley) and demanded disciplinary action. As discipline, the new newsroom chief, Phil Carroll (an old friend from Saigon) yanked me from my assignment as overnight shift chief and put me back on the assignments desk. It was almost a "don't throw me in that briar patch" moment. But the contretemps probably did affect my future career path – Carroll had been angling to get me the assignment as correspondent in Rome, and that fell through. If Kingsley and VOA Director Ken Giddens had not been prevented by Civil Service rules, they would have thrown me out the door.

> VOA had never covered any vice president on a full-time basis, but I felt it likely that before long, Nixon would be out of the White House, and a relative stranger, Jerry Ford, would be the leader of the United States government. We assigned a correspondent to Ford full-time, so our audience would come to know more about this man, and less than a year later, when Nixon resigned, I believe the transition was more acceptable to our audiences because of that decision.

Back on the assignments desk, I successfully argued for what I thought was an important step. Vice President Spiro Agnew resigned in a tax and graft scandal, and House Minority Leader Gerald Ford was appointed to replace him as vice president

After Nixon resigned in August, 1974, the onus was off covering Watergate. Those on the staff and in the administration who had been so adamant in their defense of him seemed chastened by the turn of events, and even welcomed my next assignment, which was to be full-time coverage of the Watergate cover-up trial. The trial started October 1, 1974 and did not end until New Year's Day, 1975. VOA had one of 60 assigned media seats in Federal Judge John Sirica's tiny courtroom. Other than media, only 20 or so members of the public could attend the trial at any one time and usually there was a long line waiting for the chance. VIP's could get in without waiting – it became the hottest ticket in town.

From a September 30 scene setter:

The final chapter in the Watergate affair may be written in a trial scheduled to begin Tuesday in a Washington Courtroom. Nearly two years and four months after the break-in at the Democratic National Committee office – at the Watergate building in Washington – five men will go on trial for conspiring to conceal, or cover up, responsibility for the break-in.

The formerly high-ranking defendants in the case include the attorney general in the Nixon administration, John Mitchell; and Mister Nixon's two chief aides, H. R. Haldeman and John Ehrlichman. Two less well-known defendants also on trial will be Robert Mardian, a Justice Department official at that time, and Kenneth Parkinson, who was a lawyer for the Committee to Re-Elect President Nixon.

Another person who will figure strongly in the trial – indeed who will be at the very center of the trial – is former President Nixon. He was not indicted for the cover up because he was in office at the time and he has since been pardoned by President Ford. But he has been subpoenaed as a witness, both for the defense and by the special prosecutor's staff. There is some question whether Mr. Nixon will appear in court, due to his health. (He didn't.)

The prosecutors plan to play many of those secretly-recorded White House tapes to show there was a conspiracy to conceal responsibility for Watergate.

The first step was to impanel a twelve-member jury. Judge Sirica told prospective jurors the trial might take three months or longer and the jury would be sequestered – kept incommunicado – during that period. It took nine days to pick the jurors and it was done in a closed courtroom.

Chosen were six black women, three white women, two black men and one white male, ranging in age from 23 to 68, winnowed down from an initial jury pool of 335 prospects.

The marathon began October 16 — 48 days of trial, 81 witnesses. The parade started with John Dean, the government's star witness, the former White House counsel who had been the first to break with the President, and whose phenomenal memory for names, dates and conversations was never challenged in eight days of testimony and cross-examination. He was followed by E. Howard Hunt, a flamboyant former CIA operative and writer of spy novels – one of the seven original Watergate burglars — who testified that he lied to hide the White House involvement in the break-in, in exchange for promises of "hush money" to support families and lawyers and the eventual promise of amnesty.

The existence of those secret White House recordings had been revealed in the earlier Senate Watergate hearings, and in the course of the trial, the jurors, lawyers, media and spectators would spend 20 hours wearing headphones, listening.

> The quality of the tapes was poor – there were noises, interruptions, low spots, often impossible to make out without an accompanying transcript. But, in one of my reports, I noted: "the recordings convey the mood and the sense of those White House conversations far better than the printed transcripts of the conversations. The inflections and the tones of voice – even the pauses – take on new and clearer meaning."

The trial ground on through November and December, with a two-day break for Christmas Eve and Christmas day, when the jurors were allowed to have their families visit their hotel and exchange gifts – all under the watchful eyes of U.S. Marshals to prevent them from discussing the case. The day after Christmas, it was back to work.

For those three months, I was at the courthouse all day, every day. I never went near the office, but filed two or three correspondents reports daily trying to encompass the mass of material in reports no more than two minutes long. It all ended on New Year's Day.

Backgrounder report filed January 2, 1975:

The historic Watergate cover-up trial has ended with conviction of four once mighty figures of the Nixon administration. What has come to be known as Watergate began on June 17, 1972 with a burglary and electronic bugging of the Democratic party headquarters in Washington. Two and one half years later, a jury of twelve ordinary citizens of Washington heeded the call of prosecutor James Neal to "balance the account and close the ledger of Watergate."

The jury did just that. Deliberating carefully and methodically for fifteen hours, the jurors sifted through nearly three million words of testimony from 81 witnesses and returned guilty verdicts against four top Nixon aides. (Lawyer Kenneth Parkinson was acquitted.)

Seven men had been arrested for that Watergate burglary and eventually went to jail for it. Prosecutors contended that a conspiracy began on the day of the arrests – among Mitchell, Haldeman, Ehrlichman and others — to confine the blame to a low level. Mister Nixon, of course, never went to trial, and after his resignation in the face of sure impeachment, he was granted a full pardon by President Ford. But the Watergate trial, in effect, was a trial of Richard Nixon as much as it was of his key aides.

Two months later, Judge Sirica sentenced Mitchell, Haldeman and Ehrlichman to prison terms of from 8 months to 30 years, Mardian 10 months to three years. Only former Attorney General John Mitchell had any comment after the sentencing. "It could have been a hell of a lot worse," he said, adding a sardonic comment about his estranged wife, "They could have sentenced me to spend the rest of my life with Martha Mitchell."

The media had a workroom in a basement storage area of the Federal Court House in Washington. On New Years Day, as the jury was finishing its deliberations, a big poker game was started around a press room table to while away the hours. I played for a time, but was sitting out the final hand when one of my colleagues showed me his hole cards. He had four kings, and the pot was growing enormous. At that point, a court aide came running down the hall to tell us that Judge Sirica was on his way to the press room to visit with the media (he had pointedly not talked to the press during the three month long trial). Not wanting to be caught gambling within the austere confines of a Federal Court House, the players scooped all the money and cards off the table into a wastebasket and hid it away before the judge's arrival. My friend never collected on his four kings, and I have no idea what became of the pot. The jury came back a few minutes later and there was work to be done.

The trial was the climax of my Washington tour, and I felt vindicated – that the Watergate coverage we had fought for, and suffered over, was correct and right. Newsroom Chief Bernie Kamenske said in a rating report: *In reporting the Watergate cover-up trial, VOA News was never wrong, slow or trivial. We are not the only news organization which can make this claim, but we are one of the few that can. Bob Chancellor's reports and his work with the news desk or our news items is the reason we can make this assertion. His presence at the court room was the crucial difference.*

Alan Heil remarked in a 1974 rating: The (newsroom) refurbishing project is a monument enough in itself to a man for a year's work, but Mr. Chancellor again demonstrated his reporting skills in his coverage of the Watergate Cover-up Trial.

There were still some stories to be done in Washington – follow-up reports on Watergate affairs, a political conference by conservative activists, a meeting of the World Bank and International Monetary Fund, and congressional hearings.

I spent the next three months as a general assignments correspondent, but it was all downhill after the trial.

Perhaps I should have recognized it as a omen when I was assigned to cover a symposium on U.S.—African economic relations, sponsored by 82 various organizations and 25 members of Congress. One of the speakers was Ambassador Paul Bomani of Tanzania, who said: *It does not take a genius to see that a marriage of the United States' need for raw materials and Africa's great wealth in natural resources will lead to a happy matrimony.* But, he added, *the industrial nations must learn how to accommodate to a new world economic order and must find a way to restore and accelerate development programs for the one billion poor of the world.*

It was only a few days later that Kamenske and Heil called me into the office and announced their plan to send me to Africa to head the Nairobi bureau for VOA. African coverage had always been considered a backwater in the news division, which was very focused on the Soviet Union, Europe and China, and their neighborhoods. The correspondents in Africa had always worked for the Africa Division instead of the newsroom, and the Africa Division put on its own English language programs to the continent instead of the World Wide English broadcasts beamed elsewhere.

I was not really interested nor enthralled by the prospect. But Heil and Kamenske appealed to my ego, saying that "Africa should be a "world story" for the Voice of America instead of being handled in a narrow regional view," and adding the crowning accolade: "There are few people better suited to raise this sense of news consciousness of the African story." So I was sold – besides it was a chance to escape Washington.

I learned a lot about the law during those three months. I filled several spiral note-books with almost minute-by-minute notes of the testimony. I devised charts for quick reference to the comments of each witnesses, and a log of the number of days and hours of court time. In idle times, I also tried to estimate the exact dimensions of the courtroom by counting the ceiling tiles – I forget now what the final numbers were.

The family was not as easy to sell. Africa had never been on Linda's list of places to visit, not like Tokyo had been. Kim was driving, in high school, and had a boyfriend. David was deeply involved in his band. Craig and Steven had lots of friends in the Bowie neighborhood. They were all well on their way to being typical suburban kids. In later years, I was glad we made the decision to uproot them again before that happened – I think in the long run they agreed.

We made a final trip back to Missouri to say good-bye to relatives. Unfortunately, Linda's father had become ill and was hospitalized. We stayed in Springfield as long as possible to see how he did, but then had to leave to make our deadlines. He died the day we started back to Washington – Linda got word at an overnight stop in Columbus, Ohio, and made a quick flight back to Springfield while the kids and I proceeded on to DC.

This time out, we were not going unprepared. I spent five weeks in intensive Swahili language training (very little of which stuck). Swahili was my fourth foreign language, after some Japanese and some Thai and some college Spanish, but in my mind, they all ran together and I was never able to use any of them very much.

I had several friends who had served in Africa and Linda and I spent a lot of time questioning them about what to expect. Could I take my red convertible, would that be safe? Could an elephant step through the ragtop? Is there danger from wildlife? John and Katie Roberts, who had worked in Kenya, were particularly helpful. They had done a lot of camping in Africa, and John assured me that a lion will not enter a tent to pursue a person-meal (an assurance that will be tested in a time to come).

I transferred to the African Division for a month, to learn about their programs and their needs, and spent three weeks at the Foreign Service Institute's African Studies Course.

I would learn in time that the Africa Division had a prodigious appetite for correspondents reports. Their half-hour program would not use any item that was not about the continent and with only three correspondents there, it was a gaping news hole to be filled. Often they would use two reports by the same correspondent in the same program, and I never agreed that that sounded good.

This time, we would be ready – although we learned eventually that you are never really ready for Africa.

CHAPTER 23 — AFRICA

We arrived in Nairobi in the middle of the night —we would learn over the years that almost all flights from Europe, or to Europe, or from South Africa, or to South Africa, arrived in the middle of the night.

Getting to that midnight arrival had, in itself, been a challenge. We had spent nearly two weeks between Washington and Nairobi by visiting London and Rome in true *Europe On Five Dollars A Day* fashion.

We were met in London at 7:30 in the morning by my brother Steve and his wife, Kay, who were there for one year on an exchange teachers' program. They were living in a small flat on the west side, somewhere in the vicinity of Hounslow and Twickenham. They were driving a small Morris Minor station wagon – so from Heathrow airport we traveled in their car and a taxicab. Their flat was too small for the six of us, but we also had an invitation from VOA London correspondent Ron Grunberg and his wife, Sally, to use their apartment on Wimpole Street, in the center of the city. It, too, was too small for our mob, so we left Kim, David and Craig with Steve and Kay; and Linda, Steven and I took another taxi to Wimpole Street.

In those five days in London, we learned the tube, or subway, system well – Steve and Kay would ride in from the suburbs on the train with our three kids; Linda, Steven and I would meet them and we toured the city — Buckingham Palace, London Bridge, the Tower of London, a Thames River cruise, all the tourist sites. We walked a lot. At the end of each day, after dinner, the suburban folks would board the train and we city folks would return to our Wimpole Street flat. We had a wonderful visit.

Steve and Kay's exchange program was not really-fair — they had to live in expensive London on the English teacher's salary; and he got to live in St. Louis county on theirs. At the end of their year, they took their little Morris Minor across the channel to Europe and toured around. Their tickets back to the states were from Amsterdam, so they just parked the Morris at the airport and left the keys in it, abandoning it. It may still be there.

On to Rome and even more transportation problems. Correspondent David Lent, an old friend from Washington, met us at the airport with a motorcycle. His wife was back home in Germany for the summer and had taken the car, but his apartment was large enough for us all. Again, a taxi for the majority of us while Craig rode with Dave on the bike. We followed that pattern of transport for several days, taking turns riding tandem on the BMW while the others traveled by taxi to the Vatican, the Spanish Steps, to the VOA office, the Catacombs and other tourist sites. Linda told her mother: *"Rome is our city. It was just the experience of a lifetime."* It all made me sort of sad that I had never been able to land the Rome assignment which I wanted so much.

David Lent took great delight in teasing us all about our ongoing reservation: "I have never even heard of Zambia Airways. Who do you suppose flies those things." In time, he would learn, first hand.

The Chancellors do London. L-R: Kim, David, brother Steve, Kay, Linda, Craig, Steven and Bob

Our original plan had been to go on to Beirut, but Washington sent a cable warning us not to go because of the civil war and the destruction it had caused. Alan Heil wanted me to pass through there because he had in mind that might be my next assignment after Nairobi. We tried to change our destination to Cairo, but could not get a hotel reservation, so we just camped with Dave for six days.

Kim came down with a boil while at Dave's two story apartment, and he carried her up and down the stairs. Because airlines are occasionally kind of fussy about infections, we wrapped Kim's leg in bandages and told them it was a bad sprain. They put her on the plane in Rome in a wheelchair, and assigned her three seats so she could prop her leg up.

Our midnight arrival at Jomo Kenyatta airport in Nairobi in mid-July was spectacular. We were met by an attendant with a wheelchair to take Kim off the plane. She could hardly walk.

We, as usual, had our 15 or more pieces of luggage when we were met by two strangers, who would become well-known to us: VOA Nairobi bureau assistant Lawrence Kibui and VOA correspondent from Abidjan, Ivory Coast, Doug Roberts, who had been filling in while the Nairobi bureau was vacant. Doug was the son of Ned Roberts, who had been the troublesome Public Affairs Officer in Tokyo.

In the office station wagon and a taxicab, the tired, wrung-out Chancellors were taken to the 680 Hotel in downtown Nairobi. Time enough tomorrow to see our house, the city, Africa and meet our servants, both left behind for us by my predecessor, David Williams.

The morning after our arrival in Nairobi, we moved from the 680 to our house on River Road, in the Westlands neighborhood. It was the best part of town to live in and the area most convenient to the Nairobi International School. The house was a rambling, four-bedroom ranch style structure, right on the banks of the Nairobi River, which was not much more than a babbling brook. Unfortunately, we knew we would not be allowed to stay there very long because the house had been sold, but it made satisfactory temporary quarters.

And we met Joseph and Magdalene. Joseph was the housekeeper and Magadalene had been the baby ayah, or babysitter, for the Williams family. They were a nice couple and we wanted to keep them employed, but we had no need for a baby ayah, so we made Joseph the cook and hired Magdalene to share the housekeeping chores with him. Joseph really couldn't cook much – biscuits, and bacon and eggs, roast beef and chicken curry were about the limit of his talents. Magdalene didn't want to be a housekeeper – she absolutely refused to clean toilets — but she was convinced to take on the job and we said who did the toilets was between the two of them.

Doug took me to the VOA office, which was on the fifth floor of a downtown building which housed the American Library on the ground floor and the U.S. Information Service offices on the fourth floor. The VOA office had been a three room penthouse apartment one flight up from the fourth floor offices, a walk up. Although a little inconvenient, it had a nice rooftop garden opening off the correspondent's office (the former living room). Kibui used the second room as his office, files and newspapers were stored in the former kitchen, and the third room was set aside for future expansion.

The Public Affairs Officer in Nairobi was Richard Cushing, who lived just down the street from our house. Cushing had previously been Deputy Director of VOA and we had visited with him in Japan. He was a journalist at heart and gave me lots of good story ideas with no interference.

VOA assistant Larry Kibui was a Kenyan, a former reporter and editor with Voice of Kenya radio and the Kenya news agency, and a journalism graduate of Northwestern University in Chicago. He was invaluable for his contacts in Kenya and for his insights into the national culture and politics. He was a member of the Kikuyu tribe, the predominate group in Kenya, an important factor. He stayed with VOA during the entire four years of our tour in Kenya. His English was too accented to be a broadcaster, although he could do reports in Swahili and could send telexed reports and background information to Washington in my absence.

Until my arrival, the correspondents had used a radio studio on the fourth floor, operated by an Asian staff member of USIS. But I vowed to change that as soon as possible, and installed the amplifiers, mikes and other equipment so I could do feeds to Washington from my office. That was a lot less complicated than worrying about the presence of a technician, and allowed more flexibility in filing times.

There was one big story looming in East Africa at the time of our arrival – the Organization of African Unity was scheduled to hold its annual ministerial conference and heads of state summit meeting in nearby Kampala, Uganda. The host was to be the notorious Ugandan strongman-leader Idi Amin Dada. Doug had arranged some briefings for me about Uganda, Amin and the OAU, and then took off. Within a few days, on the 16th of July, I was off to Kampala – in my mind, going to the home turf of Idi Amin was as frightening a prospect as my first trip to Saigon.

Typically, I left town just as Linda was preparing to send our four off to school and to begin house-hunting. Fortunately for us she met the Pritchett family. Jim and Deanna Pritchett had four boys; Curt a year older than Kim, Brian a year younger, Eric and Darren who were closer to Steven's age. They had been in Nairobi for a year and the kids had attended school there the previous year. Their kids and ours hit it off immediately and became close friends, and the family was a great help as Linda got settled in.

Jim Pritchett was off in Kampala, too. Jim was in East Africa on a two-year contract for a Kansas City-based outfit trying to market free-lance television coverage of Africa. I envied him because he had worked at WDAF TV in Kansas City – the place I had always wanted to work. Jim and Deanna were both from Oklahoma – fellow midwesterners.

I did not get to know Jim as well as Linda knew Deanna those first few days in Kampala, until he got sick with the flu. I had been booked into the Speke Hotel with some other members of the media – Jim, being a free-lancer instead of a staff correspondent, had been housed in a university dormitory. After the first week of the OAU conference, I made a quick two-day trip back to Nairobi and offered my hotel room to ailing Jim.

I returned to Kampala for the summit meeting, which brings me to the subject of Idi Amin. He was a huge, ignorant buffoon, who also was one of the scariest and most fascinating people I have ever met. He had been an army sergeant who climbed up to Chief of Staff when he came to power as head of the government in a coup. He ruled brutally, mostly by terrorizing all his opponents and critics. But at the same time, he could be charming and funny. I remember thinking of him as a cobra – mesmerizing but deadly.

He had been trained by the British military and served with them in Burma. He also had trained as a paratrooper in Israel, but he had come to dislike Israel because of his new-found friendship with African-Arab radicals such as Libya's Muammar Gaddafi. In a misguided attempt to reform Uganda's once bustling economy, he had thrown out of the country the Asians who had run most of the businesses and technical facilities.

African presidents mostly held their noses when Amin hosted the annual OAU meeting, but it was Uganda's turn for it, and he was the current Ugandan leader, so he was to become the next year's Chairman and chief representative of Africa to the world. In the end, only 19 of 42 African heads of state came to summit.

Correspondents Report, July 17: *Uganda's economy is said to be in difficulty, but that's not evident to the delegates. The hotels appear to have large stocks of food and liquor.*

The Ugandan government has recently imported many of the accoutrements required for an international conference including as many as two hundred new automobiles.

During the OAU, a new color television system was inaugurated in Uganda, one of the first in Africa. Amin drove the first car in a five-nation commemorative road rally, and of course, he won. He staged a mock military invasion of an island in Lake Victoria to demonstrate Uganda's military prowess and to demonstrate his readiness to lead an all-African war against South Africa. The message was clear, since the VIPs watched from a place called "Capetown View." But nothing matched the mirth occasioned when Amin arranged to be carried into a reception at his home on a sedan chair borne by four white English residents of Kampala.

I joined three other Nairobi correspondents to drive back to Nairobi, and we cheered when we crossed the border out of the country. This was not the last I would see of Idi Amin, but I would not return to Uganda until nearly four years later when he was overthrown.

Back in Kenya, our family and the Pritchetts took off for a visit to the beaches of the Indian Ocean at Malindi. It's a six hour drive, but it took us longer because we left the highway and traveled back roads through the Tsavo Game Preserve. It was our first viewing of the real unspoiled Africa, and we marveled at the wildlife, especially elephants and cheetah close at hand along the Tsavo River.

Amin's war on Capetown notwithstanding, the biggest issue in Africa at the time was the effort to bring black rule to Rhodesia, and early in August it was announced that a constitutional conference between the white minority government of Rhodesia and the African nationalists would be held at Victoria Falls in Zambia.

Correspondents Report, August 12: *The site chosen for the talks is one of the most spectacular in Africa, just meters down the Zambezi River from world-famous Victoria Falls. Apparently a luxury railway coach to be provided by South African railways will*

be parked on the seventy-year-old bridge, one hundred thirty meters above the swirling waters. The constitutional talks will be accompanied by the roar of the one hundred meter high waterfall known as "Musi O Tunya, or smoke that thunders."

I flew to Lusaka, the Zambian capital and drove a rented car 200 miles south to Livingstone on a highway that was paved on only one lane – when two vehicles met, which was rarely, one would have to pull to the dirt alongside and eat dust. This un-brave American yielded to oncoming traffic more than his share of times.

I was accompanied on the drive to the falls by Phyllis Johnson, a Nairobi-based correspondent for Canadian radio. But she didn't return with me. At Livingston, she hooked up with a very left-leaning British journalist, David Martin. They established housekeeping in Lusaka, and I would visit them often, usually for a spirited game of backgammon with David. Years later, in independent Zimbabwe, they established a publishing house and remained in the good graces of what became an oppressive regime.

Getting news out of Livingstone was difficult. The government had installed some telex machines, but decent phone lines were unattainable. Hotel rooms were scarce and I ended up sharing a room several miles from the conference site with a white, Afrikaans-speaking reporter from Johannesburg.

Correspondent's Report, August 22: *The Zambezi River is symbolic because the river divides black Africa from the white-ruled south. Rhodesian Prime Minister Ian Smith – who unilaterally broke away from Britain to maintain his white minority government – will sit down at the conference table with black nationalists whom he once said he would never meet.*

The talks achieved about what was expected: nothing. Most observers believed a settlement could not be achieved without some blood-letting, and it took five years to prove them right.

It would have been ludicrous even ten days earlier

to suggest John Vorster, the South African Prime Minister, would come to Zambia, but he did. Accompanied by Zambian President Kenneth Kaunda, he crossed the bridge and the two tried to spur on the talks. Their presence was described by one of the nationalists as that of trainers accompanying prizefighters to the boxing ring. Their encounter was the one high point of what otherwise proved to be a disappointing affair.

When the conference at the bridge ended, and the railcar was withdrawn, most journalists decided to lean back and enjoy the warm weather around the hotel pool. But in Ethiopia that day, the long-time

ruler, Emperor Haile Selassie, died and I just knew VOA would want coverage of the funeral of this long time ally, who, after all, had traveled to Washington for the funeral of John F. Kennedy.

I sped back north to Lusaka, not yielding the surfaced lane this time, and bullied my way aboard a British Airways charter flight carrying school children to London, with a fueling stop in Nairobi, only to be told by VOA, "No, we aren't interested in that story."

While I was running back and forth like a fully charged lunatic, Linda had searched, but not located a house we wanted. I filed some follow-up Rhodesian stories and a couple of local items, and we made some local sightseeing trips. We started with the Nairobi game park, just outside the city, where we saw our first lions, giraffes, baboons, zebra and ostrich. Over the years, we would visit the Nairobi park in any spare moment. We also drove to the Great Rift Valley and Lake Nakuru, home of thousands of pink flamingos.

The Pritchetts and Linda and I were invited, along with most of the foreign press corps, to a free weekend at The Ark, a game-viewing lodge in a deeply forested area near Mount Kenya, and the elegant Mount Kenya Safari Lodge. We saw our first leopard at the Ark, as well as 50 elephants gathered around a water hole and salt lick. We even saw a bongo, one of the rarest of African beasts, like a large antelope with black and white stripes.

It was a dizzying pace that July and August, and that's when I had my heart attack – September fifth. I hadn't been in this mad place for two months and already it was trying to kill me.

It occurred on a Friday night about midnight. I had taken the VOA car to a nearby club to bring David and Craig home from a disco dance, when suddenly I felt very ill – nausea, headache, soreness and shortness of breath. We were only three blocks from the house, but I pulled to the side of the road; I could drive no farther. I sent Craig running down the street to get Linda while David stayed with me as I laid across the car seat panting. Linda immediately called the Pritchetts, who came quickly and Curt drove Linda and me to Nairobi Hospital. Thank goodness he knew where it was – that was one of the things we had not yet learned.

As we arrived at the emergency room, I told Linda I was sure I was having a heart attack and

Members of the foreign press enjoy a free lunch at the Mt. Kenya Safari Club. Jim Pritchett is closest to the camera on the left, Linda is next to him, then Italian News Agency correspondent Nino Alimenti. Deanna Pritchett is closest to the camera on the right, British free-lancer John Worrall is next to her.

not to let them mess around with a bunch of other stuff. The doctors confirmed it, and slapped me into the hospital for what would be a two-week stay. My doctor was Victoria Bradshaw, a tough little English woman, who happened also to be the physician who attended Kenyan President Jomo Kenyatta. I was in the best hands available in Nairobi.

Dr. Bagshaw asked me, "Do you smoke?" "Yes." "Well, you don't any more." Later she relented somewhat and allowed me to smoke a pipe or cigars, if I would not inhale. She was convinced my attack was because I was a hyper type-A individual, although neither Linda nor I would have described me that way. But I had spent the better part of the previous year as a hyper type-A individual, with the Watergate trial, Africa training, language classes, packing and moving, visits to two European cities, two trips to the OAU in Kampala, one to Victoria Falls and my frantic trip back to Nairobi. The five-thousand-foot altitude might also have contributed to it.

I vowed to live a calmer life, and Dr. Bagshaw – affectionately known as "Baggers" – helped by prescribing little yellow mothers' helpers known as Valium. The kids thought I was delightful when I was zoned out on mellow yellow. She predicted – correctly as it turned out – that the attack wasn't a pattern likely to repeat itself, and that damage to the heart was minimal. It was what she called a "young man's heart attack" – I was 39 – and what others have described as "God's warning to slow down."

While I was in the hospital, Linda found a house. It was on the wrong side of town (as in Bangkok) but it certainly met our needs.

Linda, letter to her mother, October 21, 1975: *We have now moved into it and we all dearly love it – it's the roomiest house we've ever lived in (six bedrooms, plus den, but we are using one of the six for a kid's den and we have our own) 45,000 square feet of lawn and garden, three bathrooms, a huge terrazzo patio, a covered back porch, another back porch off Bob's den, a garage, a new kitchen we had done ourselves, a breakfast room, and a living/dining room. All of this is*

on one floor...it just goes on and on.

I wish you could see me at my typing right now. I've moved the typewriter out onto a card table under the covered part of the patio in the back garden. It's a gorgeous, bright sun-shiny day and I'll bet I can see 50 different kinds of flowers, trees and shrubs right in our back garden. We have about 70 rose bushes scattered throughout the yard...I have bright orange nasturtiums, orange, crimson, red,, white and yellow bougainvillea, iris, cosmos, three kinds of marigolds, petunias, poinsettias, daisies, cactus, jacaranda trees with lavender blossoms, flame trees, orange trees, purple bushes that are solid with blossoms now, primroses, jasmine, hibiscus, wandering Jew and ferns everywhere.

There was school bus service and the kids were settled into their routine. The school took up fifteen acres in the middle of a coffee plantation on the outskirts of Nairobi. The buildings were round structures, with pie-shaped classrooms. It had a swimming pool, tennis and basketball courts and a playing field.

By then, I was easing back into work, covering stories from Nairobi, and back into driving. By December 2, I was allowed to start traveling again, and headed off to Lusaka for nine days to cover Rhodesia talks and the ongoing civil war breaking out in newly independent Angola. Lusaka seemed to be the base for all the African liberation movements to come to posture and postulate, since Zambia shared borders with Angola, Rhodesia and also with newly independent Mozambique.

There was a great deal of interest among the press in Lusaka about mercenaries reported to be fighting in Angola. One day a group of us were sitting around the Inter-Continental Hotel, when a short, young American free-lance reporter came in and announced ecstatically, "I have found my mercenary." That was my introduction to Rick Tompkins. He had been working out of Lusaka for several weeks for one news organization or another, but planned to move to Nairobi when events and opportunity permitted.

Poor landlocked Zambia seemed to suffer more for the struggles going on in its neighboring states than did the neighbors. It was nearly impossible to export its main sources of revenue, food and copper, because the borders were closed in all directions. Zambian President Kenneth Kaunda had more motivation than most to get the struggles ended. He was interesting to watch – an emotional man who never wore a suit and tie, only a safari suit, always clutching a white handkerchief. I first heard the southern Africa national anthem, used in Zambia and later South Africa – an old hymn called "Nkosi Sikelele Afrika" or God Bless Africa – when Kaunda sang it at the opening of a parliamentary meeting, with tears in his eyes.

President Kaunda came to Nairobi to discuss the Angola situation with President Jomo Kenyatta, who was the elder statesman of African independence. At the end of the visit, they held a joint news conference at the airport – it was the first and only time anyone could remember Kenyatta submitting to press questions. He expected to be revered and respected, and when Jim Pritchett asked him some innocent, innocuous question, Kenyatta glared across the room and demanded: "Why do you want to know?" Jim wisely shrugged and said "Never mind."

Rick Tompkins came to Nairobi, too, and began working for Associated Press. Eventually, he would become a part-time reporter for me, too. He spent a lot of time covering the civil war in Somalia, and gained his nick-name "Fragger" there, when he was spotted sitting on a tank, casually tossing a fragmentation grenade from one hand to the other. Later, he would move on as a free-lance stringer in Iran

Rick's wife, Jean, moved to Nairobi from California and sort of adopted Linda as a surrogate mother. Jean had a lot of problems, mostly with drinking, and she and Rick fought a lot. She moved back and forth between Nairobi and California a couple of times, before she just stayed in California and divorced Rick.

My release from Nairobi Hospital had not ended our association with that institution. Just a few weeks later, David was taken there for an emergency appendectomy. His incision became infected and he spent two weeks there, in the same room I had occupied. Linda received high praise from dear old Dr. Bagshaw – she said she usually hated to deal with American women but that Linda had been remarkably level-headed and calm during two family emergencies. At that, she had not seen the last of the Chancellors – in time Craig would break his foot in a motorcycle accident and Steven would be in the hospital with malaria. Linda said she would be next if the hospital would only install a psychiatric ward.

While David was in the hospital, Linda spotted in the hallway an old school mate of hers from Springfield, and who also was a fraternity brother of mine. Gary Hill, we learned, was living in Nairobi and traveling the continent for the Jacuzzi company of Little Rock. We tried to get together socially a time or two, but he and his then live-in girlfriend did not seem interested in pursuing any relationship. Perhaps he didn't want to associate with me, thinking I was a spy and might damage his credibility in Africa. Or he was a spy (as I always suspected) and was forbidden to be around a journalist.

Our first Thanksgiving dinner in Kenya was celebrated with Jack and Carolyn Hart. He was Georgia and Fred's pastor at First and Calvary Presbyterian Church in Springfield, visiting Nairobi to attend the World Council of Churches conference. Also gathered around for a turkey dinner were the Pritchetts, and Jim's cameraman Jim Dunn. We were all driven into fits of hysterical laughter when Dunn was digging into a pile of mashed potatoes with the edge of one of Linda's prized Thai bronze dinner forks. The tines broke off the fork, and Dunn calmly remarked, "I've never done that before." That became a catch phrase around our house for years.

The parade of visitors continued. We had a house guest for Christmas – Sally Grunberg, who had lent us her apartment in London. She came from a strict Jewish family in the United States and had never experienced Christmas before. We had a scrawny little potted Christmas tree – thanks to a campaign being conducted by an American friend.

News Feature, December 22: "Pledge your Christmas tree to Naivasha" is the slogan Mrs. (Nancy) Crooks has adopted for her campaign to restore a devastated grove of trees in Kenya's Great Rift Valley. The story of the Naivasha trees began early this year when several large acacia, or thorn, trees were cut down on the outskirts of the town to make way for a power line. The few trees legally cut led to an orgy of tree cutting, chopping and charcoal-making, until the once stately grove of 238 green barked trees had been reduced to stumps. Mrs. Crooks suggestion: If everyone would buy a live potted Christmas tree instead of a cut tree, then donate it to Naivasha after the holidays, the growth could be restored....

There's no way of knowing where the project will lead, but if someday you're driving north through Kenya's Rift Valley between Nairobi and Nakuru and you come across a large grove of evergreen and thorn trees and you decide to stop there for a while to rest, remember that it was Christmas, 1975, when that grove of trees was reborn.

After Christmas, the whole family was able to head back to the beach at the port city of Mombasa for a vacation, in a rented beach front house. It was especially good for Linda and me to get away from Nairobi – for the kids, it was a routine affair, they had been traveling and seeing a whole lot more of Kenya than we had.

Kim had been to the coast with some other girls during the Thanksgiving holiday period, going both ways by train. Steven had been on a trip to northern Kenya with a school group. Craig and a friend had been all the way into the Samburu

country of far north Kenya, with a British friend of the family and the same trio was preparing to climb Mount Kilimanjaro just across the border in Tanzania. Only David had missed out on the travel because of his appendectomy.

Nairobi's landmark, the tower of the Kenyatta Conference Center.

In the picture below, center, the tower can be seen on the horizon by this lioness resting in the Nairobi game park no more than five miles from town.

Bottom: An elephant looks both ways before crossing the main highway between Nairobi and the coast.

CHAPTER 24 — OPENING THE SOUTH

I was introduced to a new, once forbidden country in February, 1976. I was back in Lusaka trying to keep up with the situation in Angola for what turned out to be a month-long trip and it was expanded to include South Africa. To this point, VOA correspondents had been prevented from going to South Africa – partly because the policy officers and State Department felt our presence there would signify U.S. government recognition of the regime. There was a large American diplomatic presence in South Africa, and it never seemed logical that the presence of one more American would mean that much. While I was in Zambia, someone in Washington relented and I was given instructions to head on to Johannesburg, but to keep in close touch with the American Ambassador there, because he was reluctant to have VOA running around in his country.

I was elated at the prospect. Jim Pritchett had been there and reported back what an interesting and prosperous country it was. My reaction was sort of like it had been going to Australia from Bangkok — civilization.

Ironically, despite the tensions between racially divided South Africa and the black-ruled states to its north, South African Airways provided service to Zambia. I flew to Johannesburg and then on to Capetown to consult with the Ambassador. I also spent a good deal of time touring the Cape of Good Hope area – I thought then, and still do today, that it was one of the most beautiful places I had ever seen. Apparently I convinced the ambassador I was not going to create problems and he welcomed me with a couple of really good story ideas.

Correspondents Report, February 22: *For years, South Africa has gone without television, but the country was turned on in January and shows every sign of staying turned on. Television came...after many years of a determined political policy to keep it out. The ruling National Party refused to even consider it – terming the medium a monster that could get out of control and that could introduce social mores counter to the South African grain. Thus, there was the irony that Africa's most developed country was one of the few on the continent without television service.*

A report on a disturbance at a black university,

Johannesburg skyline, 1976

prepared by a South African court justice, also surprised, intrigued and bothered the country.

> Backgrounder, February 26: *Justice Snyman submitted his report to the parliament saying he had found " a deep seated and alarming anti-white feeling on the campus. He said [the situation] has given rise to black abhorrence of the policy of separate development.*
>
> *South African novelist Alan Paton, in a Johannesburg Star article, says the Snyman report is an important social document. It is a report on the state of the nation, on a country as divided as any other on earth.*

To me, the biggest surprise was that Justice Snyman or any other member of the white regime was surprised. This particular backgrounder gained me kudos from Alan Heil in Washington, calling it a good symbol of the breakthrough into South African coverage. But there was a down side to this breakthrough – South Africa coverage would become more and more demanding on the time of what was supposed to be the East Africa Bureau, and would become the main destination of my travel for the next three years.

I spent most of March and April in Kenya experiencing the tribulations of living in the third world. There was the paper shortage – no toilet paper available anywhere for several weeks, but plenty of Kleenex. We entertained ourselves by going to movies and out to dinner and running back and forth to the school, which was becoming a problem. It was owned and operated by some U.S. university/correspondence college/diploma mill and its faculty was pretty poor. Kim was a junior, David a sophomore, Craig a freshman. We were hoping for a change – a group of American and Canadian residents, helped by their governments was trying to buy the school and improve it to American international school standards.

Financially, we were a lot better off in Nairobi than we had been in Washington. Linda found food to be especially low-priced, but we missed some American goods such as pickles and salad dressing that just were not available. Another missing commodity was peanut butter, which I love – but I solved that problem when I found a

supermarket in Lusaka and brought home a stash of Peter Pan. The mail to and from the United States was slow, getting packages could take months, but we learned to substitute and get along.

David and Kim were preparing for a school trip over Easter – the train to Mombasa, a flight to Zanzibar, back to Dar es Salaam in Tanzania, and home to Nairobi by bus. The really bad news in our circle was that the Pritchetts were leaving in May — the Kansas City television company was abandoning its free-lance television project. Curt had left early to return to school in the States. He was Kim's best friend and she really missed him. Other close friends also were preparing to leave.

> Linda wrote her mother *"at least half of the kids' friends are leaving after this school year and that only makes them feel that Africa is worse than they had originally thought, which was pretty bad. Even Steven complains there is nothing to do here – after you've seen so many animals, even that gets tiresome."*

Henry Kissinger came to visit in April – not us, Africa — but he sure put Nairobi in a swirl with his entourage of security people and reporters. Ostensibly, he was there for the United Nations Conference on Trade and Development (UNCTAD), but more importantly, he was looking into the prospect of some of his famous "shuttle diplomacy" to try to resolve African issues.

I pressed Linda into service at the office, monitoring newscasts and watching the wire services, while I watched what the Secretary of State and many other Foreign Ministers, were up to. Linda was even asked to help shop for souvenirs for Kissinger to take home to his wife, Nancy. Coverage of Kissinger was a full court press – VOA even sprung for an hour long satellite feed of his full speech which suggested creation of a billion dollar international development fund. I filed dozens of stories, not only on Kissinger's public statements, but background briefings "by a senior official traveling aboard the secretary's plane" – code for a Henry Kissinger briefing.

I followed along as he made a quick trip to Lusaka, part of a whirlwind eight-nation tour, where

Henry Kissinger and Jomo Kenyatta

he pledged America's unrelenting opposition to the white minority government in Rhodesia. As he left the continent after 13 days, he said he was leaving with a firm impression that African leaders recognize there had been a significant change in American policy. The ending impression was that the United States and the Ford administration had finally focused on Africa – a focus that would intensify in the months and years ahead.

Another high level American official came to Nairobi in Kissinger's footsteps. Secretary of Defense Donald Rumsfeld linked his trip to the growing Soviet military presence on the continent and the surrogate Cuban troops in Angola. A senior U.S. official (Rumsfeld) said the U.S. and Kenya had agreed on the sale of 12 F-5 supersonic jet fighters to Kenya. (In fact, Rumsfeld interrupted a Kissinger background briefing and upstaged Kissinger with this information.) This marked a change for Kenya, from a very low-level military establishment trained and supplied by Britain to a military alliance with the United States. The cold war

had spread to Africa — uniformed U.S. military trainers were on their way.

When UNCTAD ended, I finally got an opportunity to make my first (and last) trip to Ethiopia, and I was able to take Linda with me. She had been stuck in Nairobi for nearly a full year so she really enjoyed the trip. Lots of good shopping for local crafts and jewelry, and an embassy-run commissary where she was able to stock up on American goods: *"make up and drug store items, records, wrapping paper, pencils and notebook paper, tools, screws, thumb tacks, candy, gum, socks, a toaster, cake mixes, pudding and sauce mixes, paper and plastic stuff, baking chocolate – oh what fun,"* she reported in a letter to her mother. She had wanted to visit Ethiopia ever since she did a story about the Ethiopian ambassador to Japan while working for the Okura Hotel magazine.

By now, it was time to prepare for the July, 1976 version of the Organization of African Unity ministerial and summit meeting, to be held in the Indian Ocean island nation of Mauritius. There was a good deal of levity among the African press corps that the African leaders would be meeting in, and housed in, several beach front resort hotels, all owned and operated by a South African corporation. But we were all eager for the assignment, which meant three weeks of basking on the beaches of Mauritius. Little did we know that our presence there would cause us to miss one of the biggest stories to hit East Africa in many years.

Tensions had grown considerably since the previous Kampala summit. Fighting was intensifying between nationalist guerrillas and the white Rhodesian government. The civil war in Angola continued. Students in the South African black township of Soweto had taken to the streets in riots against their education system.

Mauritius was not a very big island, less than 800 square miles, but it was hard to work there and get around because the roads were narrow, winding asphalt tracks, following the seacoast through dozens of small villages. The meetings took place in the capital, Port Louis, radio broadcasts were sent from another town twenty miles away, and the press was housed in a resort on the far northeast corner of the island in the South African-owned

Le San Geran resort hotel, at $700 per night, low season. The people were surly, the service was poor and it rained constantly. Many hours were wasted getting from place to place. So much for the island paradise.

It was to be Idi Amin's moment in the sun as the presiding chairman of the OAU. But before he could leave for the summit, a hijacked Air France plane with 275 people aboard had been allowed to land at Entebbe, Uganda's main airport near Kampala. More than half the hostages had been released, but about one hundred, all Israeli citizens, were still being held captive in an airport building. Amin came to the OAU and reported on the situation, saying he had allowed the plane to land for humanitarian reasons. The captives, he boasted, did not want him to leave Kampala, adding, "If you don't see me very much, it is because I have a problem to solve." So saying, he returned to Kampala on Saturday night.

As it turned out, Amin did not have to solve the problem. Israeli commandos solved it for him. Flying from Israel, airborne commandos conducted a daring raid on Entebbe, freeing the captives on the Sunday morning of July 4th, with the loss of one Israeli, one captive and several Ugandan defenders. African leaders at the summit professed to be shocked by the Israeli action – Amin sent a message back to Mauritius alleging his country had been invaded by Israel, with the connivance of neighboring Kenya. The leaders even issued a resolution condemning Israel for the rescue mission.

Of course, nearly the entire East African press corps was out of pocket in Mauritius during the raid. Phones and telexes began ringing in Nairobi, and wives and office assistants were pressed into service to report what they could of the events at Entebbe. Not that there was much to report – most of the news of the raid was coming from Israel.

That Sunday morning, July 4th, also happened to be the United States bi-centennial and my old friend, Ray Kabaker, had put together an elaborate list of requested coverage of the holiday from many different vantage points. As I got on the phone line at the radio station after a hectic day of trying to piece together what had happened at Entebbe, and what Amin had said and done, and what the OAU leaders intended to do, Kabaker came on the line and asked: "Well, Bob, do you have a bi-centennial story for me.?" I just laughed.

Back in Nairobi later that month, there was increased tension along the Kenya- Ugandan border, with each side accusing the other of massing troops at the frontier. I traveled with a group of reporters to the border crossing point at Busia. There were some Ugandan refugees seeking to escape, but not much otherwise. Although there was no outward tension, we were told by Kenyan officials that visiting western journalists were in danger of being kidnapped by plain clothes members of Uganda's secret police, known as the State Research Bureau.

Our home phone in Nairobi was out of service for nine weeks that summer, resulting in a lot of errand running. Linda remarked in a letter to her mother: *"I know for a fact that Kenya is the very best country in Africa, with the exception of South Africa, and it sure makes me wonder what the others are like."* We had brought the red Chevelle convertible to Nairobi with us, and we had the office station wagon, and Linda and I kept both of them going most of the time.

Kim was concentrating on her college plans, as she was preparing to enter her senior year at the Nairobi International School. She really liked Drury College in Springfield, and was offered the opportunity to live with Georgia and Fred if she enrolled there, but she also was looking at six other Missouri schools. She did not want anything too big, like Southwest Missouri State or the University of Missouri, because she had spent most of her life in small, intimate schools.

David was still involved in the music scene, and had been a member of a pretty good local band, playing some parties and nightclubs, until their drummer moved away. Craig had found a job running a disco for our British friend, Pete Wood.

Linda reported to her mother: *"Steven is playing tennis and swimming almost every day at the club — in fact his social life puts us all to shame. His girlfriend comes to get him in her parent's chauffer-driven Mercedes three days out of five and they go to the club, the movies, swimming at the Hilton, etc. His older brothers should have it so good."*

We had new best friends in Nairobi. Ben and Mary Ann Whitten had moved to town and Ben served as the regional librarian for USIS. He traveled the continent as much as I did, and was installed in the third, spare office room at the VOA penthouse. Mary Ann had been appointed librarian of the school, which had been purchased by the Canadian-American group and showed promise to improve. Kim was asked to work with Mary Ann to help get the library organized.

We also had made a lot of friends among the foreign press group. One really worthy of mention was John Osman, the BBC correspondent. We had first met at the OAU in Kampala and had become close, even though we worked for competing international radio stations. John had been around Africa for many years, had done a tour for the BBC in Washington and liked Americans. He was a great raconteur and storyteller, and could keep an audience enthralled for hours with tales of Africa and of his coverage of the Royal Family in London.

One story about John I love to tell: He could talk incessantly. One time, it was said, he was making a long, fourteen-hour drive from Johannesburg to Capetown as the passenger in the car of another journalist, who I will refer to as Ray. John gabbed nonstop for nearly twelve hours, but finally the conversation lulled into silence for a while. As they were driving through a small town, John spotted a Coca Cola sign, which prompted him to say: "That Coca Cola sign reminds me…" Ray interrupted him with the shouted plea, "John, would you just shut the hell up!" John fell silent again. Later, someone asked John how the drive to Capetown had been. "It was very pleasant," he reported, "and Ray is a nice chap. But he has some strange hang up about Coca-Cola."

As I have mentioned several times before, old friends kept showing up. Lou and Kayleen Polichetti, our good pals and beach mates from Thai-

land, came through Nairobi on their way to Malawi, where Lou would be the Public Affairs Officer.

We were able to sneak away to the Kenya coast again, this time back to Malindi, but once that vacation was over, and the kids were headed back to school, it was time for me to head back to South Africa.

Letter from Linda to Georgia, September 7: *Bob is in South Africa, for how long is anyone's guess. I can't complain much really – he hasn't traveled nearly as often from here as in any of our other posts.*

I have fallen into another job – just like every place else we've lived overseas. Same thing I've always done – write for a magazine. This time the name is VIVA and it's a Kenyan-published women's glossy. This is the hardest I've every worked for a story. People make appointments here and don't keep them and you spend three times as much time and energy as you would in a more polite society. Even in Thailand where people are considered very slow and lazy, they are very courteous and helpful and wouldn't dream of not showing up for an appointment.

P.S. Bob called from Johannesburg a couple of night ago and reports that he is getting along fine, although bored and ready to come home. He'll have to stay at least two more weeks now that Kissinger is coming out again.

Correspondents Report, September 17: *Secretary of State Henry Kissinger has arrived in Pretoria – the highest ranking American ever to visit South Africa. Shortly after his arrival at an air force base just outside the South African capital, Secretary Kissinger was taken to Libertas House, the official residence of Prime Minister John Vorster. There the two men will hold talks and a working dinner. The Secretary of State is in South Africa to learn the results of a meeting earlier this week between Prime Minister Vorster and Rhodesian Prime Minister*

Ian Smith. The big question remains whether the American Secretary of State will himself hold talks with Prime Minister Smith.

The meeting with Smith did take place the following day. Smith "just happened" to be in South Africa to attend a soccer match. Kissinger presented Smith with a peace plan to consider, saying that the time for change has come.

Back in Nairobi at the end of this shuttle, those "senior officials traveling with the Secretary" warned that the peace arrangement, which apparently had been accepted by black African presidents and the Rhodesian regime, could still come apart. And predictably, it did, because the U.S. election just five weeks later swept a new President, Jimmy Carter, into office, and Henry Kissinger was out of the game.

I spent most of the rest of the year in Kenya. The demand for coverage of South Africa had slackened because VOA had obtained the services of a stringer, Barry Wood, to cover the day-to-day events, such as the Soweto student rioting.

I did make one more trip south in November, when Senator Dick Clark, making an eleven nation African trip, went to Mozambique to visit refugees from Rhodesia. I had never had an opportunity before to enter Mozambique, and jumped at the chance to accompany him. The democrat senator said he was not speaking for the incoming Carter administration, but it was expected that as chairman of the Africa sub-committee of the Senate Foreign Relations Committee, he would be influential in the months ahead.

The election of President Carter was greeted enthusiastically in Africa: most observers believed a Democrat in the White House would be more amenable to the black position in seeking a settlement favorable to them in all of southern Africa's trouble spots. Kenyans identified with Carter as a farmer, as a man ambitious enough to start from the bottom to gain the presidency and as a friend of black people.

Also notable on this first visit to Mozambique: New York Times Johannesburg correspondent John Burns and I were detained for half a day by police, because he was taking pictures of empty shop windows in Maputo. I smuggled some film out of the country for him the next day, and he was allowed to return to Johannesburg a couple of days later.

While I was away on this trip, an accident occurred which could have been a disaster to our family, but fortunately was not. And hidden away in South Africa and Mozambique, I didn't even know about it until I returned home. On November 29, 1976, Kim and David were on the train from Mombasa, returning home after a Thanksgiving holiday trip to the beach. In the middle of the night, the train plunged off the rails into the raging floodwaters of the Tsavo River in Tsavo Park, killing 29 people. The train was carrying 600 passengers, including 17 students from the International School as well as delegates attending a United Nations UNESCO conference in Nairobi.

None of the American kids were killed or injured, they were in the eighth car, and only the first seven cars plunged into the river and were submerged. Most of the victims were Indian children who also had been on a school holiday. It took several hours for word of the accident to get back to Nairobi, where Linda and other frantic parents were waiting for the train's scheduled early morning arrival. At midday, the Embassy finally arranged a van to take some of the parents to Voi, the nearest town, where Linda spotted David among a bus load of passengers being taken to Nairobi. David said that Kim was okay, too, but Linda didn't see her until 8:30 that evening when she got back to town.

Linda told her mother about receiving a Christmas package from Steve and Kay. It arrived in October, international mail, at the main post office. It took the better part of an hour for the postal officials to find it, and it had a customs tag on it saying it contained three T-shirts, one jar of peanut butter, a package of pancake mix and a necklace, value $16. By the time customs duty and a storage fee were added in, the Kenya Post Office demanded a payment of $12 for this $16 package. *"When we opened it at home, we were congratulating Steve and Kay on their foresight in shipping early for this coming Christmas – but lo and behold, it was from LAST Christmas."*

CHAPTER 25 — 1977 AND ANDY

The interest of the Carter administration in reaching some sort of settlement in Rhodesia was signaled quickly after the inauguration. Andrew Young, the newly appointed U.N. Ambassador, was dispatched to the continent two days after he was sworn into office. I was in Lusaka to cover a meeting of the OAU Liberation Committee, and headed quickly for Tanzania, which was Young's first destination.

Young, the first black American to hold the United Nations post, was a close personal friend and early supporter of fellow Georgian Jimmy Carter. Because of that personal connection and his past experience as Martin Luther King's aide, African expectations were very high. Young said he hoped to influence American policy. "I hope you don't expect too much, but I hope you get a lot" (of results).

I accompanied Young to the island of Zanzibar where he was to attend a celebration marking a new joint political party with Tanzania. The two entities, former Tanganyika and the island of Zanzibar had joined in 1964, and under President Julius Nyerere had had remarkable political stability but poor economic performance under his version of African socialism. Young hoped to meet with many African heads of state at the Zanzibar celebrations, but for the first 24 hours, he cooled his heels and was seen by none.

A large contingent of American reporters and television was there, because Young was the first emissary to Africa from the new administration, and after his day of waiting, Young invited us all to a news conference. He admitted he didn't have anything to say, he just felt sorry for us standing around waiting. Young eventually did meet with President Kaunda, and later, back on the mainland with President Nyerere. Both told him they hoped the Carter administration would take a bigger, active role in southern Africa problems.

His next destination was Nairobi, but logistics for his trip had been complicated at the last minute when Tanzania closed off its border with Kenya. Special permission was granted for Young and his party, including journalists, to travel overland in a convoy of cars. We stopped for a break at Arusha, near the border, and Young shopped for souvenirs – he particularly wanted a leather patchwork hat which I had found first, but I refused to give it up. As he looked around the flat plains of East Africa his reaction was much the same as any other first-time visitor: "Where is the jungle? Where are the gorillas?"

He spent a day in Nairobi and then flew on to Lagos, Nigeria – again with me right behind him. Between meetings there, he attended a durbar, a colorful festival of mock fighting, horseback riding, and whirling dancers representative of northern Nigeria. It was one of the closing events of the World Festival of Black and African Arts and Culture.

Young granted an exclusive interview to me for VOA and said he had found a real appreciation for the new concern and spirit of the Carter administration. The final event of the African Festival was a mammoth outdoor concert, featuring among other performers, Stevie Wonder. I was so tired from trying to keep up with Andy Young that I returned to the car and slept through most of the performance.

Back in Nairobi, the once promising East Africa Community – Kenya, Tanzania and Uganda – was rapidly disintegrating. The three countries had once had a joint postal and telephone service, open borders and a jointly-owned airline. But tension on the Uganda border, and Tanzania's closing of its frontier with Kenya – mostly out of jealousy of Kenya's more rapid rate of development – had doomed the community. Liberia's foreign minister, Cecil Dennis, came to Nairobi to try to mediate the dispute. We met and became good friends; he became one of my best sources of African news when we were thrown together on several occasions.

Uganda's Idi Amin caused a stir in Nairobi and in Washington one Friday in February when he announced all American citizens were to meet with him on Monday and bring an inventory of all

American property, including goats and pigs. There were over 200 Americans in the country, mostly missionaries, but also some airline technicians and teachers. His order was that none could leave before the meeting. It appeared to be his reaction to a statement by President Carter that actions in Uganda disgust the entire world.

As the long weekend rolled by and Americans hunkered down at home. Amin said they were in no danger, he just wanted to thank them for their work in his country. I continued to report the events – but in an unusual case of prior restraint – each of my reports had to be cleared by a State Department task force before it could go on the air. Perhaps that was wise, since Amin obviously was mentally unstable and it was hard to determine what might set him off if he heard a VOA broadcast. But in the end, nothing happened, and Amin turned his attention to what he called Tanzanian, American and Israeli war preparations off the coast. There was nothing to that either. But the mad man did provide a lot of grist for the news mill.

We welcomed a couple of visitors from Washington during this period. Kay Giddens, daughter of the VOA director, spent several days with us, and touring Kenya. She was a delightful young lady and a fun guest – unfortunately, just a couple of weeks later, her father was canned as VOA director by the new administration.

My boss, Alan Heil, chief of News and Current Affairs, also spent several days with us, and brought the good news that we would be extended for two more years in Nairobi after home leave.

Letter from Linda to her mother, March 14: [Alan] was one of the best and easiest houseguests we've ever had. Really a great guy – all bosses should be that way. We were all pleased with his news – the boys want to graduate from ISK (International School of Kenya) here and have their lives pretty well organized here. Since I just love the country, it certainly suits me, besides which, we are really getting to be old timers.

If things go as planned, it will be almost like having a new post. We are dickering for

another house. The building Bob is in raised its rent...so he is also moving the office to newer quarters.

The continent continued to draw attention from both the east and west. I spent two weeks in Tanzania while Cuban premier Fidel Castro, and then Soviet President Nikolai Podgorny, visited. Castro mostly wanted to play tourist and spent several days sightseeing and game-watching. Podgorny was busy laying down Soviet markers on the African chessboard, pledging support for all the liberation movements.

My coverage of Podgorny raised the ire of Bernie Kamenske back in Washington: "I have noted in your copy continued and repetitive use of communist jargon and slogans, which is not acceptable." I responded to him that there had been no complaint or comment from the editors at VOA and that his ire "reflected one of my frequent complaints, that being the lack of feedback to the correspondents in the field. Short of that, the correspondent has no choice but to assume that his material is acceptable." It was not the first time, nor the last, that Bernie and I would have sharp disagreement – ours always was a sort of love-hate relationship. He could at times be very friendly, helpful, and concerned.

Meanwhile, the West was getting ready to lay down a marker of its own. We had planned an eight-day Easter vacation at the coast, but twelve hours before our departure, VOA called and insisted that I accompany the new British Foreign Secretary, David Owen, on a five-stop tour of central and South Africa. So Linda and the kids went on to the beach on their own and I stayed behind to board a Royal Air Force Viscount jet – the British version of Air Force One.

Owen was a warm and friendly man, a medical doctor by profession, accompanied by his American-born wife. He told me he wanted an American media representative, and a VOA reporter aboard, because he was going to talk to the Africans about an Anglo-American peace initiative. Throughout the trip he was as open with me as he was with British reporters aboard. (Incidentally, on a British AF jet such as this one, all the passenger seats face the rear of the airplane – it's considered to be safer in case of an emergency.)

When we were first introduced, Owen asked me, "Are you related to…(and I thought, here it comes, that same old question about John Chancellor)…Alexander Chancellor, the chief of Reuters news service?" Here I had thought John and I were the only Chancellors in the news business.

We covered a lot of territory in that week: Dar es Salaam, Tanzania; Maputo, Mozambique; Capetown and Johannesburg, South Africa; Gaberone, Botswana; back to Johannesburg; Lusaka, Zambia; Salisbury, Rhodesia; Luanda, Angola; and Lagos, Nigeria. And there were a couple of firsts for me — the U.S. government had never before permitted VOA to enter Rhodesia because of various embargoes and the old question of recognition, but there was no stopping me this time. And the Angolan government had not permitted any journalists to enter since the start of the civil war – though in fact, we did not see much because the entire visit was to the Luanda airport.

From Lagos, Dr. Owen headed home to London and I tried to get home to Nairobi. I was scheduled on an Ethiopian Airways flight, which was delayed for nearly eight hours because of engine trouble, while we sat in the Lagos departure lounge. Finally, as the airport was closing, the airline said they would provide accommodations for the forty passengers and took us several miles to some sort of country hotel/motel. Its accommodations were round, steel huts, and its reputation was as a place where Nigerian businessmen came with their girlfriends. We were forced to double up, and I shared a bed with a black college professor from Pittsburgh – we were thrown together because we were Americans.

The next morning Ethiopian Airlines said we could stay at the motel until they got the plane fixed, but several of us mutinied and demanded to be taken back to the airport to try to catch other flights. The airline did not want to lose its paying passengers, but finally relented, and I caught a delightful Air India flight to Nairobi within an hour.

I was really beginning to hate Lagos. On my first trip there, with Andy Young, we had been put up in the Eko Island Holiday Inn which was still under construction. The elevators didn't work, and there were no doors on the rooms yet. But that was a better accommodation than the tin love huts.

Couldn't you guess that I would be back in Lagos within a month? The USIS post there was planning a traveling seminar for Nigerian journalists, and had asked for me to come and represent foreign correspondents and their work in Africa. The request came from Bill Minehart – one time chief of correspondents in Washington, the guy who kept extending my TDY in Saigon – now chief U.S. Information officer in Nigeria.

My colleague in these sessions was Dr. Floyd Arpan, a distinguished journalism professor from the University of Indiana. The seminars were held in the cities of Jos and Enugu as well as in Lagos, so I got a chance to see some outlying parts of Nigeria in the role of a traveling dignitary instead of a reporter. A cable back to Washington gave me high praise for my work in a new role:

> *"Chancellor's presentation on the techniques of international reporting was extremely informative and received with enthusiasm by the one hundred participants in the seminars. He handled himself with aplomb in response to barbed questions of "western" press practices and policies. He was forthright and persuasive in all his comments and demonstrated the high professional quality and integrity of the VOA correspondent corps."*

During this time, I also moved the VOA office. USIS lost the lease on its building This offered an opportunity to go to Agip House, a six story office building a few blocks away which housed the Reuters News Agency. I knew there would be great advantages in our news coverage by being neighbors with a full-time, fully-staffed news agency, and I found a four-room suite just down the hall from Reuters. The move was a sign of the growing independence of the VOA correspondents corps. Another sign: we always before had used USIS or Embassy communications; now we were equipping each bureau with telex machines with direct access to a telex back in the newsroom.

Not only was I able to build a real, functional studio, but I sub-let one of the office rooms to John

Osman of the BBC and John Worrall, a free-lance reporter for several British newspapers. John Worrall and his wife, Hedy, were good friends of ours – Hedy had started a very successful business designing and manufacturing women's clothing- with artistic silk-screened representations of Africa on them.

We were gearing up for home leave and for our first high school graduate. Kim was chosen as valedictorian of her graduating class, and began working on the speech she was to give. The ceremony was scheduled to take place June 18th in the plush surroundings of the main hall of the Kenyatta Conference Center. Our baby had chosen to attend Drury College in Springfield, which had offered her a partial scholarship, and she planned to live, at least for a while, with Zsa-Zsa and Grandferd.

> Linda letter to Georgia, January 21, 1977: *I can't tell you how overjoyed I am that she came to this decision. She has always had such close family ties – not only with Bob and me, but with her brothers as well – and I just felt she would be miserable completely on her own in a huge school this first year away from us.*
>
> *She had two offers to stay with people in Kansas City should she have decided on the university there. I imagine you two will enjoy getting to know Kim better, along with the entire younger set. She will probably be very popular and she has always run around with the very best crowd and steered clear of the wierdos.*

I remember just before we left Kenya for home leave, we took a Sunday drive and picnic to the lower slopes of Mount Kenya, and I felt melancholy all day – looking at this wonderful family, and knowing that we would be coming back to Kenya

without one of them. I wondered if we would all ever be together, and as close, again.

Linda wrote her mother to prepare her for how much the kids had grown and developed in the past two years .
:

> May 31, 1977 *I expect you will be fairly impressed with the whole lot – they really are very nice people. They have such good presence with adults, a by-product of living overseas, no doubt.*
>
> *Every single one of the boys' best friends are leaving for good this summer, so it will be a whole new crowd at school next year. David has said goodbye to at least five best friends in the two years we've been here and now even his girlfriend is leaving. There are drawbacks to foreign service, but all in all, I doubt any of us would trade it for a lifetime in Bowie, Maryland.*

I had been working on the itinerary for the trip home, and managed to book tickets for us, via Johannesburg and Capetown, to Rio de Janeiro, Miami, Washington and on to Springfield. I wanted Linda and the kids to have an opportunity to see South Africa and knew this might be the only way to do it.

We were in South Africa several days and I was able to show the family many of the places I had talked about and to meet many of the friends I had made there over the past two years. Their eyes were open in amazement – after two years in Kenya, South Africa was almost like being back in America. Nyoka Hahn, a former VOA Africa Division staffer in Washington was with USIS in Jo-berg, and was away on a trip, so we were able to stay in her house free of charge, although in June it was too cool to use her swimming pool. We spent a delightful afternoon and evening with William "Jake" Jacobsen and his family – he was in charge of USIS in Johannesburg and had become a good friend and source of news and advice.

The Pan American airways direct flight from Capetown to Rio, across the South Atlantic, was at that time the longest non-stop air route in the world, and there were no more than thirty passengers aboard the Boeing 707 for the nearly 12 hour journey. Oddly enough, an American diplomat in Pretoria who I knew well, Steve McDonald, and his wife and four kids were on the same flight to the same destination -- not Rio; Springfield. They too were heading for home leave, and Steve was an Ozarker. In fact, his mother had been an employee of KYTV when I worked there so many years before.

Because there were no radio beacons or landmarks on the South Atlantic air route, the flight was navigated by hourly star fixes by sextant and by dead reckoning – and because there were so few people on this adventure, our kids were invited to come forward to the cockpit to observe this process and other activities on the flight deck. Obviously the system works – on arrival in Rio, I asked the pilot how close landfall was to their intended destination, and he responded: "within 60 miles."

We enjoyed three days touring Rio, although it was too cool to enjoy the beaches. Once we reached Washington, our traveling party broke up. Kim went to spend several weeks with her best friend from Bowie High School, Pat Morgenthaler, joining Pat and her family for a vacation in Maine. David wanted to stay and spend time with some friends, so we arranged for Kim and David to meet later and fly on to Springfield together.

I had to spend a couple of days in consultation at VOA, and Linda and I looked up a lot of old friends

We spent several weeks in Missouri, visiting relatives in St. Louis, Springfield, Lake of the Ozarks and Kansas City. My aunt Phoebe and her daughters, Laura and Kristin, had moved back to Kansas City from Florida and Phoebe had married Art Popham. We took to Art immediately: He was a prominent attorney and had spent a lot of time in Kenya on game-hunting safaris. Most of his trophy animals had been donated to the Kansas City Museum and were on display in a series of African dioramas. We also made a quick visit to Fayette, Missouri, where my great aunt, Lillian Bonham Todd, lived in a rest home. The sister of my grandmother Chancellor, she had never been a warm and loveable person, and she was not much

impressed with my kids, or vice versa.

We had to be back in Nairobi by August 24th for the start of a new school year and we flew back – absent Kim – to what by then seemed like home. We traveled via Athens, where we stayed with Doug Roberts and his wife, Rashida. We visited the Parthenon and other tourist sites, discovered the great seafood restaurants at the port of Piraeus, and did some last minute shopping for supplies at the huge military exchange in Athens.

I had about six weeks to stay and work in Nairobi and that turned out to be a good thing. We hadn't been home a month when Craig had a motorcycle accident and broke his right foot. We had discouraged him getting a motorcycle for several months — in part remembering the accident Steven had had on one. But many of the American kids in Kenya did have bikes, and did a lot of motor cross and cross-country riding. Also, because the law did not allow drivers' licenses until the age of 18, we thought it might help him with transport around town.

Craig had his own money from working the disco, so we allowed him to buy a small cycle even before home leave. In Missouri, he had bought and shipped a lot of parts to tart it up. But late one Sunday afternoon, he was out riding on a main Nairobi street, without permission, and his bike was hit by a car driven by a Kenyan lawyer. If a lawyer is the worst person to be involved with in an accident, a Kenyan lawyer in Nairobi is even more so. The accident was the lawyer's fault, but he blamed the young American kid and never paid a dime for medical costs or damages. Craig recovered quickly after hobbling around on crutches for six weeks – the motorcycle never again ran and ended up being given away along with all those shiny new parts from America.

Linda had an accident just a week later. Our Chevelle had a dead battery one morning so she borrowed the new VOA office car, a Ford Cortina, to take the boys to school. Craig was in a cast and could not ride the school bus. Another Kenyan driver ran her off the road and did not stop. The Cortina ended upright, but crossways, in the bottom of a concrete storm culvert, kinked in the middle. Fortunately, no one was hurt, it could have been serious. We towed the new car to the Singh Brothers, a family of Sikh mechanics who we had often used, and they completely rebuilt it – they dismantled it all the way down to the frame, and straightened each part, and re-assembled it.

I dissembled a bit in reporting the accident to VOA – saying the VOA vehicle had been in an accident, forgetting to mention who was at the wheel. They never knew the whole story until two years later, when my successor, Sean Kelly, campaigning for funds to buy a new BMW for an office vehicle, told Washington that the correspondent's wife, not the correspondent, had wrecked the office car. There was nothing wrong with the Cortina, the $2500 repair job had been totally successful, but Kelly wanted a newer, fancier vehicle.

A new house on Riara Road in Nairobi.

The hotel business continued unabated. Nyoka Hahn from Johannesburg and her boyfriend spent a couple of days with us, before moving out to tour Kenya. Our friends, the Polichettis, came to Kenya

from Malawi for a vacation and stayed with us a couple of days before heading to the beaches at Mombasa. When they returned to Nairobi a week later, we were in the process of moving to a new house – I remember Lou grumbling because there was no hot water for a shower at the new place.

The new house, just a couple of blocks away, was a luxurious, white two-story mansion, with five bed-rooms, an office, and a huge American-style living kitchen. It had a beautiful garden, and even a greenhouse. Its owner was a Zanzibari, Omar el Haj, who was a manager for the Intercontinental Hotel. He was being transferred to Saudi Arabia. He wanted more in rent than VOA would pay, but being a fan of VOA, and trusting that Americans would take good care of his pride and joy, he cut the rent for us. The move was hectic because as we were moving in, Omar was still packing and moving out, and his cat was having kittens in an upstairs closet.

By mid-October, I was scheduled to go to South Africa for two weeks. Linda remarked in a letter than it was a good thing, "Bob could use the rest." But it turned out to be more than a two-week tour – I was away for more than six weeks. And in the course of the next year, I would spend almost as much time in South Africa as in Kenya. Barry Wood, our stringer had returned to the United States. For some reason, VOA could not, or would not, bring itself to assign a full-time correspondent to South Africa, but wanted full-time coverage of events there.

South Africa was feeling the pressures for black independence that had been prevalent before in Rhodesia, Namibia, Mozambique and Angola. The strong, well-entrenched white government began to crack down on dissent. Right after I arrived, the government banned twenty human rights organizations and closed down the country's largest black newspaper. Seven of those people arrested were white civil rights activists, and all were banned. They included a newspaper editor, five ministers and a university lecturer.

During this time, I met and interviewed Arthur Ashe, the young, black American tennis star who was the Wimbledon champion in 1975. He was in South Africa to raise funds to provide recreational facilities for non-whites in the country. Blacks in South Africa, he said, welcome outside pressure on the government, but he was concerned the pressure was pushing formerly liberal whites toward a more conservative view.

But the real focus during this time was on the Steve Biko trial. Biko, a magnetic young leader of the black consciousness movement, had died in a Pretoria prison in September — the twentieth black to die in detention in eighteen months. The minister of police at first dismissed Biko's death as being from a hunger strike, and uttered to the press a particularly callous remark: "His death leaves me cold." There was worldwide attention in November when a formal public inquest opened into Biko's death, and it quickly became evident that he died of head injuries at the hands of police inquisitors.

The three-week inquest was a chilling exposition of police brutality. A police special branch major, gaunt, thin-faced, wearing dark sunglasses, testified that Biko was kept naked in an isolated cell for eighteen days, then chained to a window and interrogated for eighteen hours. He may have received his fatal head injury in a scuffle with interrogators, the officer said. Once Biko fell into a coma, without medical attention, he was placed on the floor in the back of a police Land Rover and driven 500 miles to the Pretoria prison hospital, where he died. The inquest ended with the conclusion "no one was responsible."

Correspondent Yearender, December 22, 1977: *It's customary in year-end reviews such as this to look ahead with a degree of optimism, but the situation developing in South Africa leaves little ground for optimism. Recent events there can only result in an increasingly hostile situation between South Africa and the West unless there is a significant change in the system, and although the South African government is always talking about change, there is no indication that it is prepared to make the degree of change required to satisfy world opinion.*

Those views, at the end of 1977, would still hold true seven years later when I wrote my final South African story.

West African correspondent John Roberts, was scheduled to take home leave in December and January, leaving me as the only correspondent on the continent. VOA wanted me to stay on in South Africa through December and January, but I absolutely refused. So VOA dispatched David Lent from Rome to cover the eight-week interim. I wanted to be with my family in Nairobi, and to see my daughter, Kim, who was returning to the family fold for the Christmas vacation period.

Kim was settling in nicely at Drury College, but she sure was missed in Nairobi — especially by Linda since she was stuck being the only female in a house with three boys and an occasional husband. Steven also missed Kim a lot, and wrote her several letters on activities at school and in general.

One adventure he relayed to her: In November, Steven and some friends were in the Nairobi Hilton Hotel after a movie when they heard that reggae/rock musician Bob Marley was staying there. The never-shy Steven and his companions went to Marley's room and somehow talked their way past two bouncers. Steven said he wanted to talk to Bob Marley and was admitted, even having pictures taken with him. His friends had to leave, but Steven stayed on for half an hour and Milly Jackson joined the group. As he reported: "I get kissed by Milly Jackson and I talk to a bunch of musicians who played and sang. I even sang along."

Linda was not happy with my long absences – by the end of the year, I had spent a total of 152 days away from home, not counting the time we all traveled on home leave – but she kept more than busy trying to get the boys everywhere they needed to be for their busy social and school lives.

Kim arrived just a couple of days before Christmas, bringing gifts and goodies from the "real world." I had finally gotten out of South Africa and I also was able to bring goodies from a different "real world." Kim had more than a month to spend with us, and after Christmas, we all headed off to the beach at Malindi to begin our fourth year in Africa.

Not unexpectedly, the trip to the coast was another adventure. We were tooling down the highway in the convertible, top down, when we had a tire blow out in the middle of the Tsavo Game Reserve.

121

David was not with us, having gone on ahead by train, but Mel Dario, a friend of Kim's had taken his seat in the car. OK – blow out, big deal. While Steven and the ladies waited in the shade of a thorn tree, Craig and I changed the tire, and we headed onward.

Not twenty miles later, another tire blew out. No more spare. Stranded in this semi-arid place, we sent Craig to our rescue. He and I stood at roadside until a car stopped and offered a ride, which Craig took about 30 miles back to the town of Voi with instruction to get a tow truck, or a tire repair truck, or someone to replace two tires. We waited several hours at the roadside, until Craig triumphantly returned in a service truck with two new tires. And the trip resumed.

We made it to Malindi and spent our first night of holiday vacation, only to find the next morning the car had a dead battery. Craig and I hitchhiked into town and got a repair truck to deliver us home with a new battery. Then I headed south along the coast to the Twiga resort to retrieve David – only to have another blowout on the return trip. Fortunately, this time, we had a spare. But that was the old Chevelle's last trip to the coast – from then on, we used the VOA station wagon for our travels.

When Kim left at the end of January – all tanned and rested – it was a tearful departure because we didn't know whether she would be able to come back for the summer. In fact, we were not even sure if we would be there by summer.

By February 12th, I was heading back to South Africa, and this time, I took Craig with me. He had become more and more of a disciplinary problem, at school and at home – exacerbated, no doubt by the loss of his motorcycle and all the trouble he got into because of that accident. The Embassy doctor had contacted his counterpart in Pretoria, and thought Craig might benefit by some psychological testing and evaluations to determine the cause of his problems.

I was determined to be firm with Craig on this trip, but also to try to be a friend and a closer father than I had been in the previous couple of years. Craig was not much of a reader – he was too antsy for that – but as we settled in for the flight to Johannesburg, I handed him an adventure novel (*First Blood* by David Morrell) and told him: "Read. You've got nothing else to do for three and a half hours." And he did. And he loved the book, (but he still is not much of a reader today).

With the frequent long stays in South Africa, John Roberts and I had both gotten into the routine of renting short-term apartments in Johannesburg instead of hotel rooms. With sitting areas and kitchens, it allowed a much homier atmosphere for three or four-week stays. So Craig and I moved into one of those apartment. He met and managed to charm all of my friends and colleagues in Joburg, and spent many hours with me at the office when he was not meeting with doctors.

He was with me about three weeks, and despite the seriousness of the trip, we had a good time. And it seemed to help him – perhaps the personal attention as much as the medical. (In later years, Craig would admit that the trip did straighten him out, and may well have saved his life.)

Of course, news intervened. A new peace treaty was about to be signed in Rhodesia, and for the first time, VOA wanted to send a correspondent there to cover it. I didn't know how long I was going to be away and didn't want to leave Craig in Johannesburg on his own, so we cut his trip short and put him on a plane back to Nairobi.

However, I had been in Rhodesia for only one day when VOA decided I should return to Johannesburg immediately – apparently the diplomats did not want anything that appeared to be a long-time VOA presence on the forbidden ground. Craig could have stayed on with me for another ten days. But it probably was time for him to get back to school and get on with his life.

David, I think, resented the special attention Craig got and wondered why he had not been troublesome enough to deserve such a trip. In fact, a year later, after David had graduated from high school and was at loose ends in Nairobi, I tried to get him a visa and work permit for South Africa, where he could have worked in the local music scene. I even had other work lined up for him and a South African guarantor for his visa – but the government of South Africa would not grant him permission to come.

CHAPTER 26 — FINGERS AND PETE

That guarantor for David was about as loyal a South African citizen, and an insider Afrikaner as one could seek. James Van Der Merwe, also known as "Fingers," was the chief telegrapher with the South African Post and Telegraph Department. Many years before he had happened on to a lucrative sideline business, known as "News Services." Using his position within P&T, he was able to provide office space, telephone and telex service to many foreign correspondents based in South Africa. Office space was free, so long as you used his telex service (to which he added a hefty surcharge).

Fingers had offices both in Johannesburg and Capetown, and also provided a relay service from other African countries – you could telex to "Fingers Joburg" and depend on him and his employees to relay your information on to Washington, New York or London. Even when the offices were closed, he had a telex in his home on a wine estate in Paarl, and would relay news from there. The nickname "Fingers" was a reflection of his keyboard skills – he may well have been the fastest man on a keyboard anywhere.

Both John Roberts and I had been using News Services since we started spending a lot of time in South Africa. We didn't use the telex much, but Fingers was able to obtain a scarce private telephone line for our office so we could do direct voice feeds to Washington. As with my arrangement with Reuters in the Agip House in Nairobi, working out of News Services, alongside Associated Press, CBS, the Times of London, Newsweek, and other media greatly improved our reach and coverage – all of us in the News Services family would protect the others.

In March of '78, we lost a real good friend when Pete Wood moved back to England. We had met Pete early in our stay through Craig, who worked for Pete running his disco. Pete Wood was a 40-year-old English bachelor, who had been in Kenya several years teaching at a technical school. He almost became a member of the family – sometimes he was even around too much, but he was a great help and companion to Linda during my long absences. At first, I was suspicious of his motives – especially toward the boys – but we became convinced that he was just friendly, perhaps lonely, and was seeking some family life of his own.

We entertained his mother and aunt when they visited from Britain and we commiserated with Pete when his love life went awry. Linda helped him a lot preparing resumes and job applications for his return to England. Strangely enough, after being close for those many years, once he left Nairobi, we never again heard from him.

I got home from South Africa (Craig's aborted trip) on March 12, and four days later I was off again because Andy Young was coming to Zambia. He said he planned to be on the continent until President Jimmy Carter's planned visit at the end of the month – so much for my plans to stay home for a while. I followed Young on to Tanzania, and he even stopped by Nairobi for a couple of days, so I got to visit home.

As Ambassador Young departed for Lagos, Nigeria, where he would meet up with the President, I flew out to Monrovia, Liberia, which was to be President Carter's second stop on the continent – a brief, four-hour stop. Liberia was a unique African country, founded by freed American slaves. It kept close ties to the United States, used American currency, and its flag closely resembled that of the United States. Although President Carter became the first American president to make a state visit to sub-Saharan Africa, he was the second American president to visit Liberia – Franklin Roosevelt had stopped off there enroute home from Casablanca in 1943.

My role in coverage of the Carter visit was undramatic. All the U.S. networks had pooled to buy a satellite circuit – a so-called white line -- from the press room in the Liberian Presidential Palace back to New York, and I was appointed to be the manager and guardian of the white line until reporters, including VOA's Philomena Jurey, came to the press room to use it. I didn't even see President Carter.

I went home to Nairobi, and except for two quick trips, I spent the rest of the month of April and most of May in Kenya. I went to Tanzania for two days for a visit of Secretary of State Cyrus Vance and my old friend, British Foreign Secretary David Owen.

At the end of April, Australian reporter Stewart Sommerlad and I flew to Khartoum where we both got our first look at Sudan. That was in one of those periods when Sudan was trying to make friends with the West instead of enemies. What I remember most about Khartoum is how hot it was. Mid day temperatures reached over 130 degrees, and although it was a dry heat (as all desert dwellers like to say) Stewart and I could do little more than stagger to the British Club and stand in its swimming pool.

I filed a report in April from Nairobi on the worsening situation in Ethiopia, where more than 300 Americans were leaving the country after the closure of the U.S. Information Service, the military assistance group and other facilities. The correspondents of Reuters, AFP (French news agency) and the Washington Post also were expelled.

My report stated: *"coming just a month after the government take over of the Lutheran Church operated Radio Voice of the Gospel, the action will leave the outside world with virtually no information about events in Ethiopia.*

This observation did not sit well with the Ethiopian government, which described my reporting as *"false and distorted propaganda against the Ethiopian revolution by VOA's Nairobi correspondent. The Radio Voice of Revolutionary Ethiopia is actively engaged in bringing objective reality and achievements of the revolution to the outside world while imperialist agents such as BBC and VOA often attempt to despise our revolution."* Well, so much for going back there.

With most of the foreign eyes gone, the Ethiopian government opened its long-expected campaign to recapture the breakaway province of Eritrea. Using diplomatic sources in Nairobi, I was able to file several reports keeping up with the unseen war.

The World Health Organization came to Nairobi to announce they were making one last search of the Ogaden Desert region of Somalia for smallpox cases. Officials said they believed smallpox was a disease of the past. The last known case of smallpox had been reported in Ethiopia in August, 1976.

South Africa's famed heart transplant surgeon, Dr. Christian Barnard, visited Kenya to operate on an eight-year-old girl, and took on the role of unofficial goodwill ambassador. He said of Kenya and South Africa, "We should be friends and exchange technological, cultural and trade experiences. We should have diplomatic relations."

Another South African also visited: Black actor and playwright Winston Ntshona was in Kenya to play a role in the movie *Ashanti* being filmed there. While glad to be free of apartheid for a while, he was not interested in escape. "Africa, for me, is in a state that is like the backyard of my home – it needs some weeding and the man to do it is myself. I don't think it's wise to leave my filthy yard for someone else."

Kim managed to come back to Kenya for the summer vacation. She arrived early in June, just in time for David's high school graduation, and just a few days before I was sent down south again for another long seven-week assignment with only one week-long break. Linda had cajoled and manipulated and gotten Kim a summer job at the American Embassy, working as a secretary in various departments, so Kim wasn't bored and Linda again had female companionship.

I did manage to get in some trouble while I was down south. I made another visit to Rhodesia to see if the interim bi-racial government was working and making progress toward its year-end independence date. It was questionable whether it was working.

Instead of flying directly back to Johannesburg, I decided to see some of the countryside. I flew to Bulawayo, the second largest city, which is near the border with Botswana, with intentions of riding the overnight train south to the Botswana capital of Gaberone and spend a day with a friend there who worked with USIS. All went well until the train crossed the border at Francistown. Botswana customs/immigration/police dragged me and another young American off the train. They said I didn't have a visa (although none was required of Americans in Botswana), but primarily I think they were just suspicious that a white American was riding on a train that rarely was used by white anybodies. Or they were looking for mercenaries.

We were taken to the Francistown police office – not arrested, just detained. I asked them to call my USIS friend in Gaberone, and to contact the personal assistant to the President of Botswana, who knew of my travel plans and with whom I had an appointment. After several hours, we were cleared of suspicion and taken to the Grand Hotel to await the next day's train. As the story goes, "There are only two hotels in Francistown: The Grand, which ain't and the Tati (pronounced tatty) which is."

I attended a United Nations symposium in Lesotho – an independent kingdom completely surrounded by South Africa – on the subject of exploitation of blacks and prison conditions in South Africa. One notable point of the conference: it fell on the 60th birthday of Nelson Mandela, who at the time was in the sixteenth year of his imprisonment at South Africa's Robben Island. The conference, of course, called for Mandela's release – an event that was still seven years in the future. Through a confederate, Mandela had sent a message to the conference: "We do not expect to be released."

In this period, I also made my first trip to Southwest Africa, now known as Namibia. Its independence from South African control was the other burning issue in southern Africa beyond Rhodesia. It had been a German colony, lost to British protection at the end of World War One, and originally became part of the Union of South Africa (but not part of the Republic of South Africa, as later established by the white-ruled regime). International efforts to bring independence to SWA/Namibia seemed to be gaining more headway than in Rhodesia. A U.N. special representative was in the capital, Windhoek, on a fact finding trip. There was the likelihood of an eventual United Nations peacekeeping force and a local newspaper discussed the possible influence on quiet local life and particularly local girls in an article titled "Lock Up Your Daughters."

Correspondents Report, August 4, 1978: *this capital city of Windhoek is a pleasant little city of 60,000 people. It's a mix of old German and international modern buildings, a 90 year old town surrounded by low mountains. As people went about their usual activity on Friday, shopping, working and preparing for the weekend, this reporter watched and wondered, are they aware that things will never be the same again? But a white businessman, thinking about the security situation and the threat of intensified guerrilla warfare if the United Nations effort failed, said, "They can't get those troops here too soon."*

AP photographer Mitchell Osburne and I drove from Windhoek across the desert to the port city of Walvis Bay on the fabled Skeleton Coast, and returned to Windhoek on a back road through the desert hills. We stopped and got out of the car on a hilltop, looking at our lonely, isolated surroundings, with no sign of human life anywhere, and no sound except the wind blowing across the rocks, and I had a fleeting thought: "Some day I want to come back here and camp."

In fact, I did, but that's a later story. Also, I met up again with Mitchell Osburne, nearly 10 years later, in the middle of the Mississippi River. That, too, is a later story.

I did get back to Nairobi for the last ten days of Kim's summer visit, and we all took off for a beach vacation.

Back in Springfield, Linda's step-father, Fred Hunt, spent the summer running for election to the State legislature. We sent in three absentee ballots from Nairobi. Unfortunately, Ferd did not win in the August primary, but he had the consolation of knowing he was the only candidate with a group of supporters in east Africa.

Kim had been gone less than a week when perhaps the biggest Kenyan story of our time occurred. Jomo Kenyatta, the revered President, died at the age of 89. Fortunately, I was in town at the time. Linda heard about it and called the office, but I wasn't there and Larry Kibui had no idea where I was. It was lunch time and Linda made a reasoned guess, and found me at the Akasaka, a Japanese restaurant where I had sushi once or twice a week. I went to the office immediately and began filing news stories and features about Kenyatta and a long obituary.

Kenyatta was an African legend, one of the pioneers of the move for independence of African nations. Known affectionately as "Mzee," or wise old man, he also had earned the title of "elder statesman of Africa." He had been jailed by the British for leading the Mau Mau rebellion against British rule. In the years since Kenyan independence in 1963, the country under his leadership had been marked by economic growth, stability and peace rarely equaled in Africa.

His death began a week-long lying in state and mourning, while thousands of Kenyans stood in line outside State House to pass by his body. Dignitaries began arriving for the funeral, including six African presidents. President Carter sent one of his sons as well as Andy Young and Supreme Court Justice Thurgood Marshall. Britain was represented by Prince Charles.

For years, cynics had predicted chaos in Kenya when Kenyatta died, but that did not occur. Instead, it was a period of calm and dignified mourning. Vice President Daniel Arap Moi was sworn into office, although his stewardship of Kenya would prove to be less benign or stable or progressive as the Kenyatta days. In fact, it was not long before Kenya began to slip toward becoming just another African banana republic.

Things were changing for the VOA correspondents corps. While we all had always considered ourselves pretty independent from the embassies and USIS, Washington in its wisdom wanted to make that independence a matter of fact as well as belief. So our status was changed; our official and diplomatic passports were taken away from us, we were to obtain ordinary visas like other journalists, live off the local economy, and all support from the embassy and USIS was to be ceased. Of course that worked better on paper than in fact — for example, the U.S. government still was responsible for our health care. An elaborate and complicated system was set up so our operations were financed out of the Paris VOA bureau.

We lost the use of the diplomatic pouch, and military APO mail just as it was coming to Nairobi, and those correspondents in posts with a PX or a commissary lost their use of them, but we were given no additional compensation to make up for that loss of low cost goods. As a practical matter, it didn't really make any difference – those who considered VOA to be a propaganda organ still considered it so; those who thought we were independent, reliable journalists, continued to think so. It was a typical bureaucratic move by Washington; it just made things more difficult.

Linda's take on this change: *"it's just a bunch of hooey – VOA will still end up having to answer to every bureaucrat in the State Department and out in the field. We'll end up having to pay out of pocket for the privilege of working for the Voice – wait and see."*

Correspondents for other organizations had expense accounts, and could entertain news sources on the company's dime. VOA did not have expense accounts and didn't get the representation allowance given to U.S. diplomats for official entertaining. As Linda predicted, it became "out of the pocket."

The change did create a problem for Linda. After Kim's successful summer working at the Embassy, Linda applied there for an open position as a fill-in secretary. There was some question whether she would be allowed to "work for the government" under these new circumstances. After several exchanges of cables with Washington, she was hired, and remarked in a letter to Kim that now that she had a job, it was pretty certain we would get transferred.

Indeed, a transfer was coming, but not immediately. VOA finally announced it would open a bureau in South Africa and I applied for it, figuring I had spent nearly half of the last two years there and was best qualified for the job. But I didn't get the assignment; VOA had closed the Rome bureau and planned to transfer David Lent to Johannesburg. It was *déjà vu* all over again – back in 1974, in the newsroom, I had been promised the Rome bureau, but instead, it went to David Lent.

Meanwhile, until the bureau opened, there was still Johannesburg to cover, and I headed south again for another three-week stay. South Africa's stern Prime Minister, John Vorster, resigned and eventually was succeeded by an equally stern, and equally conservative Defense Minister, P. W. Botha — although in Botha's defense, he was the Prime Minister who eventually worked with Nelson Mandela to bring change to South Africa. Vorster's last act before resigning was to reject the U.N. peace plan for Southwest Africa/ Namibia – so concern about all those peacekeeping soldiers and the threat to Windhoek's daughters was to no avail.

I had the great privilege to spend most of the months of October and November in Nairobi. That was fortuitous, because Tanzania and Uganda were warming up for what would become a war to overthrow Idi Amin. Uganda seized a piece of land along Lake Victoria, Tanzania won it back, but the ill feeling from that incident would lead in the months ahead to a full-fledged invasion of Uganda by Tanzanian troops and Ugandan opposition forces. The activity led to a report from Nairobi, titled "The Press and The War:

Correspondents Report, November 7, 1978: *Anytime a group of African-based foreign correspondents get together, they will eventually begin to grumble about the difficulty of covering African wars. Someone usually will comment, with only slight exaggeration, that no correspondent in Africa has ever*

heard a shot fired in anger, and it appears that African governments intend to keep it that way…In the Ugandan-Tanzania war, Tanzania has said that no foreign based journalists will be permitted to come to Tanzania to cover the event – either in the war zone west of Lake Victoria or even in the capital

In the early days of independent Africa, during the Congo war and the Nigeria-Biafra war, correspondents were allowed close to the scene, but since then first hand reporting of African wars has been very rare and then often by accident. In fact, the Ugandan – Tanzanian war is somewhat easier than the others to cover since the telephone links from Nairobi are still open to Tanzania and Uganda and correspondents can telephone contacts in both capitals to supplement the diet of one-sided communiqués they hear from the two national radio stations."

Perhaps this is the place to put one of those ofttold tales about foreign journalists in Africa, as relayed by the late British correspondent, Edward Behr and repeated frequently at journalist watering-holes. At a time of the Congo rebellion in 1960, the former Belgian colony was in total chaos, hundreds of people in the countryside were killed, maimed and tortured by rampaging tribesmen. Dozens of Belgian and French nuns were among the victims, subjected to rape. The plight of the white nuns shocked and intrigued the West and captured much media attention. United Nations troops finally brought some semblance of order to the interior of the country, and the nuns were being evacuated to home. Behr writes of a newly-arrived journalist seeking information at an airport, in his book titled: *Anyone Here Been Raped and Speaks English?*

Behr also described wonderfully a phenomenon about journalists that I have often failed to describe adequately:

"I have always been struck by the fact that reporters, relaxing and drinking together, are always swapping stories about what happened, and that these stories are funnier, truer and more revealing than anything they write for their media. It is those

nonessentials, often far more entertaining and, ultimately, significant, relegated to our tight little incestuous reporters' circle, become bar room gossip, often unprintable, usually scurrilous and always self-deprecatory, that makes any gathering of newsmen a hilarious and memorable occasion.

In those words, Behr captured what was the most fun about his, and my, chosen career.

Letter from Linda, September, 1978: *Things are blessedly quiet in Kenya, after all the horrendous conjecture about what would happen when Kenyatta died. The former vice president seems to be a shoo-in and everything is very orderly. The state funeral and all the ceremony that led up to it were dignified and worthy of any first world country. I was very proud of the people of this country for remaining calm, even when Idi Amin showed up for the funeral.*

School has resumed, thank heaven. Now I only have David hanging around all day. We have to make some decisions pretty quick about what he intends to do. The visa and work permit for South Africa were turned down flat, so we are rethinking our plans. It would be so much easier if he would just start school like everyone else, but he's got this bee in his bonnet about assuming responsibility for himself for a time to see if he can hack it. I'm all in favor of it, but it's sure hard to plan from thousands of miles away.

Craig is busy being a senior this year. He is taking a class in composition, one in economics, drama, art and two periods of swimming. Doesn't sound too back-breaking...the trouble is, he's in his fourth year of this one school and he has taken practically every course they have to offer. Steven is taking the regular ninth grade subjects, plus Spanish, and a really nifty African studies class that involves lots of field trips and extra-curricular activities.

I made another two-week trip to South Africa in September – there was nothing really pressing going on, but it seemed to have become ingrained in the VOA mind that someone had to be there at all times. The trip was cut short, however, when I received a call that Linda was going into the Nairobi Hospital for surgery, and I quickly returned home. Linda told her mother:

"I sort of got him home under false pretenses, as it turned out. Bob got in on Thursday night after I had called him, but the operation was such a minor nothing that it wasn't even necessary for him to be here"

But my return coincided with a total shutdown on correspondents' travel while VOA waited for Congress to approve the budget, so for the next two months, I remained in Nairobi, filing stories based on wire service reports, except for a three-day foray to Zambia. As it turned out, that two week trip to South Africa was the last of the extended trips – by the time the budget was approved, David Lent had taken up residence in Johannesburg. Although I was disappointed not to get that job, it was a relief not to have to make all those long trips.

CHAPTER 27 — MCGOVERN AGAIN

My next and last extended trip began very unexpectedly with the African American conference in Khartoum.

Correspondents Report, November 26: *This conference – bringing together more than one hundred African and American government officials, businessmen, journalists and academics – is the largest ever sponsored by the independent African-American Institute. The last African American conference held in Africa was in Lesotho two years ago. At that time, Jimmy Carter had just been elected President of the United States and there were great expectations of a new American policy. In the intervening two years, American policy toward Africa has changed – becoming much more active. But American efforts have recently been frustrated.*

Senator Dick Clark of Iowa, the retiring chairman of the Senate Africa subcommittee, was one of those attending. He had lost his office in recent elections – a victim, he said, of single-issue politics, that being his support of abortion rights, and a general shift toward conservatism. He had been a staunch supporter of change in U.S.-Africa policy, but he felt the majority belief in the United States was that the Carter administration had gone too far. The growing wars of liberation in Africa, he said, were seen as terrorism and the Cuban-Soviet involvement on the continent was causing concern.

Accompanying Senator Clark was Senator George McGovern, the unsuccessful 1972 democratic presidential candidate. Clark was trying to convince McGovern to take over the Africa subcommittee, but McGovern said he knew nothing about the continent and wanted to look around before committing himself. He planned a fact-finding tour of six countries to follow the A-A conference and that seemed to me to be an opportunity for a story by following along.

Andy Young joined part of the tour as well. They spent a day in Ethiopia – where I was not welcome and was refused entry – then went on to Tanzania, where I was. The visitors had a front-porch meeting with President Julius Nyerere, who said he was still focused on the "continuing serious threat" posed by Idi Amin in Uganda.

(President Nyerere wasn't planning to receive McGovern — just another American politician, he said, until his Foreign Minister, Ben Mkapa, heard my report on the Clark-McGovern transition plan, and told Nyerere, who quickly changed his mind.)

After Tanzania, McGovern's itinerary included Mozambique, Rhodesia, South Africa and Angola, and as a veteran of the '72 campaign, I was welcome to accompany him. There were reminders of past political battles along the way – in Mozambique, one of the embassy staffers had previously worked in a McGovern campaign and handed the Senator a schedule, typed on an old campaign letterhead.

McGovern certainly got a wide variety of views in his fact-finding; from President Nyerere urging that the only solution in Rhodesia was the Anglo-American plan; to Rhodesian guerrilla leader Robert Mugabe who told him that America could best serve the liberation of Zimbabwe by becoming uninvolved.

In the Rhodesian capital, Salisbury, McGovern endorsed the Anglo-American peace plan and said he did not see any evidence that white minority leader Ian Smith was dealing in good faith with black officials of the interim government.

In Johannesburg, McGovern challenged the South African government to join the free world by solving its racial and ideological problems. In the only speech of his tour, he said the United States can no longer look at southern Africa in outmoded cold-war terms and the leaders of the region must be more sensitive than ever to the changing realities around them. "We in the United States have learned that freedom and security are not necessarily conflicting interests."

Correspondent's Report, December 8: *Senator George McGovern has visited the controversial and endangered South African squatters city of Crossroads, near Capetown. Crossroads has become a symbol in South Africa – a place where black people have been holding out against government pressures in order to live normal lives in normal family units.* (South African government policy was that these Africans were living illegally in a white area, and they made frequent forays to destroy their huts in an effort to drive them back to tribal homelands.) *Senator McGovern appeared to have gone to Crossroads prepared to be sympathetic about the plight of people forced to live in shanties in a squatter's camp. But by the time he left, his view had changed. He had become sympathetic with people who wanted to stay in and improve their homes. The houses he visited were clean and neat and nicely appointed, considering the materials the residents had to work with. He said, "I can see why they want to stay here."*

In a departure statement at Johannesburg, McGovern had this prescient summing up: "Time is running out on South Africa. Apartheid (racial separation) will not survive the present century. Either apartheid will be yielded peacefully by the white power structure, or it will go out as slavery did in the United States a century ago, in a sea of blood."

Angola was acting reluctant to allow me into the country, but McGovern was insistent that as a member of his group, I should be included, especially after I had been blocked from Ethiopia. Other reporters following McGovern would be allowed in, but my admission to Angola hung in the balance until the last moment.

McGovern was adamant that if a correspondent for the United States radio network could not come to Angola, neither would he. I was given a copy of one telegram sent to the Angolan government on McGovern's behalf – after they had protested that there was no room to accommodate the VOA correspondent. McGovern had responded: "VOA correspondent Chancellor can share my room if necessary." With that, the way was cleared for me to go to Luanda. I got my own separate hotel room. The Angolans were clearly pleased with the visit of Senator McGovern. They want to establish diplomatic relations with the United States immediately and they saw him as an ally in that quest.

Senator McGovern was told the Angolan government, little by little, was trying to improve things – my impression on this first, and only, visit to the capital was that there was certainly plenty to be improved. Four years after independence, many shops and buildings were empty, and there were shortages of many items, food, transport, even light bulbs. The traveling press was put up in what had once been a pretty beachfront tourist hotel on a spit of land reaching out into the Atlantic. Water was available only a hour a day, so we saved a stock in empty beer bottles. Meals were served by the hotel twice a day – the only item available at any meal was some sort of mystery meat stew. This, in a country rich in oil, diamonds and other resources.

What my colleague Doug Roberts had described as one of the nicest cities in Africa prior to independence, was now a dismal place. This was due in part to the Portuguese, who upon granting independence in 1975, had packed and taken away nearly everything, in an act that can only be characterized as bitter retribution. There also was a strong element of mismanagement by a black government unprepared for leadership, and an ongoing civil war in the countryside that would not end for another decade.

McGovern's trip through Africa was a class act. And for me, there was a bonus, because the only possible return flight was from Luanda to Paris, and I had the chance to visit civilization and do some Christmas shopping before returning home to Nairobi.

I learned a neat trick from one of McGovern's friends who was travelling with us. It was announced that the temperature in Luanda was 28 degrees Celcius, and everyone wondered how hot that was. "Twenty-eight equals eighty-two," the friend said. "And if you remember that, you can always convert Celsius to Fahrenheit, or Fahrenheit to Celsius by adding or subtracting from 82=28." Try it, it works.

The year was ending well in Kenya despite the disappointment of not getting the Johannesburg assignment. It turned out that neither Craig nor Steven wanted to leave Nairobi anyway. Linda really seemed to enjoy her work at the Embassy. She was there several days each week, and reveled in the fact that she could still type fast and generally get along well in a working environment after so many years away from it. Craig had become the miracle boy of ISK, the International School of Kenya. After being so much trouble the previous year, he was doing his homework, behaving, and even made the honor roll. David and Craig had put together a band and got a couple of jobs playing a disco at a local hotel, even put Steven to work a couple of times as a percussionist. (He played tambourine, a skill he no doubt learned from Bob Marley.)

We were really getting to be the old-timers in Nairobi – most of the press people and USIS people we had started with had moved on. Some were even coming back around again: AP's Andrew Torchia and wife Marian, who had transferred away to Lisbon, came back to the Nairobi bureau, and we would see them again at a later point in life. The Whittens had been transferred to Tunisia.

> Ben and Mary Ann Whitten with Bob and Linda in San Diego. We also have met up with these Nairobi friends in Paris, Jerusalem, New Orleans, Texas and Missouri.

We had to weather our first Christmas without Kim, and staggered through a round of holiday parties in Nairobi, and were ready for rest and relaxation. Kim spent the holidays with Georgia and Fred, Betty and Pearson, in Springfield; and miracle of miracles, both ends managed to get gifts sent to the other

There's no better way to start a new year than at the beach, so by January 3, 1979, we were at Diani, on the coast south of Mombasa, for a two-week stay. Alas, Africa caught up with us at the coast the first night there – we were robbed. Burglars came in the middle of the night and ransacked the house while we slept. It was locked, and had bars on the windows, and we never figured out how they got in, unless they slipped a small child through the bars to unlock the door.

We lost my camera (still containing pictures of David's graduation) and all my lenses, two tape recorders, a shortwave radio and lots of small stuff, but we were lucky we didn't wake up, or we might have lost our lives. The next morning, we found a Coke bottle wrapped in a sock, which probably would have been used on the head of anyone who had awakened and tried to interfere.

Toward the end of January, I went back to Capetown for a few days to report on a human rights conference. I don't remember why I was there instead of David Lent, but I was.

One report I did, on the press and human rights, was a big hit back in Washington – I received kudos not only from News and Current Affairs Alan Heil, but a note from VOA Director Peter Strauss, which was a first for the African tour.

I cut the trip short because I was having persistent back pains. This had started the previous August – I remember feeling the first twinges of it while standing for several hours outside the Union Building, the main government building in Pretoria, waiting for some meeting or another to wrap up. I had had some physical therapy treatments in Nairobi, and even spent one week in complete bed rest, but the problem never really went away. The Embassy doctor talked for a time about sending me to an army hospital in Germany, but the orthopedist there was on leave, so he decided to send me back to South Africa for treatment in March – more physical therapy and a CAT scan which showed that I had a ruptured disk. I also took advantage of my presence there to have some dental work done.

Back in East Africa, the impending war between Uganda and Tanzania was beginning to heat up. Nairobi was the best place to be for that story, because there were still telephone links to both capitals, and there was a strong Uganda liberation political front in Kenya, including our family dentist who eventually would return to Kampala and a cabinet post. Early military action was confined to the border area near Lake Victoria, but Kampala began to suffer power outages as saboteurs sneaked across the borders to blow up power lines. By February, Tanzanian troops led by Ugandan exiles, had started a march up the highway fifty miles into Uganda, west of the lake.

The exile community in Nairobi kept the world's press informed of events – often we in Nairobi knew what was going on before folks in Kampala did. VOA and BBC became the primary source of information for Ugandan citizens.

Amin was desperately calling for a U.N. Security Council intervention, and the foreign ministers of the Organization of African Unity wrung their hands over the situation. There were hopes in Amin's government, and fears elsewhere, that his allies in Libya might intervene with troops. But by then, Amin's defense was a lost cause.

By April 5th, Kampala was surrounded.

Correspondent's Report, April 6: *The anticipated final hours stretched out into final days as the invaders advanced – as they have for the past six months – very slowly and deliberately. President Amin was defiant to the end. In a Friday afternoon broadcast on Kampala radio, he said he is a true Ugandan and will never run away from Kampala, and will never give up. Even as that speech was being broadcast – and the radio said it was live – there were persistent reports that the Ugandan leader was preparing to flee the country to exile perhaps to Libya. His departure would mark the end of*

an eight year and two month rule that has been one of the bloodiest and most ruthless in Africa. Hundreds of thousands of people are believed to have been killed since he took control.

The liberation of Kampala was completed on April 11, and Amin fled – to Saudi Arabia, where ten years later he died in exile..

Along with some other journalists, on a charter plane, I arrived in Kampala April 18th. We bribed our way past roadblocks with packs of cigarettes into the devastated city. The war was still continuing in the north as the invading force pursued Ugandan army elements toward the Sudan, and there were massacres along the way by the retreating force. I was back where I had started my African coverage.

Residents and officials in Kampala praised VOA's coverage of the war. The underground leader in Kampala of the Save Uganda Movement asked how VOA knew so much about SUM and its activities. He noted that every time SUM did something, VOA reported it and more Ugandan soldiers were added to the roadblocks around Kampala.

One other quick Ugandan tale: on May first, I joined five other correspondents for a quick trip from Nairobi by charter plane to the border town of Busia, where Kenyans and Ugandans were free to cross back and forth, and which had become a vital point for supplies to Uganda. As our plane was landing at Nakuru, in Kenya, for refueling at the end of our trip, the pilot overshot the runway in a heavy downpour, hit an embankment and skidded 300 yards before coming to a stop at the edge of a road embankment. No one was hurt, and another plane eventually was dispatched to bring us home in time to make our deadlines. But in a typical reckless fashion, local Nairobi newspapers heard about the crash before we got home, and began calling the journalists' wives, who were unaware of the situation. That, by the way, was the first, and only, plane crash of my career.

In May, Linda and I finally had the opportunity to make a long-planned and often-delayed trip by road to the Serengetti region of Tanzania. Linda had said in a letter to her mother, *I will really have a fit if I have to leave this part of the world without seeing the Serengetti and Ngorongoro crater.*

Oldovai Gorge

A ten-day conference on refugees was being held in Arusha and the long-closed border between Kenya and Tanzania was opened for those attending. We drove to Arusha, spent a day or two at the conference, then hired a Land Rover and driver to take us touring in one of the great wildlife areas of Africa – one that had not been seen by many tourists for four years because of the border disputes.

We spent our first day enroute to Lake Manyara, stopping to look at game at every opportunity. The first-rate tourist hotel there was empty of guests. The next day, we drove, mostly cross country, to the Ngoro Ngoro crater, one of the most pristine animal sanctuaries there is. Again, we were the only tourists and were welcomed warmly. The next day, we headed out again, across the Serengetti Plain, noted for its mass mi-grations of wildebeest and other animals, headed for a third, empty game camp. Enroute, we drove through the Oldovai Gorge, where the Leakeys had made most of their important archeological findings about early man.

During the entire four-day trek, we did not see another person except those staffing the three lodges where we stayed. It was one of our greatest African experiences and provided many memories as we neared what we thought was the end of our life in Africa.

We knew we were leaving because VOA had already listed the Nairobi post as open beginning in July. We didn't know yet where we would go next – either back to Washington, or possibly to Jerusalem, for which I had applied and lobbied. But the Jerusalem job was not open until the following January. I suggested to Washington that I had a lot of home leave accumulated which I could use, plus I needed to take some medical leave to do something about my still-aching back.

As Linda and I discussed it – and suggested to Washington – we could move temporarily to Springfield while on home and medical leave, Steven could attend one semester of school in Springfield and pick up those credits he would never be able to get overseas, such as American history and driver's education. During leave, I could take the Middle-East studies course at the Foreign Service Institute to prepare myself for Israel, and hit the ground running there at the start of 1980. And wonder of wonders; Washington agreed.

With the Ugandan war over, and David Lent in South Africa following the Rhodesia situation, work was winding down in Nairobi. I was tired of the Africa story anyway, after four years. Sean Kelly, a former colleague from the Vietnam days, had been assigned to Nairobi.

I had one more assignment to complete – the Organization of African Unity annual summit was scheduled for July 7th to 14th in Monrovia, Liberia. I had enjoyed my brief visit there during President Carter's trip, and wanted to return for a final OAU. Monrovia was a fun and funky place to visit, given its Black American heritage and free-wheeling attitudes.

Accommodations in Monrovia for the OAU were stretched to the maximum. The government had even hired an old cruise ship to tie up in the harbor to provide housing for some of the media. Fortunately, I was able to share a room at the much more convenient Intercontinental Hotel with Reuters correspondent Peter Sharrock, with whom I had worked very closely in Nairobi.

Rental cars were at a premium during the summit, but somehow, the American Embassy wangled one for me. It was a long, black Cadillac, with fins, leather seats, a tape deck with loads of American rock music, and a driver. I never did figure out who the driver really was, but he bragged of working for one of Liberia's biggest gangsters, and he did carry a pistol. One evening, he pulled up in front of a popular café and night club, got out and said the driver of a car parked in front: "My man, You will have to move, we want to park there." And the other driver moved.

I had become friends with American-educated Cecil Dennis, the Liberian Foreign Minister, who had been a very good source for me at various OAU meetings, and I looked forward to seeing him again. We talked several times during the summit, and he gave me a Liberian flag lapel pin, which I cherish to this day. It was the last time I would see him – just nine months later, he was executed by a firing squad, tied to a post on a beach, along with several other government officials, in a coup d'etat that began Liberia's descent in darkness.

Kim came back to Nairobi in May, at the end of the Drury school year, and brought with her a close friend and classmate, Shannon Spicer, who was making her first visit to Africa, or anywhere else. Shannon's grandfather paid for her trip, but she was charged with doing an independent studies paper while in Kenya.

Linda was able to help with that, because she had become involved in doing publicity for a museum/culture festival in June. That put her in contact with Richard Leakey, the museum director, and with a wide variety of Kenyan artists, writers, craftsmen and painters who could help Shannon's project.

Linda's work at the Embassy had come to an end, because some overzealous official had decided that since Linda was no longer the wife of an "official American" she could not be around classified material. By the time we got that straightened out – she was eligible, and had her own security clearance – our tour was nearing an end, she was involved in the museum festival and didn't really want to go back anyway.

Linda pulled out the stops for Shannon's and Kim's return. We scheduled a trip to the Masai Mara game reserve and two overnights in a tented camp. And naturally, the girls also took off for a stay at the Kenya coast

Kim was home in time for Craig's high school graduation – the third Chancellor in three years to graduate from the International School of Kenya. Shannon headed home after a few weeks, and the whole family buckled down to the job of packing and preparing to move – this pile for Jerusalem, this pile for Springfield, this pile to sell or give away. We left behind my prized 1972 Chevelle convertible – I sold it to the mechanic, Mr. Singh, who assured me he could keep it in repair and running. It probably still is. And there was the usual round of going away parties and farewells to a land that had been our home for four years. Oh yes, we did squeeze in another couple of weeks at the coast.

Because we had so much time available, we were able to schedule our trip home via Israel, and late in July, the entire Chancellor clan boarded an El Al flight to Tel Aviv and put Africa behind us.

CHAPTER 28 — THE RENTERS

Welcome To El Al. The entertainment during our flight from Nairobi to Tel Aviv is a story that has been told many times, to friends, to realtors, to lawyers. It is a story so convoluted and outrageous that no one believes it at first hearing. And once they become convinced that it is indeed true, they say: "That story needs to be in print and in circulation." So sit back, here it is, entitled, The Renters.

When we moved to Bangkok in 1967, we rented our house at 12312 Melody Turn in Bowie, Maryland, and left our next door neighbors in charge of it as our rental agents. It could not have been a better experience – we had two different renters in the course of five years, both of whom took excellent care of the house, and the second renters who, in fact, improved the house by installing wall-to-wall carpeting and drapes.

Thus heartened, as we were preparing to move to Nairobi in 1975 after three years back at home, we decided to follow the same course, and began looking for renters. We were asking $400 per month in rent, with a two-year minimum lease – that was well within the market for burgeoning Bowie, for a house that by now had four bedrooms, a large living room, a big family kitchen/dining room, a huge recreation room and a swimming pool in an enclosed back yard, flanked by a brick patio.

For some reason, however, our ads in the paper just attracted weirdos. We had two women, with a passel of children between them, who said they "lived an alternative life style." We know, now, what that meant. We also had a young man, 18, and his girlfriend. He was a legally emancipated minor – as a result of suing his parents – and he and his sweetie wanted to live there and use the recreation room as a rehearsal hall for his band. We figured any kid that would sue his parents would be a problem renter.

It was a family home, in a family neighborhood, and we wanted a normal family to move in. Then, almost like a gift from Heaven, it seemed, came what looked like a normal family.

The father described himself as a self-employed electrical engineer. He was a little pasty-faced, and he had a white patch above his lip where he apparently had once had a mustache. But he seemed bright, and certainly was interested in the house. The rental rate was no problem.

He brought his wife and their three children to meet us. His wife's clothing seemed a little out of style and she a little prim – wearing stockings and high heels just to look at a house, a frilly dress and a mop of dark hair in curly ringlets. She said virtually nothing – he did all the talking for the family. In hindsight, they were a little strange, but they were a family, not a rock band or a pair of alternative lifestyle women. We introduced them to our neighbor/agents, explained the circumstances and signed a lease immediately. In fact, we were so pleased about this "normal" family that we lowered the rent to $360, and received a one-month security deposit.

The renters did not move in until July 1, 1975, after we had packed and were enroute to Nairobi. The very first inkling of the trouble to come was in a letter from our agent/neighbor, who wrote that they had moved a huge van-load of furniture and stuff into the house. The mover said the load weighed more than 40,000 pounds, about twice a normal household. It was so heavy that the moving truck made indentations in the driveway. The mover said he was concerned that too much weight was being moved into the second floor of the house and could damage it.

She also was concerned about this weight and asked for an inspection, as allowed by the lease, to make sure the house was not being damaged. The renter refused this right of inspection, at one point telling her that he was doing "top secret work" that she might reveal. Eventually, the neighbor husband was allowed to check the house and determined that most of the heavy stuff was on the ground floor and was doing no damage. I advised them to forget it and let the renters live in peace.

He paid the rent regularly on time, although he did insist on making rental checks to both my agent and to me, resulting in confusion at the bank because the checks were not properly endorsed (they did not contain my signature).

Our neighbor/agent told us of a strange pattern of life there. For example, the children never came outside, never used the brick patio nor the pool, which stood empty. The girls were enrolled in the neighborhood school, which was adjacent to the back of our lot, but they didn't walk there. Every morning, he would load them into his car in the closed garage, then pull out and drive them to school. The boy, even though he was school-age, was never seen and was never enrolled in school.

They did not use the neighborhood mail delivery – they kept a post office box and all communication to them went there – even written communications between them and the neighbors next door.

Two years passed and we came back to Bowie on home leave. Linda and I went to the house, insisted on an inspection, and were welcomed in. The stories were correct – there was a lot of stuff in that house. The 12 by 20 living room and the 16 by 24 family room both were crammed. There were boxes stacked ceiling-high everywhere, and books, machine tools, filing cabinets, with narrow paths among the stacks to navigate from place to place. More boxes, and file cabinets lined the walls of the kitchen/dining area, and the hallways and along the walls of the upstairs bedrooms. Two long extension ladders were propped up along the railing leading up the stairs. Our home looked like a warehouse.

It was difficult to understand how five people could live or move around among all that stuff. We were still trying to be friendly with them because I didn't want to have to find a new renter, and I remarked that I didn't know how they managed to live around all that stuff. His response was that they just hadn't had a chance to get settled in (after two years) and would get the place straightened up eventually. We raised the rent to $400 per month, because of inflation. He accepted immediately, signed a new lease, and we moved on with our lives and home leave – much to our neighbors' distress.

Two years later, we were again enroute back to our long 1979 home leave. Prior to leaving Nairobi, I had written the renters that we had decided to sell the house, partly for tax reasons (Maryland was insisting that we should pay state income taxes even though we did not reside in the state) and partly because of our agents' continuing concern about what her neighbors were up to. A great deal of suspicion and enmity had been created between the two households. The neighbor was convinced that her telephone had been tapped, after she had made inquires with the schools and the welfare department about the apparent nonexistence of the son.

I contacted a real estate agent about listing the house for the sale, and described to him the circumstances. He said we would have to have them move out before the house could even be listed or shown, because it certainly could not be shown when it was packed to the rafters with their stuff. Nothing had changed – it was still stuffed, perhaps even more so than on our previous inspection.

I reiterated to the renter that we planned to sell the house, but we would give him first option to buy it if he wanted, but if he didn't, he would have to move out so we could list it. In our conversation and in a later letter, I offered to sell it to them for $70,000 if a sale agreement could be completed within 30 days, $72,000 if it came after 30 days, and $75,000 if the house became listed on the market. The renter indicated he was interested and would get back to me.

We hoped to make the sale during our four-month leave in the states. While we spent that fall in Springfield, the renter acknowledged that he would be unable to make an immediate purchase, so on the advice of our realtor, I gave him 30 days notice to vacate. He didn't vacate. I tried writing him and calling him, nearly daily for three weeks, and never received any response. So, in October, 1979, I authorized our agents, to obtain a lawyer and file an eviction action to remove them. They had our full power of attorney and a contract giving them authority to act on our behalf.

That began a long series of legal challenges. The renter filed a countersuit against the agents, claiming he was being defrauded, and challenging their authority to bring the eviction action. He kept referring to what he said was an oral agreement he had with me to allow him to stay on in the house. There had been no such agreement.

He did not have a lawyer, he represented himself, and drafted several long pleadings to the court opposing eviction. Our lawyer observed at the end of the year, "Obviously, he has nothing else much to do than to abuse you and the court system in this case."

He filed a motion with the Prince Georges County Court, asking for a jury trial on the eviction, claiming he would be damaged more than $500 if forced to move out. He cited a Maryland Appeals Court case from April, 1975, affirming the right to a jury trial in an eviction case if damages totaled more than $500. Unknown to us, he had rented our house soon after that Appeals Court decision.

Our lawyers learned that Appeals Court decision resulted from a case our renter had brought against another landlord in 1973 under very similar circumstances. In that earlier case, he had been evicted, but continued to pursue it to the Appeals Court. He obviously intended to win this time. His previous victim had been a military officer who rented to them while going on an overseas assignment and wanted his home back after retiring from the service.

Just before we left for Israel, I went back to the house with my brother, Sam, and son David, but no one would respond to our knocking at the door. (That visit was later characterized by him as harassment and threatening, prompting him, he said in court documents, to have to stand guard duty at all times.) That same day, we ran into his wife, at the shopping center and in a brief, strained conversation, she acknowledged receipt of the notice to vacate and stated that they did not plan to move, had done nothing to find other housing and could not move until the summer of 1980.

By now, early in 1980, we were already on assignment in Israel. He filed suit against Linda and me in the Federal District Court, contending that since we were "residents and citizens of the foreign country of Israel" the federal court has jurisdiction, and the eviction should not be heard in local court until the federal case was resolved. In time,

he would allege in Federal Court filings that he had been damaged to the extent of $3 million by the actions of the Chancellors.

The Prince Georges County Court ruled in February, 1980, that he was entitled to his jury trial. The flurry of filings and statements and interrogatories continued through the spring and summer. It finally was set for jury trial to begin July 21, 1980, at Upper Marlboro, the Prince Georges county seat. I flew back to Washington, at my own expense, to attend and to testify. Son David attended all the court sessions with me.

The trial took four days! He acted as his own attorney and wasted many hours of the court's time fumbling through his papers and making motions and objections. The neighbors and I all testified and were all cross-examined by him.

On the third day of the trial, he began presenting his case, and called himself as the first and only witness. Apparently the excitement and the approaching culmination of his quest since 1973 overwhelmed him, because as he prepared to step up to the witness stand, he collapsed into a heap onto the floor. Paramedics were called into the courtroom immediately and he revived – he had fainted. The Judge, I think, suspected he was feigning, perhaps to delay trial. The judge ordered the jury to go to lunch, but had all 12 jurors pass by the witness stand on their way out of the courtroom to see that he was alive and well.

In the afternoon, he began his testimony and rambled on, as he had in all his court filings. Our lawyer only asked a few questions in cross-examination – the key question being, "Do you expect Mr. Chancellor simply to hand over his house to you?"

Final arguments were held the morning of the fourth day and the jury retired to deliberate. They were out a couple of hours, and then went to lunch. Immediately after lunch, they returned a verdict in our favor, to evict our renters. Later, jurors told us they had decided in our favor in just a few moments, but decided to withhold their findings until afternoon so they could get one more free lunch at county expense.

The Judge ruled damages of $5,350 for us, and in addition ordered the renter to pay our legal and travel expenses, saying "this proceeding was brought in bad faith, without substantial justification and for the purpose of delay." We received $3200 of the judgment, which represented back rental payments which had been deposited with the court. We never received the balance of the judgment nor any expenses.

The neighbors and David and I celebrated our victory. But it didn't end there. After the judgment, there was still no sign that they were making any effort to vacate the house, and on July 29th, the judge issued another order to the sheriff that husband, wife and any others in the house be physically removed from the premises. Deputies came to the house to remove them. For some reason – perhaps because of his past erratic behavior – the deputies became concerned that he might be an armed threat. The SWAT team was dispatched, entered the house, and ordered the them out.

And it still didn't end there. The deputies had no power to remove the 40,000 pounds or more of stuff inside – that was the landlord's responsibility. I began calling moving companies to do so, but none of the legitimate, regular movers such as Mayflower would touch an eviction matter. Finally, I found a small, independent mover in D.C. which specialized in such matters. "Oh, yes sir, we like to do evictions," their representative said on the phone, and within a few hours, several tough looking guys from the inner city were on the scene, carrying all the renters' possessions to the curb.

The city ordered the dispossessed to remove them from the curb within 48 hours or the trash department would haul it to the dump. He rented a truck and he, his wife and the kids started loading the stuff by themselves. There were several truck loads. We sat on the neighbor's lawn and watched, At one point, he came over to me, smiled, and said, "Well, I gave you a good fight."

The amount of goods in the house – especially the hundreds of tools, many still in their original boxes – intrigued the sheriff's deputies, thinking they might be stolen, or that this was a fencing operation. They took down several serial numbers and investigated, but discovered that he had purchased everything and that he had carried massive expenditures on his Sears card which had been paid.

In retrospect, we made one mistake. We should never have had the movers put all that stuff on the curb. We should have gone back to court and gotten an order to seal the house and confiscate the goods to satisfy the monetary judgment. But I had already been away from the job more than a week and needed to get back to Israel – thus we blew our chance to recover all our costs.

David, who was living in Washington at the time, moved into the house and did some clean up and painting, while it was listed for sale. Eventually, it did sell, for $67,500. In 2004, its value was $350,000.

But the story still does not end yet. In August, 1980, the renter appealed the Prince Georges Circuit Court jury verdict and the judge's order for him to pay expenses. The verdict was upheld, but the award of legal costs was overturned. In November of that year, he was back in Federal court, demanding production of all "documents" originated by me or Linda making any reference to them.

I was prepared to pursue a counter-suit in Federal Court for malicious prosecution, slander and defamation of character unless he dropped his federal suit. He did not respond to my lawyer's letters and the matter apparently ended. His last filing still listed a post office box in Bowie, and no phone number. I can only assume he by then had found another landlord to haunt.

If there is a moral to this story, it is: get references, and check them.

CHAPTER 29 — ISRAEL, A FIRST GLANCE

Ladies and Gentlemen, our El Al flight is now on final approach to Lod Airport in Tel Aviv. Please fasten your seat belts and put your trays in the upright position. We hope you have enjoyed our in flight entertainment, The Renters, on the trip from Nairobi. May I be the first to welcome you to Israel.

We loved Israel from the first moment of arrival. It would be a while before we would become disillusioned. The six Chancellors received a special VIP arrival treatment. We were called off the plane first and a limousine met us at the stairway to take us to Immigration and Customs, while other passengers loaded aboard a bus. We were greeted by Charles Weiss, the long-time VOA correspondent in Israel, and an even longer-time resident of the country. His first words to me were, "I don't want to leave here, but VOA is making me do so."

Charlie had been among the original settlers in Israel after World War Two – he worked aboard one of the ships that sneaked Jewish refugees from Europe to midnight landings along the coast of what then was a British protectorate. He had been there since independence, working as a freelance journalist. VOA was one of his early clients and only in recent years had hired him for a staff position. One requirement of being on VOA staff – and eligible for retirement, medical care and other benefits – was that he would have to rotate from Israel to other assignments, as did all VOA staff correspondents.

He really was reluctant to do it, but his wife, Harriett, who was a high-powered public relations executive and spent much of her time in New York, had prevailed on him to grab the opportunity for an assured future. They owned a house in Jerusalem – a rarity among correspondents. They hoped that I, as the new VOA correspondent, would rent their house, which we did, using it both as residence and office.

Our arrival was late at night, and Charles took us immediately to the American Colony Hotel, in a former pasha's palace on what had once been the Arab side of Jerusalem. The American Colony was and still is one of the most wonderful hotels in the world – not fancy, not large – but small, homey and friendly. On the way to the hotel, we drove past the west wall of the old city of Jerusalem – a scene that would do credit to any movie set. Charlie said "I'll be back to join you for breakfast – they have the best breakfast in Israel." He was right about that – served in a courtyard just outside our rooms, it was a buffet that went far beyond any other breakfast, with fruits and cheeses, wonderful breads, and middle eastern delicacies alongside the bacon and eggs.

Our two adjoining rooms were enormous, and we would learn later, were by far the best in the hotel. We awakened at dawn by the Muslim call to worship coming from a mosque just beyond our window. Properly fed, we began the first of five days of touring and becoming acquainted with what would be our future home, come January, 1980.

First stop was the Weiss house, at 64 Hanevi-im Street, just a couple of blocks from the old city wall. It was unique, quaint and historic. It was in a compound, owned by the Russian Orthodox Church, which contained two other buildings, housing three other families. It was questionable whether the Weisses really owned the house, but they had some sort of long-term agreement from the Russians to live there, and to rent it out as if they owned it.

It was an old Turkish building, two stories, fronting directly on Hanevi-im, the Street Of The Prophets, but with the entrance off the driveway into the compound. The original part of the house was more than 100 years old, the rest 60 to 80. The living room at the front had an arched, domed ceiling, where I once counted 17 different arches. The entrance from the side came into a hallway, with the relatively new and modern master bedroom to the left, and to the right, a bath and two steps down into a large kitchen. Two more steps took you back up from the kitchen to the living room. There was a narrow, winding staircase which went to two upstairs bedrooms and a large open living area. There were full bathrooms on both floors.

Charlie had set up his office in one end of the kitchen, at a massive built-in desk. A teletype machine clattered away on a landing/balcony about

64 Hanevi-Im (Street of the Prophets), Jerusalem. The driveway to the compound is through the gate, and the Weiss house is just to the right of the gate. Entrance was made from the back side, with a small garden area off the driveway, and a larger, disputed garden on the other side of the drive.

half way up the stairs. The upstairs bedrooms were occupied by the Weiss children, who also used the sitting room there. All the floors were intricate tile. Windows opened to the front street both upstairs and down, and to the driveway area. Harriett had maneuvered to fit a washer and dryer into the upstairs bathroom on a shelf cantilevered out over the bathtub. The kitchen was large and modern, with a bar separating it from Charlie's work area.

The house was charming, although small and cramped. It would be big enough for Linda, Steven and me – the other kids would be remaining in the United States after home leave, except for occasional visits to us in Jerusalem. Charles had carved out a patch of lawn and a garden across the driveway in an open area at the front of the compound, and early on warned me that Sarah, another resident of the compound, did not agree that the garden was his. She complained to us about it from the day we arrived and once in a fit of rage, tore out the pipes Charles had installed for a drip irrigation system.

Charlie took me to the Government Information Office, which was just a couple of blocks away from the house. There, everyone was warm and cordial and efficient as they briefed me on the hows and wherefores of covering news in Israel. We toured the West Bank, visiting Bethlehem and Jericho. The kids discovered the old walled city, and explored it fully. The whole family was treated to a traditional Sabbath dinner at the Weiss home with the candles and incantations and tradition that accompany that meal.

We were all introduced to Jan Ziff, who was Charlie's assistant, and who would work for me as a helper and translator. Jan was a British Jew, who had been in Israel several years and had many contacts. She also had an Arab boyfriend, which seemed to mark her as open-minded. She came from a good family – her step-father was a noted symphony conductor back in England.

Even though he was Jewish, Charlie, too, was very open minded and liberal. He had over the years cultivated a great number of contacts and friends among the Arab community as well as in the government.

When we left for the United States at the end of five days, we were really enthusiastic about Israel and looking forward to returning in January. It seemed like everything was in place for a successful assignment: a home, an office, a VOA car, a knowledgeable assistant and a good list of future contacts.

I should have been aware of a quotation from Mark Twain regarding the Holy Land: "Christ has been here once. He won't come back here again."

We were in Washington only a few days before the family split up in several directions. David decided to stay in Washington to seek his career, and signed up for computer classes at Montgomery County Junior College. He boarded at first with Nancy and Sandy Rosenblum, our good friends from Tokyo days, who had a son David's age. He took a part-time job in a pizza restaurant not far from Rosenblum's.

Craig had decided to seek his fortune in Texas, and took off to join Jerry Dale Dixon, who had been a classmate and friend at the International School of Kenya. Jerry's father had been in East Africa working the oil exploration fields in the southern Sudan and the two boys were sure they could get jobs in the Texas oil patch.

Kim, Linda and Steven headed on to Springfield, where it was time for Kim to begin her junior year at Drury College and where it was time to enroll Steven for a semester at Parkview High School. Linda's assignment was to find us a two or three bedroom apartment near Parkview and her parents, for our impending four month residence in America. I stayed on in Washington for more consultations at VOA, and to spend several sessions with an orthopedist who felt he could help with my back problems.

While in Washington, I also bought my third red convertible – a 1979 MGB which I intended to drive back to Missouri and then ship to Israel. I also had some major provisions to obtain for the house in Israel: a new bed, a new washer and dryer. David and I went to the mover's warehouse where our household goods were stored. We had gone to Kenya with only a limited shipment of goods and furniture, while in Israel we would be required to provide our own furniture, so we spent a day sorting through our belongings, picking which to send to Israel and which to put back into storage.

My visits with the orthopedist were not very successful. He was a specialist in bad backs, who had been recommended by Alan Heil and Bernie Kamenske. He looked at my South African CAT scans, fitted me with a back brace, did some cortisone injections into my spinal area, but finally came to the conclusion that surgery would be re-

quired to correct the ruptured disc. I chose to have that surgery done in Springfield, where I could be with my family, and headed west in my shiny new sports car.

Linda had rented a nice, furnished two-bedroom apartment on South Campbell street, just a block from Parkview. By the time I got to Springfield, Steven was in school, taking American History and drivers' education, and had found a part-time job delivering a weekly shoppers newspaper. Linda had borrowed linens and pans from Georgia and Aunt Betty and rented a television set.

I set up office on a card table in the corner of the kitchen, and began a long series of correspondences with our renters. And I immediately began searching for a surgeon for my back, settling on Dr. John Ferguson, a neurosurgeon who had gained a good reputation for disc repair at St. John's hospital. It was a micro-surgery technique, he explained. A small incision would be made over the affected vertebrae and the offending disc material would be plucked away "sort of like picking crab meat out of the shell." But it would take several weeks of slow recovery and limited activity. The surgery was done successfully, and except for some soreness, it was wonderful not to hurt anymore.

Linda and I both enjoyed the semblance of a normal American life after four years in Africa, and she was especially glad to be able to spend time with her longtime friend Martha Hutchison. We spent a lot of time with Georgia and Ferd, and with Betty and Pearson, and made a couple of trips to the Lake of the Ozarks to visit Dad and Martha. We also had a lot of shopping to do, to stock up for Jerusalem.

A month of this idyll had passed when we got a call from Craig. He and Jerry Dale were penniless and homesick in Dimebox, Texas, working hard carrying pipe at a supply yard and sleeping in Jerry Dale's car. Jerry Dale wanted to go home to Midland-Odessa and after a few minutes of conversation it was evident that Craig wanted to come back to his family in Springfield. When Linda said come ahead, he boarded a bus within a few hours and arrived a day later.

It was a good thing he was there. My uncle Skipper Johns died in Fredericktown, Missouri. I wanted to go to the funeral, but was not yet allowed to drive or ride in a car. Craig was more than willing to take his mother in the new red sports car, so they went to the funeral and had a nice trip.

So, what to do about Craig? He did not want to return to Israel with us, where it would be difficult to find work or go to school. He did not want to start college yet. Grand-Ferd to the rescue. He had a friend who operated a oil well service company in Casper, Wyoming, who was always looking for energetic young men to work for him in the booming oil patch. Fred contacted him, vouched for Craig's good character, and he was hired. He stayed with us in Springfield until the end of the year when we bought him an old car, packed all his belongings, and waved good-bye as he headed off to Wyoming.

We had a wonderful Christmas in Springfield, saw some snow for the first time in five years. My brother Sam and his wife, Linda, drove out from Maryland to spend the holiday with us, bringing with them a full bushel of Chesapeake Bay oysters, still in the shell, as a special treat. David joined us also – he still had a ticket valid from Washington to Springfield and was entitled to a ticket from Springfield to Tel Aviv, so he planned to go with us to Israel for a couple of weeks before returning to work and classes in Montgomery County.

Immediately after Christmas, we packed up, said our final good-byes, dispatched Craig to the wild West, and Linda, David, Steven and I prepared for our December 31st flight to Israel, via Boston, with a stop over in Paris. My back didn't hurt anymore and I was eager to get back to the new job.

We knew we were traveling on New Years Eve, but that had never been a major cause of celebration with us. It also was the dawning of the new decade of the 80's. I went to sleep almost immediately upon take off from Boston, but suddenly was awakened and reminded of the New Years holiday when somewhere over the north Atlantic, the TWA crew members and passengers began a conga-line dance up and down the aisles of our 747.

We became more aware it was a holiday when we arrived in Paris. Only a skeleton crew was working at DeGaulle Airport and taxicabs were scarce. When we got checked into Chateaubriand Hotel, we were hungry and surprised to find that none of the restaurants in Paris were open. Finally, out of desperation, we took a taxi to the Hilton Hotel and feasted on a good old American hamburger at its coffee shop instead of the anticipated gourmet French meal.

I had been in Paris once before, after the McGovern trip and was eager to show the sights to Linda and the boys, so we spent the day visiting Notre Dame, the Eiffel Tower and the left bank and walking around the nearly empty city. The next day, I hooked up with VOA's Paris correspondent, John Bue, a wonderful, charming American who had been in France for many years, and he took us to an out-of-the-way French restaurant where we finally got our gourmet meal.

I spent some time talking bureau finances with Rosie, who handled accounts for all the bureaus under our new non-official status, while Linda, David and Steven toured the Louvre. We did some more touring on a four-hour bus trip around the city and a two-hour boat ride on the Seine. January 4th, we departed for Tel Aviv – our scheduled flight had been delayed by fog so we had to make a fast, last-minute connection via Rome and did not have time to haunt the wonderful duty-free shops at the airport.

Yes, it snows in Israel. Steven and Linda look at this one shortly after our arrival, later in the year a one-foot snowfall.

CHAPTER 30 — LIFE IN ISRAEL

Charles Weiss met us again, and again we went back to our same rooms at the American Colony, but this time I was there as a working correspondent, not a tourist. Linda described our temporary home – where we would live nearly three weeks – in a letter home:

"Our rooms are simply wonderful – two connecting rooms, each as large as a small ballroom, with oriental carpets, inlaid mother-of-pearl tables, huge copper trays on legs for tables, domed ceilings 22 feet high in the center, a lovely garden and patio out the front door and a view of the new swimming pool out the back windows."

I hate snow almost more than anything, but like the black cloud that used to follow "Joe Btfsplk" in the "Lil' Abner" comic strip, snow must love me, because it follows me everywhere. Our last night in Paris, there was a light snowfall, which is very unusual there. And there was a light snow our second day in Israel. Later in the year, Jerusalem would experience a foot-deep snowfall, which paralyzed the city. In our future lay unusual snowfalls in Johannesburg and Austin, Texas – at least it never snowed on us in Bangkok or Nairobi.

I was to overlap with Charlie for about three weeks before his departure to Washington, where he was going to work on the VOA assignments desk, tracking and consulting with foreign correspondents such as me. Almost immediately, within two days, there was work to be done – Israeli Prime Minister Menachim Begin was scheduled to fly to Egypt for a summit meeting with President Anwar Sadat. Charlie had booked two seats on a press flight – it was on an Israeli C-130 transport plane, with nylon bucket seats – a mode of transport I had used a lot in Vietnam — not a comfortable ride.

The summit wasn't in Cairo, but way south on the Nile River at Aswan. It was a great opportunity to see a part of Egypt seldom seen by tourists, and we were given tours of the Luxor Temple ruins and the underground tombs of the Pharoahs in be-

tween news briefings and meetings. The three-day summit also provided a chance to meet and get to know my colleagues in the Israeli foreign press, who would become good friends in a closely knit professional community.

Steven began classes at the Anglican School, just two blocks from our house, the day I left for Egypt. Harriett Weiss took Linda and David under her wing, introducing Linda to many people and places to shop. Jan Ziff was also a great help to Linda, taking her and the boys to the old city and other places around Jerusalem. After Aswan, David helped me set up office in the empty Weiss house (it never would really be regarded as the Chancellor house) although we continued to live at the Colony, where we and the staff became fast friends.

I did not like the idea of working out of the kitchen, so I took one of the upstairs bedrooms for an office, and used the outer sitting room for an office for Jan. We moved the news wire and telex machines up from the stair landing. David and I put together a small studio for sending feeds. The other upstairs room was Steven's. David returned to Washington before the end of the month and soon was working in the news operations studio at VOA, taking in news feeds from various correspondents, including me. That gave us a chance to chat frequently.

At the end of Steven's first day of school, he came back to the hotel with Jerry Cooley, a new friend and classmate who had also just moved to Jerusalem – from Springfield, Missouri. His father, Bob Cooley, was an archeologist at Southwest Missouri State College and had brought the family to Israel for a six month sabbatical while he explored the ruins of the Arab quarter of Jerusalem. We got together with Bob, Eileen and Jerry many times, and became good friends. Visiting the sites of Jerusalem with a trained professional archeologist is an education beyond compare.

Linda quickly learned about the work habits of the Middle East.

She told her mother in a letter: *"Unfortunately, the work time is so short here – the Jews don't do anything from sundown, Friday until sundown Saturday; the Arabs begin on Saturday and then the Christians take off Sunday. The entire town closes down noon Fridays, reopens Saturday night, but by that time, the other religions are observing their Sabbath. Then on top of that, everything closes daily from 1 until 4 for lunch. Honestly, it's nearly impossible to get anything accomplished."*

I always felt that Israel, with its polyglot population of former Europeans and the resident Arab population, combined to create all the efficiency of the Middle East with all the charm of Eastern Europe – that is, none. But the work schedule did not fall in line with that inefficient pattern of life. For VOA, Friday always was a big day of story demand as producers tried to put together programs in advance so they could have a weekend, although very little was going on in Israel on Friday. Saturdays we could usually plan on quiet time, but Israel came back to life on Sunday, usually with a cabinet meeting to be covered.

The information department had a system called "the golem" – that's Hebrew for "monster." The golem was an automated calling system to all registered correspondents in the country, and answering its ring would bring a recorded announcement of something from the government or the military. Nearly every morning, the golem would ring with a report on some bombing or attack along the north border. There's the first story of the day, even before breakfast.

By noon, we were all at the information office for military briefings and a daily press conference by a spokesman for the Foreign Ministry. There's story number two. After lunch, a quick visit to the Arab West Bank to get their side of events – the mayors of the West Bank cities were particularly open and helpful to the foreign press. Third story of the day. Then there would be some evening event – perhaps the Prime Minister making a speech to some visiting delegation. Story four. Then to bed, to await the next morning's golem summons.

Despite all this, Linda wrote her mother January 17th: *"Life seems good right now and we certainly haven't changed our minds about Israel or Jerusalem – we do love it."*
That would begin to change, as from this letter dated July 16: *This place just keeps me hopping constantly, if nothing else but to keep this house from falling apart around our ankles. I finally got the washer and dryer and after only four weeks, got both of them installed in the upstairs bathroom. The trouble is that the washer tends to leap when it is the least bit out of balance. That wouldn't bother me much except that it is on a four foot high ledge behind the bath tub and we've already had one near disaster when the darned thing leaped halfway off said ledge.*

Downstairs we have a slight water problem. Our outside wall is three feet thick and it has taken almost four months for the winter rains to work their way through. So in the middle of dust and dryness from outside, I'm cultivating mold and mildew all over the place

Israeli women wander into the driveway to take our plants – so far today, three different ladies have walked right up to the plants and grabbed a handful right out of the ground. The inflation rate for the past twelve months has hit 125%. We have enormous chains with padlocks woven through all the patio furniture – it looks dreadful, but we've lost three wicker chairs and umpteen potted plants. They also are shocking trespassers. We have people unlocking the gate into the garden and going in to make themselves at home. All in all, this is the craziest place I have ever lived."

As difficult as the working situation and living situation was, we still enjoyed traveling and sightseeing in Israel. We made several trips to the Mediterranean beaches north of Tel Aviv. There the waves would wash away the dirt embankment of what had once been a dump for the Roman city of Tiberias, and we could pick up pottery shards and tiles that were 2000 years old. We liked Bethlehem a lot, and would go there to sightsee and to shop.

Shopping for fruit in Jericho

One of our favorite day trips was to the West Bank town of Jericho – reputedly the oldest city in the world – where we would eat delicious Arab lunches and buy oranges and papaya fresh off the trees. And we made several trips to Nazareth and the Sea of Galilee, where the fish called "St. Peter's fish" (same as the "tilapia" we got in Africa) was delicious at lakeside cafes.

There was so much to see in a small country, where you could go end to end in just a couple of hours – Roman coliseum ruins, ancient churches, and stunning vistas of the hills and deserts. During the summer, when Kim was there, she and I took a one-day trip all around the country – to the coast, to the northern border with Lebanon, to the west bank, and home – a total of 300 miles, all in one day's drive.

We had a VOA car which was a little Suburu station wagon. Linda drove it most of the time, and I used the MG for most of my work travels. I had retained my Missouri license plate, SNK-948, in order to avoid getting local registration, and it was often seen in West Bank towns. The Missouri license helped too, because Israel had different plates for the Israeli side and the Palestinian side – no one could take exception to a car and driver which they could not identify.

In the course of my work there, I came to like and admire the Palestinians much more than I did the Israelis. I felt they were getting a raw deal, many of them run out of their homes and lands by the Israelis, who continued to encroach on Arab lands by creating hundreds of Jewish settlements (fortified villages, really) in the midst of the Pales-

tinian lands. And they were much nicer, friendlier and more gracious than the Israelis. I had had a great deal of exposure to apartheid and racism in South Africa, but was shocked to learn that the same existed in Israel, where I expected better.

The Palestinian-Jewish schism was always present: in nearly every conversation and nearly every news story. It was no wonder that the Holy Land had been subject to wars and conflict through most of its history – both sides wanted the same piece of land. Someone once described it as "the too often promised land." Then, in 1980, the Israelis had the guns and the power, and occasional terrorist bombings and mortar firings across the border were the only Palestinian answer.

We never much worried about terrorism in those days, but we were careful and prudent. When Linda would travel to Tel Aviv alone, she often would pick up an armed hitch-hiking Israeli soldier at a bus stop to accompany her. We had one little bomb scare at our home when I noticed the trunk lid of the MGB was slightly ajar. The bomb squad came and carefully opened the trunk, but found nothing – it probably had been opened by someone looking for something to steal.

In June I received word that my father had died while he was working on the yard at the Lake of the Ozarks cabin, and I immediately made arrangements to go home for his funeral, which was in Boonville. Martha had planned to have his service at the funeral home there, but I convinced her that a service would be much more appropriate across the river at Clark's Chapel, where he had gone to school and to church as a youngster. The cortège crossed the bridge into Howard County, past the family farm house to the Chapel, and afterward, back across the bridge for burial beside mother in Boonville.

It was a nice service in which the preacher talked, fittingly, about bridges to the past and to the future. David flew out from Washington with me, Sam and Linda drove to Boonville, Craig drove down from Wyoming, and Steve and Kay were there from St. Louis. Despite the occasion, we had a nice reunion. I was pleased to see how much Craig had filled out and matured from his work in the Wyoming oil fields.

Kim spent that summer with us in Israel, working at the American Consulate. Craig took a week's vacation and used his last airline ticket to come see us at the same time. He could, and should, have stayed with us longer, because as soon as he got back to Casper, he was laid off and began looking for another job. Also, during that July – after only two weeks at home -- I had to fly back to Washington for the aforementioned Renters' trial.

Fred Hunt, playing American tourist in Israel.

We had other visitors, too, during our time in Jerusalem. My aunt Phoebe and her husband, Art Popham, came to Israel to stay with us. They had tried several times to visit us in Nairobi, but had never made it. Linda's mother and Fred also came to visit – I don't think Fred was ever very keen about touring Africa, but he was enthused about coming to the Holy Land. Ben and Mary Ann Whitten visited from their new post in Paris, as well as VOA correspondent Doug Roberts.

In March, Linda had written her mother, extolling the benefits of a visit to Israel: *You are going to love this place whenever you decide to come. It's just like stepping into one of those pictures in the Bible. History is just everywhere you look and just to be able to go to those places you've read about all your life – Jericho, Bethlehem, Nazareth, Tiberius, to say nothing of Jerusalem – well, it really is the trip of a lifetime*

Something else that is enchanting in this city is the different people you see on any

walk down the street. The orthodox Jews in their old-fashioned black outfits with the side-curls bouncing, the Greek Orthodox priests in their tall head gear and black robes, the Arabs with their robes and Lawrence-of-Arabia headgear, the Armenian women in their embroidered dresses, the hundreds of soldiers, both boys and girls looking about 15-years-old with their military gear and rifles. And yesterday, I saw a Jesus freak in the regular white Jesus robes, dragging a cross with him with tennis shoes peeping out from under his garments. What a place.

With marketing like that, it's no wonder we had lots of visitors. We developed quite a tour routine. My part was to take visitors – nearly trembling from all the tales they had heard about war and terrorism – to visit the West Bank while I explained the on-going struggle. Israel had always gotten such good press in the United States; it was eye-opening for visitors to be shown the other side of the issue.

We also became acquainted with Richard and Susan – another couple who would get more than one chapter in our lives. We met them at a dinner party hosted by Eric and Bridget Silver. Eric was a British correspondent and long-time Israel resident. We worked together on a lot of stories and often cruised the West Bank in the MG.

Richard Weeks was a tall, gaunt man of about 35, who worked as a U.S. Consular officer, issuing visas. He had joined the Foreign Service after the Navy, where he had been in one of those hush-hush jobs eavesdropping on other country's electronics. For a long time, I suspected that he might be working for the CIA, but I was never sure. When we met them, he and Susan were just preparing to go to Cyprus to be married. If Richard Weeks was a "spook," his marriage to Susan must have given the spy agency fits. She was self-described as a "Jewish American Princess." Her parents in San Francisco were wealthy – her father had developed Adolph's Meat Tenderizer. Susan had been a footloose wanderer for most of her adult life; had one unsuccessful marriage, and had settled (temporarily) in Israel. Short, blonde, buxom, and pushy, she was irrepressible and uninhibited, never reluctant to say what she thought regardless of the consequences. She did not fit the mold of an Official American Wife.

Susan created one near crisis when she told off visiting American Congressman Robert Dornan of California, calling him demagogue. She drank too much at parties and got too loud. But she and Richard were fun to be with and we became friends.

It was because of Susan that Linda had the opportunity to go to Cairo. Susan had a Jewish-American friend named Vi, who operated a popular restaurant and bar near the King David Hotel in Jerusalem. Vi was a flamboyant red-head, who jangled because of the several pounds of gold jewelry she wore at all times. She was about as quiet and restrained as Susan, who was a frequent bar customer.

We were all in Vi's one evening – Linda and I, Richard and Susan, and VOA's Cairo correspondent, Gil Butler. Vi was sitting with us when Gil noted that he was about to go on leave and his apartment in Cairo would be vacant for a month. "Why don't you use it and visit Egypt," he said to the gathering in general. Vi immediately said she would, and before the evening was over, had convinced Linda to join her. Within a week, both were on their way, and had a wonderful time for the mere cost of an airline ticket.

I did not have to travel nearly as much from Jerusalem as I had in Africa, or Asia but some of the trips were memorable. Early in the year I flew to London, to join with Special Ambassador Sol Linowitz, who was making a presidential mission trying to find a solution to the Middle East problem. The issue, then as now, was that of autonomy for the Palestinians in Israeli-occupied territory on the West Bank. Then, as now, the United States government was urging settlement of the Palestinian issue so it could improve its relations with Arab nations in view of problems in Afghanistan and Iran. That trip took us to Cairo, Saudi Arabia and Tel Aviv.

Visits by foreign journalists to Saudi Arabia were extremely rare, and I took advantage of my presence with Ambassador Linowitz to send a back-

ground report on the kingdom. This came just two months after Arab militants had attacked the holy shrine of Islam at Mecca, which had come as a shock to the King who was considered the keeper of the holy places.

Correspondents Report, February 4:
In Riyadh, there are construction projects everywhere. It looks as though nothing is completed because so many projects are started that there are many delays in their completion. Manpower is part of that problem: Saudis, by and large, do not do manual labor and fully one-third of the total population of six-million-plus is made up of foreign workers attracted to Saudi Arabia by two-year contracts and the prospect of making a lot of money fast. These workers, from Korea, the Philippines, Thailand and India as well as the more traditional migrant workers from Arab neighbor states, usually are without families and have no long-term stake in the society. But they do work hard toward the goal of turning the desert kingdom into a modern industrial state by the end of this century.

Despite continuing talks, the Israeli government held firm in its policy of supporting Jewish settlements in the occupied Palestinian lands of the West Bank. One flash point was the town of Hebron, south of Bethlehem, site of a proposed *Yeshiva*, or religious school, for soldier-students occupying buildings in the center of the Arab town's market. There was a Jewish settlement just up the hill, and frequent clashes between the settlers and the Arabs in the market. The United Nations Security Council censured Israel for the settlement policy – even the United States voted in favor of it.

A month later, Arab terrorists attacked an Israeli kibbutz, or collective farm settlement, on the Israel-Lebanon border. After a nine-hour siege, Israeli troops stormed the guerrilla-held children's dormitory. The five terrorists were killed, as were three Israelis.

The Israeli government was certainly conscious of bad publicity. In August, Palestinian prisoners at several prisons started a hunger strike to protest the deaths of two hunger strikers. The event led to violent demonstrations in Jerusalem and protests throughout the West Bank. The government arranged a press tour to Nafha Prison, in the Negev desert, south of Beersheba.

Another big continuing story was the government versus the mayors of several Palestinian cities. Several of these mayors, in Nablus, Hebron, Halhul, Bethlehem and Gaza, had become friends as well as good news contacts, and two, Fahd Kwassme of Hebron and Mohammed Milhem of Halhoul, were ordered deported from the West Bank to Jordan. Appeal of their expulsion went on for five months while they lived at the passenger terminal at the Allenby Bridge border crossing to Jordan. Eventually, the Supreme Court ruled against them and they were deported.

Is this politically incorrect? Bob and Linda in Palestinian garb

Mayor Milhem was an especially close friend. A tall man with intense blue eyes – not a militant, but certainly committed to the Palestinian cause – he would spend hours in conversation with me at his office and even accepted an invitation to a party Linda and I held at our home on the Israeli side of the line. Another equally good friend was Elias Freij, the Christian/Arab mayor of Bethlehem who somehow managed to toe a narrow line and remain in the country.

Coverage of Israel was never easy. In addition to the relentless pace, the VOA correspondent there was subjected to frequent criticism and harassment – not from the Israelis nor the Palestinians – but from editors and producers in Washington. It was, from their standpoint, an important story, but covering it was made more difficult by this constant second-guessing. Charles Weiss contributed to a lot of this – from his position on the assignments desk, he tended to micro-manage my work. The culmination of all this came in September, when war broke out between Iran and Iraq.

VOA did not have a correspondent either in Iraq, or in Iran, where American diplomats were still being held hostage, and thus we were required to report the hostilities from sources on the far periphery, including Jerusalem. One of those reports nearly ended my career.

Based on a briefing by both American and Israeli officials, I filed one report on the strategic importance of the Hormuz Strait, which links the Indian Ocean with the Persian Gulf and the gulf's oil producing states. Hormuz had been described as the jugular vein of the industrialized world, because 40 percent of the world's oil passed through it – blockage of the waterway was a big concern.

> Correspondent's Report, September 23: *Israeli analysts believe it would be difficult to block the strait with anything less than a show of military force, which would likely draw a response from the United States, France and other Western powers. The Pentagon notes that the United States is pursuing a course of neutrality in the area, but that American warships do operate in the area, passing through the Straits. In June this year, the United States and Oman concluded a military and economic agreement, giving U.S. military forces access to Omani air and seaport facilities. There are no bases, or U.S. forces in Oman.*

Some one in Washington took strong exception to the phrase "passing through the Straits" and called on me to change the report. I repeated the report, deleting that phrase, although I had no doubt that U.S. warships operating in the area, and visiting Omani seaport facilities, undoubtedly had passed through the straits in their normal course of patrolling. But that did not satisfy my unknown critic –

the demand was made that I also add this line to the report: "And contrary to my previous report, the June agreement does not provide for American patrolling in the area."

This sort of *mea culpa* would be unprecedented to the Voice, or for any other news organization, and seemed excessive. Even if I was mistaken, mistakes generally were taken care of issuing a corrected or rewritten version of the story. Someone wanted to make me wallow in my error, and I wasn't prepared to do it. News and Current Affairs Chief Alan Heil called me during dinner that evening – saying I must re-issue the report with the requested apology. I thought the report must have set off alarms at the White House or State Department and the devils were descending on VOA, but Alan would not tell me who or what was bringing this unusual pressure. After a long discussion with a very insistent Alan, I finally said: "within a few minutes, you will either have the report as you insist, or my resignation. I'm not sure which."

In the end, I went up to the office and reluctantly filed the report with the apologia as demanded. It was several months later when I learned from a secretary that all the pressure and demands were coming from newsroom chief Bernie Kamenske, not the White House or National Security Council or State Department. He was having one of his temper tantrums, which got worse when I refused to do his bidding. There was no national emergency. Had I known at the time that it was only Bernie I might well have sent in that resignation instead.

Obviously, Israel coverage was beginning to wear on me, and Israel life was beginning to wear on Linda. In the fall of 1980, David Lent transferred away from Johannesburg to Eastern Europe – he apparently did not much want the assignment that I had wanted so badly. Although it was unusual for a transfer to take place so early in a tour, I immediately applied for reassignment to Johannesburg. Until then, I had not considered myself one of the "old Africa hands" who could not get the continent out of his blood. We had willingly and eagerly departed Nairobi. But I found that I did miss it some, and anything would be better than the Middle East. Perhaps, it was to the mutual relief of Washington and me, that my transfer was approved. But I

could not leave Israel until a replacement for me was found, and Margaret Kennedy, the African desk news editor, was sent to Johannesburg on temporary duty until I could get there in December.

In the meantime, the Iran-Iraq war was continuing, and Israel-based foreign correspondents were being admitted to Iraq – the usual method was to travel across the Jordan River to Amman, Jordan, obtain a visa there and go by road to Baghdad. I went to Amman with Bill Claybourne of the Washington Post. He obtained a visa after just a couple of days, but I remained in the Jordanian capital, cooling my heels and waiting. I waited more than two weeks while the Iraqi embassy said it was working on a visa for me both in Baghdad and in Washington, but it never came.

Eventually we gave up, and after filing a series of three reports on Jordan, I boarded a flight home. Despite all the waiting there, I didn't have the opportunity to visit one tourist destination that had always been high on my list – the temples of Petra carved from red sandstone cliffs. And because of a border regulation, I could not just take a taxi back across the Jordan River, but had to fly out to Greece and make a connection to Tel Aviv. At least the misadventure got me a couple of days in Athens, one of my favorite cities.

I made two journeys to Turkey, the first in April for some long-since forgotten conference and to get acquainted with the country, and the other after a military takeover of the government in September

The first trip to the capital, Ankara, became somewhat of a personal adventure, because the Turkish internal airlines were on strike. I arrived in Istanbul intending to take an overnight train to Ankara if the strike was not settled. It wasn't. I went by taxi from the airport to the rail station across the Bosporus – to the Asian side of Istanbul. I was several hours early for the train and the station was nearly deserted. And no one spoke any English. The Turkish language is one that seems to have no resemblance to any other language, and written, it is just indecipherable.

I remembered my father telling me once that he had a recurring nightmare in which he was in a place where he could not communicate with anyone, and

I thought: "I am living my father's nightmare." By standing at the ticket window until it opened, I finally got the message across that I wanted a ticket to Ankara; and with that in hand, I went immediately to board the train, even though it would not leave for several hours, fearing that I would miss a departure announcement. Fortunately, once the train was underway, I met a Turkish businessman in the bar car, who spoke English and had been to the United States, so we had a nice, long conversation about Turkey.

Once in Ankara, I fared pretty well. I hired a taxi at the train station, an old Chevrolet, and the driver spoke English. He had once worked as a driver for the U.S. Embassy and had purchased his Chevy from a departing diplomat. I hired him forthwith for the duration of my stay, and he took me on some tours of the Anatolian highlands around Ankara. I also hired a young Turkish-American freelance reporter to help me, and to serve as a future stringer for VOA.

Whatever the story was in Ankara, it was quickly overshadowed by the failed American attempt to rescue the Embassy hostages in Iran. VOA wasn't interested in much else and there was not much I could contribute from Ankara. I certainly was concerned and interested in the Iran hostage crisis which had started the previous November when we were in Springfield – one of the hostages was Kate Koob, a good friend of mine who had been the information officer in Lusaka in the past.

By November, Linda, Steven and I were wrapping up what was a record-short VOA tenure in Israel, and preparing for Johannesburg. It had been a revealing exercise. We still loved the country and its attractions but we had trouble liking the government, the situation and some of the people. Furniture was loaded, belongings were packed, the little red MGB was taken to the port for shipping to South Africa. We needed to time our departure between the end of Steven's semester at the Anglican School, and the start of a new semester at a school I had found near Johannesburg.

My heart was warmed when my foreign press colleagues threw a surprise *bon voyage* party for Linda and me, using mostly duty-free booze which had been purloined from our house. Charles and Harriett Weiss decided to sell their house to Eric and Bridget Silver. The Silvers also adopted our white cat, Cassie, who over the years had made several long trips, from Bowie, to Nairobi, and on to Jerusalem. With loss of the house, it became necessary to find new, temporary, offices for my successor, Ron Pemstein

After another ten days at the American Colony, we were on the road (or in the air) again – this time to territory well known. Songwriter Mac Davis wrote that "Happiness is Lubbock in your rear view mirror." We could sing the same thing about Israel – although just two years later, enroute to home leave from Johannesburg, we would visit Jerusalem again to see old friends and haunts.

Just a little red MGB with Missouri plates, wandering in the Israeli wilderness. I figured this car spent a lot more time at sea than on the road: by sea from the factory in England to the dealership in Maryland; by sea from the U.S. to Israel, by sea from Israel to South Africa, and by sea back to Houston, Texas. And in case you are counting, this is red convertible number three.

CHAPTER 31 — BACK TO AFRICA

Jan Smuts Airport in Johannesburg felt like home when the three remaining Chancellors arrived from Tel Aviv on December 6, 1980. There was no one to meet us – Margaret Kennedy had already departed for home, but I knew my way around here. We rented a car and drove into the city, to the office parking garage where Margaret had left the VOA car. We retrieved that car, transferred our baggage and prepared to take the rental back, when things began to go wrong. The office car wouldn't start: dead battery. It was late on a Saturday afternoon, and it took a long time and a lot of phone calls to get a tow truck to bring us a new battery and get us started. We still had not even checked into our hotel. Welcome back to Africa.

I had booked us into an apartment hotel on the edge of downtown, in the Hillbrow area, in a tall, circular building called Ponte City. We had an apartment on the 40th floor. Linda wrote to her mother: *The view was breathtaking. The problem there is that you can't get outside without taking two elevators down, and by then, the weather may have changed."*

So we began the familiar task of looking for a house, and getting acquainted with a new city. We were there well before Christmas and were able to get a tree, buy some gifts and celebrate the holiday on a warm, sunny midsummer day in the Southern hemisphere.

Rental properties were scarce. We were told of a lovely vacant house near the Johannesburg Zoo in Parktown North – the part of the city where we wished to live. Linda became acquainted with the owner, Edith Neickau, a new widow who was moving out to a townhouse. She wanted to sell her home, with its huge lawn, swimming pool and tennis court, but agreed to rent it to us furnished on a monthly basis until it sold, or until we found another place.

We moved there in three weeks, and stayed for two months, living with bare necessities until our shipping could be delivered to a permanent address. We did manage to have a dinner party

cookout for 16 people soon after moving into Edith's, to take advantage of the tennis court and pool and to pay back some folks who had entertained us on arrival.

Linda wrote: *"I must say we just love it here. I must be a colonial at heart, because I feel most at home in Africa, of all things. The life is just so gracious and easy, the people are so friendly – both black and white — to Americans. It must be one of the few places left where Americans are not only welcome, but really made over like royalty. Steven is delighted with the place as well. He is so impressed with the friendliness after Israel and that rude bunch."*

Eventually we found a rambling three-bedroom house on Verdi Avenue, in Risidale. That was really too far from the center of the city and from the center of activities, but the rent was right, so we took it. The landlord was a psychiatrist, who had purchased the house as an investment, and in terms of upkeep, it showed. Edith remained a good friend, and we had dinner with her several times at her new townhouse and at our home. She was particularly fond of Steven.

Steven got enrolled and started school in January, and Linda went to work at the American Consulate in Johannesburg as a well-paid typist. She pointed out to her mother that for a South African, (either black or white,) typing is considered beneath an educated person, so there are no typists around. She was paid $3.75 per page, compared to a dollar per page she was paid by the United Nations in Israel. "I will get about $150 for 15 hours work – that's almost as good as being a plumber," she said.

Steven began classes at Woodmead Academy, a private school just beyond the far northern suburbs of Johannesburg. It was a unique place as the only fully-integrated high school in South Africa. About half of its students were Africans; about half the students boarded at the school. Steven lived at home and commuted by school bus. Woodmead School taught the South African curriculum, but with a much more liberal syllabus than available in South African government high schools. It quickly became apparent that the South African curriculum was far advanced from that of the International School of Kenya, or Parkview in Springfield, or the Anglican School in Jerusalem, and Steven struggled to catch up and keep up.

He attended one full academic year there – from February through November. Remember, their summer season in the southern hemisphere is November through January and that is when schools take vacation. It became evident that Steven was not going to make it at Woodmead and we began to consider how, when and where to send him to a boarding school back in the United States.

Early in our stay, I attended the annual general meeting of the Foreign Correspondents Association of South Africa, and was elected secretary of that organization at that first introduction. I also got into the swing again of reporting.

What the policy of the Reagan administration would be toward southern Africa had been an unanswered question since the previous November's election when Ronald Reagan defeated Jimmy Carter.

Correspondent's Report, January 19:
Whites in South Africa are jubilant over the prospect of a Ronald Reagan administration. But blacks in South Africa and elsewhere on the subcontinent are skeptical at best. A black leader of South Africa, Anglican Bishop Desmond Tutu, has this description of white South Africa's reaction: "They
are cock-a-hoop (unrestrained joy) about Reagan. It's an axiom here that anything that the whites like and welcome as good, the blacks are going to dislike and find bad."

There have been minor changes in South Africa in the past few years and more are promised. Although blacks here believe these changes fall far short of what is required, they are prepared to credit international pressure, led in part by the Carter administration, for at least the awareness in South Africa that there must be some change. And they fear that the Reagan administration will ease off on that pressure, out of a greater concern about perceived Soviet strategic gains on the continent.

David Lent had retained our relationship with Fingers and his News Services organization, and my first days back at the office were a homecoming of sorts, renewing acquaintanceships with many former colleagues. Not much had changed in the South African story in the year-plus interim – still apartheid, still government reluctance to give any ground to African representation, still occasional protests and violence. The South African government was still in dispute with the United Nations and the western nations over independence for Southwest Africa/Namibia.

What had changed was Rhodesia. It was now Zimbabwe. Salisbury would soon be renamed Harare. During the year I had turned my back, real independence appeared to have come. Former guerrilla leader Robert Mugabe was now President Robert Mugabe – his rival liberation leader, Joshua Nkomo, also was in the government, but eclipsed by the Mugabe faction. Former white Prime Minister Ian Smith was still in the country, and still sitting as a member of the bi-racial Parliament. The hopes of the West and of neighboring African states were high that Zimbabwe would become a shining example of what independence could bring to an African state. It certainly had the potential, with rich farm lands and a cadre of white farmers who were very successful. During its isolation by the outside world, Rhodesia had developed a strong manufacturing sector – a country deprived of the chance to import refrigerators, for example, had learned how to make its own.

We had not been back long when the Zimbabwe government and the United Nations scheduled a massive economic conference in Harare. Although independent and potentially rich, the country needed an infusion of outside capital and outside expertise in order to thrive. Beyond a good story, it seemed a good opportunity to reacquaint myself with the country and to learn about the new regime. Steven was in school and old enough to fare for himself, so Linda was able to travel to Zimbabwe with me.

We loaded our suitcases into and onto the red MGB, which had arrived from Israel, still bearing Missouri license SNK-948, and headed north. Linda had never had much of a chance to travel with me before, so we looked forward to this opportunity. We crossed the border without incident, and visited the ancient Zimbabwe ruins. Great Zimbabwe, as it is called today, is the remnant of a once large city – a stone walled enclosure nearly 300 yards in circumference. The walls are 36 feet high and as much as 15 feet thick.

In colonial times, white rulers refused to believe that this massive structure – the largest ancient structure in southern Africa — was the work of natives of Africa, crediting it instead to the Queen of Sheba or a northern race coming into Africa. Great Zimbabwe had become a potent symbol of the African nationalist movement, while the white minority government suppressed findings of historians that Africans had built it between the 9th and the 14th centuries. "Zimbabwe" means "stone dwelling" in the native language and its political and historical significance provided the name for the newly independent country.

It was strange, even spooky, touring this historic site – there were no other visitors because tourism had not revived since the war for independence a year earlier. We found that elsewhere in the country – we also were the only guests in a unique hotel built for white Rhodesian vacationers in the eastern hills of Zimbabwe near Mozambique. That area had been a hot spot for fighting for control of Zimbabwe, since Robert Mugabe's guerilla had fought from sanctuary across the frontier.

In Harare, we stayed in the Meikles Hotel, long a landmark of the city, first opened in 1915, and the hotel of choice for journalists, diplomats and business travelers. It had retained its stature as one of the finest hotels in Africa, even with the addition of a modern towering wing of rooms and conference center. We were fortunate to get a room in the older section, packed with antiques. Meikles was noted for its dining veranda overlooking the adjacent park. I covered the conference while Linda visited the sites and markets of the city, picking up several stone carvings.

In addition to covering the conference, I did a series of interviews for inclusion in a 15-minute documentary that Paula Wolfson was preparing for April, to mark the first anniversary of Zimbabwe's independence. I supplied tape of Prime Minister Mugabe, taken from a long speech he made to the economic conference, and talked to others, such as Lord Soames, the British Governor who had overseen the transition between the white minority government and the guerrillas. Soames said it really had been "a remarkable year, there is a lot yet to be done, but Zimbabwe almost can be seen after one year as a oasis of stability in southern Africa." This was a prediction that the ensuing years would find to be seriously flawed.

One disappointment in Salisbury/Harare was that in re-naming most of the city's streets to honor African leaders and freedom fighters, "Chancellor Avenue" near the old British Governor's mansion had been changed, although the old sign remained for a while.

I talked with former Prime Minister Ian Smith about the exodus of several thousand white Rhodesians, who had left for South Africa and several Commonwealth countries. I spent some time with former rival guerrilla leader Joshua Nkomo, who I had been around many times, and who always seemed a more moderate and affable person than Mugabe. In the early months, Nkomo had been dismissed from the post of Home Affairs Minister in the Mugabe government.

In February, there had been fighting near Bulawayo between the men who had once fought under Nkomo and those who served under Mugabe – fighting that had to be broken up by the remnants of the white Rhodesian army. "The violence," Nkomo said, "like many of Zimbabwe's problems, is a result of the war. Ours is a country born of blood."

I discussed Zimbabwe's economic future with a very impressive spokesman, Minister of Economic Planning and Development, Bernard Chidzero, who predicted that after three years, Zimbabwe would not be asking for assistance from the international community, but would begin itself to contribute to the process of giving aid to other countries. You can check your history books to determine the validity of that optimism.

The Director of the U.S. Aid Agency, Peter McPherson was there – the first top official of the new Reagan administration to visit Africa, and he pledged aid of $75 million a year for each of the next three years.

Linda and I enjoyed the Zimbabwe trip, enjoyed the escape from the tensions of Israel, and appreciated the opportunity that we now had to travel together to some of those spots which only I had been able to visit before.

Because road travel was so easy in the wide expanses of southern Africa and I could always tuck Linda free into a hotel room paid for by VOA, she accompanied me on trips to Botswana, to Lesotho, and to Capetown and South Africa's garden coast. VOA travel regulations were strict – they would not pay for wives to accompany correspondents, nor for their meals, while we correspondents were on a per diem rate which usually was not quite high enough to cover costs. We always had to certify that hotel rooms were required because we were not provided U.S. government housing in places visited, and had to certify that any porter fees were for carrying "heavy government equipment" – in other words, correspondents otherwise should carry their own baggage.

Short trips to Capetown were frequent – five or six times a year. And traditionally, one of those trips was a long, two-week stay in January, for the opening of the Parliament. While Pretoria was the administrative capital of South Africa and the government offices were there, Capetown was the legislative capital. Every January, all the government Ministers and key aides would pack up from Pretoria and move operations to Capetown for a month. For reporters, it was an opportunity to get to know some members of the government better – everyone seemed to be in a better mood along the sunny sea-swept coast.

Linda flew back to the United States in May for Kim's graduation, *Magna Cum Laude*, from Drury College. The flight was at our expense, and I couldn't go, because I couldn't get away from work that long; because we couldn't afford two round-trip airfares; because someone had to stay in Johannesburg with Steven, and because we were scheduled for a home leave at the end of the year. I was certainly sorry to miss Kim's day of achievement.

Linda and Aunt Phoebe stayed in Kim's dormitory room during graduation. Afterward, Kim and Linda flew out to Wyoming for a visit with Craig, and then before Linda headed home, she, Georgia and Fred helped move Kim to Austin, Texas, where Kim had decided she wanted to make her life and career.

Linda also visited many old friends in Washington and spent some time with David. He had just been hired to manage the computer operation at Catholic University (where he had interned). She wrote her mother: *"Was I ever impressed. I just don't see how he managed to get as smart in just 21 years that he can run all those computers and even fix them when they go haywire."* David also was still working part-time at VOA as a night time operator in the operations studio – thus I got many free opportunities to talk with him while sending in news feeds.

One of my first tasks in South Africa was to hire an assistant, as had been approved by Washington. Even though VOA correspondents were no longer attached to the official U.S. establishment, assistants had to be hired through the local U.S.

Embassy personnel system. After looking at several applications, I selected Zodwa, a young, well-educated black, a resident of Soweto, who had gained some experience in journalism with Johannesburg's black newspaper.

Her hiring created some stir among the South African owners and operators of News Services, because no black had ever worked there except as a janitor. I wanted her because of her extensive contacts in the black community, whereas a white would simply talk to those same sources I could talk to. However, Zodwa did not work out – she was frequently late or absent and did poor work with administrative duties. I finally fired her when I found that she was copying my reports to VOA, and submitting them under her own byline to a Soweto weekly paper.

Enough of the experiment with political correctness. I hired American Claire Hone to work for me. She had some experience as a journalist and was married to Steve Hone, a Newsweek photographer and good friend. She stayed with me several months, but then she and Steve moved to the United States.

I next hired Paul Robinson, a young, white, bookish South African, a recent university graduate who wanted to be a journalist. Paul worked out well for VOA and even got to the point where he could file protective news items to Washington when I was out of town. He left after a time to take up a job as a news stringer in Harare because he was facing conscription into the South African army.

Next up was Dee Rissik, a white photo department assistant at the *Johannesburg Star* newspaper. She had little or no training as a journalist, but had ambition and boundless energy. She and her husband Nigel became social friends as well as work place friends. She was with me for a year, but quit to take a job as a film producer.

My last assistant was Delia Robertson, a friend first, who worked at the U.S. Consulate. I had some hesitation about her credentials as a journalist, in fact, I had passed her over to hire Dee. But Delia, too, was energetic and efficient, and I hired her just as my four year tour in South Africa was nearing its end. Delia obviously got along as well with all my successors as she did with me, because at last report, she remained at the VOA office for a long time, while writing books on the side.

Independence for Southwest Africa/Namibia was at the top of the international agenda for South Africa – the Reagan administration showed no signs of pressing the government for serious reform at home. Assistant Secretary of State for African Affairs, Chester Crocker, became a frequent visitor, but his attention was focused on Namibia under a policy he termed "constructive engagement." He paid scant attention to the situation in South Africa itself. Crocker did not like to talk to the press – he would slip into South Africa for talks with the government and slip away quietly. He often did not stay in hotels, but with a long-time friend, South African newspaper editor Tertius Myberg. I learned this, and also learned Myberg's home telephone number – and on several occasions, I called directly to Myberg's house, asked to speak with Mr. Crocker and got some exclusive information.

A United Nations conference was convened in Geneva – the first such talks in 30 years – to discuss implementation of a peace plan, which included a cease fire and supervised elections within a year. Namibia basically was a U.N. problem: the territory had been a German colony, given over to British protection after World War One, then handed over to South Africa by Britain before the Nationalists seized power and established apartheid. It had never been intended for it to be a South African possession.

The so-called terrorists of Namibia were guerillas of the Southwest Africa Peoples Organization, SWAPO, who operated primarily out of neighboring Angola, immediately to the north of Namibia. The South Africans were supplying arms and support to UNITA, a break-away Angolan liberation movement which waged a 25-year war against the leftist government in Luanda. It was a thousand-mile-long, tense border, with frequent forays across it by both sides.

One impediment was that Angola received financial support from the Soviet Union, and several thousand Cuban troops were there to provide physical support. South Africa was paranoid about the Cubans, arguing that South Africa itself was the intended target of an onslaught directed by Moscow. The black African front-line states, meanwhile, were equally paranoid about the presence of South African troops in Namibia and along the Angolan border.

Journalists from Johannesburg visited the border region on several occasions – some even were allowed across into UNITA-controlled territory, but I never did. I had been impressed with the UNITA leader, Jonas Savimbi when I first met him back in Lusaka several years earlier. The effectiveness of this Chinese-trained medical doctor and guerrilla leader is evidenced by the fact he was able to exist for more than 25 years of fighting in the midst of Africa. There is an old African expression: "When elephants wrestle, only the grass gets trampled." Savimbi obviously was more than grass. (The Angola civil war finally ended after his death in 2002 with 500,000 Angolans dead and millions more impoverished and displaced.)

There's that red car again, parked outside the Union Building, the main government office, in Pretoria, South Africa.

Correspondents Report, August 27, 1981:
The frontier between Namibia and Angola is a long and tense border. The line stretches from the Atlantic Ocean to the tip of the Caprivi Strip in the very center of the African continent. It passes through desert, swamp and heavy bush, heavily populated and virtually unpopulated stretches of land, following rivers and the lines drawn by colonial planners.

In June, 1981, I had my first chance to go back to Kenya. Sean Kelly, who had replaced me in Nairobi, had moved on to another post, and a new correspondent, Hugh Muir, was on his way to Nairobi and a first overseas assignment. The opening of the Organization of African Unity annual summit meeting was scheduled the same day as Hugh's arrival, and it was felt he would need help with such a major event.

I knew at Kenyatta Airport that things had changed in Kenya since Kenyatta's death and Daniel Arap Moi had consolidated his hold on power. I was asked for a bribe in order to clear customs – something that never would have happened under Kenyatta. I refused, and was waved on through anyway. But in discussing this incident with a friend in Nairobi, he observed that Kenya currently was like a sugar cube, sitting on the edge of a saucer full of coffee, slowly dissolving and crumbling.

Muir would learn this firsthand a few months later, when a female friend of his was visiting from Washington. Hugh was driving a BMW sedan, which Kelly had obtained for the office car, and he and his companion were followed home from a downtown restaurant. The car pulled in behind Hugh's vehicle, trapping it up against the gate. When Hugh and his companion refused to open the car door for the inevitable robbery, the pursuers shot at them through the car window, killing the visitor. That, too, would not have happened so blatantly in Kenyatta's time.

There were in South Africa internal pressures for internal change. One of those voices was Harry Oppenheimer, the leader in South African gold and diamond mining, as well as real estate and other business interests. By far the richest man in a rich country, his Anglo-American Corporation was said

to responsible for more than 25% of South Africa's total private sector output.

One year, Anglo-American reported on its annual diamond production — so many thousand carets of stones. I asked what that amounted to in volume; turned out to be about one load in a pick-up truck.

Linda and I had the chance for a couple of other excursions in those busy first months in South Africa, as did Steven. The three of us were included in an outing for the foreign media conducted by the information section of the Department of Foreign Affairs, to visit with Afrikaner farmers in the far northeast of the country, near Mozambique. About 50 of us in all were flown to the area aboard a South African Air Force Hercules transport early on a Saturday morning, and were guests at a large community gathering/picnic.

That gave us the opportunity to have conversations with many of these folks, mostly successful, large-scale farmers. After the big community gathering, we broke up into small groups and went away with host families. Linda, Steven and I and one other couple went with one family to their home, where we toured their farm, conversed, had dinner and spent the night. After breakfast the next day, the larger group reconvened, and the media group and our escorts boarded busses for a motor tour of the countryside, and up to the Mozambique border, before flying back to the Air Force base at Pretoria.

Steven also had the chance to go to Zimbabwe. One of his Woodmead schoolmates was a white Rhodesian, son of a doctor at Mtale in eastern Zimbabwe. Rather than spend weekends in the dormitories, Nick Walker often came to our house and became almost a member of the family. During one break, he invited Steven to come back home with him to Zimbabwe for several days.

And then Linda and I got the chance to go to Sun City and see Frank Sinatra. Sun City was in one of the so-called tribal homelands — a reservation in effect — set aside for one of the country's many black groups. This particular homeland, north and west of Pretoria, named Bophutaswana, was made up of a lot of non-contiguous areas of land that was not of much value for anything, including farming. By holding to the fiction that these "homelands" were independent and the blacks had their own countries and governments, the white government was hard pressed to exert much control over the homelands. Thus, the homelands began to open casinos which were forbidden in South Africa -- much as the Indian reservations in the United States have done.

Bophutaswana had a contract with a white South African hotelier, Sol Kerzner, to develop a hotel/resort/casino in it's homeland, which was close enough to the population centers of Pretoria and Johannesburg to attract a large number of fun seekers. The aim also was to provide work for the blacks in their homelands. Kerzner spent many millions building his Sun City resort and casino. In true Las Vegas fashion, part of the resort was a large theater, and somehow he managed to book Frank Sinatra as the opening act for the opening week of Sun City.

It was always a bit of puzzle how Sinatra was persuaded to do this. Many entertainers viewed the homelands as a farce designed only to perpetuate South Africa's racial separation policy, and refused to perform anywhere in South Africa. Sinatra was one of those who had a strong pro-civil-rights record in the United States. But he and his advisers bought into the fiction of the "independent homeland" and agreed to perform.

Kerzner had an active public relations program in South Africa and invited many representatives of the media, both local and foreign, to the grand opening of Sun City; and to Sinatra's show.

I will let Linda tell the rest of it, as she did in a letter to her mother in July:

"There was a short press conference of Sinatra's manager about noon, and he said we could come to the door at rehearsal time, but it wouldn't do much good, as the big man never, ever saw the press. We dutifully went, however, and they let us in to his rehearsal. There he was, not 20 feet away from my very eyes, belting out the likes of "Bewitched," "New York," and "My Way."

It was unbelievable to have a star of that magnitude just right there in front of me and giving a concert for some 25 people. Not only did he sing for 45 minutes, but then he sat down on the edge of the stage and talked to the press for another 20 minutes in a very casual, informal way. I tell you, I was impressed. He looks very good and his voice was strong and clear.

We went on to the concert that night, along with almost 5,000 other people and although I enjoyed it immensely, I'll never forget that rehearsal when I felt like he was singing to me privately.

A strange story relayed by Linda to her mother: *"We are the proud owners of a white Persian cat. Right after our return from home leave, Bob and I went out to the SPCA to get a kitten for [our cat] Scarlett, whose brother was killed by a car earlier this year. Believe it not, the SPCA had not one kitten in the whole place, so we came home rather dejectedly, planning to look in the newspaper or somewhere for a kitten. Well, upon our return, there was this magnificent white Persian sitting on our front porch! He came right in, had lunch, curled up for a nap on the sofa and has been our constant companion and most favorite cat ever since.! I have since had him to the vet, where I was told he was about eight months old and he had all his shots and was neutered, and not in all this time has anyone ever come looking for him."*

Note: we named him "Flake," and he moved back to Texas and then Missouri with us and lived a long happy life. He was the most relaxed, laid back cat we have ever known. But how did he know we needed a kitten?

CHAPTER 32 — THE WORKING PRESS

As a member of the News Services family, I was well connected with the foreign press contingent in South Africa. Others sharing the offices at 52 Simmonds St. in downtown Johannesburg included the Associated Press bureau, Newsweek, CBS News, the Washington Post, and the British newspapers, the Guardian, the Times of London, the Daily Telegraph and the Financial Times. A couple of blocks away was the Reuters News Agency office, where I also had some close friends and colleagues (including Rob Batsford, with whom I had worked a lot in Zambia) and the New York Times bureau headed by future NYT Managing Editor Joe Lelyveld. Journalists from both these places would meet many evenings at a bar called "The Guild Hall," halfway between the two.

I had been active in the foreign press association in Israel, and had not been in Johannesburg a month when the Foreign Correspondents Association of South Africa held its annual meeting and elected me secretary. The next year I was elected vice president and then president; and I spent 18 months in that office. Although it was a lot of work, it greatly increased my contacts with government officials, who preferred to deal with the foreign press in a large organized setting rather than on an individual basis. Often as the representative of the foreign press, I would have to protest some action or another by the government or try to win some concession or a coverage situation.

We were still in our first year when old faces began showing up from old places. The AP sent Nairobi bureau chief Andrew Torchia to Johannesburg to run its bureau, replacing Bill Nicholson, who went to ABC television. Nino Alimenti, the Italian news agency correspondent in Kenya, also moved south. Dan Yett, the USIS regional librarian in Nairobi, who had replaced Ben Whitten, was transferred to Johannesburg. And Richard and Susan Weeks were sent to the American Consulate in Johannesburg from Jerusalem. Through Susan, we made another close friend, a Canadian doctor, Sandra Allaire.

I worked closely with all the AP reporters:

Nicholson, Torchia, Jim Smith, Jim Peipert, and particularly a reporter/editor named Terry Anderson. Several of us played poker each week with Anderson (who usually won). He usually was desk-bound in the AP office, but I remember one day, when there had been a plane hi-jacking and the released hostages flew to Johannesburg, we went to the airport together. He exalted in being out on a story, and a few months later, seeking more action than Johannesburg offered, transferred to become bureau chief in Beirut, where he was captured and held prisoner for seven years. Terry was replaced by Tom Baldwin, whose talented wife, Tony, did some work for me and other radio stations as a stringer.

Another media colleagues was Bill Mutschmann, a CBS cameraman and producer. He had spent years in Rhodesia and had a British/Rhodesian wife, Doreen. They were good friends socially. Bill, nicknamed "Mutters," had his own airplane, and often would arrange charter flights for a group of journalists to some outlying town for a story.

There is one of those "small world" stories about Bill. He and Doreen were building a retirement home on the Algarve coast of Portugal, and one day Bill mentioned in conversation that he hoped to install a hot tub at the home. "I can do it cheaply," he said, "because I have a close friend who is the Africa sales representative for Jacuzzi." I interrupted to ask if his Jacuzzi friend happened to be Gary Hill (Linda's high school classmate and my fraternity brother, who we had run into in Nairobi Hospital). Yes, Bill said, he and Gary had shared a house in West Africa.

Another reporter I admired a lot was Marsh Clark, the bureau chief for Time Magazine. We had more interaction with Marsh and Pippa socially than professionally, but Marsh and I had one thing in common: we were both Missourians. He came from the politically prominent Clark family, which had produced a Speaker of the House of Representatives; I was descended (distantly) from the Stark family, a competing clan that produced a Missouri Governor.

Bob and Jack Foisie on the job

Jack Foisie of the Los Angeles Times, and his wife, Mickey, were other close friends – I had known Jack since Vietnam —as was Peter Hawthorne, who was a free lancer working for both BBC and Time. Vick Aiken of NBC-TV and his bride, Leslie, arrived from Tel Aviv.

One of the first things I did as president was change the name of the press organization to "Foreign Correspondents Association of Southern Africa," due to black Africa's suspicion of anyone directly connected with South Africa. I'm not sure it made a whole lot of difference, but I felt better about it, especially when I traveled north on the continent.

The Foreign Correspondents Association had a couple of memorable annual meetings. My first year in office, it was at a colleague's home, around the pool, and irrepressible Susan Weeks – with more than a full load of wine – chose to skinny dip the length of the pool, doing the back stroke, in the presence of such luminaries as the government information minister.

The next year's bash was in the backyard of Nino Alimenti's home (no pool for Susan) under a huge tent. I had invited Bishop Desmond Tutu and was surprised when he attended. I thought it only fitting that he say grace before we tucked into a catered meal of shrimp and lobster and lots of good South African wine. The diminutive Bishop climbed atop a chair, and said something brief in the Xhosa language – it sounded like "Ooga booga click clock." Then he grinned, looked heavenward, and said: "He understands." It was really a classy performance under those raucous circumstances.

In November, 1981, we started out for our first home leave from South Africa, after the end of Steven's school year. It was the start of a packed, six-week trip. Linda, Steven and I flew to London, landing at Heathrow Airport, and made a connection via helicopter to Gatwick Airport for a direct flight to Dallas, Texas, where we were met by Kim and her room-mate, Becky Bergland. Becky had been a good friend of Kim's at the International School of Kenya, and had gone to college in Minnesota, but had been convinced by Kim and other ISK alums to move south to Austin.

We all crammed into their apartment on First Avenue in Austin, and Linda and I got involved in house-hunting. Since we had the proceeds from the sale of the house in Bowie – and it would be taxable as a capital gain if not reinvested in another house – we decided to buy a house in Austin, and rent it to Kim and Becky. We found a four-bedroom home with a pool, on Bend Cove, near Barton Creek in south Austin. The shared rent, with the addition of another room-mate or two, would be cheaper than their apartment. It also provided us with a legal address in the United States.

One of the goals of this trip was to find a school for Steven. Linda had written her mother about it:

We are all three adamant about getting him back to the States to pick up credits he has lost by studying things like Middle Eastern history, Hebrew, Afrikaans, Voortrekker (Afrikaner) history and all the silly stuff they feed kids abroad. What he really needs is American history, French or Spanish and geography. He can give you a complete history of the life of a Masai warrior, but I'll bet he hasn't a clue whether the Rhine flows through Germany or Peoria, Illinois.

Enroute to Missouri from Austin, we stopped at a private boarding school in Denton, Texas. We had been in communication with them, they had agreed to accept our student, and it was our favorite choice. But upon visiting there, school officials were reluctant to admit him because of his recent grades. Over the next few days, we mutually agreed that that was not the school for him. In Missouri, we visited Kemper Military Academy at Boonville and a fancy private school in St. Louis affiliated with Washington University. Students at the St. Louis school were reading Greek classics, in Greek, and that sounded a bit beyond Steven. Kemper wanted him, but we felt the Kemper facilities were run down, and we were skeptical of the military school environment.

The search continued, mostly by long distance phone, until we settled on Villa Oasis boarding school at Casa Grande, Arizona, and we committed to enrolling him there after the Christmas break.

We spent that Christmas in St. Louis, with brother Steve and Kay, and their children, Chris and Alison. We managed to make a real family reunion of it: David flew in from Washington, Kim flew up from Austin, Craig and Donna flew in from Casper. Steven was with us, and Aunt Louise came up from Fredericktown.

After Christmas, Linda, Steven and I drove back to Texas to complete the house purchase. Linda and Steven flew to Phoenix to enroll Steven in his new school. It was a traumatic day for Linda, to drop off her baby at a place he had never seen, in the middle of the Arizona desert, and then get on a plane back to Texas. I met her in Dallas, and we headed again for Missouri.

Our next mission was to buy a car for David, which we found in Springfield, and Linda and I drove it from Springfield to Washington to deliver it. This trip came during one of the coldest, snowiest winters in U.S. history. I remember a TV weatherman showing a map of the United States, all white from the Rockies to the east coast, and he noted: That white stuff is not clouds, it is a snow cover as photographed from space.

The car was a little Chevy Monza two door hatchback. We had all of our luggage, plus of lot of stuff we had purchased to take back to South Africa. And we were carrying to David one of his prized possessions – a three-foot-tall wooden carving of a very well endowed old African man. David had requested the carving as his graduation

present in Nairobi. It had been shipped to Springfield when we went on home leave in 1979. It lived in Fred's office for a year or so (and gathered giggles from office visitors who were advised to look under the robe the statue wore). Tucked in between the two seats of the Monza, the little "big man" was enroute home to his owner.

We did the usual round of Washington meetings and reunions with old friends before heading back to South Africa. I also did a television tape interview with Herman Nickel, the newly-appointed U.S. Ambassador in Pretoria, for airing on South African television.

Once again we traveled via Paris, and stayed with our friends, Ben and Mary Ann Whitten. By this time, I was in my Texas land owner mode, and got off the plane wearing a huge Stetson hat Kim had given me for Christmas. I had a lot of fun talking about the "ranch" we had bought back in Texas – the four-bedroom ranch style house, with swimming pool, on Bend Cove.

After all that home leave activity, it was almost a relief to be back in South Africa and back at work. And it was a new year, 1982, and our first year with an empty nest. Linda began working part-time at News Services, clipping and filing stories and doing basic research for several of the British correspondents.

Before home leave, we had contracted with a local service to provide house sitters for our place in Johannesburg – far safer than leaving a house vacant and unattended. We interviewed a young couple that was recommended by the agency, and agreed they could live in our house during our absence. Linda reported the bad results in a letter to her mother when we got back to Johannesburg:

On arriving home, we find that our house sitters were not quite the genteel folk we thought – neighbors reported wild parties, furniture in the pool, vile language, cats not fed, servants fired, etc. Took me awhile, but I finally got the place put right side up and the gardener and the maid both came back with even more horrendous stories. On top of everything else, they broke some of my Palestinian pottery and drank every drop of liquor in the house, and it had been under lock and key.

Our landlord, Dr. Van Osleyn, decided to raise the rent on the house on Verdi. He didn't want to spend any money to fix it up (or to put a security and privacy wall across the front, as most houses in Johannesburg had). Instead, he wanted us to move to another, huge house he owned closer to the city center. He announced this scheme to move us to the big house, which cost nearly double the rent on Verdi, and when I responded that we couldn't afford that much rent, added: "It won't cost any more than this one once I raise the rent here." I blew up, all but physically threw him out of the house, and Linda and I began house hunting again.

We found a neat, older house at 2 Park Avenue – just a couple of blocks from Edith's old place by the zoo, in the Parktown North neighborhood where we had always wanted to live. The owner had lived in it while he did an extensive remodeling, and now was ready to move on to another project. He jumped at the chance to put it under lease to the U.S. government. The house had three bedrooms and a den – we only needed one bedroom, but kept a second equipped for Steven or guests, used the third as a TV room, and the den as an office. There was a huge kitchen with every modern convenience imaginable. The hallway and bedrooms had retained their old pressed-tin ceilings. Between the living room and the office/den was a little room we converted into a full-time bar.

We were short some furniture, so Linda and Susan Weeks began shopping for antiques to fill it out. They found a teakwood opium bed which was converted into a sofa, and a tall, dark dining room buffet. Marion Torchia helped me find an antique armoire with stained glass windows, which we used for a bedroom closet. Those items are still in our house today and are among our most prized belongings. There was a pool out back in a tiny yard, a basement garage for the MG, and a servant's apartment with a full bath including a tub, which was a rarity for South African housing.

We moved, and set up our gardener from Verdi in the servant's apartment. Apartheid regulations did not allow Africans to live in the white parts of the city unless they were registered as servants living in their "master's" compound. Enoch only worked for us two days a week, but he was a gentle and honest man whose family lived several hundred miles away on a tribal homeland. I was glad to have him there to watch over things, especially at those times when I was traveling.

We had a maid, too, an older African woman named Lillian, who lived in Soweto and commuted by bus to work for us two or three days a week. She was a level-headed woman, who was constantly concerned about her grandchildren growing up and surviving in the rough streets of Soweto and was also concerned that any trouble could result in her family being booted out of their government-owned two-room house in Soweto. Here arose an opportunity for us to again repay Walt McClughan's tremendous favor to us so many years earlier.

A typical Soweto house

The government announced a new program which would allow the blacks in Soweto to purchase their government-owned houses, giving them a stake and permanency that they had never had before. Of course, very, very few of Soweto's blacks could even consider the $2000 cost of buying. It seemed like a good idea to Linda and me, and we talked to Lillian, who was eager to be a homeowner. So we gave her the money to buy her Soweto home – she swore it was just a loan that she would pay back someday. She never had the wherewithal to do so, and we never really expected it, but we felt good about helping her improve her life and the future prospects for her family.

Civilization was being extended to Soweto in other ways, too. Soweto was a separate, black city, set aside for Africans, about ten miles from Johannesburg. It had a population of more than one million, and its residents had spent their lives in darkness and cold, knowing only the light of candles, the heat of coal or kerosene.. Electricity was to be supplied to the black township

Number Two Park Avenue was a great little house for parties, and we entertained there often with small dinners and larger affairs. Our guests were a mixture of diplomatic and journalistic folks, and our living room and bar were a frequent stopover for drinks and snacks after a show or some other event.

Fingers at News Services had arranged for the installation of a telephone line to Park Avenue (which was a rare accomplishment in Johannesburg). But it was listed as a News Services telephone and billed directly back to him. Fingers, in turn, would bill the VOA bureau for telephones (both at home and at the office) but never with an itemized bill, just a monthly lump sum. With a large number of overseas phone calls going to the United States from both home and office for feeds of news materials, it did not take long to recognize that a few phone calls to kids in the United States would not even be noticed.

Federal regulations for Americans overseas set out an allowance for installing draperies in newly leased housing. Linda had drapes installed in the living room when we moved to Park Avenue, only for me to be informed by one of VOA's officials that VOA would NOT pay for drapes. I made several representations to the VOA brass about this, quoting chapter, verse and page number of the regulations, only to be told "We don't care what the regulations say, VOA will not buy your drapes."

Instead, Fingers purchased our drapes, and charged the cost back to VOA in four successive month's telephone bills. Once, several years later I told a VOA administrator, who had been sympathetic to our argument: "VOA bought our drapes. I challenge you to find the expenditure." My rationale then, and still today, was that it was the VOA brass that were not following the regulations, we were only finding a way to uphold them.

We have on our living room floor to this day, a beautiful hand-woven wool carpet from Ethiopia. We first saw this carpet in the home of the Public Affairs Officer in Addis Ababa in 1976. Later, when all the U.S. officials were run out of Ethiopia, most of those furnishings were shipped to a warehouse in Nairobi. Also stored in that warehouse was a carpet which one of my Nairobi predecessors had purchased, but someone, in their zeal to clean out the warehouse, had thrown away the VOA carpet. When we needed a carpet for the second Nairobi house, and the VOA carpet had been lost, we were offered the Ethiopian carpet instead, and accepted it. When we moved to Israel, it went along, then on to South Africa, and somehow it followed us home to the United States

In March, 1982, a big trial was scheduled in the district court at Pietermaritzburg. A group of South African mercenaries, led by the legendary soldier of fortune Mike Hoare, had tried to foment a coup in the Seychelles, but were driven back, and were arrested when they reached South Africa. (That was the story that so enthralled Terry Anderson.) They were to be tried — a good international story. The court room in Pietermaritzburg was tiny, and would hold only a dozen journalists at a time. The Foreign Correspondents Association was allotted three of those seats, but it was up to us to parcel them out. We did, by a drawing each day of the trial if there were more than three applicants.

The large contingent of us was staying at a hotel in Pietermaritzburg, and the owner was so glad to have the business that he paid to install a telephone line and loudspeaker at the hotel, so those who could not get into the courtroom could at least hear the proceedings. And the Mayor of Pietermaritzburg was so happy to have this large crowd of foreign journalists in their town she held a reception for all of us. As president of the FCA, it was my duty to respond to her welcome speech, which I did with these words: "It's so nice to be greeted and welcomed to a place. Usually, the government wants to throw us out."

We were able to take another long trip in May. We drove a total of 2667 miles, stopping the first day at the dusty little country town of Graaf Reinet. We went on to Capetown touring the wineries and the scenic Cape of Good Hope. We headed east, across the south coast of South Africa, to the beach resort of Mossel Bay and then to the Beacon Island Hotel at Plettensburg. We headed home via Port Elizabeth, and Bloemfonteine.

One source of entertainment was Johannesburg's Market Theater in a building that for 70 years had served as the city's fruit and vegetable market, and which had been converted to three auditoriums. It was one of the anomalies of the apartheid state.

Correspondent's Report, November 20, 1981: The Market Theater has been described as a major force in South African theater. Many of its productions have been experimental, avant-garde and controversial. It has provided a home for black theater in a country with a wealth of black theatrical talent. It has been a repository of political drama in a country not noted for its tolerance of political criticism. One controversial play which opened at the Market, "The Island" went on to win the coveted Tony Award when it played in the United States.

In November, I made another trip to Zambia and on to Nairobi. In Lusaka, they were holding another of the innumerable conferences on independence for South Africa. The highlight of that trip was to meet Oliver Tambo, who was a close friend and colleague of Nelson Mandela, and who served as the African National Congress representative to the outside world. He was a fan of VOA and made it a point to talk to me at a reception about how things were going back in his homeland. He also introduced me to his aide, who over the next couple of years would become a good source. He was a very bright, impressive young man, named Thabo Mbeki, who later would become Mandela's vice president and eventually the President of South Africa.

In Kenya, the story was the United States Navy making its first ever port call to Mombasa. I joined up with AP's Jim Peipert, who had recently moved to Nairobi from Johannesburg. An aircraft carrier and four support ships pulled into Mombasa, and suddenly the quiet harbor town that I was so familiar with began to look like Norfolk, Virginia, with sailors in white uniforms everywhere. They swarmed the bars, the beaches and took off for game viewing safaris. They were a well behaved 4000 sailors and there were none of the anticipated incidents.

The day I was to leave Mombasa, fly to Nairobi and make a connecting flight back to Johannes-

burg, Kenya Airways stopped all domestic flights for some reason. Normally it wouldn't bother me to spend another night or two at the beach, but there was something pressing I had to get back for (I don't remember what, but there was always something pressing). At the Mombasa airport, with no planes flying, three of us decided to rent a car and drive back to Nairobi, up a highway that certainly was familiar to me.

We were making good time up the dreaded highway, past Tsavo Game Reserve, when the Avis car ran out of gas. I should have known better, and should have filled the tank at Voi when I had a chance. But there we were, stranded along the highway, a familiar feeling. We flagged down a passing vehicle which was headed for Nairobi, transferred our luggage, and left the rental car at the roadside. I made my flight that night to Johannesburg, after sending the keys and a note to Avis, telling them they could find their car somewhere south of Nairobi along the highway. Apparently they did, because I never heard any more about it.

Above: Interviewing soldiers in Namibia.

Below: I often was able to get Linda accredited as the VOA photographer.

CHAPTER 33— OKAVANGO AND A TEXAS VISITOR

Steven returned to Johannesburg for the 1982 summer vacation. We hoped to find him a summer job, but nothing materialized except busy work. He helped some friends move, he tended bar at friends' parties, and he cleaned houses and swimming pools. He was not without transportation – the Yetts had gone away on home leave and left their car with him to use. And Linda was working for the British newspapers, in the Newsweek office, and occasionally typing for the U.S. Consulate; so Steven took on the task of doing the shopping and errands, which was a big help.

Bill Mutschman came to the rescue with a proposed trip of a lifetime. One of his colleagues had just returned from the Okavango Swamp in neighboring Botswana, and Bill proposed that Linda, Steven and I join him and his wife, Doreen, and visit the Okavango. He would fly us up in his Beechcraft if we would share expenses for the plane, and he would make all the arrangements. So, in July, we were airborne to Maun, the biggest town in the Okavango region.

The Okavango is an unusual area – half of the year, it is a totally dry and barren grassland, but in the summertime, rains to the north in Angola would gather into rivers that headed south into the near-desert conditions. The dry grasslands become a water wonderland, studded with thousands of tiny islands that are no more than hilltops in the dry season. The abundant water concentrates the usually widespread wildlife onto these hillocks, and fish miraculously appear in the waters. Grass and trees and brush and reeds burst into green for the three-month wet season.

Travel in the Okavango is by *mocorro*, or low canoes, hewn from solid logs, propelled by pole, navigated and operated by Botswanan tribesmen. From Maun, we had flown to XaXaBa camp, (pronounced Kah-Kah-Bah) at the edge of the swamp, where we stayed one night in a thatch-roofed hut as our four boat party was outfitted. The next morning, we headed out into the Okavango, seated on the bottoms of the low-riding *mocorros,* with the water and reeds sliding by silently almost at eye level. It was quiet and peaceful, and after a couple of hours in the tippy craft, we began to feel quite at home.

We spent three days and two nights in the swamps and never saw another human, just our party of five, a guide, and four boatsmen. We camped at night on the hilltops. Shelter was provided by stringing a rope between two trees, and attaching to that rope mosquito nets that reached to the ground and were tucked under the edges of foam mattress pads. We ate around a campfire, while

the mosquito net tents swayed in the firelight like encircling ghosts.

Our second night out was when we met the lions. During various excursions ashore, we had seen signs of lions, usually pug marks, or tracks, in the mud as they traversed from one hillock to the next. At our second encampment, our boatsmen had caught some fish and were smoking them over a nightlong fire to preserve them.

Do these mosquito nets count as tents? Are tents really safe from lions? Do lions know it?

We were all asleep, when about midnight, Doreen got up to go to the bathroom on the far side of a large tree near our tents. She screamed "lions!" and we were all immediately awake. As much as her scream scared us, it scared the lions even more – they turned and ran away from the camp area toward which they had been headed. Later, we heard the splashing as they crossed to the next island. No one was harmed, but it put our nerves on edge.

Were we in danger? To this day, I don't know, but I don't think so. I think they were attracted to the fish. Besides, I had been told many years earlier that lions would not attack people in tents, or would not enter tents to grab people. I don't know if that is true, or if the lions knew it, or if our string of mosquito nets qualified as lion-repelling tents. But there wasn't much we could do about it anyway, except to put some more logs on the fire and crawl back into the safety of our sleeping quarters.

What was perhaps most disconcerting was that we had no guns with us – the white guide, a displaced Rhodesian, did not carry a weapon and neither did the boatsmen, although their leader did have a rickety old spear. They all admitted that they had never before had such an experience.

The next morning we tracked the lions and found that they apparently had been crossing our island, when they stopped and made a 90 degree turn toward our camp, probably to investigate the smell of cooking fish (or the smell of sleeping people). There were four or five of them – one had run to within 20 feet of Doreen's tree when she spotted it and sounded the alarm. The lion had skidded to a stop, turned on his tracks and they all ran away. We photographed the paw prints – the largest one was six inches across, and Bill somehow made a mold of it, which Doreen later converted into an ashtray.

The next night, by plan, we were back in our hut at XaXaBa camp (no electricity, but with flush toilets) and the following day we boarded our plane and flew on to Savuti camp in the Chobe game reserve. We were at Savuti two nights, sleeping in tents, and watching hundreds of animals, including many elephants, during the day at the Savuti River watering hole.

Our last night at Savuti, Bill suggested that Steven should see Victoria Falls since we were so close. So at morning, instead of heading south to Johannesburg, we flew northeast to the largest waterfall in the world. I had seen the falls from the Zambian side several years earlier. It was Linda's third trip to the falls – she had been there on a quick trip with Beverly Yett, and on a bus excursion from Salisbury, but to fly over the falls in an airplane is the best way to view and appreciate this spectacular sight.

After the flyover, we made an unannounced landing at the town of Victoria Falls and once we convinced the authorities we were just tourists, not spies or mercenaries, we bummed a ride into town and booked into a hotel. We spent the rest of the day touring around the falls by foot. The next day, we flew back to Johannesburg, where it was time to get Steven packed up and on his way back to school in Arizona.

Even though Steven had spent the summer vacation with us, he was also authorized to come and visit us over Christmas. Kim, too, had one authorized round trip to South Africa from her last year of college. We were looking forward to both of them coming and then Kim upped the ante: She had a new boyfriend, by the name of Jeff Carter, and she had convinced him to come to South Africa with her. We hadn't met Jeff, but had heard about him in letters and figured this must be a serious relationship. Sometime in mid-December, we went to Jan Smuts Airport and picked up Steven, Kim and Jeff, with plans for a great holiday showing them around South Africa.

There had to be a game-viewing trip, especially for Jeff, so we booked three days at Londolozi, a wildlife refuge well to the east of Johannesburg. Linda and I had been there previously, and had even taken visitors there. Kim and Steven, of course, had seen a lot of wildlife in Kenya, but animal watching in the game reserves is always a delight.

Richard and Susan Weeks heard about our plans and asked if they could join us on this safari. They knew and liked both Kim and Steven. Linda was reluctant – she was, after all, about to entertain what might prove to be her future son-in-law and she wasn't sure she was willing to introduce this young man to our uninhibited friend. Susan pleaded and begged, and eventually Linda relented, extracting a solemn promise from Susan that she would behave. "Oh, yes. Absolutely!"

The day after the kids arrival, we were on our way to Londolozi in a two car caravan. Enroute, we stopped at roadside for a picnic breakfast – Susan, good to her word so far, had prepared a feast of bread, cheese, deviled eggs and fruit. We were enjoying this repast, marveling at the beautiful open countryside, and getting acquainted with Kim's still-shy boyfriend, when suddenly there was the loud report of an explosion nearby. We all looked up and around us, and Susan asked: "What the F--- was that?" Then we all looked at each other, and at Linda's stern countenance – Susan had done it again. But then we all broke out laughing – the ice had been broken.

Susan remained on moderately good behavior the remainder of the trip, except one night at the game reserve when we heard, and then saw, the rare sight of two lions mating. She could not help but make several lewd observations about animal behavior.

After Londolozi, the five of us (without Susan and Richard) headed to Capetown in a VW van I had borrowed. Kim was insistent that we must stop over in the town of Kimberley, noted for its huge open pit diamond mine. She needed to buy souvenirs containing the town name. We spent several days touring the Cape area, staying in an apartment owned and maintained by Newsweek.

From Capetown, we drove across the south coast of South Africa – what was called the Garden Route – along the Indian Ocean, and headed inland back to Johannesburg for Christmas.

Kim and Jeff had to head back to Austin right after Christmas, but we felt we had had the opportunity to get to know our prospective son-in-law. Steven was able to stay on in South Africa well into January before his school resumed.

Linda and I celebrated our 25th wedding anniversary in March, '83, in Johannesburg. Susan Weeks said she had never known anyone to be married for 25 years to the same person, thus the event deserved a big party. Susan and Richard organized it all at their house, with some cooking help from Linda. We invited about 100 of our closest friends to attend. We filled a bathtub with ice and bottles of South African wine, about one bottle per invitee, plus we had a full bar. Most of the 100 attended, and ate and danced until the early morning hours. Most also brought Silver Anniversary presents, which we had not expected, and after most of the guests had left, Linda and I, Susan and Richard, and a few other night owls stayed up until well after dawn, opening gifts and doing a full recap of the festivities. We all had a great time.

Somehow, in May of 1983, we were eligible for home leave again. (I never understood why exactly, but when the round trip tickets were offered, we took them.) This time, it was just Linda and me traveling, and we made a return trip to spend five days in Israel. Back in the American

Colony, which was really beginning to feel like home. We visited favorite haunts and several favorite restaurants, including The Gondola in Jericho. For the first time in our footloose life, Linda and I both caught a terrible case of dysentery, which stayed with us for a week or more. We flew to Houston, where we were met by Kim and Jeff, and went on to Austin. During our stay in Austin, Jeff and Kim announced their plans to get married the following year.

One primary objective of this home leave trip was Steven's graduation from high school, so Linda and I flew to Phoenix, and headed for Casa Grande. It was my first visit to the school, and Linda's only return since dropping her baby off in the desert a year and a half earlier. After graduation, the three of us, in a rental car, headed north to visit the Grand Canyon. From there, we followed back roads on the west side of the Rockies – the back slope – even farther northward to Casper to visit Craig, and his girlfriend (and future wife) Donna Fowler.

From Casper, we flew to Springfield and a visit with Georgia and Fred. Steven headed on to Austin, where he planned to live with Kim and Becky in the Bend Cove house and attend Austin Community College. Linda and I made our obligatory trip to Washington for consultations, and to spend some time with David. We returned to Johannesburg from the six weeks of home leave at the end of June.

My Texas ranch-owner persona had become more than just a running joke. In Washington, VOA had a whole new top management team as a result of the Reagan administration. During my meetings with the new Program Director, Sid Davis, a former NBC news executive, and with Gene Pell, the Deputy Program Director for news, they revealed they had plans for a great expansion of domestic U.S. coverage for VOA's worldwide audience, and within those plans was the idea of a Texas bureau, to cover the space program and news in the southwestern United States.

They said they had me in mind for the Texas bureau, and that it probably would occur after the next South African tour of duty. It almost seemed to make buying the house in Austin make sense.

Linda and I both were thinking beyond four years in South Africa to: What? – with the kids now all in the states, did we really want to stay so far away with another foreign assignment. Texas sounded like a chance to be closer to the family, and still avoid the dreaded idea of reassignment to Washington.

I made two trips back to Kenya during 1983. The first was to help a newly-assigned VOA correspondent there, Dan Robinson, get settled into a new office, and help set up his studio. The Foreign Correspondents Association of Kenya had somehow wangled a whole floor of a new office building in Nairobi, and had installed offices for most of the foreign press, and a press club lounge. It was a great setup for working there.

While there, staying at the Intercontinental Hotel, I met a Finnish racecar driver, Rauno Aaltonen, who was in Kenya preparing for a forthcoming Safari Rally. He invited me to spend a day with him as he prepared for the race, and we headed down the Mombasa highway to the Tsavo area. He was part of the Nissan race team, and offered to take me out for a run over part of the Safari Rally track – not a track, really, or a road, but a set of rutted tire tracks across the barren landscape. He put me in the passenger seat, belted me in, and we took off at 160 miles an hour across the plains. We had an intercom, with head sets and lip mikes, so we could talk to each other. I had rigged a tape recorder to the headset to try to record his comments and make a story of it.

I have never been afraid of fast driving – in fact I have been known to do so myself. But there is a big difference in my daring 80 MPH, and crossing open country on a dirt path at twice that speed. I learned that he was looking much farther down the road than I was, as he anticipated the next turn or bump. At one point he said, "See that open ditch up ahead on the left? I am going to skid up onto my two right wheels to get over the hole." By the time I figured out what he was talking about – the ditch was nearly a mile ahead – he was already up on two wheels while my side of the car was in the air over the ditch and settling down on the far side. I wasn't aware scenery could go by that fast. We drove for about an hour – I enjoyed every minute of it. But the tape re-

cording didn't work because there was too much background noise to hear his commentary.

The Safari Rally had started in 1953, 4000 miles across Kenya, Uganda and Tanzania, to mark the inauguration of Queen Elizabeth, It had become a big annual event in Kenya, attracting many racing teams from Europe, although most often, it was won by a Kenyan citizen, a Sikh named Joginder Singh or Ugandan Shektar Mehta. The race has been described as the "most exacting test for mankind and machine yet devised in the world of rallying," as cars and driver slog through mud and choking dust, crossing deserts and climbing mountains, and crossing the equator several times. My friend Aaltonen did not win that year – in fact, he never won it but finished in the top ten 12 times. That in itself is an accomplishment because 90 percent of the cars that start each year never finish.

During this same trip, I was scheduled to travel from Nairobi to Mauritius for national elections there. As I was boarding the plane, I ran into a black American musician, who had been performing in the Intercontinental Hotel bar. We began talking, and sat together on the flight. At Port Louis, where I had a rental car waiting, I offered him a ride into town, where he had several performances scheduled. We stopped for lunch and when we returned to the car, discovered it had been broken into and his guitar stolen. He was devastated – an itinerant musician without his guitar is not going to make any money in Africa. We went immediately to the police headquarters and reported the theft. There's one advantage to a small, island culture – everybody knows everybody else, and within 24 hours, the police had recovered his guitar and he was back in business.

Computers entered our working life about this time. Apple computers were available in South Africa at outrageously high prices, but were not commonplace. The Associated Press bureau was the first place I watched a computer in action in a news gathering setting. The reporter could take notes on the screen, then over-write it with a finished story, press a button and transmit it automatically to London or New York. It was not necessarily very good for Finger's telex business, but no one at News Services had moved that far into the 20th century.

VOA had been searching for years for a way to get hard copy of correspondents reports as well as voiced versions, so they could be quickly transmitted to the language services for translation. That was the reason that all the bureaus had been outfitted with telex machines. The correspondent, or his assistant, would type his story onto the telex and send it at about the same time as voicing a report – the really efficient manner was for the correspondent to compose his report on the telex and read from the printout rather than retyping 400 words.

VOA correspondents entered the computer revolution when Washington sent out a machine, called the Teleram PortaBubble to all bureaus. It was about the size of a standard typewriter, with a typewriter style keyboard. The monitor was a small, eight-inch screen, placed just above the keyboard. And it linked to Washington via an acoustic coupler – a set of rubber cuffs on top of the machine that a telephone would fit in. It had a printer port, so the correspondent could print out his story, but for breaking stories, I usually wrote and then read the piece from the tiny screen. The bubble memory, an early form of RAM, would hold about forty reports, then had to be cleared. The PortaBubble was described as a portable, but it really wasn't. It was too bulky, and too fragile, for the rigors of travel, and it had to be plugged in to an electrical outlet.

The PortaBubbles were delivered to each bureau by a young lady named Debbie, who worked in the VOA computer department. She was sent carrying computers to four posts in Africa – Nairobi, Johannesburg, Abidjan and Cairo – with no overseas background, and she experienced a lot of difficulties getting the equipment through customs at various airports. She trained each of us in the PortaBubble's use and then moved on to the next post.

Later, in the mid 80's, each correspondent was also assigned a Radio Shack TRS-80, which was becoming the standard machine for journalists everywhere. We called it a "Trash 80" but most users loved them. The Trash 80 was not much larger than today's laptop, and was fully portable, operating on batteries. But it was really limited in storage space, and its monitor was an LCD screen that would contain only eight lines of copy. To read a report from it, the correspondent would have to become very adept at scrolling down the page while broadcasting, but that was about the only way to use it because its printer connection was slow and unreliable.

Trash 80's were discontinued by Radio Shack before 1990, but some are still available on the internet from collectors. Only once have I seen a reference to a PortaBubble for sale. I was still using the PortaBubble in the Southwest bureau when I left VOA in 1989. The VOA news operation had gone into computers in a big way – all the typewriters were replaced with work stations, and stories were written, edited and transmitted around the building via electronics.

While I am on the subject, let me describe the correspondent's bag of tricks. Most of us traveled with two cassette tape recorders, plus microphones, cords and other paraphernalia, including in my case, a set of connectors for almost any electronic hookup or public address system. I also carried a shortwave radio to listen to VOA and other news, and a 50 foot length of wire to hang out a hotel window to improve shortwave reception. All that plus a portable typewriter, or once back in the U.S., the Trash 80. It made about a 40 pound load in a shoulder bag – I dared not trust that equipment to the luggage compartment.

The general method of sending voiced material while on the road was to take apart the telephone (much to the distress of hotel operators and phone company technicians), attach alligator clips to the two contacts in the mouth piece, plug the other end of the alligator clip cord into the tape recorder, and play back the tape. Sometimes, the TRS 80 could be hooked up the same way to transmit text. If I was in a place for more than a couple of days, I would take apart the wall connection box of the telephone, and hook alligator clips, or bare wires, to the terminals inside, and feed that way, so I could continue to use the telephone as well.

CHAPTER 34 — A MEDIA CONFRONTATION

It was getting more and more difficult to work as a foreign journalist in southern Africa. South Africa was beginning to feel more international pressure to change, and the government was getting tougher with perceived transgressions by us. Several correspondents were expelled from the country and as president of the Foreign Correspondents Association, it was my responsibility to make entreaties on their behalf, and mollify the government as much as possible to avoid further expulsions. Even more frustrating than the expected anti-press attitude of South Africa was the fact that the black African states to the north – the self-described "front line states" – also were cracking down on foreign reporters, particularly those of us who were based in South Africa.

They felt that by being based in the south, we were collaborating with the regime there – although the real reason was that communications and facilities were much better, and travel connections were simpler. There began to be talk that South Africa-based correspondents would not be allowed to travel to or work in the more militant black states – and in time, that restriction came to fruition in Zimbabwe, but not elsewhere.

As FCA president, I was invited by USIS in Botswana to speak on this subject at a seminar, attended by journalists and public information officials from several of the front line states. The seminar heard lots of appeals by liberation movements for the media to "get with the program," to support independence movements; and lots of criticism of the foreign press for what they considered negative reporting.

Excerpts from my talk, entitled: Problems of the Foreign Press in Covering Southern Africa, April 29-30, 1983:

I am concerned about recent developments vis-à-vis the foreign press in southern Africa, and unfortunately, I have no reason to be optimistic that things are likely to get better in the days to come. I think, in fact, we are seeing the beginning of a period of increasing tension between the regimes of southern Africa and the foreign press; sad and tragic as that may be, but the campaign against the foreign press is growing in South Africa and other parts of the continent. The idea is beginning to take strong shape that the way to get rid of bad news or unpleasant news is to get rid of the people who bring the bad news and unpleasant news – to kill the messenger. It doesn't surprise me in South Africa, particularly because we know that it's an autocratic regime. But it does surprise me some of that countries of black Africa that have achieved independence, seem so willing to return to the autocracy that they have just recently gotten rid of.

I have no argument with the concept of a new information order that supplies more information to third world countries about third world countries, but my reading of the new world information order is that the third world hopes to impose its bias on the information that the rest of the world gets. In other words, news should be favorable, journalists should generate good publicity about the third world. We have heard here of "developmental journalism" In my view... developmental journalism is not journalism, it's advertising and public relations for a government. It's a nice ringing phrase – it means getting the people "on side" to boost development, but I don't think that's what journalism is about.

This brings us to the question of the South Africa-based correspondents. As I said, there are about 90 of us. And there is some growing sentiment in the black republics of southern Africa to keep us out. Somehow, there is the mistaken belief that basing in South Africa is a commitment on the part of the journalist to the deplorable apartheid system in South Africa – that by being there, we are somehow a part of apartheid, or have become friends of apartheid. This simply is not true. And it is an unfair judgment to place against us.

To boil it all down to the essentials, the [problems faced by the foreign press] are: lack of access, lack of trust, lack of understanding. Lack of access to countries – the foreign press cannot report fairly or accurately about those countries that it cannot enter. Nor can it report as well without access to people – ministers, bureaucrats, businessmen, experts – who know, and who feel free to relate what the given situation is. Lack of trust: that perhaps is the reason for lack of access -- the paranoia that the foreign press is out to get you, when really the foreign press is merely out to get the facts.

I cannot boast that my comments were well received – the mood of nationalism was too strong in the room. The African participants, led by Zimbabwe's Director of Information, Justin Nyoka, put forward a series of resolutions criticizing western news coverage of the region and <u>declaring objectivity as a myth.</u>

Three Americans involved in the seminar – University of Missouri Journalism School Dean Roy Fisher, USIS Public Affairs Officer for Botswana Tom Martin and me – felt the resolutions compromised our integrity as journalists. They were political declarations with which we should not be associated. After a long argument, and several abstentions, the three of us shocked the gathering by walking out on the meeting rather than be so associated.

Justin Nyoka presents an interesting case. For many years, he was the Rhodesian correspondent for the BBC African Service and was widely respected by fellow journalists on the continent. Then he disappeared – apparently kidnapped – during the liberation struggle in eastern Zimbabwe, and his grieving colleagues took up a collection to provide for the education and care of the apparently-departed colleague's family. Voila! At the time of independence, Justin re-appeared as a radical member of Robert Mugabe's government – he had crossed the line and joined the guerrillas. From then on, he forgot, or ignored, his background in, and friendship for, the foreign press, and became its strongest antagonist in Zimbabwe.

What I was alluding to in my seminar statement came true five months later when the Information Ministers of six black-ruled states decided to bar South Africa-based foreign correspondents from working in their countries. Zimbabwe applied the new rule immediately, while Botswana, Mozambique and Zambia ignored it.

In the FCA, we blamed Zimbabwe for instigating the prohibition and asked for a meeting with the Harare government over the issue. They refused, but four officers of the Foreign Correspondents Association boarded a chartered jet to Harare anyway, to try to force the question.

The four of us – Marsh Clark of Time, Edgar Denter of the German news agency, free-lancer Peter Hawthorne and I – had no idea what sort of reception we would get upon our arrival. In fact, they were friendly and there was no confrontation. We were given one-day visitor permits. But officials were adamantly opposed to our protests. We met with Justin Nyoka and with U.S., British and German diplomats. The Minister of Information and the Prime Minister were unavailable, or disinterested. Nyoka said exceptions might be made in certain circumstances, but in the months that followed, exceptions were rare, and rarely sought.

It was my last trip to Zimbabwe, which caused VOA no serious harm because by then we had established Andrew Meldrun as a stringer there. And before he was expelled, Andrew, too, learned about the new form of journalism.

CHAPTER 35 — CHRISTMAS IN THE DESERT

I got back to Kenya one more time, in November, 1983. Our new Nairobi correspondent, Dan Robinson, had planned a vacation with his wife, which coincided with the scheduled return to East Africa of Britain's Queen Elizabeth.

She and Prince Phillip had been at the Treetops Lodge, a game-viewing location north of Nairobi, in 1953, when she was informed her father, King George, had died and she was now the Queen of England. That ascension to the throne had become a part of Kenyan lore, but she had not been back to Kenya since. And now on the 30th anniversary of that event, the royal couple was to return to Nairobi and to Treetops.

In my view this was a story that needed to be covered, but Robinson refused to change his vacation plans, so I volunteered to go do it. I wouldn't have missed it – it was a colorful and nostalgic several days – not real hard news but a great human interest story. The Queen rode by train from Nairobi north, giving her trademark little wave from the doorway to thousands of Kenyans who turned out at trackside. There were more than 100 journalists there to cover her return, mostly from British newspapers, and a handful of Americans.

The journalists did not stay at Treetops but we were at a nearby tourist hotel and were kept fully briefed on her visit. Back in Nairobi the next day, it was announced the Queen would hold a reception for the foreign press covering her visit. It was held at the Governor's Palace, which was the Nairobi home of President Moi and the place where President Kenyatta had lain in state.

We journalists were advised that coat and tie were required, we did not have to bow or curtsy, that we would shake hands with her gently when she offered her hand, and that we should not initiate any conversation, but to follow her lead in conversing. And it was all off the record – no stories and no quotes.

I put on a coat and tie, I met the Queen, I did not bow or curtsy, I shook her hand gently when she offered it, and she initiated some innocuous conversation about who I worked for and why I was there, and I asked her how she was enjoying her return trip to Kenya.

I had a longer conversation with Prince Phillip – he asked about VOA, and when I explained it was the American version of the BBC World Service, he seemed interested, and was curious why VOA would be covering what would appear to be a British internal story. I explained that we broadcast back to a large audience in Africa, and that anything the Queen did in Africa was of great interest to the Africans, particularly anything with the historical context of this visit. Regrettably, I was never able to obtain a picture of that audience, even though there was a palace photographer present.

Christmas of 1983 was approaching – and it was looming as the empty nester's first Christmas ever without any children or any other family with them. It showed promise of being a sad, melancholy day. To avoid that, Linda and I decided we would avoid Christmas altogether – no tree, no decorations, no parties, no gift exchange – and take a trip to a place where Christmas would not intrude. We would go to the desert of Southwest Africa/Namibia.

VOA had authorized purchase of a new office vehicle, and we traded the decrepit old Citroen sedan in for a new Opel (Chevrolet) station wagon. I rigged the back of the station wagon for camping, with foam mattresses and curtains on the win-

dows. We purchased camping equipment and extra fuel and water tanks to carry on the rooftop luggage rack. Two spare tires and wheels were added to the rooftop, and from a medical institute, I purchased a snake bite kit to guard against a possible encounter with denizens of the desert. We studied the maps and two weeks before Christmas, we took off, heading west from Johannesburg.

The plan was to camp along the way for a couple of nights, and then check into a hotel or inn in major towns for a chance to shower and eat a prepared meal. Our first destination was Augrabies Falls National Park in South Africa, just south of the Namibian border, named for the Hottentot word for "place of great noise." Here, the Orange River, which winds its way from east to west across two thirds of South Africa, drops more than 400 feet into a granite chasm and flows on toward the Atlantic Ocean. Just 30 miles upstream, at the town of Upington, the Orange River is wide and placid. We stayed at a campground in the national park and explored the rim of the canyon.

Another, larger canyon was ahead of us as we crossed the border into Namibia. That destination was the Fish River Canyon, second in size only to America's Grand Canyon, 100 miles long, 16 miles across at its widest point, and 1600 feet deep, with sheer rock walls. We camped along the rim at a picnic site, sleeping in the back of the station wagon. During the late evening and early morning hours, we looked out on the spectacular, but barren surroundings, and watched a beautiful sunset across the canyon. There is a hot springs resort on the floor of the canyon, but it is closed during the summer months because the temperatures there are unbearable.

Namibia is a huge country, an area larger than Texas and Arkansas together, with a population of less than 2 million. It's named for the Namib Desert, which stretches the entire 1200 mile length of its Atlantic coastline and is the oldest desert in the world. It is bone dry – most moisture is derived from huge fog banks that sweep in when the cold Benguela current of the Atlantic clashes with the hot air over the coastal desert. It is stark emptiness and desolation, but with spectacular desert and mountain landscapes.

Namibia had 2400 miles of highway, but only the main roads were two lanes and paved. The rest were wide, hard gravel roads without ruts or bumps, because there were no moisture to cause them to deteriorate. We drove on those roads a lot, 200 miles at a stretch, with no towns or facilities along the way – which is why we carried extra gasoline in our rooftop tanks. And, again, it was rare to see another vehicle or another person.

Our destination beyond Fish River Canyon was the Atlantic coast, and the town of Luderitz. It's an old German town, established as a seaport in 1883, and much easier to reach by sea than by road. The highway runs 100 miles west from the nearest inland town, across an absolutely barren desert. On both sides of the highway are signs warning travelers not to leave the road, because it's a restricted area to protect diamond mining. The restricted area is 50 miles deep from the coast inland, and nearly 400 miles long from the border north to Walvis Bay. Diamonds in Southwest Africa are occasionally found on the surface, along the beach but the primary mining area is at the border town of Oranjemund, which is a totally restricted area – no visitors.

The vast expanses of restricted area are to keep people from traveling overland and smuggling diamonds away from the mines or even finding them. I had visited the Oranjemund mining operation a few months earlier with a group of foreign correspondents, escorted and watched constantly by officials of the Anglo-American mining company. At Oranjemund, giant bulldozers push the desert sand out beyond the surf line to build temporary dams, and scrape down to the bedrock underlying the beach, where the diamonds are plucked from pockets in the rock. Once an area has been picked clean, the surf is allowed to re-cover the rock with sand, and the mining moves on up the coast.

Luderitz looks completely out of place. Surrounded completely by desert sand, the town is made up of dozens of buildings in the 1800's German style. It looks like a Bavarian village that was magically picked up from the German countryside and set down intact in this forbidding place. A few miles inland is the ghost town of Kolmanskop. Once the home of 700 families and the headquarters for the diamond mining operation in the early 1900's, the people went away and the blowing sand began to take back the streets and buildings. Because of the dry conditions, abandoned houses stand intact, with sand dunes building up in the corners of their rooms.

The ghost town of Kolmanskop

We also planned to visit two other coastal cities, Swapkomund and Walvis Bay, 300 miles to the north, but because of the restricted area, it was necessary to drive several hundred miles inland, then north, and then back westward to the coast. Enroute, we stayed at Hardap Dam, near Marienthal, where a dam across the Snake River has created a fifteen-square-mile lake. It is by far the largest water storage facility in Namibia, and its shores are ideal for fishing and boating.

We drove on to Windhoek, the capital, which I had visited many times before in the course of covering the political struggle for independence in this strange colony. We stayed two or three nights at the Kalahari Sands Hotel, enjoying civilization after our days living in the back of a station wagon. The better part of one day was spent in a rock shop, picking through and buying specimens of quartz, agate and desert rose. Southwest Africa is blessed with an extraordinary assembly of rocks, gems and precious stones.

We then headed back toward

At right, view from "my place."

the Skeleton Coast —so named for the whale skeletons which washed ashore during whaling days, as well as for the ships wrecked on rocks in its massive surf. We took the back road to Swapkomund – the same deserted road I had traveled several years earlier with photographer Mitch Osburne. Linda and I stopped and camped at the very spot where I had made my earlier declaration to revisit. We did not see another person or another car during the nearly 300 mile drive west from Windhoek, and through Bosua Pass. We set up camp under a grove of trees near the edge of the road about 4 P.M. and sat back to enjoy the solitude. Not another vehicle came by all day nor all night. The silence was deafening and awesome.

I have only one regret about that campsite. Someone had left there on the ground a perfect set of spiraling Kudu horns, about a yard long. I wanted to take them with me, but I was uncertain if their original owner might sometime come back to reclaim them, and was a little concerned that their possession might be illegal. So, reluctantly, we left camp the next day and left the horns where they lay.

At Swapkomund we camped along the beach, with the wind blowing in off the Atlantic so strongly that I had to erect a plastic drop cloth shield between the car and a post to even be able to light our camp stove. The beaches are expansive, but the water, fed by the Benguela current coming north from the regions of Antarctica, is cold. You

175

experience a strange mixture of hot desert sun and a chill sea breeze. Swapkomund, like Luderitz, has a large collection of old German-style buildings, but it appeared to belong in its setting – the nearby sand dunes did not seem to be as big a threat to this thriving, pleasant town.

However, just to the south of Swapkomund, on the road to Walvis Bay, the largest sand dunes in the world flank the highway and provide a playground for sand surfers. We visited the Namib River – which flows under the sands toward the sea, and only occasionally breaks the surface with puddles of water. But the river course is lined with green trees and shrubs feeding off the underground waters. It was there that we looked at several Welwitschia plants. Growing low to the ground, they look like some sort of desert cactus, but actually are a dwarf tree that requires no rainfall to survive but absorbs some moisture from dew through its leaves. The plant does not flower until it is at least twenty years old, and a plant three feet across can be hundreds of years old – they will live one thousand years.

We spent Christmas Eve in a dumpy, harborside hotel in Walvis Bay, a major port for cargo and fishing and at one time, for whaling ("Walvis: is German for "Whale Fish"). Walvis Bay had been a British colony at the time the Germans controlled all the rest of Southwest Africa, giving the British a hammer-hold on the German colony. It remained a point of contention in the 1980s –

while South Africa often stated its intention to grant independence to Namibia, the South African government said it would not turn over Walvis Bay because it had not been part of the original German holdings. Eventually, however, Walvis Bay did become part of Namibia.

Our Christmas hotel had made only a bare gesture toward the holiday, with a string of colored lights hanging above the bar. After a welcome shower, Linda and I had a few drinks and a steak dinner, wished one another a merry, but unusual, Christmas, and left the bar/restaurant to a lone sailor, a girl he was trying to pick up, and the girl's ten year old daughter, who should have been spending Christmas Eve in better circumstances.

We camped along the beach again before heading inland. North along the beach of the Skeleton Coast we visited a seal rookery, where thousands of seals, babies and adults, lived on rocks just off the beach. Heading back toward Windhoek, we jumped north toward an area called Twyfelfontein, an area of strange rock formations, shale mountain outcroppings, and a jumble of large rocks with a collection of primitive engravings on them. But the relentless heat in this area of the Namib desert soon sent us scooting back toward civilization.

Back in Windhoek there was a lot more to see, but we were running out of time and energy, and made the decision to start heading back home. Even sticking to the main highways, it was a three day drive back to Johannesburg – our last night out, we camped in a municipal campground of some unmemorable South African town. It was New Years Eve, and the celebration consisted of someone in the campground setting off a string of firecrackers at midnight.

We were back in Johannesburg to begin 1984, and what would be the final few months of our life in Africa and our life overseas.

There were big family plans for 1984 – Kim and Jeff were getting married on April 28. Early in April, Linda left South Africa for good. She was going home to Austin to help with wedding preparations. I followed a couple of weeks later, because I had a bride to give away, but I could not be away from the job very long. The wedding was an occasion for another big family reunion – Craig and Donna came from Casper, David from Washington, Georgia and Fred and Betty and Pearson came down from Springfield, Phoebe and Art from Kansas City, brother Steve and Kay from St. Louis, brother Sam and Linda and their new baby, Emily, from Maryland. Even our good old friend from Saigon, Wayne Hyde, flew in from Washington to attend.

After the wedding, Linda and Steven moved in at Bend Cove and our long unseen goods from storage were shipped to Austin. I had to go back to South Africa for three months to continue working until a replacement was named for me, and in place, because by now I had been appointed to head the new Southwest bureau. Most of our belongings in Johannesburg had been packed for shipment or sold, leaving me with just the bare necessities until I could close up the house and go home, too. I finally returned to the United States for good in August, 1984.

During those last three months, my Aunt Phoebe and Art finally made it to South Africa for a tour that they had been anticipating for several years, and I had a chance to do one more round of tour guiding in a country that I had come to know pretty well. Art joked that on their last day in Johannesburg, someone came to take the bed they had been sleeping on, and which had been sold. "We couldn't have stayed any longer," he said.

My replacement was Mallory Saleson, a newsroom writer and Washington correspondent for VOA, who had spent a good deal of time covering the White House. Johannesburg was her first foreign assignment. Mallory and I overlapped for about a month, while I showed her the ins and outs of South Africa coverage, and introduced her to some key figures, including Bishop Tutu, Dr. Motlana, the Soweto leader, and we flew down to Durban to meet Zulu chief Gatsha Buthelezi.

I remember well the morning we were sitting in Bishop Tutu's office at the Anglican Church headquarters in Johannesburg. As we talked, he was awaiting a phone call from the United States, and when the phone rang he picked it up, and said "Hello. New York?" Then turning to Mallory and me, he flashed his pixie grin, and said: "White man's magic."

The last story I sent from Johannesburg was a long background report, recapping my eight years of coverage of Africa. It was not very optimistic. There did not seem to be any progress being made in resolving South Africa's political problems – despite some surface changes, apartheid still was in control, blacks were still repressed, the guerrilla war and terrorism were intensifying.

Kenya, which had shown so much promise during the Kenyatta days when we lived there, was slipping back into the ways of other African states, with corruption and crime growing daily. Zimbabwe, despite the early predictions, did not seem to be evolving as had been hoped. The former Portuguese colonies of Angola and Mozambique were still mired in backwardness. There was a cynical expression often used by Africa correspondents regarding African politics and independence movements: "One man, one vote, one time." That prophecy seemed to be coming true.

Background Report, "South African Retrospective," July 20, 1984

When I first came to South Africa, in February, 1976, this was a country running scared. Its army had been beaten by Cuban troops during an expedition into Angola and forced to retreat. A few months later, rioting broke out in the black township of Soweto and it seemed for a time that the nationalist government had perhaps lost control of the system of apartheid or racial separation, which had been imposed over the previous quarter century.

Today, by contrast, the ruling Afrikaners are very much still in control. The government openly boasts that the country is a regional super power. The Prime Minister has been accepted in western European capitals and officials say 'It may be arrogant, but as a regional power, we demand that the Cubans leave Angola."

That, in itself, has been a major change in a society where the basic dispute is over change. But the change most often argued about is reform. The white ruling elite of South Africa will say that reform is taking place. The opposition, both black and white, will say it is not. The government cites as reform the new tri-cameral legislature that will begin meeting later this year. Opponents say it is a sham because it avoids the major issue of this country — how to deal with blacks, who make up 70 percent of the population and who are excluded from the so-called reform.

Sham or reform, the new constitution is significant in that a racially-obsessed country is letting non-whites into the corridors of power. But change in South Africa falls far short of what is demanded by the local majority or the international community. At the same time, it far exceeds what the conservative Afrikaner is prepared to give willingly. It has led to a spilt – probably irreparable – in the Dutch emigrant society that came to this tip of the African continent 350 years ago and who now consider themselves 'the white tribe of Africa."

What change is there? Elevators and park benches are integrated, but there still are white and non-white signs on busses and toilets. There are international class hotels where blacks can use the dining room, but not the dance floor, and most black people still have lunch from a carry-out counter. Blacks in urban areas are being encouraged to purchase their homes and electricity is being brought to Soweto. But the group areas act still sets out racially segregated neighborhoods and the richest black entrepreneur cannot escape Soweto. Blacks are allowed to form labor unions in the industrial city of Port Elizabeth, but beaches are still restricted by race

Some of the rules have changed and more may change in the years to come. But the attitudes that created those rules have not changed. South Africa remains a self-indulgent society, divided into haves and have-nots along racial instead of economic lines. No one in power has even hinted at a willingness to go beyond the limited sharing of political power with mixed race and Asian people.

But there is no one able for force greater political change. "One man one vote" is a hollow slogan with no strength behind it. South Africa is a European level industrial state, which has proven it is not vulnerable to boycott or sanction. The entreaties and the shouts from the black states come from enemies too weak to harm South Africa and they are getting comparatively weaker.

In time, demographics will catch up with South Africa. When the black population outnumbers the whites by 15 or 20 to one, the sheer weight of numbers will force additional reform. The economic dependence on the black worker will help it along. But that change will come slowly – it will be given only grudgingly. It could come violently or quietly, but it won't come soon.

In fact, change came somewhat sooner than I anticipated. Nelson Mandela was released from prison in February, 1990 and the first free elections were held in April, 1994. Ten years had passed since I left. By then, I was long gone from VOA.

This time, when I left Africa, I was sure I was leaving for good. I was ready to become an American again, and I was looking forward to the challenge of working in the Southwest bureau. I looked forward to covering my own country with the same intensity and curiosity that I had applied to some 35 others. I knew I was leaving behind many good memories, and good times and good friends and perhaps the most fulfilling years of my career. But I was ready to go.

CHAPTER 36 — TEXAS

A whole new country to learn. My first assignment as chief of the new Southwest Bureau was the Republican National Convention, to be held in Dallas late in August, 1984. I had never covered a national convention before and was looking forward to the experience.

Convention coverage was a big deal for VOA and I was to be one of nearly 50 VOA reporters, anchors, producers and engineers assigned to the Dallas convention. I flew to Dallas early in August, just to get acquainted and get the lay of the land. I applied for Dallas Police Department press credentials (not necessary for the convention) and drove around, locating landmarks and important sites.

I figured with Dallas's past history of political violence (Kennedy in 1963) that it would behoove me to know where the police station was, and Parkland Hospital, among other things. I toured the Dallas Convention Center, and visited the hotel that VOA advance planners had booked for our team. I also had been asked, unofficially, to scout out some good restaurants for the VOA staffers.

To insure security, and thwart demonstrators, a two-mile-long chain-link fence was erected around the convention center, creating protests that protestors would neither been seen nor heard by convention goers. The convention center, the size of five football fields, was expecting 4,000 delegates, 9,000 spectators and 10,000 journalists.

In fact, I had actually started my Texas political coverage in Dallas several months earlier. While back in Texas for Kim's wedding, I had been asked to take a couple of days to fly to Dallas for one of the Democratic Party candidate debates between former Vice President Mondale (the eventual nominee and loser to Ronald Reagan in a landslide) and others. Joined there by Ed Conley from Washington, I learned that the new American press corps had changed from the hard-drinking, hard-driving journalists I had known previously in the McGovern campaign, or in Vietnam or Africa. The new breed, Ed explained, didn't repair to the nearest bar after an event such as the debate, instead they went to their hotel rooms and studied and read books. That was an unusual lesson to have to learn, and it certainly made press reporting in the United States a lot less fun that it had been abroad.

I played only a peripheral part in the convention coverage itself – other reporters had been assigned the more exciting floor coverage, or to the anchor sky-booth overlooking the convention floor. VOA had work facilities including a newsroom and studio in a trailer in the basement of the convention center as did all the radio and TV networks, and the major newspapers. As a rule, I would go there first thing in the morning, and pick up an assignment to go elsewhere in Dallas, to a news conference or a luncheon speech by the Republican candidates and administration officials who packed into the city.

I attended a party-sponsored seminar for 200 foreign visitors from 20 countries, which was addressed by administration officials such as Secretary of State George Schultz and U.N. Ambassador Jean Kirkpatrick. Secretary Schultz created some stir when he said "we are going to campaign hard all the way" – a no-no because Secretaries of State are supposed to stay out of political fights. Later his spokesman in Washington clarified that Schultz would not take part in day-to-day campaign activities. VOA political types thought I should not have reported that much, but I had been there and I had him on tape.

The Republicans organized another conference of about 400 Asian-American groups devised to rally people of Asian descent away from their traditional support of the Democrat party. And a 16-year-old Vietnamese refugee girl, who had escaped by boat from Vietnam just three years earlier, became one of the darlings of the convention when she recited the pledge of allegiance at the opening night ceremony to a standing ovation.

The Chinese ambassador to Washington took strong exception to a platform plank pledging support for the people of Taiwan and urging self-determination for Hong Kong. I was asked to provide interviews for the Estonian language service with two invited guests, Estonian emigres, one an executive with the Boy Scouts national headquarters in Dallas. I covered all these events – I had become VOA's foreign correspondent at the convention.

In between two trips to Dallas I sandwiched in a visit to the Alamo in San Antonio, to fulfill a Washington request for an interview with the chair of the Alamo Committee of the Daughters of the Republic of Texas. This had been prompted by a history buff in Illinois, who questioned the Daughters' manner of maintaining the site and wanted public and private support to wrest the site away from them. I got the interview, but management of the fortress, which is sacred to most Texans, never changed.

Things were running at about the breakneck pace I had expected when I returned from South Africa. I was charting entirely new waters in setting up the Southwest Bureau. VOA had long had domestic bureaus in New York, Los Angeles, Miami and Chicago, but other than a brief experiment in Boston, Texas was the first new bureau to be established in 20 years.

Spending some time in Washington, enroute from Johannesburg to Austin, I was told of the grandiose plans Washington had for the bureau. In time they anticipated assigning a Spanish-speaking correspondent to the bureau as well as me, so the Southwest could help in coverage of Mexico and Latin America. I also was to get a full time assistant. The Latin American division was particularly high on the idea, because the Miami correspondent concentrated most of his efforts on Cuba and the Caribbean. It looked like a place where I could grow a little empire and really deserve the title "bureau chief" instead of being a mere correspondent. Unfortunately, most of this was to never happen.

Temporarily, I was setting up office in the fourth bedroom of our "ranch" in south Austin, installing a second telephone line, renting office furniture while three teletype machines spewed out yards of news in the garage. Two newswires were fed by separate phone lines (that made four lines into the house) and one was fed by a small satellite dish on the roof. Linda and I had the master bedroom at the back of the house, with direct access to the pool and the yard with its 40-some trees. Steven, who was attending Austin Community College, had the front bedroom, and we even had a guest room and frequent guests among all this activity.

While in South Africa, I had become fascinated with the subject of foreign correspondents, and had written to the journalism school at the University of Texas, telling them of my plans to move to Austin, and my interest in being involved in some sort of center for the study and support of American correspondents serving overseas. And the University had responded with some interest. Once back in Austin, I hoped to be able to obtain office space for VOA in the spacious Communications Department building, using the studio facilities of the NPR station which the university operated from there, and perhaps contribute to that longer time goal of a center for foreign journalism. There was even some interest in that, but as time

2602 Bend Cove, Austin, TX, the ranch where the VOA Bureau should have stayed.

went by, it became clear that neither of these were going to happen.

Despite that, I still felt Austin was the logical place to establish the VOA office, while the bureaucrats in Washington had their eyes set on Houston. The Washington Post had created a new bureau in Texas, and their correspondent had chosen Austin for many of the same reasons I argued: the rich and growing University of Texas was a great source of expertise on many subjects of interest, especially Latin America. Austin was the state capital and center of political events. It was central and travel was as easy from there as from either Houston or Dallas – either by road, or by Southwest Airlines, which had flights nearly every hour to every major city in the state, for fares of no more than $40-60. A major new computer and electronics research facility, known as MCC, had recently been established in Austin after a spirited nation-wide competition, making Austin the Silicon Valley of the south. Unspoken was the feeling that Austin would be a much more pleasant place to live – besides, we already had a home there.

But VOA Washington had become difficult to reason with. In the time I had been in South Africa, a whole new top management team had come to power in VOA with the Reagan administration. VOA had a new director, Richard Carlson, a political appointee, a chubby light-weight right-winger, whose professional past primarily consisted of being a flack, a PR operative, for a San Diego savings and loan group and working for Hollywood gossip columnist Louella Parsons.

Sid Davis, a former NBC news executive, was Program Manager; Davis had brought in Ed DeFontaine, a former AP radio chief, to be Director of News, and DeFontaine had brought in Don Henry, then an unemployed newspaper writer, to be the assignments editor. No one that I knew from my previous 23 years at VOA was in the line of authority, and none of these new people knew me or much about my previous VOA service. And none had much, if any, experience with foreign news or foreign news consumers.

There was constant Washington pressure for me to move operations to Houston. I was able to buy a few months in Austin, and I spent a lot of time in Houston to demonstrate to Washington that I could cover anything in that part of the state that was newsworthy and important through frequent travel, use of the telephone to record interviews and with the wire service material. I also subscribed to two Houston daily newspapers, as well as two from Dallas and one from Austin and the New York Times, all delivered to our doorstep at 2602 Bend Cove each morning. Along with the wire services, I had plenty to read.

I even toyed with the idea of keeping the house in Austin, and renting a small apartment in Houston where I could spend most of the week, and commute home on weekends (or for Austin occurring stories). But that scheme ran afoul of government travel regulations – to receive per diem while traveling to and working in Houston, I had to have hotel receipts and an apartment rental receipt would not work. And I also could not claim per diem for news trips back to Austin (when I would stay in our home) because that was not allowed. So in the spring of 1985, I took Linda to Houston with me for an extended stay during a space shuttle mission, and we began to look for houses there, preferably in the vicinity of the Johnson Space Center, which had taken on the central rationale for coverage in Houston.

In the meantime, the 1984 presidential election campaign was underway, and Texas was expected to attract its share of the national campaign – more from the Republicans than the Democrats. As a Reagan-Bush sweep began to appear inevitable, the Mondale campaign apparently wrote off the state. The Republican vice president seeking re-election, George Bush, declared Texas as his home state. Bush's residency was always subject to some question: he had lived most of his life in Washington, spent his summers at a family compound in Kennebunkport, Maine, and his only Texas residence was a suite at the Houstonian Club Hotel and Health Fitness Center he used whenever in Houston – a fact that Democrat vice presidential candidate Geraldine Ferraro pointed out with some glee.

Bush adamantly defended his choice of home and voting location. "I'm a Texan," Mr. Bush declared. "I've lived there since 1948. I go there when I can." He was sometimes described as a

Texas oil millionaire, but by Texas terms, he was certainly in the low range of the "oil rich." Most Texans accepted him – except those opposed to any "Yankee;" those who believe that no northerner can ever become a Texan.

I accompanied Bush to a campaign appearance on the Texas Tech University campus in Lubbock, and I traveled to San Antonio where former democratic candidate Jesse Jackson tried to persuade Hispanic and black voters to vote for Mondale. Jackson also was critical of the Reagan administration's South Africa policy, calling it a "moral disgrace." I had other opportunities to report back to Africa, mostly from Texas newspaper editorials which increasingly were taking note of events in South Africa and calling on the U.S. government to tighten the pressure on Pretoria.

The Hispanic vote was a big issue in Texas, where like California, Hispanics made up 20 percent of the voting population, and I returned to San Antonio to do a report on a non-partisan voter registration and education project.

I was in Houston Election Day, November 7, to watch Bush vote and to report live from an election watch party. The vice president was in a buoyant mood all through the day, starting when he voted after standing in line for 17 minutes with other citizens at his neighborhood polling place.

Between the convention, the election and three space shuttle missions, I covered a lot of other news from the southwest, some in Houston, some from Austin, to demonstrate that the capital city was a viable location for the bureau. I will not attempt to detail all these items, but it will give you an opening sentence from several to demonstrate the scope of material done. Some is serious, some a little more light-hearted.

September 19: A 33 year old Pakistani businessman has pleaded guilty in Houston to charges that he tried to export illegally electronic devices that could be used to trigger nuclear weapons.

September 20: The Hispanic Chamber of Commerce of the United States is holding its annual convention in San Antonio, to focus on the special problems of the Spanish speaking businessmen in this country. Defense Secretary Casper Weinberger was preparing to travel to San Antonio when first reports of the Beirut Embassy bombing were received. He called the bombing another example of the type of terrorist attack to which the world is subjected.

September 25: In American culture, it is always assumed that fishermen are going to exaggerate the size of their catches. But in Texas, it has gotten so serious that legislation is being considered to outlaw the lies of anglers. Fishing for the elusive bass has become a big sport on the lakes of the southwestern United States, and there are now many bass-fishing tournaments and contests with prizes reaching as high as one million dollars.

September 26: Texas billionaire H. Ross Perot has purchased a 13th century edition of England's Magna Carta for permanent display in the United States. The one-page document, hand written on sheep skin and bearing the seal of King Edward the First, has been purchased for $1.5 million.

October 1: The President of Peru, Fernando Belaunde-Terry, ending a trip to the United States and the U.N. General Assembly, visited the University of Texas in Austin. He called on universities here to help find a solution to the economic problems of the third world.

October 30: Two convicted murderers were executed in the United States early today – reviving the controversy over capital punishment.

November 30: The University of Texas announced that Mrs. Jehan El Sadat, former first lady of Egypt, will launch the Liz Sutherland Carpenter distinguished visiting lecture program January 31.

December 7: A concerted campaign is gaining strength in Texas to abolish the state's blue laws that prevent shopping on

Sunday. It started in Houston with a revolt taking place against the law, particularly during this busy season of Christmas shopping.

December 7: Texas Stadium, the home of the Dallas Cowboys, is the stadium with the hole in the roof. It's known to gridiron football fans in the United States by fans who follow the Cowboys and it's known to millions of television viewers overseas because the stadium with the hole in the roof is one of the scenes of Dallas shown on the screen during the opening credits of the Dallas TV program. Now, a plan is underway to close the hole in the roof.

December 7: The U.S. Justice Department has filed suit in Federal Court in Washington to overturn restrictive deeds used in a Houston housing area to deny civil rights to blacks.

December 12: One of the treats of Christmas in the United States is the offering of unusual gifts. VOA's southwest correspondent Bob Chancellor went to one of the sources of the unusual – the Nieman Marcus department store in Dallas. The company's vice president, Keith Nix, describes this year's top of the line. (Actuality) "This year, what we have to offer is a desk made to duplicate your favorite steer or horse. Now don't laugh...." The price, about $65,000 and the department store already has orders for six of them.

December 14: Residents of the city of Bartlesville, Oklahoma are uniting to oppose the financial takeover of the oil company which is their town's main employer. T. Boone Pickens is a successful and flamboyant Texas oil man. But he may not have reckoned on the reaction of 28,000 citizens to his proposal to buy up stock and take over the Phillips Petroleum Company. He has become Bartlesville's favorite villain.

December 19: The states of Texas, Nevada and Washington are the finalists, of a sort, in a federal government program an-

nounced in Washington. But the honor is something none of the states want – to be the site of a nuclear waste facility. Texas governor Mark White was not pleased. He said sparks will fly before the people of Deaf Smith County are allowed to glow in the dark.

December 28: The administrator of the Texas Alcohol Beverage Commission has outlawed two for the price of one drink specials. The organization, Mothers Against Drunk Driving, has welcomed it as a first step.

December 28: Mexican demonstrators protesting against alleged election fraud have blockaded a bridge across the border to Texas. The cities of Eagle Pass, Texas, and Piedras Negras, Mexico, 120 miles southwest of San Antonio – are separated by no more than half a mile of river, but since Wednesday afternoon, the bridge connecting the two neighboring towns has been closed to cars and trucks. Six to eight thousand cars usually cross daily on the bridge.

Linda and I were both fans of novelist James Michener. We had met him in Japan, and I was delighted to find him in Austin, where he had been working on his novel "Texas." I was granted an interview, and went to his home, and met his wife, Mari, where I even helped her by changing a couple of light bulbs while he was busy elsewhere.

There had been a lot of controversy over whether Michener had done all his research on Texas himself, or whether it had been done by intern/helpers at the University of Texas, with which he was affiliated. During our interview, I wanted to throw him a softball question about this issue, so I asked "How do you work? How do you amass so much information?" He stood up abruptly, announced "The interview's over, I will not be insulted" and stomped out of the room. Mari, who was still puttering around the room, asked:"What did you do to him? He is a national treasure." I tried to explain that I was only trying to help, but she never asked me to change any more light bulbs. I never bothered to send a story on the aborted interview. And I never read "Texas."

One continuing story I got interested in, and our Latin American services were interested in, was that of the Sanctuary Movement. Several nuns, clergymen and lay-people in the Tucson, Arizona, area had been indicted for aiding illegal immigrants from Guatemala and El Salvador who said they were fleeing persecution and war. I made several trips to Tucson before and during their trial, and became well acquainted with the Rev. John Fife, who operated the small Southside Presbyterian Church in Tucson. His usual garb was cowboy boots, jeans and a western cut shirt. During one interview he asked if I would like to meet some of the illegal refugees he and others were helping. "Yes," I said, and he took me to a room just behind the pulpit of his church, where about 20 were living.

The Reagan administration opposed granting asylum while the churches said they were following their religion putting them in direct opposition to federal law. In the end, eight were found guilty of alien smuggling charges, but received light, or suspended, sentences. The movement of providing "sanctuary" to aliens fleeing persecution spread to hundreds of churches and even cities across the United States.

In the midst of a very busy first few months in Texas, our son, Craig, announced in Casper, Wyoming, that he and longtime girlfriend, Donna Fowler, planned to be married November 19, 1984. Linda and I flew to Casper for the wedding, and to take delivery of a new Ford pickup truck. A pickup is a right of passage for all Texans, and I had been

shopping for some time, not quite finding what I wanted. It had to be new, a Ford (all Texas pickup trucks are Fords) a three-quarter-ton vehicle, with extended cab and four-wheel drive. This was because I planned to install a camper on it and wanted four-wheel drive so we could drive on the beach. So, as we were planning our trip to Casper, I asked Craig to look for my dream truck there, and he found it. I sent him a deposit to hold it – our plan after the wedding was to drive it back to Missouri for a visit, and then home to Texas.

Craig and Donna had a wonderful, small wedding, with just us and some of their friends in Casper. Craig, by then, was working for the gas company; the oil field work had petered out a four years earlier. They had no honeymoon plans, although they both had a week off. Craig was insistent I was not going to drive away in a new truck without him spending some time riding in it. So they joined us, on their honeymoon week, on a trip from Casper through Colorado. They jumped into the cramped back seat of the extended cab and we took off for several enjoyable days touring the Rockies.

On Thanksgiving Day, we dropped the newlyweds off at the Denver airport for a flight back home, and we headed east across the flats of Colorado and Kansas toward Missouri. We had to drive slowly because the truck was still in its break-in period, so that first night, we only got as far as Limon, Colorado, near the Kansas state line. It was Thanksgiving night – where to celebrate with a holiday dinner? The only open restaurants in Limon, we were told, were two truck stops, one of the east edge of town, one on the west. We went west – it was not the best holiday meal we had ever had, but it may have been one of the most memorable

CHAPTER 37 — SPACE

One key element of the Southwest bureau's mission was to provide coverage of NASA's space shuttle program, which was controlled from the Johnson Space Center in Houston. I covered my first shuttle flight, designated 41-D, just a week after the end of the Republican convention in Dallas, and there were two more before the end of 1984. I was joined in that first flight by our Chicago correspondent, Paul Francuch, who had been doing the Houston end of all previous shuttle flights and was relieved to no longer have that burden.

I had not been involved in any space program coverage since the Apollo moon mission, when I was sent to Australia in 1968. Having been overseas most of the ensuing years, I had not even seen much television coverage of space missions, except occasional film of a launch on news programs in Kenya, Israel and South Africa. I had never seen a launch of the space shuttle, and knew virtually nothing about the shuttle program. Thus, I faced a tremendous learning curve to catch up with a program that required nearly hour-by-hour reports on VOA. The space program had a high priority with the Voice – it was a program that reflected well on the United States among foreign audiences.

Mission 41-D, by the shuttle Discovery, was the 12th in the series of manned space shuttle flights. There was a convoluted rationale for naming the missions – something about which ship, and which fiscal year it was planned in – but I have forgotten the details of that, and anyway, usually just referred to them in numerical sequence and by the name of the individual ship. I often remembered them later by some unusual occurrence during the flight – for example, my first one was noted because a large blob of ice formed on the outside of the ship near a vent, and crew members and flight controllers on the ground spent a couple of days trying to dislodge it by basking that portion of the ship in the sun, and eventually knocking it off with the shuttle's robot arm.

VOA's method of covering missions involved 20 or more people. Launchings were broadcast live from the Kennedy Space Center at Cape Canaveral, Florida, by a crew of writers, broadcasters and engineers sent down from Washington. All pre-launch activity was in the hands of the Florida NASA staff. Shortly after blast-off – you may have noticed during launches — as the shuttle clears the launch pad, the mission commentators announce "Houston is in control now," and the mission commentator changes to a person in Houston.

Our coverage would follow the same pattern – the VOA crew in Florida would do the launch and any wrap-up stories and then the correspondent in Houston (often just me) would take over from that point onward. When landing time came several days later, Greg Flakus, the Miami correspondent, would travel to the Cape to report the landing, if it took place in Florida, or the Los Angeles bureau would cover it if the shuttle landed in the California desert.

News wanted a new, short 45-second report, nearly every

hour, and every couple of hours a long 2 ½ minute report wrapping up the mission so far. Our only break would come at night – when the astronauts went into their 8-10 hour quiet time and sleep period, we could also get some quiet time and sleep on the ground. TV networks covering the shuttle missions also followed this pattern, and worked out of trailers parked on the Johnson Space Center grounds, with their own satellite uplink dishes. Television pictures and the audio commentary on the mission were fed to the space center public information office and distributed to the networks and all journalists covering the flight.

Those of us without trailers worked in a temporary newsroom set up at tables in the lobby of the JSC auditorium and visitor center museum. The lobby had an extensive display of former space memorabilia: a lunar lander, a moon buggy, displays of space suits worn over the years, a mock up of the earlier era orbiting space laboratory called SpaceLab plus numerous maps, charts and explanations. The tourists continued to visit the center even during missions, and would peer around the dividing screens to watch the hubbub of the press and radio people at a long row of temporary tables.

NASA made it as easy as possible for the journalists covering the flights – usually 30 or 40 of us in the early days. At our tables, we would watch the mission downlink television, and record the mission control commentary for possible actualities or sound bites which we would include in the news reports which we fed by telephone from special phones lines installed for the media along one wall of the lobby. Briefings at the end of each eight hour shift in mission control would be conducted in a small auditorium across a plaza from the museum in the public information building. If we missed an actuality, or wanted the full version of a briefing, the PIO office would provide it very quickly. And the public information specialists were always available to us to answer questions.

On some flights, especially those that had foreign participants or experiments aboard, VOA would send some language reporters to Houston to do their own reporting in their own language. Occasionally, Washington science writer Brian Cislak would come to Houston also – that was especially helpful on those scientific flights when operations continued for 24 hours on orbit. As the Houston bureau chief, it was my responsibility to make hotel reservations for any visitors – I stayed in hotels too, during my time of living in Austin, and I became the guide to the visitors to tourist sites and restaurants. A mission of five to seven days would be a busy time of intense work.

My nearest table companion in the newsroom was Doug Ross of KPRC radio in Houston, who had been covering the shuttle since the first flight. Also nearby was the group from the Space Institute, who would come to Houston from all over the country as volunteers, offering a full-time 24-7 commentary on an 800 number telephone circuit which was dialed up by space fans everywhere. All these folks were very cooperative and helpful to the new kid on the block as I struggled to catch up and figure out what was going on.

Also of great assistance was Carlos Byars of the Houston Chronicle – he had been covering space for many years, had great contacts throughout the space center, and was always very generous in sharing information. I also received a lot of help from Frank Seltzer, who was working for CNN TV – we became friends because previously he had worked in the VOA operations studio and I had talked to him many times in sending overseas feeds.

One entertaining element on each flight came as flight controllers in Houston sent a message to the ship to wake them up and start the day after a sleep period. It became a tradition, and a challenge, to find a portion of a recorded popular song that had some connection to the flight's mission. This, too, was always recorded and gave us working radio folks our first actuality of the day.

Another element of most missions was to prepare us for the next mission. The crew appointed for the next mission would come to the information center for a news conference for all of us at JSC, which was also broadcast to the Cape and to NASA headquarters in Washington. After the news conference, those of us interested in getting tape or more information, would be assigned to small rooms in the information center – often one journalist to a room, occasionally two – and the astronauts would be brought to us one-by-one for 15 minutes of interview and chatter.

The poor astronauts would usually be asked the same questions in each of a dozen interview rooms, and would patiently respond to each. They were willing to talk about the mission plans, what they saw as the most important items, what each specifically would be doing, and – to a limited degree – what were their personal feelings about flying the shuttle and the space program.

This gave those of us who were regulars at the space center an opportunity to meet and feel like we knew many of the astronauts. Some of them we met on several different occasions for different flights. And there were always some that were favorites, either because they were particularly personable and/or especially helpful. Among those were Bob Crippen, the most senior of the shuttle astronauts, Bob (Hoot) Gibson, and Charles Bolden, one of the few black astronauts.

I remember Bolden particularly: during one interview, we were talking about his up-bringing as a poor black kid in the South, and he teared up as he talked about the importance of education to himself, and to future black youngsters. I admired his courage to show such emotion; most astronauts tried to keep the "stiff upper lip," "right stuff" demeanor. After several successful missions, Bolden went on to become the Director of NASA.

Crippen was one of those I interviewed in my first day of round-robins, and I am afraid I asked him a lot of dumb questions as I struggled to understand how the shuttle system worked, with its capabilities and limits. He was very patient to explain things to me in the simplest of terms. I hope that in future encounters he felt I had learned a bit and asked more intelligent questions. Around NASA, the motto was, "There are no stupid questions," but surrounded by knowledgeable, experienced space reporters, with all news conferences broadcast everywhere on television, stupid questions just felt like stupid questions.

All this material would be saved up, and used for scene-setter stories after the current mission and prior to the next one. Once I learned what to ask, and what to look for, I could usually pick 5 or 6 actuality-laden long advance reports on the next mission. After a flight ended, the crew would fly back to Houston for a reunion ceremony at nearby Ellington Air Base, and then conduct a post-flight news conference. There was no shortage of material on the space program, and VOA used it all.

Ellington AFB was no longer in use by the Air Force, but it was home field for the astronauts, most of whom were pilots, who flew high-speed jet trainers to various meetings in Florida, Washington and elsewhere. Those astronauts who were not qualified jet pilots would fly along as passengers in the sleek T-33 jets. When we lived nearby, it was a great thrill to hear them buzz overhead at low altitude on a takeoff or landing at Ellington. The air field also was used by the Texas Air National Guard, and was the landing location of choice for Vice President Bush when he made his frequent trips to his hometown of Houston.

One time when the space shuttle itself was being ferried back to Florida from a California landing, piggy-backed on a 747 jet, it landed at Ellington, after making a long, slow low-altitude pass over the space center and along Nasa 1 Road, the main thoroughfare in the area.

I had my first opportunity to watch a shuttle launch in January, 1985. The flight of Discovery was the 15th in the series, and the first one controlled by the military. Thus, it was nearly all secret – once launched, there would be no information about it until it returned. For that reason Washington decided not to send its usual crew to Cape Canaveral, and sent me instead. The launch time was not even announced, we were just given a three-hour window during which it would be sent up, and we were never told its mission, although it was generally believed it would launch from low earth orbit a military spy satellite and send it to a higher orbit from which it would watch the earth below.

The first launch date was set for January 23, but ice and cold weather delayed it two days. In the interim, I was able to tour the Kennedy Space Center, and up and down the Florida coast, where I had never been before. There was no requirement for a live launch commentary, since the exact launch time was not known. My assignment was simply to file news reports about preparations, the launch, then wait for the landing back in Florida. I was not prepared for the spectacle. I cannot describe it any better now than I did in a report filed then to VOA.

Correspondents Notebook, January 25, 1985:
This reporter has covered space stories over the years from the VOA newsroom in Washington, from the Johnson Space Center in Houston and once, during the first moon landing, from a place called Parkes, at a radio telescope in the Australian outback. But never before had I witnessed a launching – I'm sorry, Houston and Parkes, but nothing you offer can match the thrill of watching a blast off at the three-mile range.

I was warned in advance to be prepared for the sound, and it is awesome. The roar rolls across from the pad, a deep throaty roar that makes your skin creep and shakes the ground beneath you. As the rocket climbs skyward, it crackles and bangs and pops, along with the roar.

I was not prepared for the visual spectacle. The TV cameras are usually in close, so you can see the shuttle gradually diminishing in size as it climbs from view, but nothing can convey the brilliant orange intensity of that flame. It almost hurts to look at it and you think you should feel the heat.

The Kennedy Space Center is a place of superlatives. The mobile launcher platforms which carry completely assembled shuttles and their rockets from the assembly building to the launch pad, lift, hold and move the largest, tallest and heaviest known portable structures in the world. The vehicle assembly building is the second largest structure in the world. Inside its doors is an open area nearly 50 stories high, so large that rainfall can develop inside the building.

The landing: Well you might think it is like watching that of any aircraft, but the 80 ton spacecraft comes down in an eerie silence, with no power and appears to drop to the runway at an alarming rate. The 200 mile-per-hour glide must be right for a perfect landing the first time – there is no circle and try again.

The secrecy of the military mission was very frustrating for those NASA officials who had in 45 manned space flights been encouraged to make everything public. At one briefing, a flight controller was asked about the upcoming Defense Department mission, and he responded: "No comment." And then he added, laughing, that was the first time he had ever been permitted to give that answer. It also was very frustrating to the media.

I was to witness another launch a few years later, after interest had waned in the shuttle program. To save money, VOA decided not to send its usual crew to the Cape. This time, I was able to take Linda with me, and she shared the thrill of the event. This time, VOA had me on the air, live, for the launching, and I have to admit I again was so taken with the spectacle that I was nearly tongue-tied and several times lapsed into dead air.

The shuttle flights continued through 1985, with the same routine – a Washington-based crew covering the launches, and then I would pick up coverage from Houston.

Up to the end of the year, I had conducted 84 astronaut interviews as they prepared for upcoming missions, and countless NASA and astronaut news conferences, both pre- and post-flight. I had covered three missions flown in 1984, nine in 1985, and two early in 1986. Most of them involved the deployment of two or more satellites from the shuttle payload bay. Three were Spacelab missions, which had operations 24 hours each day while on orbit, with alternating shifts of astronaut/workers. A couple of exciting flights had long space walks, in attempts to repair, and later, to retrieve, errant satellites. And there were the unusual passengers: Senator Jake Garn, Congressman Bill Nelson, and French, Canadian, German and Vietnamese flyers.

An ambitious year was planned for 1986 – 15 shuttle flights, a fourth shuttle to be added to the fleet, two new launch pads to be available, British, Indonesian and Indian flyers anticipated, and deployment of the Hubble Space Telescope. They were even interviewing journalists to be the first journalist in space and the betting was that Walter Cronkite had the inside track.

During 1985, had NASA announced its plan to send a teacher on a future shuttle missions, and began a competition and screening process to select the lucky teacher. I was sent to Las Vegas for a teacher in space conference where many of those candidates were attending and did some interviews with aspirants, as well as with veteran flyer Chuck Yeager, one of the conference speakers. And after her selection, I did several interviews with the successful applicant, Christa McAuliffe, as she entered her astronaut training.

Of course, it was her flight, on the shuttle Challenger which was launched that fateful, frigid Tuesday morning of January 26, 1986, which exploded shortly after takeoff, killing all seven flyers, and bringing the shuttle program to a nearly three year halt. By then, we had moved to the Houston area, living in Seabrook about three miles from the Johnson Space Center. We could receive the NASA television pictures on our cable system at home, and I was still working from a home office. Because of the high interest in the "teacher" flight, there was a larger-than-usual VOA contingent at Cape Canaveral, and I did not have to be at the Space Center for a couple of hours after launch. Linda and I watched the lift-off from home, but the instant I saw that column of smoke and then the billowing orange flash of the explosion, I started packing up my gear and headed for JSC – I knew something bad had happened and Houston was going to be in the middle of the story.

In the early few hours, no one was sure what had happened, but I asked one long-time NASA information officer what would happen next. He correctly predicted that the accident, whatever its cause, would prompt a delay of many months in the shuttle program and a full-scale inquiry. That certainly was prophetic

Within a couple of hours after the crash, reporters started pouring into the newsroom at the Johnson space center — many of them covering their first space story, with little background knowledge of the program. Some had been at nearby New Orleans for the Super Bowl two days before the launching and were sent directly from there.

Soon it was announced President Reagan would come to the Johnson Space Center the following Monday, February 3, for a memorial service for the fallen astronauts, and even more journalists poured in. I put Linda to work that day — I was confined to the newsroom filing a constant stream of reports, but she was able to roam outside into the press area and stood just a few feet away from the president during his moving speech and personal talks with the astronauts' families.

There were still space stories to be covered after Challenger. The formal inquiry was held in Washington, but revelations there led to follow up stories at JSC. After the cause of the crash was determined to be a leak in one of the solid-fuel rocket boosters used to lift off the shuttle, there was to be a series of stories about efforts to redesign and test the rocket segment joint that had leaked fire because of the ultra-cold launch day in Florida.

Bob at the space shuttle mock up, used for astronaut training. It was just across the parking lot from the VOA trailer office and usually was open for visitors.

I made some trips to the Wasatch Mountains of Utah, where Morton Thiokol was testing its re-designed rocket motors.

One cause of the crash had been that the O-rings connecting the various sections of the solid rocket booster were too cold and allowed propellant to burn through. The re-design required that it be no colder than 40 degrees, while the Challenger had been rushed to launch on an 18 degree day. On the day of the final test at Wasatch, the ground temperature was close to 50 degrees, but it was breezy, causing a wind chill reading of about 35. It took a lot of questioning and arguing within the ranks of the gathered "space science" reporters to convince them that huge stack of metal cylinders did not feel wind chill, only reporters.

There were changes in personnel as well: many astronauts quit the program due to frustration over the delays they saw coming in their immediate future. (Some may also have been affected by what appeared to be a cavalier attitude toward safety in NASA that had prompted a rush to keep up to schedule and launch Challenger on a day when many thought better of it.)

I was back at my post in Houston to cover the return to flight. – it would be two years and eight months later, September 29, 1988, before the shuttles would fly again. And I covered a couple more flights early in 1989.

Sometimes, if you knew the right people, you could play with NASA's toys, as Craig and Donna learned on a visit to Houston. At the controls of the space shuttle training mock-up.

CHAPTER 38 — AFTER THE CRASH

Throughout 1985, VOA Washington had continued to insist that we move my operations out of Austin, to Houston. We moved the last week of October, 1985. This was only three months before the Challenger crash, which seemed to threaten the very need for a Houston bureau.

During that summer, I flew back and forth several times to Tucson keeping up with the Sanctuary trial, which ground on day after day, week after week.

We were still in the post-Challenger lull in early fall of 1986. As we were nearing the end of the federal fiscal year, I got a call from Joe Chapman on the assignments desk. "We have a lot of travel money left over in this year's budget," he said. "Can you think of a trip that you can take for two or three weeks and help us spend a couple thousand bucks?"

That didn't even take much thinking. Just recently, Bill Moyers on Public Television had done an excellent series on the U.S.-Mexican border region, with its problems and its promise. I suggested that I could take a similar look at the border region for VOA, and Washington immediately agreed. I took Linda along in our big pickup truck for the first of what would be several extended trips through the South and Southwest, mostly writing features about America, during the slow period after the Challenger crash.

We drove west to El Paso and starting at boundary monument number one, where the eastward border becomes the river, and the westward border is a line drawn across the sand. We headed back east along the Rio Grande River, crossing the river fourteen times, on every bridge, on foot, on a raft and once in a Border Patrol airplane. I filed stories about border towns on both sides — their problems and their prospects.

We wrote about the Tigua Indian tribe which lives on both sides of the river; floated the Rio Grand River through Big Bend National Park; and ended the journey at the Gulf of Mexico near Brownsville, Texas

A lone stop sign on the beach marked the end of the 1,969 mile-long river border.

The concept of features, or Americana, was a popular one at VOA, and the border trip set off a series of requests, and a new freedom, to go out on the road and seek out this type material.

I had had only had limited opportunity to do this sort of work before. Early in 1985, someone had requested a ten minute feature on the why and how of Mardi Gras in New Orleans, and Linda and I spent ten delightful days there before and during the celebration.

Some time during this period I did my first and only interview of a U.S. President (other than Richard Nixon back in St. Joseph and idle chit-chat with George H.W. Bush). And even at that, it was an ex-president, Jimmy Carter. He had been defeated in his re-election bid by Ronald Reagan, partly because of the U.S. diplomats being held captive in Iran. There is evidence that Reagan envoys made a deal with the Iranians to hold on to the captives until after the election — they were released on Reagan's inauguration day. It wasn't too many months before the Reagan administration was tangled up in Iran-Contra — in effect, the U.S. government was buying the freedom of Americans held captive by Iranian allies in Beirut by supplying weapons to Iran.

Carter had been silent about the controversy but finally agreed to talk about it. VOA arranged a 15 minute satellite link from Carter's Houston hotel to Washington, and I, and a reporter from the Christian Science Monitor, interviewed him. The main question: did he feel vindicated by what was happening in Iran-Contra. The answer seemed to be "yes," but Carter was too much a gentleman to crow about it.

February and March, 1987, found us heading for Dallas (story on the Trade Mart), Fort Worth (stockyards and interview with Tandy/Radio Shack president), Wichita Falls (the city, its growth, and the training of international air force pilots), Albuquerque (atomic bomb museum and Indian health issues), Carlsbad, New Mexico (visit the underground salt mines being considered for nuclear waste storage), and Cloudcroft, (a mountain resort where one can hide from the desert heat). We also visited the cowboys at Waggoner Ranch, the largest contiguous ranch in the world, with 529 thousand acres.

We were out again in June, to Oklahoma, for the large Red Earth Indian festival and pow-wow, and visited nearby Guthrie, an early 1900's frontier town where nearly every early brick structure is still intact. The town is occasionally used as a movie location. And Guthrie was the jumping off place for reenactment of the Oklahoma land rush.

In July we went to Arkansas, visiting Texarkana, which sits on the state line, and where numbered streets are different, depending on which state you are in. Then on to Washington, Arkansas, an abandoned pioneer village that once was a jumping off point for people heading to settle in Texas.

As much travelling as we were doing, that big old Ford pickup was getting too expensive, so we bought an economical Chrysler Le Baron. The car was more than paid for by the mileage allowances we accumulated during our touring America period. Shown above at White Sands, NM.

Digging for diamonds near Hope, Arkansas. Two stories revisited Little Rock's heritage as a holdout against school integration. We visited the Ozark Heritage Village at Mountain View.

We made a couple of trips into Louisiana to do stories about Cajun culture, and the upcoming gubernatorial election. I wrote a feature on the state's skyscraper capitol building.

In February, 1988, we headed toward Dixie, where I did an interview in Atlanta with Mayor Andy Young. We visited the home area of the Cherokee Indians before they were pushed to the West. We reported on the space camp conducted by NASA at Huntsville, Alabama. I also did a story at the famed black college, Tuskegee Institute, where scientists were studying growing hydroponic sweet potatoes as possible food for long-term space travel.

In July, we were headed west again, to Canyon, for the performance of pageant "Texas" in a natural amphitheatre in Palo Duro Canyon; Albuquerque again; the cliff dwellings at Mesa Verde National Park, the Royal Gorge Canyon in Colorado and finally, I made it to Four Corners.

We visited the Navajo reservation, where I interviewed Peter McDonald, a 59 year-old businessman serving as chief of the Navajo tribe.

In November, Linda and I went to Florida for the second of the resumed space flights. It was another hush-hush military mission, but it gave her a chance to watch the spectacle of a launch and since the launch was delayed several days, we had time to explore parts of the Florida coast.

I flew down to Harlingen, Texas, to cover an air show put on by the Confederate Air Force. I did a feature story from Lubbock about the Texas wine industry.

At the Rothko Chapel in Houston, a quiet museum showing fourteen huge panels by artist Mark Rothko, I had a reunion with Rev. John Fife of Tucson, and with Bishop Desmond Tutu, who was the speaker at the tenth anniversary re-dedication of the facility.

In Las Cruces, New Mexico, I interviewed Clyde Tombaugh, the astronomer who discovered the 9th planet, Pluto, in 1930. Unfortunately for him, some 80 years later, scientists have downgraded Pluto to less than a planet; it's now considered a "dwarf planet."

At the University of Utah, I discussed "urban legends" with Jan Brunvand, a professor and folklorist who identified and wrote three books about this phenomenon long before Snopes and the internet.

I spent some time in Waxahachie, Texas, just a few miles south of Dallas, where the government planned to build a $5 billion underground super-collider atomic testing facility. It would be in a seventeen-mile-long tunnel, which would encircle the old restored town. Residents hoped the influx of scientists would enrich the town, whose main claim to fame to that point had been the use of its old houses and neighborhoods as sets for several movies. Because of budget issues, the project never got off the ground, or factually, under the ground.

Kenny Rogers, Dollie Parton and Willie Nelson did a show on the grounds of the Johnson Space Center, so Rogers could introduce a new song about cowboys in space. We went to San Antonio for the grand opening of a Sea World attraction a long way from the sea.

Along the U.S.-Mexico border, Lake Amistad is a flood-control reservoir on the Rio Grande River, near Del Rio, Texas, jointly owned by the two countries. "Amistad" is the Spanish word for "friendship." Nearby is the town of Langtry, where Judge Roy Bean once served out justice west of the Pecos River.

Another trip to Oklahoma City involved the world's largest auction of used airplanes, and a reunion at the local museum of U.S. and Soviet space flyers of the 1975 Apollo-Soyuz joint space flight.

One day, President George H. W. Bush mentioned in Washington that he had called a friend in Lubbock, Texas, for an assessment of how things were going. And I flew to Lubbock to have lunch with and interview the president's friend, Robert Blake.

And in Dallas, I visited and wrote about Southfork Ranch, the fictional home of J R. and the Ewing family. It's a real privately-owned ranch home, but was being developed into a tourist attraction, visited by half a million TV fans each year. By the way, the house was a whole lot smaller than it appeared on TV.

I also covered the 25th anniversary of JFK's assassination in Dallas; with the opening of the museum on the sixth floor of the Texas Book Repository building.

I did a story on the Battleship Texas being readied as a tourist attraction near Houston. I reported on on changes in the alien asylum program.

For five days, beginning on Christmas Day, 1988, I went to Beeville, Texas, to cover President-elect George Bush's annual hunting excursion. The accompanying press entourage never saw the President-elect during this period, but we played a lot of poker while hanging out. This all occurred in a period in which I had requested annual leave, so, I had to request a special exemption to carry that leave forward into 1989, where eventually I was paid for it.

I received an unusual telephone call at the bureau at some point during 1988. This was during the early days of "Glastnost and Peristroika" in the Soviet Union, when the Russian people were beginning to feel the end of years of oppression. The caller identified himself as a Houston businessman, and he simply said: "Congratulations."

"Congratulations, for what," I asked.

He responded, "Congratulations, you won."

Still uncertain what he was talking about, I asked, "I won what?"

"Not you, but VOA. You won the cold war." I had never quite looked at it with that perspective, but perhaps he was at least partially correct although I had never really considered myself as a foot soldier in the cold war. I thanked him for his thoughts while assuring him I had not done it single-handedly. But, it was a nice thought.

Early in 1989, I did a story that had another Russian hook. Kempton Forest, a Texas real estate investor, had been a B-17 pilot in the waning days of World War II. His plane was forced down over Poland by a Russian fighter pilot. Once on the ground, and identified as friendly, Forest's aircraft was repaired by a Soviet crew, headed by a female engineer, who also was the fighter pilot's new wife. In the week the repair took, the three formed a wartime friendship, and when Forest flew back to his unit in Italy, he carried as a souvenir a damask tablecloth. It had been a wedding present to the newlyweds, and they signed and inscribed on it "May your return be as smooth as this cloth."

Forest said he though about them often after the war, but his efforts to find them during the cold war were to no avail. But he was in Leningrad on a cruise in 1987, was interviewed by the Novostny News Service, and a few weeks later heard from his Russian friends. They turned out to be Anatoli Kozhevnikov and Tamara Kozhevnikova. She had achieved note as a writer and film producer, he retired as a Lt. General, with decorations as an air ace and test pilot. Forest returned to the Soviet Union in April, 1988, for a warm and tearful reunion, still carrying the inscribed damask. He described himself to me as "an ambassador of table cloth diplomacy.

On the waterfront at Memphis, Tennessee, during the Great Steamboat Race. The Mississippi Queen is in the background. The story of the steamboat race — which turned out to be my last assignment — is in the following chapter.

Over the years, I designed and built several broadcast studios for use by me and other VOA correspondents; in Bangkok, Tokyo, Jerusalem, Nairobi, and Johannesburg. But the epitome was the one, below left, at the VOA trailer on the Johnson Space Center at Houston. It had full flexibility to record incoming phone calls, record two-way telephone interviews, and send reports out to Washington by telephone, with the capability of sending four tapes and a voice down the line in a single broadcast. An audio engineer at NASA wired it all up for me.

CHAPTER 39 — BEGINNING OF THE END

Linda went with me to Houston in 1985 for a couple of prolonged shuttle missisons, giving her the opportunity to get acquainted with some of my colleagues at NASA and with the Johnson Space Center and its neighborhood. We began looking at houses in the vicinity, and soon found one we liked a lot. We wanted something within a few miles of the JSC and near the water of Clear Lake and Galveston Bay. And it had to have a swimming pool, as we had in Austin. We were spoiled by then about pools — we had had them also in both houses in South Africa.

The corner house at 323 Cedar Lane, in the El Lago subdivision, just a block away from Clear Lake and NASA 1 Road, was not even on the list of those we were to look at this particular day. But we were parked in front with our agent looking at the list of prospects and it beckoned to us. We were intrigued by its roofline – it had a set of windows in what appeared to be a two-story atrium. It had a lockbox, and was available for showing, so we made a spur of the moment decision: "Let's look at it." It was cool inside on a very hot day and the house was so inviting that we both fell in love with it immediately.

The atrium was over a large living room that was the very center of the house, almost like an indoor patio. Its floors were brick. There were three carpeted bedrooms down the left side of the atrium/living room, and a large dining room, kitchen, breakfast area and master bedroom suite along the right side. The back wall of the living room was all glass, looking out onto a patio and pool. A two-car garage and a spare room were adjacent to the pool. It was even within our price range—if we could sell the house in Austin. We decided to buy it almost immediately.

That was easier said than done. In the end, it was nearly a year before the house in Austin sold. This all came during a total real estate bust in Texas, due to the tremendous drop in oil prices. That was why we could afford 323 Cedar Lane, but also why it took so long to sell the Austin house, and why we spent a year making double house payments. Steven was still attending classes at Austin Community College, and working in telemarketing at the same time, so we left him in the Austin house, with a small refrigerator and some furniture, to show it and keep it clean until sale.

Washington had been so adamant that I must move to Houston that, without my knowledge or any warning, they had sent an administrator to Houston one weekend when I was away from Texas covering a story in Arizona. I had been looking around for potential office space, something halfway between the city and JSC, and near Hobby Airport which served most of the Southwest Airline flights in and around Texas. But despite my looking and my recommendations, this administrator contracted with the General Services

Administration for office space for VOA in the Rusk Federal Courts Building in downtown Houston.

To make matters worse, he even went to an office furniture store and purchased desks, chairs, filing cabinets and other equipment for a three-office operation. It was all moved and stored immediately in the proposed VOA office suite in the 8th floor of the Federal Building. If they were thinking at all, they still had in mind an English speaking correspondent/bureau chief (me) plus a Spanish-language reporter and an office assistant.

Once this was all done – it only took him a day and a half – the administrator went back to Washington and informed me by phone of the wonderful things they had wrought for me. The first opportunity I had, I went to Houston to see these wonderful things. The suite was on the 8th floor alright, at the back of the building, with one window overlooking the parking lot. It was tucked between a freight elevator, and a private passenger elevator reserved for the Federal judges who had their offices nearby on the same floor.

The space was not large enough – the stored new furniture filled it wall-to-wall, and that was without any people or any activity. There was no space for a broadcast studio or for wire service teletype machines.

The offices were impossible to find, behind two doors that closed off portions of the hallways, in a maze that led to the back of the building from the public elevators in the front. Some of the corridors were blocked because they housed the judges. Because the federal courtrooms were in the building, there was strict security at the front entrance. Anyone coming in – other than employees – had to step through one of those airport security devices, and have any handbags searched.

I was outraged and told Washington so. I proved how inaccessible the space was by getting a colleague arrested there. Soon after we took up residence in Seabrook, we were visited by Ruben del Castillo and his wife. He was a Spanish-language reporter at VOA, and was considering and being considered for, transfer to the new Houston bureau. I took him to the Federal Building, and past

security, and challenged him to find the VOA office by room number. I warned him that it was a difficult challenge, but gave him a head start by telling him it was on the 8th floor. And then I waited in the lobby outside the building manager's office.

Ten minutes hadn't passed before security guards brought Rueben to the manager's office. He had been apprehended after being spotted on security cameras, wandering around in what appeared to be an aimless fashion, on the 8th floor, opening various doors and approaching the vaunted judges' inner sanctum. My point was made – how would anybody from the public who wanted to have any dealing with the VOA Southwest News Bureau manage to get past security and cameras and guards and closed-off corridors to get to the VOA offices. With a great deal of delight, both Rueben and I called our respective home offices in Washington and reported on the day's adventure.

Despite this, Reuben still wanted the job, and Linda and I wanted him and his delightful wife to join us in Houston. But he didn't get it; the Spanish position was never filled -- even after I convinced Washington that I should move to another part of the building, and got established in a suite of proper-sized and located offices. Throughout my time in that building, one office and desk and chair remained open and empty for the Spanish reporter who never came.

The new location was a great improvement. It was on the front of the building, with two windows and a view out at part of the fantastic Houston downtown skyline. It was also near the elevators and easy to find, although visitors still had to go through the lobby security process. It had three office areas, a room for a studio and a closet for the wire machines. There was parking in a city owned garage across the street, for which I, and all visitors, had to pay.

There were other hassles. The General Service Administration was reluctant to allow me to install an outside phone line. They thought I should use the government telephone service, even though it was less reliable and subject to all sorts of restraints on long distance. The bureau used a lot of long distance phoning. They also were reluctant to allow me to install a television antenna on the roof, because my co-tenants in the FBI office, had a satellite dish up there and my antenna might interfere. Nor could we install a satellite dish for possible use in broadcast circuits. I never won that fight, so I was never able to set up a system to record all the local TV newscasts and I was never able to watch NASA television in the downtown-bureau office.

Then there was the fight with Washington over having an official car with a U.S government license plate on it. Perhaps they thought they were doing me a favor, but I much preferred the flexibility of using my own vehicle (the MG was a lot more fun to drive than some stodgy old Chevrolet sedan). I wouldn't be allowed to take the government car home, some 45 miles away, but only to a nearby fenced motor pool in a rough part of town. And I couldn't even park my own vehicle inside the fenced area when I was using the government car – I would have to leave it parked on a neighborhood street.

Still Washington was insistent, until I called my old friend David Hitchcock in Washington. He was the former deputy Public Affairs Officer in Tokyo, he and his family had shared our beach house there, and he had been PAO and a good friend in Israel. He now was the chief administrative officer of USIA and quickly saw the stupidity of the assigned car plan. He made a call, and nothing more was ever heard about the car. Was I making some enemies in Washington? You bet, and there were more to come.

One of my demands for moving the VOA operations from Austin to Houston, and from the convenience of my house to a downtown office building, was that VOA provide me the assistant that the bureau was promised. I went through several applicants who were listed as government clerk typists on the federal register, but none had the sort of journalistic experience I wanted. I finally decided to hire Tommy Jones – he at least worked at VOA, and came with high recommendations from a friend of mine in Washington who had been his supervisor. I talked with Tommy on the phone about the job and he was enthusiastic to come to Houston and take it on.

Tommy was a tall, thin black man, about 30, who had lived in Washington, D.C. most of his life. He was married and had a two-year-old son, Brandon, who he said he wanted to get away from the District and all its crime and drug problems. He also said he wanted to get himself away from a "bad crowd" that he had fallen in with. I hired him and in the early summer of 1986, Tommy came to Houston, to be followed in a few weeks by his wife, Maylene, and Brandon. I found them an apartment near NASA, in the same project where I had stayed several times during long space missions.

Tommy Jones and Brandon

The downtown office was not yet finished, so I set Tommy up in a spare room of our house and he began work. He was a good worker: loyal, diligent, enthusiastic, and a nice guy. We became friends, and when his family arrived, they became friends too. Once the downtown office was opened, Tommy went there each day and manned the phones, handled the finances, cleared the teletype machines, learned how to operate the studio, and began learning about journalism. This gave me the flexibility to come in to the office, or spend time at NASA, or even out of town.

Tommy was a great sports fan (and I was not), so I had him cover some sports events requested by VOA, such as an interview with Houston Rockets basketball star Akeem Olajuwan, and some fun events, like covering the 1986 Major League All-Star Baseball game. He even had a press pass to the Astro's ballgames and could dip into the press buffet before each game.

Things were running along nicely in the Houston bureau. So, of course, you can anticipate that this, too, is about to end. In December, 1986 – just a week before our first Christmas in Houston – VOA called to announce they planned to close the Houston Bureau, effective January 31, 1987 as a budget-cutting measure.

I was furious and frustrated. We had not even yet sold the house in Austin, and here we were making payments on two houses in Texas, where two years earlier, the powers in Washington wanted me to be. They had disrupted Tommy Jones and his family's lives: Maylene had quit a good job in Washington to move to Houston. A lot of money had been spent establishing the office, and installing a studio downtown. And they didn't even have an assignment for me: "Oh, we'll put you back in the newsroom, somewhere."

So, I wrote a letter to Senator Lloyd Bentsen of Texas, asking him for support. I noted that the bureau had only been established two years earlier, at great expense, in order that VOA could follow its Charter mandate to "present a balanced and comprehensive projection of significant American thought and institutions," and to report news from "beyond the Beltway." I noted that it would cost more to move Tommy and me back to Washington than would be saved in a bureau budget that only ran to $15,800 per year plus salaries, which would continue.

I added in my letter: "The resumption of manned space flight in another year will be important. In the past year, this bureau has followed closely the efforts of NASA to recover its momentum. In addition, we have concentrated on news such as Hispanic affairs, U.S.-Mexico border problems, drug interdiction and immigration problems in the Southwest." I also naively said: "This is not a sour grapes complaint and does not appear to be a personal problem – I have had excellent efficiency ratings throughout my 24-year career with VOA." But it obviously was a personal problem – as the coming months were to show.

Sen. Bentsen made an inquiry to VOA about the matter, and was informed early in 1987 by VOA Director Richard Carlson: "In the first (budget) review, we considered closing the bureau. How-

ever, we were able to keep the bureau open for the time being by leaving the chief correspondent there, but returning his assistant to fill another vacancy here in Washington." Carlson's response was not entirely truthful; the decision had been made and then rescinded when the Senator inquired.

That decision killed Tommy Jones. He was dejected by his treatment at the hands of VOA when we put him and the family back on a plane to Washington. And within the year, Tommy was dead from a drug overdose. He had gotten back in with that "bad crowd."

And I, in a phrase borrowed from British journalists, "had blotted my copy book" – I had earned the eternal enmity of Richard Carlson. And within the year efforts would begin to get rid of me.

I crossed Carlson's radar screen again in March, 1987, when I was interviewed by a newspaper columnist in Amarillo. She had run into me at a Henry Kissinger news conference and asked for an interview about VOA and what it was doing in Texas. I thought it was a positive article about the Voice, and had even sent it in to friends at VOA as proof of effectiveness, and those friends inadvertently called it to the attention of Director Carlson. He wrote me a strong letter, denouncing me for acting as a "spokesman" for VOA and for discussing the issue of occasional interference in VOA news by outsiders. That subject occupied only one paragraph of a 23 paragraph article, but it was the one he focused on and reacted to.

Without an assistant to run the office, I insisted that we needed to close the downtown office, and finally good sense prevailed. We got permission from NASA to put a trailer/building at the Johnson Space Center, in a row with other media trailers. It was big enough that I could move all the office furniture and equipment from the Federal Building, and we had a great set up just three miles from our house in El Lago. I took the front office room, with windows on three sides, overlooking the parking lot and the Space Station Training Facility. The center room, with desk and file cabinets, was set aside for any assistant or visitor to use. The back room was divided into a room for the teletypes and fax machine; and a studio which I had installed by a NASA sound technician.

I even gained an assistant the summer of 1987. Shanna Swendson, a broadcast journalism major at the University of Texas, contacted me to ask if VOA could and would use an intern. No salary was involved; in fact, Shanna moved to the Clear Lake area for the summer, got an apartment and an evening job as a receptionist in a restaurant, just so she could work for VOA for free twenty hours per week. I had her do some of the bookkeeping and telephone work, while using her to do as much reporting and writing as she could. She had a lot of potential, but I have lost track of what she made of her career in broadcasting. The internship was a great arrangement, and one which I had hopes of continuing in future years.

But hopes of continuing anything in future years had been dashed in February, 1988, when VOA served notice that I would be retired at the end of the year. I was to be forced to retire ("selection out" is the gentle phrase they use) under a "time-in-class" provision of the Foreign Service Act under which we served. Time in class is sort of like the up-or-out challenge that career military officers face. The foreign service provision were that if you had been in the same grade or rank (I was an FS-1, the top) for twenty years without further promotion, you were required to retire. At USIA, I was a specialist as a correspondent, and the only place for us to be promoted to was the Senior Foreign Service, and very, very few specialists ever received a promotion to that grade.

Even more ironic and infuriating was the fact that earlier in the year I had been recommended by the Overseas Specialist Selection Board for a Meritorious Service Increase and had received my first pay increase in several years. A friend of mine had been a member of that selection board, and he told me privately that the board members were given no indication of my then-pending status with T-I-C and were not given much latitude to promote specialists to the Senior Foreign Service. In fact, he said, board members were not even made aware that Foreign Service Specialists were subject to selection-out. Nor was I aware of that –

I had always been under the impression that specialists were not so imperiled.

There was only one way to avoid it. There was a provision for a "limited career extension" under which a selected-out officer could be retained for three additional years "for the good of the service." I requested an LCE, which was rejected by Richard Carlson.

I filed a detailed formal appeal of the action to the VOA Director of Personnel, arguing that it could be viewed as personal discrimination against me because "it is well known by my colleagues within VOA that there is some high-level administrative animus toward me because of my efforts early in 1987 to prevent closure of the Houston bureau."

I also argued economic hardship: even two more years under an LCE would have boosted by ultimate pension by $4000 because of a new pay scale. I informally polled most of the other VOA correspondents; none of whom were aware that "we" were subject to selection out. My formal appeal was rejected by the Director of Personnel.

Before the end of the year I filed a formal grievance with the Foreign Service Grievance Board, arguing many of these same points. Because of that grievance, I was extended beyond the December 31, 1988, retirement date while the formal grievance was adjudicated. Meanwhile, I continued working.

One of the trips Linda and I took late in 1988 was to Washington, to attend a three day retirement seminar. At that point I still had hopes my grievance would be upheld, but in preparation for the worst, I delved into the issues of living on retirement and finding new employment. The seminar at least inspired me to believe that I could earn some money after retirement by freelance writing. On the long drive back to Houston, Linda and I discussed the possibilities, and even made up a long list of 50 or so possible freelance stories I could pursue in retirement. When we got home, I began to shop for computers, knowing I would need one to pursue a freelance career.

CHAPTER 39 — BEGINNING OF THE END

A wonderful story opportunity came in the summer of 1989. The previous summer, I had done a story on low water in the Mississippi River which threatened to delay the annual "Great Steamboat Race" from New Orleans to St. Louis by the riverboats Delta Queen and Mississippi Queen. In interviewing the steamboat company representatives in New Orleans, I casually remarked that I would be interested in going on and writing about a river steamer ride. I gave it little further thought.

In the late spring of 1989, I received a desperate call from the Delta Queen Steamboat Company. They had misplaced my phone number and wanted to invite me to take part as a passenger in the 1989 Steamboat Race. "No charge — Bring Your Wife." I put the proposal to Washington and was amazed when they agreed. So I began an intense period of preparation, researching and studying each of the river cities which the steamboats would visit during their ten-day cruise up the mighty river, ending in St. Louis on July 4.

The cruise was scheduled to stop for the day in Natchez, Vicksburg and Greenville, Mississippi; Memphis, Tennessee; Cairo, Illinois and Caruthersville, Missouri. I had loads of background information, and contacts arranged in each town, and as the steamboat passengers would take off in each port for sight-seeing, I would spend time doing interviews with various contacts, preparing and phoning in feature stories on these historic river towns and their economic links to the river. It was a wonderful trip, and as it turned out, a memorable way to end an interesting career. Once in St. Louis, we were met by my brother, Steve and his family, and spent a few days at the Lake of the Ozarks with them before flying home to Houston.

While on the Delta Queen, I was re-united with Mitch Osburne, the AP photographer with whom I had travelled in Namibia. He now was the official photographer for the Delta Queen Steamship Co.

I had not been back in the office a day when I got a call on July 13, that I had lost my grievance, and the mandatory retirement would soon take place. I

suggested that a couple of months would give me time to wrap things up – the response from Personnel was to be gone by July 31: "That will give you time to clean out your desk."

During this time, it had been indicated by the news and programming folks in Washington that every effort would be made to hire me back as a part-time reporter in Houston once and if retirement became effective. But once that occurred, VOA Director Carlson made it clear that he did not want me working for VOA under any circumstance, despite his previous assurances to the news executives. An engineer was sent to Houston to dismantle the studio, pack all equipment and furniture and ship it back to Washington, and arrange for the removal of the trailer from NASA. As my friend Ben Whitten observed: "They all but salted the furrows of the earth to make sure you would not return."

On my last day I sent an e-mail to most of my VOA colleagues.

My retirement from VOA is effective today. This is not something I sought. I fought [mandatory retirement] before the FS Grievance Board, but lost my appeal and was granted by Personnel just over two weeks notice…"plenty of time to clean out your desk," they said. Yes, I am a little bit bitter about ending a 26-year career with VOA in such a fashion. However, I am not bitter about the time I spent with VOA News. I believe that despite the best efforts of some, we have managed to develop and maintain an admirable news gathering and reporting organization. Except for a few occasions, I have been proud of VOA and its people. I implore you to keep up the fight for the Charter and all it represents. NON ILLEGITIMI-CARBORUNDUM. [DON'T LET THE BASTARDS GRIND YOU DOWN].

I received just one e-mail response before my e-mail service was unplugged, and I went home. The next morning, August 1, Houston and Clear Lake were hit by Hurricane Chantal. And I did not bother to report on it.

CHAPTER 40 — VOA IN THE REAR VIEW MIRROR

I remember the morning. At the ripe old age of 54, I start thinking of a new career, a new life and/or a new job. Hurricane Chantal is blowing 80 miles an hour outside, rain banging against all the upper level windows that are so attractive the rest of the time. The storm drains are stopped up, and the water is rising all the way up to the level of the front porch, just inches from making its way into the house. We find a neighborhood woman cowering on the front porch, hiding from the wind and rain, and bring her in for coffee until the storm passes.

Several apartments and businesses along the shores of Clear Lake were damaged by tornadic winds. It probably would have made a good first person story for VOA. We had been preparing for this eventuality and for working as a free lance writer. Linda took a course in photography, so she would be able to assist me as I pursued stories.

I purchased a computer, and daisy wheel impact printer (having done some homework, I learned that editors would not accept submissions from thermal printers, which most printers were, and I was not of a mind to go back to typewriters). I learned how to work MSDOS in the era before Windows.

I purchased the *Writers Handbook*, the guide to all possible outlets for freelance work, and subscribed to the monthly *Writers Magazine*. I took a weekend seminar at Rice University on public relations (where I first learned not to pick a fight with people who buy ink by the barrel). And I enrolled in a course taught by the Manuscriptor's Literary Service. Jerry and Janet Weiner were free-lance magazine writers who found it more lucrative to help other writers with critiques, seminars and book proposals than doing all that for themselves. Smart people. Their primary lesson, over several Thursday night classes: it's not the writing of the piece, it's the sale of the piece in advance by a proposal letter to magazine editors.

I began sending out "pitch" letters about some of the 50 or so subjects Linda and I had identified during our long drive back from the Washington retirement seminar. And I learned pretty quickly that "pitching" to magazine editors was frustrating and sometimes degrading. Vanity Fair and Esquire were not interested in me.

I kept my NASA credentials, and my contacts there, and I have did some prerecorded stories for upcoming space shuttle missions for the National Space Foundation, the folks who operated the 24/7 reporting over their telephone network.

A weekly Washington-based newspaper, *Space News*, used occasional pieces from me. Three articles were published there early in 1990.

One piece that grew out of NASA was published nationally in *Modern Drummer* magazine. It featured astronaut Jim Weatherbee. The 37-year-old shuttle pilot was a good amateur drummer, playing in a five member rock-and-roll band made up entirely of astronauts, calling themselves "Max Q." Weatherbee took drum sticks to space with him in January, 1990, and played on a practice pad, becoming the first drummer in outer space.

Weatherbee was in awe of, and friends with, E Street Band drummer Max Weinberg, and carried a souvenir set of drumsticks into space for Weinberg. I interviewed Weinberg by telephone about the story, and Max was invited to Weatherbee's launch from Cape Canaveral.

I got a second little item from Weinberg. He told me he was going to law school. He expected the performing side of the music business would lose him. "I am going into the other side of the music business. For 30 years I have been on this side of the drum set. By going on the other side, hopefully I will be able to make a contribution to people who have problems and need them solved."

Of course, Max never left the music business, and wrote to *Modern Drummer* that he didn't remember saying or implying that he was giving up performing. I had it on tape, but *Modern Drummer* was not going to take the word of a free-lance writer in Houston over one of the best known drummers in the music business. It did leave a sour taste.

I also got hooked up with *Food People*, a newspaper for the food industry, with a story about Austin's Whole Foods company embarking on a campaign against food additives. Another story in *Food People* concerned Stop-N-Go stores in four states upgrading their line of merchandise beyond beer and cigarettes to oat-bran cereals, gourmet pasta and bottled water.

I even had a brief (tiny) item in Gannett's *USA Weekend* on its What's Next Page, about hydroponic vegetables being grown and sold at a Fiesta Supermarket in Houston (Clear Lake City, actually). *Food People* liked the story also and featured it big in its December, 1989, issue. So did *The Produce News* — "All the news that's fresh."

The Houston Chamber of Commerce had a monthly magazine for its members, and I did three pieces for it. All were cover stories. One titled "Breaking the Deadlock" discussed how Houston developers were finding new locations for businesses and offices along the toll road system that was being built to encircle the city.

Another article for *Houston Magazine* reported on the Port of Houston and its long term ties to international trading, particularly the Japan External Trade Organization.

The third cover story was about the re-emergence of the petrochemical industry in the Houston area. In addition to the main story, I had an interesting side bar about Igloo's Playmate cooler replacing old fashioned metal lunch boxes, and being carried in by workers at the Phillips petrochemical complex in Pasadena, the same site where the original plastic was made for Igloo.

One series of stories that I thought would be a natural was "The Many Springfields." At that time, there were 28 cities, towns and villages bearing the name "Springfield." It took a lot of time and research to find out about each of them (it would be so much easier now with Google and the internet). I wrote Chambers of Commerce and newspapers in each of them asking for information and for pictures, and got responses from nearly every one. I even traced the name back to the original Springfield, in England.

With all the information and pictures in hand, I began sending out pitch letters to newspapers and magazines in or near each of the Springfields, offering a custom written piece on their Springfield and how it compared with all the others.

A long-time friend, Bob Glazier, publisher of *Springfield! Magazine* in my hometown of Springfield, Missouri, was the first to get aboard. He published it, not only in his monthly magazine, but with a slight re-write, featured it in his 1990-91 *Guide to Springfield* book.

But, I was disappointed. The story was not bought by any other Springfield; not by Massachusetts which was then the largest of the group, not in Illinois, or Ohio, Oregon or Virginia.

This free lance venture was not making much money, certainly not enough to be worth the time and effort it was taking. I think my cover stories for *Houston Magazine* paid the most, about $200 each, and they even complained when I asked them to cover the expenses, primarily incurred using the toll roads I was writing about.

I also was looking around for employment. Houston's Compaq computer company was looking for some one to handle international public relations (I should have been a natural for that — probably too old).

A nearby community college was seeking a public relations director. I applied, provided the required half dozen letters of reference, only to find the job had gone to someone else — the application process had all been about the process, they had a candidate in the pipeline.

By the end of the year, 1989, we decided we had had enough of this. Linda's step-father, Fred Hunt, assured us we could live comfortably in Springfield on my retirement pay of $30,000. On a trip to Missouri, we were struck about how much more attractive it was than the Houston area. It was that or become a Wal-Mart greeter. And the decision was made: we would move home to Springfield, Missouri.

CHAPTER 41 — BECOMING MISSOURIANS AGAIN

We had some hesitations. For one, we hated to give up the house in El Lago because it was unique and roomy. But it also was expensive — it had only single pane windows throughout, and there were lots of them, allowing the Texas heat and humidity in. Many months of the year, our air conditioning bill would run $400 or more.

We also had grandchildren nearby. Kim and Jeff Carter were in Austin, just four hours away, and they had been blessed with a son, Kyle Robert Carter, born on November 27, 1989. And after we were gone, granddaughter Shannon Kaye Carter was born October 8, 1991.

There were grandchildren also at Villa Rica, Georgia, near Atlanta, where Craig and Donna had moved from Casper, Wyoming. Justin Robert Chancellor had been born May 21, 1985, and Jenny Leigh Chancellor on July 26, 1987.

Son Steven was living in the Houston area, and was expected to soon marry a Texas girl, Karen Marie Rogers. They did marry on April 26, 1991. So there was every likelihood that we would be spending a lot of time on I-35 and I-45 making visits back to Texas.

And there was the question of weather. Houston can get very hot and humid in the summer months, but wintertime is pretty pleasant, while Missouri does have four seasons, and one of them is usually cold and occasionally snowy. And, while we didn't give it much thought at the time, we were moving into one of the most politically conservative places in the country.

The weather was offset somewhat by the fact that we would be near the Lake of the Ozarks, where my brothers and I had retained ownership of the family cabin. It was only about 600 square feet, but the previous summer we had contracted to put a big deck across the front, nearly doubling the amount of useable space.

We made a visit to Springfield early in 1990 to reconnoiter. We found a three bedroom house on the south edge of town at 4950 South McCann, which we could rent reasonably, and signed a lease beginning in April. Our intention was to rent for a year while we looked for something to purchase. The rental house had a full basement which would provide storage for our accumulation of furniture and other treasures.

Anticipating that we were going to move, we drove to Springfield in two cars, me in the lead in the MGB, Linda following in our Chrysler LeBaron. The plan was to leave the MG in Fred's barn and return to Texas together to prepare for the move.

We talked to our realtor in Seabrook, where the sales market was still slow. She suggested she could find us a short-term renter while we made sure the move was really what we wanted to do. And she would serve as our rental agent, to prevent any folks like our Maryland renters from moving in. We agreed to that plan and began the familiar task of sorting out what goes and what stays.

We moved the first week of April, 1990. It took all day to load the moving van, and we despaired if we would ever get on the road. Our goal had been to get at least as far as Dallas before stopping for the night. As we headed out, we didn't get much beyond the northern outskirts of Houston when a sudden, intense thunderstorm hit. So we pulled into a Holiday Inn in Conroe, Texas, for the night.

Again, we were in a two vehicle convoy — Linda in the LeBaron and me in the pickup truck. I had outfitted the truck with a cap, and in the back were our two cats along with some housekeeping goods we thought we might need in the first day or two until the moving van arrived. The cats were not good travelers, but they had a pan, food and water and we had figured they would be alright. But they were terrified by the storm, so we smuggled them into the Holiday Inn.

To make things worse, the motel bathroom had a leaking water pipe and about half the floor was soaked. But we couldn't call on motel maintenance to fix it, because we didn't want them to know about the two cats.

The next morning dawned bright and clear and we made an early start for Springfield, pulling in at the rental house by mid afternoon. The moving van arrived the next day and we began moving stuff into the house.

That spring we spent a lot of time at the lake. Fred had purchased a small bass boat several years earlier, which he kept in his barn behind his house. After hauling it to the lake two or three times, and taking Fred along on some other fishing trips, he suggested we just keep the boat at our dock at the lake. That seemed like a good deal. Linda and I really got into fishing, especially trolling for white bass.

We were learning a new craft. Linda had not done much fishing for years, I had done only a little in Texas with a next door neighbor who had a boat.

Linda re-established contact with her life-long friend, Martha Ferguson Hutchison, but I was not aware that I had any good, life-long buddies in town.

I still had some work to do — one last assignment of features to write for the National Space Foundation folks, based on interviews I had done with the astronauts before we left Houston. I set up an office in the front bedroom and went to work.

Fortunately, I ran out of paper for my printer, and had to go to a nearby computer store for supplies. The guy running the store said: "I know you. You were a Teke. You're Bob Chancellor. I'm Norm Hall." That was all true. Norm, a Navy veteran, had been in college and in the fraternity when I was. He told me the fraternity alumni association had become very active and was trying to raise funds for an addition to the TKE House at SMS, and invited to me to an alumni meeting.

From there, I met Jerry Nixon, who was one of the driving forces behind the revived alumni association. He had an insurance agency, and in fact, had written my first auto insurance policy back when I bought my first car. Norm Hall had tipped him to the fact that I was a retired writer. Jerry was one of those people who would not accept "no" as an answer, and quickly appointed me chairman of the national fund raising campaign, meaning I would write and publish a newsletter seeking donations from other alums. The first newsletter went out in November.

Included in this effort was Sam Mullin. He was a businessman in Bolivar and had been serving for two years as president of the alumni association. I remembered Sam from my college days; and in time he would become one of my best friends.

Others involved included attorney Lee Gannaway, who had been a couple of years behind me in college, and Gary Ellison, who ran an advertising agency and was an entertainer, who had been designated as "Missouri's Official Ragtime Piano Player."

In the meantime there had been housing developments. Linda and I looked at probably 100 houses for sale in Springfield, and had an understanding with realtor JoAnn Mitchell that we would use her as our buying agent if and when we found something we wanted. In time we did — a three-bedroom, two-bath house with a huge family room at 2152 East Berkeley. What made it particularly attractive was that it had an assumable 8 percent mortgage (and that was good in those days) with a very low down payment. JoAnn suggested jumping on it if we could.

We also were in the process of selling the house in El Lago. The temporary rental had ended and

2152 East Berkeley

some people from California had shown up, wanting to buy it. Anybody moving to Texas from the California real estate market at that time was carrying around bundles of cash — we were told that the down payment they made on our house came just from selling their sailboat. We agreed to carry their mortgage note at 9 percent, which more than covered our house payments in Springfield. The only downside came a year later, when mortgage rates dropped and the buyers refinanced, depriving us of that income stream.

So, we were home in Springfield, and in fact, lived in that house eight years, longer than we had ever been in one place before. We added a deck, we remodeled rooms, painted, refinished floors, planted a garden. We were keeping busy in our new life, while still hitting the road often to Villa Rica and/or Austin and Houston.

I remember a story Fred told me when he retired from the insurance business. One day he found himself standing in line to apply for a job as a Wal-Mart greeter when he suddenly thought to himself: "What Am I Doing?" He got out of line immediately. His advice to me: "If you ever find yourself thinking about getting a job, go lay down until the feeling goes away."

Never one smart enough to follow advice, I found myself applying for a job. Bass Pro Shops in Springfield was looking for people to take phone orders for fishing and outdoor equipment for its catalog operation. Since I was becoming an avid fisherman, that sounded like an ideal job — getting paid to talk to people about fishing. I was hired and went through their three-week paid training program and was put in a cubicle. They were pretty flexible about working hours — you could get off almost any time you wanted, but even working 20 hours a week cut into my fishing time and my fraternity time. And it didn't pay much more than minimum wage, although they promised commissions on up-selling specials to callers.

I did pretty well, but resigned at the end of six months, because they gave me a raise. It was not the fact of the raise, it was the fact that in praising my work, they increased my hourly pay by eleven cents an hour, and I felt that pittance was an insult.

But I did miss the five percent employee discount that I received at the store.

Some of my fraternity brothers, namely Karl Scholz and Steve Rule, were members of the Sertoma Club. It is a national service club, which in Springfield supported the Boys and Girls Clubs. I was invited to one of their Friday lunch meetings as a speaker — I had a little song and dance about VOA and international broadcasting, backed up with some tapes of various broadcasts. That Sertoma Club, Heart of the Ozarks, was having a membership rush party that evening, and I was invited back to it. And, I joined. I have been a member for the twenty-plus years since.

I recruited several other of my Teke fraternity brothers into Sertoma: Ed Wester, Bill Hawkins, Sam Mullin, and Conrad Griggs.

Sertoma had its own building downtown, which was used as a Bingo hall for fundraising, and all members were expected to work at least one Thursday night per month at Bingo. I learned the ropes there, as a caller, working the floor, and as a cashier, and in time, was named one of the captains, in charge of one week each month.

Another Sertoma function was the annual Chili Cook-Off, a big fund-raiser conducted jointly by all six Sertoma Clubs in town. I didn't pay much attention to it the first year or two, but in 1994, I joined the Cook-Off committee to boost its publicity. The '94 cook-off made a profit of $11,399. Two years later, profits had more than tripled, to $37,700. I will modestly take some of the credit for that: I prepared news releases, radio commercials, had a television public service announcement produced, and made personal appearances on radio and TV. By 2009, the event was almost self-promoting, and I gave up my publicity efforts. By then, the Sertoma Chili Cook-Off was generating annual profits of $140-170,000.

Also in 2009, I stopped publishing the Teke Talk alumni newsletter, which I had put out two or more times each year since my first one in November, 1990 I think I just wore out and lost interest in both projects.

But that was not all of my activity. Fraternity brother Lee Gannaway was elected Mayor of Springfield in 1995 and soon afterward, started talking to me about serving on some city board. He suggested I might be interested in the Mayor's Commission on Human Rights (perhaps because it was a pretty liberal board, and I was the only liberal Democrat he knew). I met with the Director of the Human Rights Commission and was convinced that it was not a discussion board, but one that took an active part in its mission. Commission members were appointed to hear and adjudicate various discrimination complaints concerning race, landlord issues, employment issues, and discrimination for disabilities and sex. I took the appointment and enjoyed the Commission's activities for a year or so.

At the same time, I was serving a three-year term on the board of the SMS Alumni Association. That was an easy task — the director of the association did all the work, and board members just basked in reflected glory at one or two university events annually.

Meanwhile, another fraternity brother, Gary Ellison, got me drafted onto the board of the Springfield Landmarks Preservation Trust, with which he had been working and serving. The trust had one goal — to restore the historic Gillioz Theatre in downtown Springfield. It had been abandoned as a movie house in 1980, and stood vacant, except as a home for vagrants and vandals for several years. It was in danger of the wrecking ball when a group of interested citizens got together and purchased the property with the intent to make it a working theater again.

The Gillioz was the city's last standing example of the old-time movie palace, a 1200 seat auditorium on two levels. Constructed by Monett, Missouri, road and bridge builder M. E. Gillioz, it was a solid structure of reinforced concrete and brick. It had been in operation — and the place to go — back in the time I was in college; the place where I saw "Giant" and "Picnic." I was particularly intrigued by the Gillioz because it had been designed by Larry Larsen of Webb City, the father of my high school friend David Larsen and the designer of the Civic Theater where I worked as an usher.

It was a unique property. M. E. Gillioz wanted his theater to face St. Louis Street, which was Highway 66 through Springfield, and the theater opened in 1926, the same year the national highway was designated. But Gillioz was unable to obtain enough property on Route 66 to build his entertainment palace. He did purchase a 25-foot-wide store front, and used that as a long lobby to reach to the north, where there was sufficient space for the theater on an adjacent street. Part of the problem saving the structure had been that the front, lobby, portion was owned by one family, and the rear, auditorium, portion by another.

My job for the Gillioz board, expectedly, was publicity. I devised and issued some newsletters, and put together a mailing list. It was a frustrating experience because the board had a lot of great ideas for the grand old theater, but not enough money to do them. I was only there for a year when something else came along that required me to quit the board. I am glad to report, though, that in time, the money was found, the Gillioz Theatre was restored, and is now open for business.

CHAPTER 42 — ME, A POLITICIAN?

There was an opening on City Council, and Mayor Gannaway wanted me to apply for it. Although council elections were held every other year, in a non-election year, it was up to the remaining eight members to elect a citizen to fill the empty ninth spot.

I was really, really reluctant. Gannaway assured me that he could swing the five council votes necessary to get me declared a City Council member, and introduced me to a couple of members he was certain about. He had been elected in 1995 with three others on a reform slate, but by no means did he have total control of the body.

I agreed to give it a one-year trial, until the next election. And on May 5, 1998, I found myself in a waiting room outside the City Council Conference Room in City Hall, along with eight other candidates for appointment to the council.

The other contenders included Ralph Manley, a property developer and long-time member of the Planning and Zoning Commission. He seemed extremely confident he had the nomination in the bag, and proceeded to perform as the glad handing host, introducing all the others to one another.

Other men included a realtor, two businessmen, an insurance agent, another retiree; and three women, a lawyer, an artist and a retiree. The council process was to listen to each of us make our pitch individually, then winnow the number of candidates down to three.

I was next to last to speak. I had five minutes. I gave them a summation of what I had done in my career and civic activities since returning to Sprinfield. I said to them:

"You might rightly ask: so what does being a foreign correspondent have to do with being a city councilman? I would respond that I have had a wide range of experiences and exposure to things, places and people. I have watched governments at work in some 30 countries and several states in the south and southwestern United States. None of these are likely to be issues to come before the Springfield City Council, but they are like issues that do come before the council. They require energetic study, intelligent thought and action. I don't come before the council with any fixed agenda, nor any driving demand to see some certain thing accomplished or fixed. I am not applying in order to get even with somebody. I don't have any strong concerns that keep me awake at night — I believe Springfield is a good city, and a good place to live and is generally well run."

I guess I said the right thing. I was one of the three finalists, along with Manley and attorney Nancy Lahmers. In the second round, Manley was eliminated, and Lahmers and I were tied. It took three votes before the tie was broken and I was the new council member. Later I received a nice note of congratulation from Nancy, and one of the less successful candidates sent an e-mail to the council noting that if he had been a member of the council, he would have picked me as the best candidate.

Manley apparently was disappointed, and the next day resigned from the Planning and Zoning Commission, although a year later he ran unopposed and was elected to the council.

Votes in my favor came from Mayor Gannaway, Teri Hacker, Bob Vanaman and Conrad Griggs. I had become the fifth vote to assure Gannaway's majority. The tie breaking vote came from Russell Rhodes, and the consistent votes against me were from Tom Carlson (a former and future mayor), Gary Gibson and Sheila Wright. That was the usual 5-4 voting block as we went through my first year, although many, if not most, issues were decided by a 9-0 majority.

It was never publicly discussed, nor generally known, but Gannaway, Griggs and I bemusedly shared a secret: we all three were members of the TKE fraternity at SMS.

I began a process of learning what city government was really about with meetings with City Manager Tom Finnie and other officials, and with City Clerk Brenda Cirtin and her assistant, Anita Cotter.

Swearing In, with City Clerk Brenda Cirtin.

I tended to keep a low profile in council meetings those first few months. I didn't feel a need to speak out and demonstrate how little I knew. But as the months went by, I began to get more assertive on some issues that interested me.

Service on the council was hard work and very time consuming. We had an hour-long lunch meeting every Tuesday, and a full council meeting every other Monday night that could run as long as three hours. A stack of proposals, documents, e-mails, letters and memoranda was delivered to my house every evening, and the ring binder brief case holding all the information for an upcoming council meeting would be two inches thick. I was committed to reading every document, something some of my other colleagues did, others did not.

I estimated I spent at least twenty hours every week on council business, between reading and taking phone calls. Much of the council business concerned rezoning. Even though the city had a Planning and Zoning Board, the council had the final say on every rezoning proposal. While most citizens professed to be in favor of growth and development, Springfield at the same time was going through a serious spell of NIMBY (not in my back yard). Issues always were traffic, flooding and property values. It seemed every one wanted to live on a cul de sac, or at least a low traffic street, but to be no more than a three-minute drive to banks, stores and offices.

I made it a point to view each rezoning request personally, usually by driving by, and driving around the adjoining neighborhood, although I rarely made direct contact with either side in the argument. With that knowledge, I could ask intelligent questions, and recognize BS, when the petitioners appeared before the council.

On some occasions, I did interject myself, such as at Elfindale. The nursing home wanted to add a

Gannaway's Council, 1998-99. L-R: Bob Vanaman (back to camera) Shelia Wright, Tom Carlson, Mayor Gannaway (standing) Teri Hacker, Bob Chancellor, Russell Rhodes and Conrad Griggs. Gary Gibson was not present, and I don't know who is being congratulated by the Mayor.

new wing, and a new entrance and parking lot off a residential street. The only neighbor who strongly objected was a family which was operating a day care center at their home. They were concerned about the traffic the nursing home would create on "their" street. I met with all the parties and ultimately sat down with the architect and together, we re-designed the traffic entrances and exits for the parking lot, so cars did not have to go past the day care center. Problem solved.

Did I mention that this was all unpaid? Service on the City Council was a volunteer activity. The Mayor received a $200 monthly stipend; the rest of us could be reimbursed for mileage (if we bothered to keep track of it) and other out-of-pocket expenses. The city provided us with a telephone line at home and a fax machine. Later, they provided laptops, to help cut down on the paper flow.

There was some travel involved, some of it good, some bad. A couple of times each year, we would go to Jefferson City to lobby state legislators. There was an annual conference of the Missouri Municipal League, either in St. Louis, Kansas City or at Tan-Tar-A Resort at the Lake of the Ozarks.

Linda and I had the opportunity to spend an enjoyable week in Los Angeles for a National League of Cities conference. Our delegation had been booked into the Figeroa Hotel, certainly not one of LA's most fashionable hotels, but one of its most unique. It was within walking distance of the Convention Center and across the street from Staples Arena, where we went to watch a basketball game. The Figeroa was an old structure, once a YWCA, and decorated with eclectic touches of Arabia and Morocco. No two rooms were the same; the outdoor patio-bar and pool area was lush with bougainvillea and other plantings. It did not have a restaurant, only a lobby carry-out stand. Most of the Springfield party quickly checked out and moved on to more traditional hotels, but the Chancellors and Bobby Vanaman and his wife, Lee, stayed on. We liked the laid back atmosphere of the hotel and we enjoyed touring Los Angeles and Venice Beach together.

I also flew to Miami Beach, Florida, for a convention. I had been named the council representative to the Sister Cities organization, and was invited to attend the national convention of that organization, at the famous Fountainbleu Hotel. We were treated fabulously, wined and dined, and even had a large reception at the Vizcaya Museum and Gardens on the mainland, a national historic landmark. It's setting is one of the most beautiful I have ever seen, overlooking Biscayne Bay.

Springfield's sister city at the time was Isesaki, Japan, and although I had never been to Isesaki, or even heard of it, I had great credibility with visitors from there to Springfield, because I had lived in Japan. During one delegation's visit, we hosted one of the members of Isesaki's Taiko Drumming group. During an evening off, Linda and I took him to Branson to Shoji Tabuchi's show. It just happened that Shoji had introduced a Taiko drumming performance to his show. I introduced our guest to Shoji at in-

termission, and Shoji pointed him out from the stage in the second half of the show. He was thrilled by the recognition.

There were a lot of other activities for council members and often their spouses — openings, dedications, receptions, parties — some fun and some deadly boring.

City council elections were looming in 1999, a primary in February, the general in April. Toward the end of 1998, I decided that I had fulfilled my promise to Lee Gannaway to give council a year's trial, but I was not interested in continuing to serve. Gannaway didn't say much in response, but when I told Tom Carlson my intention not to run, he said: "You have to run. When we appointed you, it was with the understanding that you would be a candidate at the next election." (I found that a strange comment, since Carlson had been one who had consistently voted against my appointment.) I guess my conscience got the better of me, and with the urging of some city staff members who had become friends, I decided to be an election candidate.

At first, it appeared I would have to run in both the primary and the general election, but one of two potential opponents took an appointment to the Planning and Zoning Commission instead. My opponent in the April election would be a business woman named Kaye Parker. She had previously failed in a run for the State Senate, but got into the council race at the behest of the police and fire unions, who had been upset with the council and the city administration over their pay. They had even picketed City Hall during one council session, an act which did not endear them to any of us.

To be listed on the ballot required petition signature of 200 citizens, and I began the process of obtaining those signatures. I received a lot of help from fellow members of the Sertoma Club. They also were a big help when we set out yard signs all over town, only to have a wet snowfall damage many of them, and force us to set them out again. I also received help from some neighborhood groups that felt I had been sympathetic to their needs, and, fairly quickly, I had the petitions in and I was a candidate, running for office.

The election campaign was pretty low key, with just a couple of occasions when the candidates appeared face-to-face. In an interview with the newspaper, I described it as a "god-awful, time-consuming job ...but the council has been productive and I would like to keep that going." Although I had been a union member myself several times in the past, I was concerned about the power the fire fighters and police unions were trying to exert.

With the help of a lot of friends, and some strangers, I raised about $12,000 in campaign funds, and before it was over, I spent all but $300 of it. Most went to television advertising, which my friend and fraternity brother Gary Ellison produced and placed in the final week before the vote. Some money went for yard signs, some for mentions on public radio as a day sponsor, some to a flyer that was inserted in the newspaper the day before the election.

Front page of Springfield News Leader, April 7, 1999.

Council incumbents keep seats

Voters retain Teri Hacker, Shelia Wright and Bob Chancellor.

By Jennifer Portman
News-Leader

The makeup of Springfield's City Council will remain virtually identical, after voters Tuesday stayed with familiar faces rather than union-backed challengers.

With all 113 precincts reporting, incumbents Teri Hacker and Bob Chancellor held on to their general council seats. Shelia Wright also retained the position of Zone 2 representative.

Mayor Lee Gannaway and Planning and Zoning Commissioner Ralph Manley both ran unopposed. Gannaway will serve a third two-year term; Manley will take over the Zone 3 chair for four years.

Hacker, a nonpracticing attorney and homemaker, won by 60 percent over swimming coach Jack Steck; Wright, a homemaker and rental property owner, beat dock supervisor Thomas Long with 63 percent.

Retiree Bob Chancellor squeaked by Planning and Zoning Commissioner Kaye Parker by a mere 83 votes. After Parker led for most of the night, the victory came as a surprise to Chancellor, appointed to the council last year.

"At 10:25 p.m. I got the shock of my life," Chancellor said. "I think people are generally pleased with the way

Steve J.P. Liang / News-Leader

City Council incumbent Teri Hacker gives fellow incumbent Bob Chancellor some encouragement at the watch party at the Elks Lodge. Unofficial final results show both won.

things are going and the way the city is run. I'm pleased to be a part of it."

Wright

The strong support of police and firefighter unions, disgruntled with the council since last year when it approved a pay increase rather than a bigger benefits package, appeared to have little impact on voters.

"I was very, very worried because there are a number of unions in my district," said Wright, who will serve her second term. "But I know there are a lot of people who are looking forward to having an independent person on council."

Hacker said she is pleased to have another term to continue improving basic services.

"It's back to the basics, the same things we've been doing," said Hacker, who was first elected in 1995 and raised the most money for this year's race. "Better traffic flow, crime prevention, stormwater and water quality improvements."

Mayor Gannaway helped me too, with an endorsement in my campaign material, and by assigning me to several ground breakings and public readings of council resolutions, to give me greater exposure in the community.

Election night, April 6, 1999, Teri Hacker and I jointly arranged a watch party at the Elks Club, and as the results were coming in, I was running behind. As a reluctant candidate and councilman from the start, I wasn't really too upset. As I told a commiserating friend, "I had something to do before the council, and I will have something to do afterward."

Teri won her race against another police-fire union candidate handily, by 60 percent. Reporter Jennifer Portman, who had been hanging around our watch party, anticipated my loss and headed over to Kaye Parker's place. When the last precincts reported in, she had to rush back. At 10:25 P.M., Bob Chancellor was the winner by a mere 83 votes out of 22,869 votes cast, leading my friends to refer to me as "Landslide Bob."

I had developed a couple of favorite projects in my council work. One was a new downtown park, which was to include an ice rink, an exposition center, a parking garage, and ultimately a hotel and baseball park. As this was developing, it carried the name of "Civic Park," but no one was happy with that. I became a member of a committee which mulled over dozens of suggestions in several sessions, and came up with the name "Jordan Valley Park," after the water stream that ran through it.

Development of the park and its facilities was a major focus of the council during my four-year elected term. I also became concerned by the continuing requests to put up cell phone towers; it threatened to make Springfield look like a pin cushion. Online, I discovered an expert in cell towers and municipal laws, and was authorized by the council to travel to Fort Myers, Florida, for a seminar he was conducting. Using knowledge from that trip, I worked with the city legal department to devise a ordinance, approved by the council, which set some controls over placement of cell towers, by using tall buildings and water towers for antennas. The expert also had suggested

hiding them in church steeples, and inside flag poles, but I don't believe we ever got that far.

Another issue of interest was to establish a citizens police advisory board. There had been a number of citizen complaints about various police actions, and the complainants were not satisfied with the results that came from police department internal affairs investigations. I was named the chairman of a five-member committee to study the matter, and working with the police department and the city attorney, we came up with a plan for a council-appointed police review board. The ordinance would require the board to receive special training before hearing complaints and their recommendations would not be binding on the police department. My stated view was "there is a catharsis involved here for the people who are mad, upset and angry." The ordinance passed and the board has been in operation ever since. Although it did not achieve all I had hoped for, it was better than what had existed before, when, as I described it: "People are seeing one thing going into the mouth of the sausage machine and nothing coming out the other end."

We also had some major conflicts over smoking and alcohol. By a five to four vote, the council rejected a proposal to sell alcohol at an arts fundraising event to be held Labor Day weekend on a public parking lot. The influence of the Baptist Church, and the Assemblies of God, which has its international headquarters in Springfield, was just too much to overcome.

The council also rejected a proposal to allow the sale of beer and wine at certain, limited events in parks: beer at city owned golf courses; wine at zoo fund-raisers, wine at professional tennis matches, beer at ice hockey games and major softball tournaments. The Assemblies of God said even such limited sales would "contribute to the decay of the moral fiber of Springfield."

After that failure, I became involved in an initiative petition process, to let the public vote on the alcohol question. Our group obtained more than 2500 petition signatures from Springfield residents. The question was placed on the ballot at the November 5, 2002, general election. It failed.

And to this day such serving of alcohol is prohibited on all city property.

Hammons Field, the Double A baseball park, is an exception, because it is privately owned and operated, and alcohol sales there in seven seasons do not seem to have contributed to any decay in the moral fiber of the community. But there is good reason that Springfield is sometimes called "the buckle on the bible belt." In 2011, voters came out again, against a movie theater that was serving alcohol to customers.

In 2002, the Health department came forward with a proposal to ban smoking in restaurants. I was opposed to that prohibition, and argued that restaurants should be required to post on their doorway that they were a smoking or no-smoking facility, thus giving the customer a choice whether to enter or not. My argument went nowhere, and the coun-

This picture appeared on a web site maintained by retired journalist Richard Grosenbaugh. Titled "Media People in the 60's," the caption read: "the fellow on the left, Bob Chancellor, is right back where he was during the 1960's. Then he was a reporter for KTTS. Now he's a member of City Council. He and Mike North of the Springfield Newspapers are shown covering a Council meeting."

cil passed a no-smoking ordinance, although it had some exceptions which took the anti-smoking lobby nine years to overcome. The ordinance, as passed, permitted smoking in private clubs and facilities, in enclosed, independently ventilated smoking areas, and in facilities where 50 percent or more of sales come from alcohol or where annual alcohol receipts are more than $200,000. It also excluded cafes with few than 50 seats. (Those

exclusions were all overturned in the same 2011 election that stopped alcohol sales in movie theaters.)

I was wearing down, being the spokesman for sin. I already had decided that I would not be a candidate for re-election in 2003. I was not prepared for four more years. Gannaway and Vanaman already had retired from the council, Teri was planning to leave, and I did not get along well with, or trust the word of, a couple of the new members.

Then, unfortunately, one of my council colleagues, Mayor Protem Gary Gibson, died. During the 2003 elections, in February and April, a replacement would be elected for his seat for a two-year term. Maybe I could do two more years, so I started circulating petitions to seek that shorter term.

I had become embroiled in a neighborhood zoning issue, in my own neighborhood. The Southeast Springfield Neighborhood Association opposed rezoning a tract of land for a funeral home. It was on the corner of Southern Hills Boulevard and Lone Pine, just a portion of a 14-acre undeveloped tract of privately owned land. The owners offered to sell the remaining land to the city, or to the neighborhood association, at $25,000 per acre in exchange for the opportunity to develop the corner lot as a funeral home. Otherwise, the owners said, they had the right, and the intention, of developing the entire tract.

The city did not want to take responsibility for the land, and the neighborhood association did not have the funds to buy it at its regular price. So the owners' plan sounded like a good deal to me. But my support of the idea only gained me an announced opponent to my goal to run for two more years on the council.

At about this time, we discovered that one of my best friends, Sam Mullin, had inoperable brain cancer. We discovered this when he was circulating nominating petitions for me — he was unable to recall his street address on a submission form, and went to the doctor to see what was wrong. His illness, which would prove fatal in about a year, led me to thinking about life — it's too fleeting to be wasted tilting at windmills at City Hall.

Within a day or two, on November 27, 2002, I announced I was withdrawing from the 2003 race. In a statement to the press, I said:

> *"When I was elected to the council in 1999, I vowed to myself and several friends that I would not seek reelection four years hence. I believed that this would permit me to use my full abilities to vote on issues before the council dispassionately, rationally and logically. I still believe that independence and freedom of action has served me and the community well.*
>
> *I don't want to run in a primary and a general election. It's just too damn much work. I'm looking forward to retiring. I've got a book to finish writing (this one) and a cabin at Lake of the Ozarks to refinish."*

I felt relief the moment I issued my statement. And to this day, I have never regretted that decision. I finished out my term in April, 2003. It had been an interesting five-year experience, having spent a career as a journalist on the other side of the desk asking questions of government officials.

At a farewell reception at City Hall, I thanked various people who had helped me, closing with:

> *And finally, my wife, Linda, who supported me, answered phones, made early meals every other Monday, critiqued my ideas, sometimes disagreed with them, flinched every time she saw my picture coming up in the paper or on TV, and who much more would have wanted to be at the lake. So now, that's what we are going to do.*

At left, there are some who say this is where all politicians should be. A new county jail building was opened, and we were "allowed" to spend a night there before its rightful residents moved in, as part of a charity fund raiser.

As council members, we were always cutting something or as below, shoveling something. Sometimes what we shoveled was dirt as at this fire station ground breaking.

Elect **Councilman** Bob **Chancellor**

Bob Chancellor
At-Large Councilman D
881-0043

√   Retired Foreign Correspondent
√   Offers Energetic Study & Action
√   Common Sense Based On Experience
√   Fair & Open Minded

"Springfield Is The Best Place In The World To Live"

This is the flyer I passed out at campaign appearances. I also sent out several thousand copies as an insert in the Springfield News Leader the day before the election.

Elect Bob
Chancellor

City Councilman At-Large

2152 E. Berkeley Springfield, MO 65804   (417) 882-4979

- Retired Foreign Correspondent and Bureau Chief for Voice of America
- Appointed to a vacancy on the City Council in May, 1998, from a field of nine candidates
- Serves on Council's Public Involvement, Governmental Relations and Oversight, and Telecommunications Committees
- Past member, Mayor's Commission for Human Rights
- Council Liaison and Board Member, Springfield Sister Cities Association
- Member of the Alumni Board of Southwest Missouri State University
- Active Supporter of Boys & Girls Club through Sertoma Club activities
- Past member, Springfield Landmarks Preservation Trust (Gillioz Theatre project)
- Married 41 years to Linda Hulston Chancellor, 4 children, 4 grandchildren

"My career as a journalist took me to live and work in many parts of the world and the United States. But when I retired, there was no question about it, we would return home to Springfield. It truly is the best place in the world to live. I am totally independent as a retiree, with no ties to any local business or profession, no fixed agenda and no interest in other elective office. I ask for your vote to elect me to the Springfield City Council. I will use good common sense with a fair and open mind to help keep Springfield the best place in the world to live."

Bob Chancellor

"Bob Chancellor's wealth of experience and his ability to understand and analyze all sides of an issue, make him an outstanding and invaluable councilman."

Mayor Lee Gannaway

Councilman Chancellor Campaign Committee--Fred S. Hunt, Treasurer

CHAPTER 43 — BACK TO THE BEGINNING

Yes, there is life after city council and working around the world, it's just a little slower and more relaxing. But it remains interesting and sometimes challenging.

After leaving the council I ended up with another job, one that paid. I had invested some money in the Sinclair Financial Group, a company that supposedly made its profits from granting loans to automobile purchasers with less than prime credit. Turns out it made its money from being a Ponzi scheme. The company was declared bankrupt, and a couple of its officers went to jail. But rather than just take the loss and collect about four cents on each dollar invested, the 1,800 investors elected to reorganize the company, make it legitimate and bring it out of bankruptcy.

Jerry Fenstermaker was appointed by the bankruptcy court to manage the new company. I met Jerry through Teri Hacker, and we became friends because he, too, had had an international career, as a banker. As the company was emerging from bankruptcy, under the name Freedom Financial Group, Jerry asked me to serve on the board of directors. That provided me with some "earned income" which I could put away in savings in an IRA.

We almost made it. FFG was making sub-prime auto loans also, using insurance money that had come out of the bankruptcy proceedings. We were able to put together a $25 million loan from a subsidiary of Goldman Sachs, at ten percent interest, and use it to make auto loans at 20 to 24 percent. We had just become profitable in 2008 when the financial crisis hit the country, and Goldman Sachs would not renew, or extend our loan. So we had no choice but to sell off the company's books and close FFG. Our efforts did make some improvement; original investors in SFG were paid off at 18 cents on the dollar, instead of the four cents that was originally offered.

Challenging as that venture into capitalism was, it does not match the intensity of PPS, or post-polio syndrome. I had first heard of this disorder back in 1985 in Houston. It is suffered by some polio survivors who have over-used their remaining good muscles to compensate for those lost to the original disease. I went to the Texas Institute of Research and Rehabilitation, and was diagnosed as one of those who was showing signs of PPS.

For forty years, I had been using my good, left leg to carry me around, in a pretty active life. Then, about at the age of 68, I began to notice weakness in my left leg. Stairs were difficult to climb, and walking long distances was very tiring. I began using a cane occasionally, especially for long distances, and then my doctor prescribed a four-wheel walker for me to use whenever I felt the need for it. I began to feel the need for it more and more, and in 2010, I went back to TIRR in Houston, where they said my strength had diminished considerably, and to use the walker at all times, especially to eliminate the risk of falling and breaking a bone, which could end up in confinement to a wheel chair.

Exercise and physical therapy will do nothing to help the disorder, because those over-worked muscle nerves will not regenerate, exercise will simply cause them to degenerate more quickly. The long-term plan is to take it easy and not get fatigued — that's the sort of advice a lazy man might welcome. But it is a damned nuisance.

We got welcome news in 2006 when our son, Steven, and his wife, Karen, decided to move to Springfield from the Austin, Texas area. With other kids stuck in Texas, Georgia and California, it was a wonderful idea to have part of our family nearby. Steven was especially enthusiastic about the plan, because he is an avid fisherman, and the cabin at the Lake of the Ozarks was beckoning.

In fact, it was now cabins. For many years, Linda and I shared the old family cabin with my brother Stephen and his family. We retirees used it during the week, then cleared out so they could use it on weekends. Then the chance arose for Linda and me to buy a smaller cabin behind the family cabin. We remodeled it, added a deck, and used it on occasions when both families were there at the same time. But we didn't like it as well, because it was not on the water, and one of the great delights at Lake of the Ozarks is being able to sit on your deck, just a few feet from the water's edge and watch the world go by. Then a second opportunity came along, to buy the cabin next door to the old family cabin. We bought it, remodeled it, and added a roofed deck which has become a neighborhood gathering place.

Brother Stephen bought out my share of the original place. Brother Sam took his share of the money and ran. Our share went into remodeling. Now there are the three cabins in the Chancellor compound at Owens Cove; Stephen and family in one; Bob and Linda in one, and son Steve, or other guests, in the small middle building.

Steve and Karen bought a house in Bois d'Arc, a small town about 20 miles west of Springfield, and he set up an office so he could work from home

selling computer programs. They were welcomed to Missouri their first winter by the ice storm of 2007, that paralyzed this whole part of the country for two weeks. Steven was making coffee over charcoal briquettes until he was able to obtain a scarce electric generator. Our house was without power for 13 days — we toughed it out a couple of days in front of the fireplace, then retreated to a hotel, and finally to the empty home of Pat and Willie Washam, who were in Florida. (Pat is a niece of Linda's stepfather, and Willie is a fraternity brother with whom I co-authored a book about the Promenaders square dance group.)

Steven and Karen's move to Missouri was star-crossed and even more disastrous. Early in the spring of 2007, his company eliminated his sales position, and he went to work selling oil products for a company in town. That made for a long commute. In the meantime, Karen was sick. She had long suffered from Crohn's disease and several other disorders. Though she was seeing several doctors, taking several medications, and had surgery, she did not seem to get any better.

The stunning disaster came on January 25, 2008, when Steven drove home during his lunch hour to

check on Karen, and found her dead in bed. Cause of death was apparently a reaction to one, or some, of the medications she was taking at the time. She was only 47-years-old. She and Steven were together for 22 years, and she had become a close, loving member of our family. She was an accomplished violinist, who had taught music in schools for 21 years. Her illness had kept her from being able to take a position teaching music to kids at the Boys and Girls Clubs.

Karen's two brothers and a sister came to Springfield for her funeral, as did Steve's sister, Kim and brother Craig. Karen was buried in Maple Park Cemetery in Springfield, not too far from the graves of Linda's stepfather, Fred Hunt, who had died in 2000, and Linda's aunt, Betty Ward, who died in the last week of 1999.

Steven eventually sold the house in Bois d'Arc and moved into Springfield. He is renting the house of Linda's mother, which was vacated when "Zsa-Zsa" had to move to a nursing home after breaking her hip.

Steven lives just a few blocks from us, because we moved into a new house in 2001. We were looking for a place slightly larger than 2152 Berkeley, but were not seriously shopping. One day in April, we were on LaMonta Avenue, in the 50-year-old Southern Hills neighborhood, looking at another house for sale, when we spotted and became interested in 3041 East LaMonta. It didn't look very big from the street, and was sort of old-fashioned looking to us, with white weeping mor-

tar brick walls, French provincial windows, and lots of trees and flowering bushes in front.

But the back was spectacular, with a big deck, a screened porch, completely surrounded by woods, so that no neighboring house could be seen. Directly behind it was a wooded flood plain which could never be built on, and, the clincher, the

Aunt Betty in her '82 Mercedes 560 convertible. When she learned of my love for red convertibles, she said she would leave this one to me. And she did, when she died late in 1999. It was like a brand new car, only 40,000 miles on it. If you are keeping count, this is convertible number five. And below is convertible number six, the 2000 Mustang at the rear. Councilman Manley was so jealous of mine that he bought himself one too.

Zsa-Zsa celebrates her 90th birthday

sweetest Verbena bush I have ever smelled. We immediately called our realtor friend, JoAnn Mitchell, who came to look at it and was impressed. Only after gaining entrance, did we learn that it had two bedrooms in an upstairs which couldn't be seen from the front, a finished basement recreation room, two large bedrooms on the ground floor, four bathrooms, hardwood floors, and two fireplaces. We signed a contract, and moved in two weeks later.

Perhaps the greatest honor of my life came on October 13, 2005, when I was named to the Webb City High School Hall of Fame. I was presented a plaque which was then hung on the wall in the school lobby along with several other notable graduates of the school. The presentation came at the annual Chamber of Commerce banquet supporting the school, and I was asked to make a short speech on the occasion. Just reading the excerpts from this speech might have saved you the trouble of reading this entire book.

Wow. Imagine me standing here with this. When I graduated from Webb City High School in 1954, I think there are a lot of people who would have been skeptical and surprised to see this night happen. I think the principal of Webb City High School would have been surprised to see this happen. (For those of you not in on the joke; the principal of the high school was my father, Bonham Chancellor.) And I think he would have been proud tonight.

I probably am unable to perform any inspiring oratory in 10 minutes, so I will just tell a story.

This is not the first time I have tried to leave a permanent impression on W.C. High School. Back when I was a sophomore or junior, the school was building a new dressing room at Hatten Football Stadium, approximately on this site where we are tonight. After practice one day, I joined several other members of the football team in putting my initials into the wet concrete of the floor of the dressing room construction project. Naturally, the principal did not take long to determine whose initials were

"B.C. He sent me, and the others, to the junkyard to buy and break into pieces an old carborundum grinding wheel, which we then used to rub onto our names until they were no longer visible in the now hard concrete. It took several days rubbing. I hope my impression on the school will be more permanent this time around.

A friend remarked recently: "I'd still like to hear, sometime, what youthful dreams began you on that journey to an interesting life, what motivated you to wander so far — at a time when that was unusual in our little world. What was your college major, for instance? What influenced you—negatively or positively — along a certain path or into certain interests and subjects ?

There is an old Yiddish proverb: Man Plans, God laughs.

The answer to that question is not all that dramatic. I didn't stand atop some chat pile and gaze into the far horizon. It's more of an issue of happenstance.

But that happenstance does have a connection to Webb City. I served in the National Guard here with a fellow from Carl Junction, Dewey Joe Phillips. A couple of years later, when I was preparing to attend Southwest Missouri State college, I ran into Joe in Springfield, where he was working in a clothing store. He was attending SMS, and was president of a fraternity, Tau Kappa Epsilon. He invited me to be rushed by the fraternity. I joined, and

in the first few weeks, another member of the fraternity was named editor of the Southwest Standard, *the college newspaper. He needed staff members. I was one of those drafted from among the fraternity pledges, probably because I could read, write, spell and organize thoughts (thanks to Webb City schools).*

I found that the newspaper was something I enjoyed doing, and I spent a lot of time doing it. You got to meet interesting people and learn about important things. It also was a neat way to meet girls – it worked for me, because that's where I met Linda.

Let me say a little more about my partner of 47 years. As Ann Richards said of Ginger Rogers: She had to do all the same dance steps as Fred Astaire, except do them backwards, and in high heels. That has been Linda's contribution to our adventurous life. While I was flitting off to one country or another, and to another story, she had to stay back, and make a home, for us and four kids, in nine cities, in six countries, and in 25 different houses, under frequently difficult circumstances.

The paths of life often have branches, and some are chosen, and some are just followed. When I left high school, my plan was to attend Joplin Junior College for two years, and then move on to the Rolla School of Mines to seek a degree in engineering, probably electrical.

A medical mis-adventure that summer led to a change in plans. And I began studies at SMS in pre-med. My grades in organic chemistry and a couple of advanced mathematics classes, led me to the decision that English, history, sociology, political science and economics were a whole lot more interesting. The college newspaper led to a job at the Springfield newspaper, which led to local TV and radio, which led to VOA. It was not a well-defined or well-planned career path – but it sure was an interesting and enjoyable path as it unfolded. I liked my job, and like many other journalists, I

have said many times, I would have paid them to let me do it. (Almost.)

I mentioned the James family, neighbors where I spent a lot of time. That was not unusual in Webb City then – almost every kid had several surrogate families. In that time, it was a living example of a slogan by Hillary Clinton – you may like her or hate her – "It takes a village to raise a child." Growing up in Webb City, it was difficult to get into too much trouble because someone always was watching, and cared. This village of 7033 people was a wonderful place to grow up. I tried, and I hope I succeeded, in keeping Webb City's small-town, Midwestern values with me as I followed the paths of my life and career.

This is a great honor. I will be hanging on the wall with some notable and important people. Fellow journalist Lisa Myers: I don't know her, never met her, but I watch her on TV and I did work for her grandfather many years ago. My 1954 classmate Jeremy Rusk – there is some pride in this room that our class of '54 is the first class to have two members of the R-7 Hall of Fame.

Finally, a thank you to the people of Webb City and Jasper County for something they did, you did, your parents and grandparents did, more than 50 years ago. The summer after my high school graduation, I came down with a serious case of polio while visiting Kansas City. My father did not have medical or hospitalization insurance then – in those days, few people did, and we faced

at least a year of serious medical bills, therapy treatments, hospitalization and surgeries. At that time, the head of the Jasper County March of Dimes contacted my father and said: "Don't worry about the cost; we will take care of it." And they did.

Now, I guess I have to keep a promise to my old friend, now deceased, Sam Mullin. When I first started writing this back in 2003 (yes, it has been that long), he said, "You must conclude it with your thoughts about the news media and journalism today." OK, Sam, here goes:

I think news, information and the media have become irrelevant today in America. The money-changers have entered the temple of truth. Newspapers are dying — I used to read 6 or 8 papers daily, now they are all the same. Recently I spoke to a group of college students about freedom of the press, and only a couple of them ever read a newspaper.

They get their news online, on blogs, on Facebook, and from e-mail. Basically they get the news they want to hear or know. Daniel Patrick Moynihan famously said that people are entitled to their own opinions, but they are not entitled to their own facts. But now, people can almost get their own facts, there is so much of it out there, that the truth is difficult, if not impossible, to ascertain.

Radio news was once an honest mode of communication; now it is just a hodge-podge of music, ads, and usually vitriolic talk.

TV news is not as bad as talk radio, but it is shallow, and the presenters just smile, giggle and neglect to inform. When did you last see someone ugly doing news?

Americans are getting the news and information they are willing to pay for, and that interests them: sports, weather and Hollywood gossip.

In their 1996 book "The Murrow Boys," Stanley Cloud and Lynne Olson relate a story about one of the Murrow boys, Eric Sevareid. "Their true medium was radio and their day was short. That thought may have been on Eric Sevareid's mind

near the end of his life as he lay in a hospital after surgery. One afternoon, he awoke suddenly from a nap and mumbled to his son, Michael, "I had the most terrible nightmare." "What about, Dad?" "Television," said Sevareid.

Foreign news has nearly disappeared from our field of view. The U.S. is still involved in two foreign wars. One in Afghanistan for ten years now, and the American print press is almost totally absent from the country. According to the Nieman Watchdog, TV coverage averages 21 seconds per newscast on NBC and not that much more for ABC or CBS. Only five newspapers and two wire services maintain bureaus there. A survey by the American Journalism Review in January, 2011, found that ten newspapers and one chain employ 234 correspondents to serve as our eyes and ears to global events. In 2003, AJR found 307. During the Vietnam war there were more than 200 American journalists in that one country alone.

VOA is a mere shell of its former self. Focus has turned to the internet and TV there, too. Recently I talked with a VOA correspondent in Houston. (Yes, they decided they did need a reporter there, after all.) He not only has to find, report and write news, but he has to carry a video camera to provide coverage for VOA television, and a computer to feed their web page. English language broadcasting to the world has nearly disappeared from VOA, and the vaunted BBC is following the same path. The most aggressive international news reporting is being conducted by China and by Al Jazeera from the Arabian Gulf states. The U.S. has a few bright spots: NPR radio is expanding its foreign coverage, PBS is solid, the New York Times is keeping its promise, even the Sunday talking head shows on network television are worthwhile.

But other than that, journalism and information is a sad scene. I once was proud to be in the news business; to say I was a journalist. Now, not so much. This may be the view of a retired journalist, or of a grumpy old retired man. But there it is, my friend.

And there it is for "Pieces of String Too Short To Save." As my brother Sam Chancellor used to remark at the end of e-mail messages: "Mind is emptied."

If the careful reader is puzzled that he/she did not see convertible number five, it is because there is not a picture of it. It was a '57 Ford Mustang (actually maroon instead of red) which I had for only a short time between selling the MGB to son Craig, and inheriting the Mercedes from Aunt Betty. And I traded the Merc for the current Mustang because the Mercedes was too expensive to operate, and had a manual top, while Ford had mastered the power top.

At right: Called the Rem house due to the name of a previous owner, son Steven and guests use it.

Bottom : The Chancellor compound on Owens Cove, Mile 8, Niangua Arm, Lake of the Ozarks, from the dock. Brother Steve's house is on the left, Bob and Linda's on the right.

Note to readers:

There should be an index here, but there isn't. Indexing just appeared to be too much of a task for a project that has been underway for eight years already. There are lots of people's names and lots of place names in here, so if you want to know if you are included, you will just have to read it.

A hint to readers:

Chapters 1 through 9 deal basically with family history..
10 through 12 begin to explain work.
13 through 20 are in Asia.
21 and 22 are back in Washington.
23 to 27 are in Africa, as are 31 to 35.
28 is the story of The Renters
29 is in Israel
36 through 40 take place in Texas and the Southwest.
41 through 43 are back home in Missouri.

Acknowledgerments

This is the place to acknowledge those who have helped with this book.

My wife, Linda, should be listed as co-author, she contributed so much to the story. She proof-read the manuscript three times in various incarnations, and had suggestions and insights.

Thanks to daughter Kim and son Steven, who read the manuscript, for their enthusiasm about it. And it was Kim who suggested the title.

Thanks also to Janet and Gary Ellison, who proved to be wonderful and insightful proof readers.

Thanks to my Aunt Phoebe, who originally inspired this project,

And to Maggie Castrey of The Book Artists group in Springfield who gave me the final push

Artist Bruce Helm picked up the title and ran with it to create a great cover.

My appreciation, also, for friends, mentors and heroes who have made up so much of my life.

Of course, I am responsible for any errors that remain: But I never make misteaks.

The author can be contacted at bobchancellor+book@gmail.com

Made in United States
North Haven, CT
08 November 2021